THE ORGANIC DIRECTORY

The Organic Directory

2004-2005

Edited by Clive Litchfield

Foreword by Hugh Fearnley-Whittingstall

PUBLISHED BY GREEN BOOKS
WITH THE SOIL ASSOCIATION

Acknowledgements

Ever since I started work on the first edition of this Directory in 1991 I have had enormous amounts of help and encouragement from a variety of people and organisations. A list follows, and if I have missed anyone out I apologise.

My partner Annie, our daughters Sophie, Lydia and Ella, Mark Redman, Paul Adams; Tom de Pass, Martin Trowell, Sam Platt and everyone at the Soil Association; Basil Caplan, Alan and Jackie Gear, Robert Sculthorpe, James Anderson at the BDAA, Dr. Mae-Wan Ho, G.P. Lawson and Jan Hurst for Mac and website help, and John Elford at Green Books for taking on this project.

This edition published in June 2004
by Green Books Ltd, Foxhole, Dartington, Totnes, Devon TQ9 6EB
sales@greenbooks.co.uk www.greenbooks.co.uk
www.theorganicdirectory.co.uk

with the Soil Association
Bristol House, 40–56 Victoria Street, Bristol BS1 6BY
info@soilassociation.org www.soilassociation.org

Copyright © Clive Litchfield 2004
Design by Rick Lawrence samskara@onetel.net.uk
Typeset at Green Books

Printed and bound by MPG Books, Bodmin, Cornwall, UK
on Corona Offset 100% recycled paper

First edition published October 1992
Second edition October 1996
Third edition October 1998
Fourth edition May 2000
Fifth edition June 2002

A CIP record for this book is available from the British Library.

ISBN 1 903998 36 0
(10–copy counterpack for retailers: ISBN 1 903998 37 9)

Contents

ENGLAND, CHANNEL ISLANDS & NORTHERN IRELAND

SCOTLAND

WALES

ASSOCIATIONS & ORGANISATIONS

Foreword

by Hugh Fearnley-Whittingstall

At a time when most of us drive Continental cars, watch American programmes on Asian-made televisions and drink Eastern European beers whilst watching Premiership soccer teams with barely a pair of home-grown legs on the pitch, you might ask 'Does it really matter where food comes from?' But there are many, very tangible, worthwhile benefits that follow from your efforts to buy organic food that's indigenous to your part of the country—ideally directly from the people who produce it.

Firstly, buying direct keeps many small producers in business. It cuts out the middleman and thereby provides farmers and craft food producers with a vital alternative to succumbing to the crushing bargaining power of the supermarkets. You are supporting small farmers, keeping the relationship between you and those who produce your food alive and contributing to the rebirth of local food economies. The 2001 report *Plugging the Leaks* showed that every £1 spent in a Cornish organic box scheme generated an extra £1 for the local economy, while £1 spent at the local Asda supermarket only generated 14p. So money spent on locally produced food effectively doubles its worth.

Those who are endeavouring to supply you with good local food—and I'm proud to include myself amongst them—undoubtedly need your support. But I also believe passionately that they (we!) deserve it. Because buying locally also contributes culturally to the preservation of local food traditions and regional varieties. Again, it's a vital antidote to the sledgehammer buying power of the multinationals that has reduced so much of our food to bland homogeneity. So buy locally and you are investing in the future of good food, with real character.

You are also investing in the safety of the global ecology. This is because the closer the point of sale to the farm, the less miles food has travelled to get to us. It has been estimated that the food in a typical

Sunday lunch bought from a supermarket could have been transported 49,000 miles—more than twice round the world. This process is burning millions of tonnes of fossil fuels and releasing greenhouse gases into the atmosphere.

Buy local and organic and you have the added satisfaction of knowing you have contributed to the diversity and vitality of the countryside around you—the very health of the ground beneath your feet. This is because organic farmers and producers are committed to a way of looking after the land that is sustainable—and that will not exhaust and deplete the soil of its natural goodness, increasing its dependence, for high productivity, on ever higher inputs of chemical fertilisers, weedkillers and pesticides.

Against this background of increasing global and local ecological trauma, what a pleasure it is, and what a comfort, to sit down to a meal knowing that the meat and the vegetables on your plate, and with a bit of luck the fruit in your crumble, have all been raised naturally, within a few dozen miles of your home—perhaps by people whose names you know.

And these are not simply altruistic reasons: they are compellingly in your own interests. Firstly there is your health. Since it hasn't been shipped and stored and carted all over the country locally produced organic food can be sold fresher, or picked riper, and will consequently be more nutritious. And it is guaranteed to be free of any chemical residues that may harm you or your family. Secondly, you can think of your purse. Research shows that organic produce brought direct from the farmer, through a farmers' market, farm shop or box scheme, is usually cheaper than similar produce brought in a supermarket.

But perhaps the most compelling reason for making these choices is sheer taste. Because you simply can't beat locally grown organic food that is fresh from the farm. It's the best food you'll ever eat—and the food you should eat every day.

In buying this book you've taken a huge step towards the enjoyment of the best food, and partaken of the antidote to industrialised agriculture. Flick through its pages and I hope you'll agree that locally produced organic produce is not a niche market, but for everyone.

With that last thought in mind, I wonder if I could ask a favour of you? When writing a foreword such as this, or addressing an audience that has gathered because they are interested in the issues I've been discussing here, it is sometimes hard to shrug off the niggling feeling that I may be preaching to the converted. So I'd like to ask you to help me out—by preaching to the unconverted.

I hope you'll spread the word about the benefits and pleasures of buying organic food locally. Take a friend along to your nearest farmers' market, or introduce them to your box scheme. Go halves with a neighbour on an organic lamb from a local producer for the freezer. When you entertain, tell your friends where the delicious food they're eating comes from—and give them names, numbers and addresses.

Best of all, buy a second copy of this book, and give it to someone as a present.

Hugh Fearnley-Whittingstall

Introduction

Why should I buy local?

Buying locally produced food helps to support the producers in your region, maintaining a well established rural way of life. It gives the local economy a boost by keeping money within the community, sustaining local businesses and creating jobs for people who live in the area. Food that is grown closer to us has travelled less distance to reach us—this means less environmental pollution. Locally produced food can also be fresher, healthier and more nutritious, having been spared lengthy periods of storage, chilling and travel. And culturally, local organic food has its own 'story', bringing a shared meaning at mealtimes and a deeper connection to the land.

What is a box scheme?

A box scheme is a box (bag, sack or net), containing freshly picked, locally grown, produce, delivered weekly to your door, or to a local drop-off point. Box scheme operators usually offer small, medium and family size boxes with prices ranging from £5 to £15. The operator decides what vegetables go into the box, and this will vary each week depending on the seasonal vegetables available. Healthy, tasty vegetables just as you would want to grow them yourself—but without the digging!

Organic box schemes are now one of the fastest growing forms of direct marketing in the UK: that is, getting food straight from the farmer to the consumer. The original concept was developed by vegetable growers to shortcut the extended food supply chain in order to sell their fresh produce direct to local consumers. Not surprisingly, a number of variations on the basic model have evolved, and there are an increasing number of home delivery businesses that buy their produce from farms and wholesalers. They may also supply fruit, dairy produce, meat, wines and wholefoods. Most schemes operate locally or on a regional basis, but some also deliver nationally. Box schemes usually source produce locally, keeping unnecessary packaging, storage and transportation to a minimum, which ensures it arrives fresh to your home.

What is a farmers' market?

Farmers' markets help local producers and processors to sell their goods direct to the public, near the source of origin, creating benefits to them and the local community. Usually held on a once weekly basis, farmers' markets place an emphasis on added value, quality and freshness. They aim for an atmosphere which is vibrant, upbeat and fun, helping to revitalise urban centres and to make shopping an enjoyable experience. Although the concept is not a new one, farmers' markets are becoming increasingly popular—more and more people are demanding quality, locally produced food, sold at a fair price to both consumer and producer.

What does organic mean?

Organic agriculture is a safe, sustainable farming system, producing healthy crops and livestock without damage to the environment. It avoids the use of artificial chemical fertilisers and pesticides on the land, relying instead on developing a healthy, fertile soil and growing a mixture of crops. In this way, the farm remains biologically balanced, with a wide variety of beneficial insects and other wildlife to act as natural predators for crop pests and a soil full of micro-organisms and earthworms to maintain its vitality. Animals are reared without the routine use of the array of drugs, antibiotics and wormers which form the foundation of most non-organic livestock farming.

Is organic food healthier for me?

"Many research publications have shown that organically produced foods have higher amounts of beneficial minerals, essential amino acids, vitamins and lower potential risks from food pathogens and mycotoxins" —Carlo Leifert, Professor of Ecological Agriculture, Director of the Tesco Centre for Organic Agriculture

Over 400 chemical pesticides are routinely used in intensive farming, and residues are often present in non-organic food. So-called 'acceptable levels' are calculated for each of these chemicals, and their risks to human health evaluated. However, surveys consistently show high and multiple residues occurring in a proportion of food samples such as baby food, spinach, dried fruit, bread, apples, celery, and chips. There is also little knowledge of the long-term effects of these compounds or of the 'cocktail' effect (the way in which their toxicity may be increased by mixing them together). The routine use of synthetic pesticides is not allowed under organic standards. Only four chemicals are allowed in restricted circumstances under Soil Association regulations.

Research has also shown that on average, organic food contains higher levels of vitamin C and essential minerals such as calcium, magnesium, iron and chromium, as well as cancer-fighting antioxidants. Even organic processed food is different—hydrogenated fat and artificial flavourings and sweeteners are banned, along with other food additives which can cause health problems.

What are genetically modified organisms (GMOs)?

Genetic modification involves the artificial insertion of a foreign gene into the genetic material of an organism in an essentially random way. There are currently two main types of genetically modified crops: those engineered to be resistant to herbicides in order to kill weeds, and those engineered to produce toxins to kill pests.

Though GMOs have been marketed for several years, scientific knowledge of the processes involved is actually at a very early stage. Very little is known about the side effects of the inserted genes' random location, how gene location is controlled, and gene transfer into other micro-organisms such as bacteria in the human gut. In addition, evidence set out in the Soil Association's *Seeds of Doubt* report illustrates that GM crops have no economic benefits and can actually harm the environment.

Organic standards prohibit the use of GMOs and GM derivatives in organic food production and in animal feed.

What about farm animals— how well are they looked after?

"Organic farming has the potential to offer the very highest standards of animal welfare. The Soil Association's welfare standards are leaders in the field"
—Joyce de Silva, Chief executive, Compassion in World Farming, 2003

Organic standards place a strong emphasis on animal welfare. Animals have access to fields and are allowed to express their natural behaviour patterns. They always have comfortable bedding and plenty of space when they are housed. Organic livestock farmers can manage their animals without the routine use of antibiotics and other drugs because they run a healthy, balanced system: not keeping too many animals on a given area, keeping a mixture of species wherever possible, and using natural organic feedstuffs. Grazing animals like cows and sheep are fed mainly on herb and clover-rich grass. Homoeopathy and herbal remedies are used widely in organic livestock management. In a case of acute illness, where the animal might otherwise suffer, a conventional drug treatment would be used.

The Soil Association is one certification body that has chosen to set higher standards for animal welfare in certain key areas, to ensure that the highest possible standards are being met. These standards are constantly under review by a group of experienced organic farmers, vets and scientists to ensure that all the farm animals are reared in optimal conditions on organic farms.

Is organic farming better for the environment?

Extensive research has shown that organic farming can be better for the environment than conventional agriculture. Surveys by, among others, the Ministry of Agriculture and the British Trust for Ornithology, have shown the beneficial effects of organic farming on wildlife. It's not difficult to see why: the pesticides used in intensive agriculture kill many soil organisms, insects and other larger species. They also kill plants considered to be weeds. This means fewer food sources available for other animals, birds and beneficial insects, and the destruction of many of their habitats.

In contrast, organic farming provides a much wider range of habitats: more hedges, wider field margins, herb and clover-rich grassland and a mixed range of crops. Wildlife is not a luxury for the organic farmer, but an essential part of the farming system, and conservation is an integral part of the Soil Association's standards.

The avoidance of artificial chemicals means organic farmers minimise health and pollution problems. They also reduce the use of non-renewable resources such as the fossil fuels which are used to produce fertilisers and other agrochemicals.

How do I know if it is organic?

'Organic' is a term defined by law, and all organic food production and processing is governed by strict standards. Producers, manufacturers and processors of organic foods have to be registered with one of the approved certification bodies and are required to keep detailed records ensuring a full trail of traceability from farm, through any processing operations, to table. Any major infringement of this results in the suspension of their licence and withdrawal of products from the market. All organic farmers, food manufacturers and processors are inspected annually, as well as being subject to random inspections.

The standards are stringent and cover every aspect of registration and certification, organic food production, permitted and non-permitted ingredients, the environment and conservation, processing, packaging and distribution. The standards are regularly updated and are then enforced by certification bodies.

To avoid any confusion with non-organic produce, most organic food is sold pre-packaged. Always check for the symbol and/or number of recognised certification bodies. Where produce is sold loose, proof of certification must be available to consumers. If the retailer cannot prove certification of the produce being sold, then find out who their supplier is and contact them to find out about their certification. All manufacturers must be registered with a certification body. Some shops pay a certification fee to register as organic in their own right. This gives an added assurance to customers. Any shop that repackages goods out of sight of customers, or cooks its own food and labels it 'organic', must also have its own licence to do so.

What about organic imports— just how 'organic' are they?

Each EU member state has its own national organic certifying authority which applies the EU regulation in that country. These approve private certification bodies, or in some cases take on the role of certification themselves. As in the UK, each certification body may apply additional specifications on top of the EU standards.

Food imported from outside Europe into the EU is subject to similar rigorous checks and standards. Imported produce must come either from countries recognised as applying equivalent standards and inspection procedures, or from identified supply chains where it can be verified that equivalent standards and certification criteria have been permanently and effectively applied at all stages. Importers and their storage facilities are also inspected and certified to ensure all their importing activities comply with the above.

Who are the certification bodies in the UK?

The organic food sector in the UK is expanding rapidly. Although over 70% of all organic products in the UK carry the Soil Association symbol, there are a number of other certifiers who, unlike the Soil Association and Demeter, operate on a profit-making basis. The certification bodies are:

 Soil Association Certification (SA Cert)—UK5

 Organic Farmers and Growers Ltd (OF&G)—UK2

 The Scottish Organic Producers Association (SOPA)—UK3

 The Organic Food Federation (OFF)—UK4

 Demeter (BDAA)—UK 6

 The Irish Organic Farmers and Growers (IOFGA)—UK7

 Food Certification (Scotland) Ltd

 Organic Trust Ltd—UK9

 CMi Certification—UK10

 FVO (Farm Verified Organic)—UK11

Organic Certification Ltd—UK12
Quality Welsh Food Certification—UK13
SGS United Kingdom Ltd—UK14

 Ascisco Limited—UK15

What do the UK codes mean?

Each certification body within the UK is given a UK code—the Soil Association is UK5. The number awarded has nothing to do with stringency standards but rather the order in which DEFRA received applications from the certification bodies. Legally, a company does not need to show a certification symbol on pack, but if the product has been produced and/or processed in the UK they must show the UK code. The Soil Association standards are among some of the highest in the world.

What are biodynamic farming standards?

You will notice that some of the producers listed in this directory are certified as biodynamic. Biodynamic farmers apply organic standards but in addition use special preparations for field sprays, and compost and manure treatments. Close attention is also paid to practical rhythms in husbandry, concentrating on closed systems. Biodynamics is a contemporary organic philosophy, following the ideas of Rudolf Steiner; it sees the whole earth as a living organism interrelating with the universe. Biodynamic produce is certified by the Demeter Standards Committee and carries their symbol, which is their trademark.

The Labelling of Organic Food

Strict EC regulations cover the labelling of organic foods, with the aim of ensuring that consumers are not misled. Natural products such as potatoes and lettuce may only be described as 'Organic' if they have been grown by a registered organic producer; they will probably be labelled 'Organically Grown Lettuce' or just 'Organic Lettuce'. The inspection system for organic producers is covered in the Introduction to this book. Manufactured goods such as bread are covered by the same regulations and will probably be labelled, e.g., 'Bread baked from Organic Flour'. Where it is not possible to manufacture goods from wholly organic ingredients, the manufacturer can use up to 5% non-organic minor ingredients—these are specified in the regulations and are recognised as not being available in sufficient quantities in organic form. So products labelled 'Organic' will be between 95% and 100% organic.

Products containing between 70% and 95% organic ingredients cannot be labelled 'Organic'. These products may use the term 'Organic' only in their ingredients list in descending weight order, e.g. Organically grown wheat (55%), Organically grown barley (15%), Organically grown oats (7%).

Products containing less than 70% organic ingredients may not use the term 'Organic' or any derivative of the term anywhere on the label. Percentages refer to agricultural ingredients; non-agricultural ingredients (e.g. water and salt) are not included in the calculations. No genetically modified or irradiated organisms are allowed in organic food products.

The UK registration body, UKROFS, also recognises all other EC certification bodies and a limited number of non-EC certification bodies that have an equivalent standard and inspection system. For all other countries, importers must demonstrate, either to UKROFS or an equivalent body in another EC country, that the food has been produced to equivalent standards and inspection systems in order for them to be allowed to use the term 'Organic' or its derivatives. A list of worldwide organic logos is available from the International Federation of Organic Agricultural Movements (IFOAM)—see under Associations listing.

How to use this directory

The heart of this Directory (pages 22–445) comprises the entries for suppliers of organic goods and services: producers, wholesalers, retailers, bed & breakfast, restaurants & cafés, and garden and farm sundries. This is followed by (pages 446–476) a listing of a wide range of associations working in the field. Finally there is the index by name of the companies and organisations listed.

The symbols for the various kind of entries are shown before each company name. Sets of symbols with their meaning are scattered throughout the Directory, depending on the space available.

Please telephone suppliers before making a special journey to visit them! Inevitably, some companies in the Directory will move premises, or even go out of business. The world of organics is changing fast.

There have been changes in recent years as regards the naming of Welsh and Scottish counties. We have used the current county and unitary authority names in this book.

Disclaimer

All the information in this Directory regarding the producers, retailers etc. and the products they grow and sell has been gathered primarily from the entrants themselves. We have not verified any claims as to whether any produce described as such is 100% organic. Please note therefore that we cannot be held responsible for any claims made as to the quality of the produce or goods offered. There has recently been a proliferation of 'Green' labelling schemes, and we advise you to satisfy yourself as to the validity of any such claims.

What the symbols mean

The symbols of the organic certifying bodies are given on page 16.

 Accommodation: this can be anything from a field for camping to a hotel with full board.

 Box Schemes/Local Deliveries: local box schemes and/or delivery services. Boxes may be delivered to the door or to a central pick-up point.

 Day Visits: generally farms open to visitors. Some may require prior booking.

 Eco Products: non-food items, cleaning materials, toiletries etc.

 Farm Gate Sales: sales of produce from the farm (may need prior notification).

 Garden and Farm Sundries: composts, seeds, tools, etc.

 Farmers' Market Stall: sales of produce from local farmers' market stall.

 Manufacturers/Processors: mainly food manufacturers and/or processors, but can be any manufacturing process.

 Importers and/or exporters.

 Mail Order Suppliers including internet suppliers

 Producers: farmers, growers etc.

 Restaurants/Cafés/Caterers. All claim to serve some organic produce.

 Retail shops.

 Textiles: clothes, nappies, mattresses, bed linen etc.

 Wholesalers and distributors.

BEDFORDSHIRE

CATLIN, DAVID
CHURCH FARM, CHURCH LANE, FLITTON MK45 5EL
Tel: 01525 861452 Fax: 01525 861452 Contact: D. Catlin
farmercatlin@aol.com
Soil Association G4481. Vegetable and salad grower delivering within a 40-mile radius of Bedford.

DAIRYBORN FOODS LTD
DAIRYBORN WAY, EATON GREEN RD., LUTON LU2 9XF
Tel: 01582 457979 Fax: 01582 400957 Contact: Billy O'Riordan
billy.o'riordan@kerry.ie
Cheese products for food manufacturers.

JORDANS (CEREALS) LTD, W
HOLME MILLS, BIGGLESWADE SG18 9JY
Tel: 01767 318222 Fax: 01767 600695 Contact: Emily Turner
www.jordanscereals.co.uk
Jordans have been producing natural cereals for 30 years, and their organic range combines superior quality, exceptional taste and support for British farming.

PRATT, SH & CO (BANANAS) LTD
LAPORTE WAY, LUTON LU4 8EN
Tel: 01582 436503 Fax: 01582 436570 Contact: Brice Lamarque
bricelamarque@shpratt.com
Soil Association P2512. S.H. Pratt & Co (Bananas) Ltd import and ripen organic bananas for the UK market.

SHERRY'S HEALTH FOODS
58 HIGH ST., BIGGLESWADE SG18 0LJ
Tel: 01767 220020 Fax: 01767 782663 Contact: Christine Soulsby
sheradbrit@aol.com
Health food shop with a wide range of organic foods, vitamins and mineral supplements, herbs, homoeopathy, aromatherapy.

SPIRIT OF NATURE LTD
UNITS 1–2, CLIPSTONE BROOK IND PARK, CHERRYCOURT WAY,
LEIGHTON BUZZARD LU7 4GP
Tel: 0870 725 9885 Fax: 0870 725 9886 Contact: Oliver Burrell
mail@spiritofnature.co.uk www.spiritofnature.co.uk
Spirit Of Nature offers over 1,000 natural and environmentally friendly products. Clothing made from organic raw material, bodycare made from organically grown wildcrafted herbs, natural and organic baby products and environmentally friendly household and cleaning products. Natural products—feel the difference.

WHOLEFOODS & HEALTH
1 THURLOW ST., BUS STATION SQUARE, BEDFORD MK40 1LR
Tel: 01234 219618 Fax: 01234 312929 Contact: Paul Martin
Extensive range of natural food products, vitamins, minerals, herbal supplements, special dietary and organic foods.

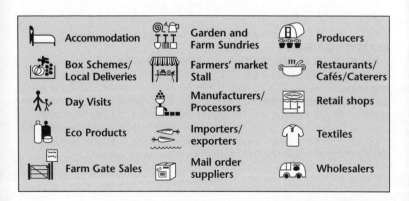

Accommodation	Garden and Farm Sundries	Producers
Box Schemes/ Local Deliveries	Farmers' market Stall	Restaurants/ Cafés/Caterers
Day Visits	Manufacturers/ Processors	Retail shops
Eco Products	Importers/ exporters	Textiles
Farm Gate Sales	Mail order suppliers	Wholesalers

BERKSHIRE

BONDUELLE LTD
5 RICHFIELD PLACE, 12 RICHFIELD AVENUE, READING RG1 8EQ
Tel: 0118 957 6020 Fax: 0118 957 6030 Contact: Vanessa Nagy
info@bonduelle.co.uk
Production and wholesaling of vegetables from the field to finished production in cans and jars.

BROCKHILL FARM ORGANIC SHOP
BROCKHILL FARM, WARFIELD, BRACKNELL RG42 6JU
Tel: 01344 882643 Fax: 01344 882643 Contact: Silvana Keen
A whole range of organic food under one roof: fresh fruit and vegetables, meat, poultry, fish, dairy produce, groceries, wine and beer etc. Local delivery.

DOVES FARM FOODS LTD
SALISBURY RD., HUNGERFORD RG17 0RF
Tel: 01488 684880 Fax: 01488 685235 Contact: Clare Marriage
mail@dovesfarm.co.uk www.dovesfarm.co.uk
Soil Association PD04. Speciality flour millers and bakers with over 20 years experience of organic food manufacturing. Ranges include home baking flours, breakfast cereals, sweet and savoury biscuits, snack bars, cakes and bread. Also gluten-free flours and biscuits.

ELLIS ORGANICS
2 BRAMLEY CRESCENT, SONNING COMMON, READING RG4 9LU
Tel: 0118 972 2826 Fax: 0118 972 4187 Contact: Aidan Carlisle
ellis-organics@clara.net www.eatorganic.co.uk
Soil Association certification Nos. E06S & RE06S. Organic food home delivery specialist for the Reading and Henley-on-Thames areas. A fantastic quality range of fresh produce, some grown on our own farm, is complemented by a full range of other totally organic groceries including fair trade, special dietary foods and Soil Association standard meats and poultry.

ELM FARM RESEARCH CENTRE
HAMSTEAD MARSHALL, NEWBURY RG20 0HR
Tel: 01488 658298 Fax: 01488 658503 Contact: Pat Walters
elmfarm@efrc.com www.efrc.com
EFRC provides agricultural and policy research, education and training
courses, a farm trail, organic, OCIS and in-conversion advisory service,
organic demonstration farm network, soil analysis, publications; also consultancy and producer groups.

GARLANDS ORGANIC
6 READING ROAD, PANGBOURNE RG8 7RS
Tel: 0118 984 4770 Fax: 0118 984 4220 Contact: Denise Ingrem
Soil Association G1619. A fantastic organic emporium with home-grown
vegetables, groceries, fine cheeses, local and British meat, supplements,
etc. Special diets, regional breads, consulting room, lovely shop, great staff.
Parking behind.

THE KINDERSLEY CENTRE AT SHEEPDROVE ORGANIC FARM
THE KINDERSLEY CENTRE, SHEEPDROVE ORGANIC FARM, WARREN FARM,
LAMBOURN RG17 7UU
Tel: 01488 674737 Fax: 01488 72285 Contact: Pippa Regan
pippa.regan@thekindersleycentre.com www.thekindersleycentre.com
Sustainable, organic and environmentally sound, the Kindersley Centre
combines exceptional surroundings with the most advanced technology
and attentive service. Set at the heart of award-winning Sheepdrove
Organic Farm, the centre is housed within a beautiful, eco-friendly building, surrounded by fields and woodlands. A range of meeting places and
adaptable seating for up to 200 people.

THE ORGANIC BEEF COMPANY
THE OLD CRAVEN ARMS, INKPEN, HUNGERFORD RG17 9DY
Tel: 01488 668326 Fax: 01488 668429 Contact: Bernard Harris
enquiries@theswaninn-organics.co.uk www.theswaninn-organics.co.uk
Organic beef farm and butchery managed with The Swan Inn—organic
restaurant, bar food and organic farm shop specialising in all organic meats
and ready meals. An integrated organic business.

ORGANICO

60–62 KINGS RD, READING RG1 3AA
Tel: 0118 951 0518 Fax: 0118 951 0519 Contact: Charles Redfern
info@organico.co.uk www.organico.co.uk
Import and distribution of authentic high quality produce supplying the
specialist organic and wholefood trade as well as fine food stores. Winner of
10 Great Taste Awards 2003. Wide range of quality organic brands and food
products: juices, pasta, sauces, babyfoods, tinned fish, dairy and gluten-free
products, veggie spreads, cordials, jams, fruit purées, oils, vinegars, soups.

PRODUCT CHAIN LTD

TWYFORD MILL, 55 HIGH ST., TWYFORD RG10 9AJ
Tel: 0118 934 4944 Fax: 0118 934 1399 Contact: The Manager
info@productchain.com www.productchain.com
Soil Association P5339; Organic Food Federation 00424/01. Product Chain
is the foremost broker/agent in the UK, having been personally involved in
the movement since 1974. Associated with most of the key brands and
players, including Martlet, Grove Fresh, Tim's Dairy, Amy's Kitchen and
more to come.

RANGER ORGANICS LTD

HOLMES OAK FARM, COLLINS END, GORING HEATH, READING RG8 7RJ
Tel: 01491 682568 Fax: 01491 681694 Contact: Theresa Whittle
ranger.organics@virgin.net
Soil Association R07M. Traditional range of English and Continental cuts of
home-produced organic beef sold at local and London Farmers' Markets.
Beef Highly Commended at the Organic Food Awards 2002; poultry winner
1999 and highly commended 2000. Rare breed poultry and laying geese.

ROCKS ORGANICS

LODDON PARK FARM, NEW BATH RD., TWYFORD RG10 9RY
Tel: 0118 9342344 Fax: 0118 934 4539 Contact: Melanie Ketch
hugh@rocksorganic.com www.rocksorganic.com
Soil Association P2150. Specialist producer of organic dilutable drinks, we
are a dedicated organic producer only.

SHEEPDROVE ORGANIC FARM

WARREN FARM, SHEEPDROVE, LAMBOURN, HUNGERFORD RG17 7UU
Tel: 01488 71659 Fax: 01488 72677 Contact: Hayley Smith
manager@sheepdrove.com www.sheepdrove.com
Driven by a passionate concern for animal welfare, wildlife preservation and a sustainable rural economy we produce our own organic beef, lamb, mutton, chicken and pork. We hang and cut all our meat on the farm and offer a bespoke service with nationwide delivery. Organic and environmentally sound, The Kindersley Centre combines exceptional surroundings with state of the art technology for meeting, conferences and events for between 8 and 200 delegates. See display ad.

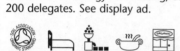

THE SWAN INN ORGANIC FARM SHOP

CRAVEN RD., INKPEN, HUNGERFORD RG17 9DX
Tel: 01488 668326 Fax: 01488 668306 Contact: Mary Harris
enquiries@theswaninn-organics.co.uk www.theswaninn-organics.co.uk
Organic beef, lamb, pork, chicken and turkey all matured and butchered on the premises. Bacon, gammons, sausages, burgers, ready to eat organic meals all manufactured on premises and sliced cold roast beef and ham. Special orders available. Over 1,000 items of veg, dairy, dry goods in stock. Ten luxurious bedrooms and gourmet restaurant. Public House, organic bar meals.

VINTAGE ROOTS LTD

FARLEY FARMS, BRIDGE FARM, READING ROAD, ARBORFIELD RG2 9HT
Tel: 0118 976 1999 Fax: 0118 976 1998 Contact: Neil Palmer
info@vintageroots.co.uk www.vintageroots.co.uk
Specialist shippers of the finest organic wines, beers, ciders, spirits and other products from around the world. Call for free brochure (Freephone 0800 980 4992) or visit our website. See display ad.

WALTHAM PLACE FARM
CHURCH HILL, WHITE WALTHAM, MAIDENHEAD SL6 3JH
Tel: 01628 825517 Fax: 01628 825045 Contact: Steve Castle
estateoffice@walthamplace.com www.walthamplace.com
Soil Association No G557 since 1989. Mixed organic farm and gardens
open to the public Mon–Fri (excl. bank holidays) 10am–4pm. Produce
available at farmers' markets and farm shop include seasonal vegetables,
preserves, meat, eggs and bread. Tearoom serves light organic lunches and
teas. See display ad.

WILTON HOUSE
33 HIGH STREET, HUNGERFORD RG17 0NF
Tel: 01488 684228 Fax: 01488 685037 Contact: D Welfare
welfares@hotmail.com www.wiltonhouse.freeserve.co.uk
Although not totally organic, Wilton House offers mainly organic or locally
produced wholesome food in its classic English town house. Elegant, high
standard accommodation with 2 beautiful en suite bedrooms from £30pp
per night.

WISTBRAY TEAS LTD
PO BOX 125, NEWBURY RG20 9LY
Tel: 01635 278648 Fax: 01635 278672 Contact: Lynn Painter
info@wistbray.com www.elevenoclocktea.com
Wistbray Teas is an exciting and innovative family business with over 100
years of passionate tea experience. Eleven O'Clock Rooibosch Tea is the
original caffeine-free tea and the Dragonfly Organic speciality range offers
high quality teas for every taste. Alternative website:
www.dragonfly-teas.com.

BRISTOL COUNTY BOROUGH

BARLEY WOOD WALLED GARDEN
THE BETTER FOOD COMPANY, THE BRISTOL PROVING HOUSE,
SEVIER STREET, BRISTOL BS29QS
Tel: 0117 935 1725 Fax: 0117 941 4520 Contact: Phil Haughton
admin@betterfood.co.uk www.walledgarden.co.uk
Restored Victorian kitchen garden open to the public, weekly box scheme
using seasonal produce from the garden. The produce is sold in the Better
Food Company in Bristol, and also direct to the public, through other
shops and restaurants. A wonderful piece of our heritage for all to enjoy,
set on a gentle southern slope overlooking the Mendips. Ideal for a family
visit—learn about the garden's history, buy the plants and produce, and
visit the tearooms and craft workshops.

BART SPICES LTD
YORK ROAD, BRISTOL BS3 4AD
Tel: 0117 977 3474 Fax: 0117 972 0216 Contact: Matthew Shaw
bartspices@bartspices.com www.bartspices.com
Bart Spices produces a range of organic herbs and spices destined for multiple retailers. We also sell bulk organic herbs and spices to other food
manufacturers. Bart Spices is a member of the Soil Association.

THE BETTER FOOD COMPANY
THE BRISTOL PROVING HOUSE, SERVIER ST., ST. WERBURGHS,
BRISTOL BS2 9QS
Tel: 0117 935 1725 Fax: 0117 941 4520 Contact: Phil Haughton
admin@betterfood.co.uk www.betterfood.co.uk
Organic grocery store based in the Centre for Ethical Trade and Creative
Play, specialising in fresh vegetables, salads and fruit from their Walled
Garden in Wrington, near Bristol. The huge range of other produce
includes a delicatessen counter and butcher's counter, dairy, all basics such
as rice, pasta and cereals, chocolate, wine & spirits and cleaning materials.

BOCM PAULS LTD

1ST AVENUE, ROYAL PORTBURY DOCK, BRISTOL BS20 7XS
Tel: 01275 378384 Fax: 01275 373828 Contact: Mike Thompson
mike.thompson@bocmpauls.co.uk www.bocmpauls.co.uk
Soil Association P2091, P2966, P4688. BOCM Pauls manufacture approved
non-organic and partially organic feeds for dairy cows, youngstock, beef
and sheep. The products are supported by specialist management services
for organic producers.

BORN

64 GLOUCESTER RD., BISHOPSTON, BRISTOL BS7 8BH
Tel: 0117 924 5080 Fax: 0117 924 9040 Contact: Eva Fernandes
info@borndirect.com www.borndirect.com
Retail and internet shop specialising in organic, natural and practical
products for pregnancy and babies. We're the experts on washable cotton
nappies! Organic range includes organic cotton and wool baby wear
(underwear, nightwear, outerwear and bedding), organic herbal teas for
pregnancy and afterwards, toiletries made with organic ingredients
(Weleda, Green People, Urtekram), organic massage oils. We are open
Monday–Saturday 9.30–5.30.

BRENDA'S

251 HOTWELL ROAD, HOTWELLS, BRISTOL BS8 4SF
Tel: 0117 929 8154 Contact: Jane Wiltshire
brenthinks@hotmail.com
A small family business selling top quality fruit and veg, organic milk and
eggs, organic boxes and a large range of organic wholefoods. Brenda's also
stocks award-winning Herberts bread including organic loaves and 100% rye
bread for people with wheat allergies. We also stock a wide range of non-
dairy products. Brenda's offers a viable alternative to the faceless supermarkets, and is an important and active member of the local community. If you
want personal service and top quality produce, Brenda's is the place for you!

BRITISH SEED HOUSES LTD

PORTVIEW RD., AVONMOUTH, BRISTOL BS11 9JH
Tel: 0117 982 3691 Fax: 0117 982 2198 Contact: Paul Billings
seeds@bshavon.co.uk www.britishseedhouses.com
Soil Association P5945. Wholesale seed merchants producing and supplying
both agricultural and amenity seed trade with conventional and organic
seeds of grass, clover and cereal varieties.

CAFE MAITREYA

89 ST. MARKS RD., EASTON, BRISTOL BS5 6HY
Tel: 0117 951 0100 Fax: 0117 951 0200 Contact: Rob Booth
thesnug@cafemaitreya.co.uk www.cafemaitreya.co.uk
Café-restaurant serving delicious modern vegetarian food using some
organic ingredients where practical. All served with love and care.
Daytimes: Wed–Sun. Evenings Tues–Sat.

EARTHBOUND

8 ABBOTSFORD RD., COTHAM, BRISTOL BS6 6HB
Tel: 0117 904 2260 Contact: Pat Clark
Friendly, local organic and fine food store selling fresh organic fruit and
vegetables, a wide selection of organic and natural groceries, speciality
chocolate, good organic breads, all locally sourced where possible. Also
household and body care products.

ESSENTIAL TRADING CO-OPERATIVE LTD

UNIT 3 & 4, LODGE CAUSEWAY TRADING ESTATE, FISHPONDS,
BRISTOL BS16 3JB
Tel: 0117 958 3550 Fax: 0117 958 3551 Contact: Frances Barnsley
sales@essential-trading.coop www.essential-trading.coop
Trade only. Essential Trading is a natural foods wholesaler supplying the
independent retail sector. Our product range is entirely vegetarian and we
carry only GMO-free products. Aiming for totally organic product range.
Registered with OF&G and BDAA. Customer careline 0845 458 1459.

FIRST QUALITY FOODS

UNIT 29, THE BEECHES, LAVENHAM ROAD, YATE, BRISTOL BS37 5QX
Tel: 01454 880044 Fax: 01454 853355 Contact: Steve Fisher
fqf@mail.com www.firstqualityfoods.co.uk
Sammy's Organic couscous in 3 varieties: Mediterranean Tomato, French
Provençal, Italian Pesto; Ma Baker Organic cereal bars in 4 varieties: Date
& Walnut, Almond, Apricot, Apple & Sultana.

FRESH & WILD

85 QUEENS RD, THE TRIANGLE, CLIFTON, BRISTOL BS8 1QS
Tel: 0117 910 5930 Fax: 0117 925 7871 Contact: Alison Powell
Fresh & Wild are the leading specialist retailer of organic foods and natural
remedies.

HARVEST NATURAL FOODS

11 GLOUCESTER ROAD, BRISTOL BS7 8AA
Tel: 0117 942 5997 Fax: 0117 924 9073 Contact: Ruth Alderman
harvest@bristolshop.fsnet.co.uk
We are a wholefood retailer specialising in organic and fair traded goods,
including fresh produce, chocolate, ice cream, tea, coffee, wine, beer.

HEART OF DEVON ORGANICS

ALBERT CRESCENT, BRISTOL BS2 0XM
Tel: 01647 24894 Fax: 01647 24894 Contact: Geoff Jones
Soil Association P6946. The largest sole wholesaler of quality organic fresh
fruit and vegetables in the South-West. Working closely with local and near
continent growers. Deliveries from M4 to Lands End.

JEKKA'S HERB FARM

ROSE COTTAGE, SHELLARDS LANE, ALVESTON, BRISTOL BS35 3SY
Tel: 01454 418878 Fax: 01454 411988 Contact: Jekka McVicar
farm@jekkasherbfarm.com www.jekkasherbfarm.com
Soil Association G5869. This farm grows over 500 different varieties of herb
and native wild flowers. The transplants are grown to Soil Association
Standards. The herb displays have won RHS Gold Medals at the Chelsea
Flower Show in 1995, 1996, 1997, 1999, 2000, 2001, 2002 and 2003. The
farm also has Open Days throughout the year and runs herb workshops.

MILLERS COFFEE BAR

55 QUEENS RD., CLIFTON, BRISTOL BS8 1QQ
Tel: 0117 914 6549 Contact: Anne Miller
Licensed café. Most of our coffees and teas are organic; we also stock
Luscombe organic drinks, Rock Home Farm and Yeo Valley ice cream.

MUNCH ORGANIC

100 KINGS DRIVE, BISHOPSTON, BRISTOL BS7 8JH
Tel: 0117 954 0808 Contact: Catherine Twine
kingscourt01@tiscali.co.uk
Make cakes, pasties and sandwiches for sale to shops in the local area. A
selection of buffets are available for outside events.

MURRAY, T & PA

153 GLOUCESTER RD., BISHOPSTON, BRISTOL BS7 8BA
Tel: 0117 942 4025 Contact: Tom Murray
Butcher and delicatessen. Purveyors of organic meats and delicatessen foods.

NEAL'S YARD REMEDIES

126 WHITELADIES RD., CLIFTON, BRISTOL BS8 2RP
Tel: 0117 946 6034 Fax: 0117 946 6034 Contact: Clare Proctor
mail@nealsyardremedies.com www.nealsyardremedies.com
Stockists of a wide variety of natural remedies and cosmetics; many are certified organic, including herbs and tinctures, homoeopathic and flower remedies, e.g. essential oils, bath and body products. Also massage oils and books.

ONE PLANET

39–41 PICTON ST., BRISTOL BS6 5PZ
Tel: 0117 942 6644 Contact: Roger Cole
roger@oneplanetwholefoods.co.uk
Vegetarian and vegan community wholefoods store selling organic, fair traded, and local produce, fruit and veg, dairy, breads, with 100% organic juice bar.

PRIMROSE CAFE ICE CREAM

BOYCES AVENUE, CLIFTON, BRISTOL BS8 4AA
Tel: 0117 946 6577 Contact: Patrick Glennie-Smith
primrosecafe@talk21.com
Soil Association P7528. Producer of small quantities of pure natural ice creams, sorbets and frozen yoghurts. All handmade on our own premises.

PUKKA HERBS LTD

14 FREDERICK PLACE, CLIFTON, BRISTOL BS8 1AS
Tel: 0117 974 4811 Fax: 0117 974 3234 Contact: Sebastian Pole
sebastian@pukkaherbs.com www.pukkaherbs.com
Specialist organic ayurvedic growers, manufacturers and producers of the highest quality organic herbal teas, tinctures, capsules and oils. We are committed to sustainable farming, fair trade and personal wellbeing.

R & B (BRISTOL) LTD

UNIT 4, BRISTOL DISTRIBUTION PARK, HAWKLEY DRIVE,
BRADLEY STOKE, BRISTOL BS32 9BF
Tel: 01454 456700 Fax: 01454 456710 Contact: The Manager
We are a Soil Association certified site (P2492) and produce organic pasta sauces for retail.

SOUTHVILLE DELI

262 NORTH ST, SOUTHVILLE, BRISTOL BS3 1JA
Tel: 0117 966 4507 Contact: Paul Wick
pgw-awe@dircon.co.uk
We are a retail store selling organic wholefoods including bread, dairy products & eggs. In addition, we have a small delicatessen carrying as wide a range of organic luxury goods as possible, including fresh olives, cheeses & chocolates. We also grind organic & fair trade coffees to order.

STONEGROUND

5 THE MALL, CLIFTON BS8 4DP
Tel: 0117 974 1260 Contact: Jackie Budd
Veggie, GM-free shop stuffed with pulses, cereals and soya plus 200 organic delights and award-winning fresh bread. Excellent organic, veggie wines and beers. Also vitamins/supplements and herbal remedies. Local where possible.

WILD OATS WHOLEFOODS

9–11 LOWER REDLAND ROAD, REDLAND, BRISTOL BS6 6TB
Tel: 0117 973 1967 Fax: 0117 923 7871 Contact: Mike Abrahams
info@woats.co.uk www.woats.co.uk
Organic natural foods grocery specialising in chilled, frozen and ambient foods, wines, beers, toiletries, natural medicines, household products, organic and natural paints, books. Mail order service available.

WINDMILL HILL CITY FARM SHOP

PHILIP STREET, BEDMINSTER, BRISTOL BS3 4EA
Tel: 0117 963 3233 Fax: 0117 963 3252 Contact: Keith Ladbrooke
Info@windmillhillcityfarm.org.uk www.windmillhillcityfarm.org.uk
We sell locally produced food including organic meat, free-range eggs, goat's milk and vegetables grown by organic methods on our inner-city farm. Open Tuesday to Saturday, 10am to 5pm.

DUDLEY, JC & CO LTD

CHEYNEY HOUSE, FRANCIS YARD, EAST STREET, CHESHAM HP5 1DG
Tel: 01494 792839 Fax: 01494 792875 Contact: Mark Dudley
sales@jcdudley.co.uk www.jcdudley.co.uk
Soil Association P4449. Importers/agents dealing in organic fruit juice
concentrates, NFC fruit juices and purées, along with frozen elderflowers
and frozen and dehydrated cranberries, blueberries and lingonberries.

FIELDFARE ORGANIC AND NATURAL LTD

THE BARNS, NASH LEE LANE, WENDOVER HP22 6BG
Tel: 0845 601 3240 Fax: 01296 622245 Contact: Sandie Calow
office@fieldfare-organics.com www.fieldfare-organics.com
Soil Association P1870. Organic Retail Guild. Home delivery of all your
organic requirements: fruit and vegetables, bakery and dairy, meat, poultry
and fish, wholefoods, wines, beers, aromatherapy and baby care.

FULLER'S ORGANIC FARM SHOP

MANOR FARM, BEACHAMPTON, MILTON KEYNES MK19 6DT
Tel: 01908 269868 Fax: 01908 262285 Contact: Sally Barwell
fullers.organics@farmline.com
Superb quality home-produced rare breed organic meat and poultry.
Resident Master Butcher, own cured ham and bacon, also eggs, vegetables,
dairy and wide range of artisan products.

GILES FOODS LTD

6 TANNERS DRIVE, BLAKELANDS, MILTON KEYNES MK14 5BU
Tel: 01908 217824 Fax: 01908 217825 Contact: David Marx
info@gilesfoods.com www.gilesfoods.com
Soil Association P5044. Chilled bakery products: primarily quiche, Danish
pastries, garlic slices (frozen), party foods (fresh and frozen). Speciality
breads, garlic bread and dough balls (all chilled).

GREAT HUNDRIDGE MANOR FARM

THE ESTATE OFFICE, GREAT HUNDRIDGE MANOR,
GREAT MISSENDEN HP16 0RN
Tel: 01494 794551 Fax: 01494 794552 Contact: Charles Mullins
Soil Association G2520. Farm: mainly arable.

HEALTHRIGHT

48C FRIARS SQUARE, AYLESBURY HP20 2SP
Tel: 01296 397022 Contact: Roger Oliver
Member of Soil Association. We stock a variety of organic products
including dried fruits, bread, cakes, cereals, pulses, rice, teas, soya milk and
soy sauce.

HEALTHRIGHT

27 HIGH ST., CHESHAM HP5 1BG
Tel: 01494 771267 Contact: Roger Oliver
Health food store selling a full range of foods, supplements, herbal and
homoeopathic remedies, aromatherapy oils, filters, cleaning products,
books, cassettes, CDs plus Bach care products.

ONLY NATURAL

41 ST. PETERS COURT, CHALFONT ST. PETER SL9 9QQ
Tel: 01753 889441 Fax: 01753 889441 Contact: Mr Sachdev
Small volume of pre-packed organic products including frozen organic
ready meals.

Europe leading resistance to GM foods

*Widespread resistance to GM foods has resulted in a global showdown. US exports of
genetically modified maize and soya are down, and hungry African nations won't even accept
the crops as food aid. The EU is implementing a more stringent labelling and traceability
programme. Monsanto is faltering financially and is desperate to open new markets. The US
government is convinced that the European Union's (EU) resistance is the primary obstacle
and is determined to change that.*

**From *Seeds of Deception: Exposing Corporate and Government Lies about the Safety of
Genetically Engineered Food* by Jeffrey M. Smith, Green Books, £9.95**

PIZZA ORGANIC LTD
54 LONDON END, OLD BEACONSFIELD HP9 2JH
Tel: 01494 677758 Contact: Mike Traszko
info@pizzapiazza.co.uk www.pizzapiazza.co.uk
Expanding range of Soil Association accredited restaurants featuring a
menu packed full of organic stonebaked pizza, sautéed pasta, gourmet
burgers, grilled fish and fabulous desserts to die for.

REDFIELD COMMUNITY
BUCKINGHAM RD., WINSLOW MK18 3LZ
Tel: 01296 713661 Fax: 01296 714983 Contact: Chrissy Schmidt
info@redfieldcommunity.org.uk www.redfieldcommunity.org.uk
Redfield is an intentional community. We grow and raise our own organic
produce as well as run courses and offer accommodation for groups.

REVITAL HEALTH AND BEAUTY
12 THE HIGHWAY, STATION RD, BEACONSFIELD HP9 1QQ
Tel: 01494 678787 Contact: The Manager
www.revital.com
Health shop.

THE ORGANIC WINE COMPANY
PO BOX 81, HIGH WYCOMBE HP13 5QN
Tel: 01494 446557 Fax: 01494 446557 Contact: Tony Mason
afm@lineone.net
Importers and wholesalers, including mail order (by the case) of organic
wines, beers, spirits, juices, and olive oils. Established over 18 years, with a
range of over 300 lines.

THE SUSTAINABLE LIFESTYLES RESEARCH CO-OP LTD

THE OFFICE, POND COTTAGE EAST, CUDDINGTON RD., DINTON,
AYLESBURY HP18 0AD
Tel: 01296 747737 Contact: Mike George
mikegeorge.lara@btinternet.com
Organic Food Federation 0071/01/981. Free range eggs, seasonal vegetables and fruit, especially Victoria plums. Occasional lamb, mutton (Jacobs sheep). Selling at Tring Farmers' market and from farm stall. Full public access to 70 acres. Farm walks through woodland to the riverside. Run by volunteers.

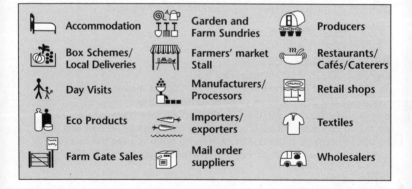

Accommodation	Garden and Farm Sundries	Producers
Box Schemes/Local Deliveries	Farmers' market Stall	Restaurants/Cafés/Caterers
Day Visits	Manufacturers/Processors	Retail shops
Eco Products	Importers/exporters	Textiles
Farm Gate Sales	Mail order suppliers	Wholesalers

CAMBRIDGESHIRE

BELSOS (UK) CEREALS LTD
38–40 STAPLEDON RD., ORTON SOUTHGATE, PETERBOROUGH PE2 6TD
Tel: 01733 362900 Fax: 01733 394111 Contact: Terry Black
terry@belso.co.uk www.belsos.co.uk
Manufacture and packing of breakfast cereals including traditional blended mueslis and baked crunchy products. Able to supply in bulk or in retail units, cartons or bags, especially own-label.

BRITISH SUGAR PLC
OUNDLE ROAD, PETERBOROUGH PE2 9QU
Tel: 08000 688022 Fax: 01733 422916 Contact: Robin Lloyd
sales@britishsugar.co.uk www.britishsugar.co.uk
British Sugar's organic range includes granulated, cane, icing and liquid sugars. The range is supplied to meet all your product requirements and provides all the functionality expected from quality sugars.

BRITISH SUGAR PLC
OUNDLE RD., PETERBOROUGH PE2 9QU
Tel: 0870 240 2314 Fax: 0870 240 2729 Contact: Richard Cogman
rcogman@britishsugar.co.uk www.britishsugar.co.uk
British Sugar Plc manufactures LimeX products which are ideal for rapid, persistent correction of acidity. LimeX contains useful nutrients and may be used in organic systems. Flexible service options meet the needs of individual customers. Email: coproducts@britishsugar.co.uk

DAILY BREAD CO-OPERATIVE (CAMBRIDGE) LTD
UNIT 3, KILMAINE CLOSE, CAMBRIDGE CB4 2PH
Tel: 01223 423177 Fax: 01223 425858 Contact: Christian Osborne
cambridge@dailybread.co.uk www.dailybread.co.uk
Soil Association P4448. We retail and wholesale wholefoods, with a good and increasing range of organic flours, grains, cereals, pulses, fruit and vegetables.

DELFLAND NURSERIES LTD

BENWICK ROAD, DODDINGTON, MARCH PE15 0TU
Tel: 01354 740553 Fax: 01354 741200 Contact: Jill Vaughan
info@delfland.co.uk www.delfland.co.uk
Vegetable, salad, herb and ornamental plants for outdoor and
greenhouse/polytunnel production. Wholesale deliveries made all over the
UK. Retail shop and mail order for gardeners and allotment holders—
on-line catalogue at www.organicplants.co.uk. See display ad.

THE FRESH NETWORK

THE FRESH NETWORK LTD., PO BOX 71, ELY CB6 3ZQ
Tel: 0870 800 7070 Fax: 0870 800 7071 Contact: Karen Knowler
info@fresh-network.com www.fresh-network.com
Trying to eat more healthily? We are here to help. We specialise in promoting and supplying organic raw and living foods and publish *Get Fresh!*
magazine, hold an annual Fresh Festival featuring many of the world's
leading authorities on natural healthy living, and offer an extensive range
of specialist books, foods and kitchen equipment by mail order, including
juicers, sprouting equipment, dehydrators and much more. See display ad.

G's MARKETING LTD

HASSE RD., SOHAM, ELY CB7 5UN
Tel: 01353 727513 Fax: 01353 624388 Contact: Paul Heaton
paul.heaton@gs-marketing.com www.gs-marketing.com
Soil Association P4445. Growers and packers of organic salads and vegetables. Growing in Cambridgeshire and the West Midlands producing the
finest quality organic produce. Sourcing product worldwide when out of
the UK season.

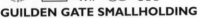

GUILDEN GATE SMALLHOLDING

86 NORTH END, BASSINGBOURN, ROYSTON SG8 5PD
Tel: 01763 243960 Contact: Simon Saggers
simon.saggers@home.pipex.com www.guildengate.co.uk
Soil Association G5970. Mixed organic smallholding offering local veggie
box scheme and guided tours. Wildflower meadow, veg & herb fields,
woodland, pond and orchards. Interesting on-site water and energy
resource cycles. A practical design for living and working in a more ecologically sound and sustainable way.

JARDINS DU MIDI

BROAD END RD., WALSOKEN, WISBECH PE14 7BQ
Tel: 01945 465556 Fax: 01945 465795 Contact: Jon Chesworth
jdmuk@dialstart.net
Soil Association P6068. A manufacturer of a wide range of vegetable purées
(garlic, ginger, chilli, onion, pepper, etc) and roasted vegetables (onion,
pepper, aubergine, courgette, tomato etc).

LANDAUER HONEY LTD

TOP BARN, FOWLEMERE RD., NEWTON, CAMBRIDGE CB2 5PG
Tel: 01223 872444 Fax: 01223 872512 Contact: Mr Steen
landauerhoney@compuserve.com www.landauergroup.co.uk
Honey refiner supplying the food manufacturing industry.

MASTEROAST COFFEE COMPANY LTD

50–54 IVATT WAY BUSINESS PARK, WESTWOOD, PETERBOROUGH PE3 7PN
Tel: 01733 842000 Fax: 01733 266934 Contact: D Baxter
info@masteroast.co.uk www.masteroast.co.uk
Soil Association P2995. Roasting, grinding and packing of fresh coffee
beans to customers' requirements.

NATURALLY YOURS

THE HORSE AND GATE, WITCHAM TOLL, ELY CB6 2AB
Tel: 01353 778723 Contact: Jo & Bob Horton
Organic Farmers and Growers reg. no. OCL 0274. Suppliers of organic and additive-free foods including meat, fish, fruit and vegetables and groceries. Full traditional butchery service. Fruit and vegetables box scheme. Free delivery within defined area.

NEAL'S YARD REMEDIES

1 ROSE CRESCENT, CAMBRIDGE CB2 3LL
Tel: 01223 321074 Contact: Ali Hunte
cambridge@nealsyardremedies.com www.nealsyardremedies.com
Neal's Yard Remedies manufactures and retails natural cosmetics in addition to stocking an extensive range of herbs, essential oils, homoeopathic remedies and reference material.

NORGROW INTERNATIONAL LTD

GRANGE FARM LODGE, LEVERINGTON COMMON, WISBECH PE13 5JG
Tel: 01945 410810 Fax: 01945 410850 Contact: Henri Rosenthal
sales@norgrow.com www.norgrow.com
Food ingredients (wide range), soya products, sugar and natural sweeteners, beans, peas, pulses, seeds, nuts, fruit, vegetables, culinary and medicinal herbs and spices, essential oils, oleoresins, plant extracts and powders. Bulk and wholesale only. See our website for full range of products.

OAKLEY FARMS

HALL RD., OUTWELL, WISBECH PE14 8PE
Tel: 01945 773387 Fax: 01945 774101 Contact: David Murfit
technical@oakleyfarms.co.uk www.oakleyfarms.co.uk
Growers and packers of organic vegetables, specialising in courgettes, pumpkins and broccoli.

ORGANIC CONNECTIONS INTERNATIONAL LTD

RIVERDALE, TOWN ST., UPWELL, WISBECH PE14 9AF
Tel: 01945 773374 Fax: 01945 773033 Contact: Edwin Broad
sales@organic-connections.co.uk www.organic-connections.co.uk
Soil Association IP1653 & G1885. Fruit and vegetable suppliers to all
aspects of the organic market. We grow, market and pre-pack, and make
nationwide deliveries of our award-winning box scheme. Suppliers to pre-
packers.

ORGANIC HEALTH (CAMBRIDGE)

87 CHURCH ROAD, HAUXTON, CAMBRIDGE CB2 5HS
Tel: 01223 870101 Contact: Jackie Garfit
www.organichealth.biz
Specialist retailer of organic, biodynamic and special diet foods. Thousands
of lines including organic fruit and veg, meat and fish, breads, dairy, vegetarian and vegan foods and lots more. Phone for details. Opening times
Tues–Sat 9am–5pm. Thurs 9–6.30.

PETERBOROUGH HEALTH FOOD CENTRE

25 THE ARCADE, WESTGATE, PETERBOROUGH PE1 1PZ
Tel: 01733 566807 Fax: 01733 566807 Contact: H Walji
We stock organic beans and pulses, dried fruit, teas, honey, cooking oils,
juices, cereals, flour, chocolate and soya milk.

PRO-VEG SEEDS LTD

6 SHINGAY LANE, SAWSTON, CAMBRIDGE CB2 4SS
Tel: 01293 833001 Fax: 01293 833006 Contact: John Burrows/ Julie Jones
johnburrows@provegseeds.com www.provegseeds.com
Wholesale and retail vegetable seed suppliers, supplying to other seed
companies, including packet seed companies and professional growers.

PROSPECTS TRUST

SNAKEHILL FARM, REACH, CAMBRIDGE CB5 0HZ
Tel: 01638 741551 Fax: 01638 741873 Contact: Phil Creme
prospect@farming.co.uk www.prospectstrust.org.uk
Soil Association registered. Charitable trust, working together with people
with learning disabilities. Provision of training, work experience and work
opportunities in organic market gardening and horticulture for people with
learning disabilities.

SMITH FARMS, RUSSELL

COLLEGE FARM, GRANGE ROAD, DUXFORD, CAMBRIDGE CB2 4QF
Tel: 01223 839002 Fax: 01223 837874 Contact: Andrew Nottage
rsmithfarms@fwi.co.uk
Arable and field scale vegetables: producer. Soil Association membership
no. G2440.

UNWINS SEEDS LTD

HISTON, CAMBRIDGE CB4 9LE
Tel: 01223 236236 Contact: Colin Hambidge
colin.hambidge@unwins-seeds.co.uk www.unwins-mailorder.co.uk
Soil Association P4413. Seedsman. Supplier of vegetable and flower seeds
to gardeners.

WATERLAND ORGANICS

WILLOW FARM, LODE, CAMBRIDGE CB5 9HF
Tel: 01223 812912 Fax: 01223 812912 Contact: Paul Robinson
www.waterlandorganics.co.uk
Soil Association G1709. Run local box scheme around Cambridge. Supply
local shops and restaurants with fruit and vegetables. Mail order strawberry
and soft fruit bushes.

CHANNEL ISLANDS

FARM FRESH ORGANICS
LA BIENVENUE FARM, LA GRANDE ROUTE DE ST. LAURENT,
ST. LAWRENCE, JERSEY JE3 1GZ
Tel: 01534 861773 Fax: 01534 861772 Contact: Steven & Linda Carter
We grow a wide range of organic vegetables and import fruit which we
supply island-wide through our box scheme. We supply pre-packed
produce to supermarkets.

GUERNSEY ORGANiC GROWERS
LA MARCHERIE, RUETTE RABEY, ST MARTIN'S, GUERNSEY GY4 6DU
Tel: 01481 237547 Fax: 01481 233045 Contact: Anne Sandwith
guernseyorganics@cwgsy.net www.cwgsy.net/business/guernseyorganics
Soil Association G1000, P1000. We grow over 40 different crops and
approximately 150 different varieties of fruit and vegetables, distributing
them to local households through our home delivery box scheme.

HANSA WHOLEFOOD
SOUTHSIDE, ST. SAMPSONS, GUERNSEY GY
Tel: 01481 249135 Contact: Ruby Farrell
hansa@cwgsy.net
Established 27 years; over 5,000 lines of quality vitamins, minerals, herbal
products (Solgar, FSC etc). Natural toiletries, sports nutrition, wholefoods,
organic products. Mail order specialists. VAT-free. Friendly, reliable service.

HANSA WHOLEFOOD
20 FOUNTAIN ST., ST. PETER PORT, GUERNSEY GY1 1DA
Tel: 01481 723412 Fax: 01481 716388 Contact: Jane Molloy
hansa@cwgsy.net
Established 27 years; over 5,000 lines of quality vitamins, minerals, herbal
products (Solgar, FSC etc). Natural toiletries, sports nutrition, wholefoods,
organic products. Mail order specialists. VAT-free. Friendly, reliable service.

JERSEY DAIRY

FIVE OAKS DAIRY, ST. SAVIOUR, JERSEY JE2 7UD
Tel: 01534 818500 Fax: 01534 818535 Contact: Janet Wyatt
www.jerseydairy.je
Soil Association P4608. Dairy product range. Manufacture, supply and marketing.

THE ORGANIC SHOP

68 STOPFORD RD., ST. HELIER, JERSEY JE2 4LZ
Tel: 01534 789322 Contact: Celina Sochaczewska
organicshop@jerseymail.co.uk
Fresh fruit, vegetables, dairy, meat and poultry, wine and beer. Full range of household cleaning materials and toiletries. Comprehensive delivery service including box scheme.

VERS LES MONTS ORGANIC FARM

RUE DE LA PRESSE, ST. PETER, JERSEY JE3 7FE
Tel: 01534 481523 Contact: Stephen Jones
Soil Association G2465 P5325. A small mixed farm producing a wide range of mixed vegetables, potatoes and eggs sold from the farm stall, box scheme and occasional farmers' markets.

	Accommodation		Garden and Farm Sundries		Producers
	Box Schemes/ Local Deliveries		Farmers' market Stall		Restaurants/ Cafés/Caterers
	Day Visits		Manufacturers/ Processors		Retail shops
	Eco Products		Importers/ exporters		Textiles
	Farm Gate Sales		Mail order suppliers		Wholesalers

ABBEY LEYS FARM

ABBEY LEYS FARM, PEACOCK LANE, HIGH LEGH, NR. KNUTSFORD WA16 6NS
Tel: 01925 753465 Fax: 01925 753465 Contact: Tim Harrison
tim.abbeyleys@virgin.net www.abbeyleys.co.uk
Soil Association G4985. Organic free range hens including Speckledy and
Hebden Black breeds. Free range duck eggs, home-grown Cheshire potatoes, fresh vegetables, fruit, farmhouse ice cream, home-made cakes,
cheese and Abbey Leys honey. Local delivery.

ALLWOOD, MICHAEL & SANDRA

BURLAND FARM, WREXHAM ROAD, BURLAND, NANTWICH CW5 8ND
Tel: 01270 524210 Fax: 01270 524501 Contact: Sandra Allwood
info@ravensoakdairy.co.uk www.ravensoakdairy.co.uk
Wholesaling milk mainly to Ravens Oak Dairy.

AROMART

28 STOCKPORT RD., ROMILEY, STOCKPORT SK6 4BN
Tel: 0161 406 7176 Fax: 0161 494 1129 Contact: Susan Goto
aromart@tiscali.co.uk www.aromart.co.uk
We are a retail shop selling natural and organic products including herbs,
spices and herbal teas.

BARBER, JB & SON

BENTLEY FARM, WHITLEY, WARRINGTON WA4 4QA
Tel: 01925 730784 Contact: Philip Barber
barber@foxbent.freeserve.co.uk
Soil Association G4565. Dairy production and beef.

BOOTHS SUPERMARKETS
STANLEY ROAD, KNUTSFORD WA16 0BS
Tel: 01565 652522 Fax: 01565 652504 Contact: J Roskell
Supermarket with broad range of organic food, clearly labelled in store.
Fresh produce, meat, dairy, Village Bakery products, many other groceries.

THE CHEESE SHOP
116 NORTHGATE STREET, CHESTER CH1 2HT
Tel: 01244 346240 Fax: 01244 314659 Contact: Carole Faulkner
carole@faulkner73.fsnet.co.uk www.chestercheeseshop.com
Specialist cheese shop with local delivery (not a box scheme). We promote
local, organic and British cheeses, particularly cheeses sourced direct from
the farm, mature and cared for in our cellars below the shop. Also organic
wine, chutneys and biscuits.

CHESHIRE ORGANICS
5 BOOTHS HILL ROAD, LYMM WA13 0DJ
Tel: 01925 758575 Fax: 01925 758043 Contact: Jackie Lees
jackie@cheshireorganics.co.uk
Soil Association R2955. Over 1,000 product lines, fruit, vegetables, bread,
dairy, grocery, gluten/dairy/sugar-free products, meat and poultry, home-
care, wine and beer. All delivered direct to your home or office.

DEER PARK FARM
FORTY ACRE LANE, KERMINCHAM, HOLMES CHAPEL, CREWE CW4 8DX
Tel: 01477 532188 Fax: 01477 544638 Contact: Martin & Sue Steer
martin.steer@lineone.net
Organic lamb (whole and half) available to order. Steer Ethelston Rural Ltd.
Rural Chartered Surveyors, Specialists in Environmental and Organic Land
Management.

DEMETER
12 WELLES ST., SANDBACH CW11 1GT
Tel: 01270 760445 Contact: Phillip Shallcross
phillipdemeter@cs.com
A shop full of organic grains, flakes, fruits, nuts, honey, yoghurts, cheese, snacks and sometimes vegetables. Also essential oils, selected supplements (Solgar etc), books, cards and prints (Woodmanstern, Prime Arts).

DUCKWORTH FLAVOURS
ASTMOOR RD., RUNCORN WA7 1PJ
Tel: 0161 872 0225 Fax: 0161 848 7331 Contact: Mike Gilligam
www.duckworth.co.uk
Manufacturers of organic fruit juices and compounds. Flavourings supplied for use in organic products.

ERLAM, JF
SUGARBROOK FARM, MOBBERLEY ROAD, ASHLEY, NR. ALTRINCHAM WA14 3QB
Tel: 0161 928 0879 Contact: JF Erlam
Soil Association G4603. Producing organic lamb, potatoes and cereals. Organic farmhouse B&B with en suite facilities and a friendly welcome.

GOODLIFE FOODS LTD
34 TATTON COURT, KINGSLAND GRANGE, WARRINGTON WA1 4FF
Tel: 01925 837810 Fax: 01925 838648 Contact: Fran Sawyer
enquiry@goodlife.co.uk www.goodlife.co.uk
Manufacturer of frozen vegetarian foods. Soil Association P2241.

NATURE'S REMEDIES
10 TIME SQUARE, WARRINGTON WA1 2AR
Tel: 01925 444885 Fax: 01925 654821 Contact: Janet Hignett
Healthfood shop stocking wide range of organic foods.

THE O ZONE

8 FRAMINGHAM ROAD, BROOKLANDS PARADE, BROOKLANDS, SALE M33 3SH
Tel: 0161 291 8862 Contact: Linda Jones & Sarah Yates
o.zone@virgin.net www.theozone.uk.com
One-stop organic shop. Full range of organic groceries, gift hampers, vouchers, local suppliers.

OAKCROFT ORGANIC GARDENS

OAK CROFT, CROSS 'O' THE HILL, MALPAS SY14 8DH
Tel: 01948 860213 Contact: M.S. Fardoonji
Organic since 1962. Grow large variety of veg and soft fruit, but offer fruit not grown here, bread by order, and eggs. All 100% organic. Delivery to CW5, SY14, CW8, CW4, CH3, WA1. Nantwich, Crewe, Chester, Northwich, Knutsford areas.

THE ORGANIC STORES

BROOKLYN FARM, SEALAND ROAD, CHESTER CH5 2LQ
Tel: 01244 881209 Fax: 01244 881209 Contact: Allan Hughes
Fruit, veg, meat, fish, poultry and much more. Discount for specialised diets. Ample car parking space and carry-out service. Home delivery, not a box scheme. Established in 1996, we only sell organic foods. One-stop organic shopping.

ORGANICFAIR

43 ST. JAMES STREET, CHESTER CH1 3EY
Tel: 01244 400158 Fax: 01244 342228 Contact: Mark Holme
mark@organicfair.co.uk www.organicfair.co.uk
Organicfair is an organic and fairtrade specialist store with a complete range of food, drink and household items and is fully licensed.
We run a delivery service and veg box scheme for Chester, the Wirral and North Wales. We are open 6 days a week from 10am to 7pm.

RAVENS OAK DAIRY

BURLAND FARM, WREXHAM ROAD, BURLAND, NANTWICH CW5 8ND
Tel: 01270 524624 Fax: 01270 524724 Contact: Patrick Brunt
info@ravensoakdairy.com www.butlerscheeses.co.uk
Soft cow Brie and fresh cow cheese.

THE SALT COMPANY

WORLESTON, NANTWICH CW5 6DN
Tel: 01270 611112 Fax: 01270 611113 Contact: Dawn Storey
dawn@thesaltcompany.co.uk www.thesaltcompany.co.uk
Importer of Red Sea salt for use in the organic industry. Packer of salt for
manufacturing and retail use.

STOCKLEY FARM ORGANICS

SMITHY FARMHOUSE, ARLEY, NORTHWICH CW9 6LZ
Tel: 01565 777492 Fax: 01565 777501 Contact: John Walton
organics@stockleyfarm.co.uk www.stockleyfarm.co.uk
Stockley Farm is open to the public and schools from March to October.
Stockley Farm Organics operates a box scheme, hand delivered throughout
Cheshire and south Manchester.

URENBIO

WOODPARK, NESTON, SOUTH WIRRAL CH64 7TB
Tel: 0151 353 0330 Fax: 0151 353 0251 Contact: Jamie Uren
james.uren@uren.co.uk www.uren.com
Soil Association P1723. Urenbio sources, processes, imports and distributes
organic ingredients for the food manufacturing industry. Re-inspection,
quality control and re-packing facility in Whitchurch, Shropshire certified
by SA.

A & N HEALTH FOODS
62 FORE ST., SALTASH PL12 6JW
Tel: 01752 844926 Contact: Janice Clegg
Wholefoods and organics, veggie box scheme, herbal and homoeopathic remedies, vitamin supplements.

ARCHIE BROWNS HEALTHFOODS
OLD BREWERY YARD, BREAD ST., PENZANCE TR18 2EQ
Tel: 01736 362828 Contact: Helen Swift
Retail shop and vegetarian/vegan restaurant selling organic and/or vegan dairy, goat's milk, cheeses, yoghurts, soya products, jams, chocolates, pasta, flour, cereals, nuts, grains, fruits, pulses, biscuits, artisan bread, preserves, honey, drinks, gluten-free products, natural beauty products, natural cleaning products, deli counter, oriental section.

BANGORS ORGANIC TEA ROOM
BANGORS HOUSE, POUNDSTOCK, BUDE EX23 0DP
Tel: 01288 361297 Fax: 01288 361508 Contact: Gill Faiers
neil.faiers@btinternet.com www.bangorsorganic.co.uk
The first certified organic Tea Room in the country, making and serving traditional Cornish yeast splits as part of our delicious cream teas, homemade cakes, biscuits and bread, and proper Cornish pasties. Beautiful location in restored Victorian house and formal garden. The first bed and breakfast premises offering accommodation, with Soil Association certified organic breakfast, in elegant en suite rooms in this magnificent house on the north Cornish coast.

BARWICK FARM
TREGONY, TRURO TR2 5SG
Tel: 01872 530208 Contact: Nick & Barbara Michell
nick@michell.fsbusiness.co.uk www.theorganicfarmersmarket.co.uk
Soil Association G7204. Producing Cornish Jersey dairy products: milk, butter, clotted cream and liquid creams from our own cows. Good healthy natural products.

BODINNICK FARM

ST STEPHENS, ST AUSTELL PL26 7LL
Tel: 01726 882421 Contact: Charles Barnecut
Organic beef and lamb cut ready for use, lamb patties and other products.

BOSAVERN FARM

BOSAVERN, ST. JUST, PENZANCE TR19 7RD
Tel: 01736 786739 Fax: 01736 786739 Contact: Guy & Joanna Clegg
joandguy@bosavern.fsnet.co.uk
Registered with Soil Association G6989. Farm gate sales open Saturdays
from 10am to 2pm, selling freshly picked vegetables, naturally reared beef
and pork, and free range eggs. All from Bosavern Farm.

BOSWEDNACK MANOR

ZENNOR, ST IVES TR26 3DD
Tel: 01736 794183 Contact: E Gynn
www.smoothhound.co.uk/hotels/boswednack
Vegetarian B&B on eco-friendly smallholding. Meditation rooms, gardens,
sea and moorland views, superb walks. Meditation and yoga retreats. St.
Ives, Tate Gallery and beaches 6 miles. Self-catering cottage also available.

BROWDA FARM

LINKINHORNE, CALLINGTON PL17 7NB
Tel: 01579 362235 Contact: Lavinia Halliday
Soil Association G4671. Bed and breakfast accommodation in our large
17th century farmhouse on lovely organic farm near Bodmin Moor.
Traditionally furnished rooms, overlooking gardens. Full English breakfast.
No smoking, no pets. From £27 per person per night.

CALLESTICK VEAN FARM

CALLESTICK VEAN, TRURO TR4 9NF
Tel: 01872 561442 Contact: P Hilton
peter@vean73.freeserve.co.uk
Soil Association G3072. Producers of organic North Devon cattle.

CAMEL VALLEY FARM SHOP

ST. KEW SERVICES, BODMIN, NR. WADEBRIDGE PL30 3ED
Tel: 01208 841343 Fax: 01208 841343 Contact: Alan Vague
info@camelvalleyfarms.co.uk
Meat, cheeses, yoghurt, vegetables, ice cream, pickles, chutneys and eggs.
bread.

CAMEL VALLEY FARMS

LOWER TREDORE, ST. ISSEY, WADEBRIDGE PL27 7QS
Tel: 01841 540767 Fax: 01841 540767 Contact: Alan & Margaret Vague
alan@camelvalleyfarms.freeserve.com www.camelvalleyfarms.co.uk
We produce and sell our own beef, pork, lamb and vegetables. We also
have a farm shop at St. Kew Highway, nr. Wadebridge where we sell other
local produce. Alternative phone/fax: 01208 841343.

CARLEYS OF CORNWALL LTD

34–36 ST. AUSTELL STREET, TRURO TR1 1SE
Tel: 01872 277686 Fax: 01872 277686 Contact: John & Rachel Carley
sales@carleys.co.uk www.carleys.co.uk
Soil Association P1584. We are an organic supermarket specialising in
locally produced fresh fruit and vegetables, meat and dairy foods. We also
import fruit and veg directly from suppliers, manufacture our own 'Carleys'
brand products and have a rapidly expanding home delivery service.

CARLEYS ORGANIC FOODS LTD

THE PARADE, TRURO TR1 1UJ
Tel: 01872 270091 Fax: 01872 270092 Contact: John Carley
sales@carleys.co.uk www.carleys.co.uk
We manufacture our own 'Carleys' brand products.

THE CHEESE SHOP

29 FERRIS TOWN, TRURO TR1 3JH
Tel: 01872 270742 Contact: The Manager
Farmhouse cheeses, handmade and unpasteurised, including organic
cheeses, from Cornwall and across the UK.

CHURCHTOWN FARM

CHURCHTOWN FARM, LANTEGLOS BY FOWEY PL23 1NH
Tel: 01726 870375 Fax: 01726 870376 Contact: M&C Russell
National Trust coastal farm selling organic beef and lamb. Extensive range available in any quantity including delicious barbecue products. Phone first. Soil Association no. G 1784.

COOMBE MILL FARM

PILLATON MILL, NR. SALTASH PL12 5AN
Tel: 01579 350315 Contact: Giles and Angela Greenhough
Organic lamb and eggs.

CORNISH ORGANICS

PENCOYS, FOUR LANES, REDRUTH TR16 6LZ
Tel: 01209 202579 Fax: 01209 202579 Contact: K Thomas
Organic dairy and beef. New farm shop opening Spring 2004. Pork, poultry, eggs, veg.

COTNA ORGANICS

COTNA BARTON, COTNA LANE, GORRAN, ST. AUSTELL PL26 6LG
Tel: 01726 844827 Fax: 01726 844827 Contact: Mike Nicholson
mikenich@gn.apc.org www.cotnaorganics.co.uk
Renewable energy demos. Wide variety of exotic and culinary vegetables, herbs and fruits. Free range eggs. Visitors welcome anytime, come and see our ecobarn along with wind turbine and solar panels.

COUNTRYSTORE HEALTHFOODS

3–5 BOND STREET, REDRUTH TR15 2QA
Tel: 01209 215012 Contact: The Manager
Two shops, one completely organic, selling a whole range of organic foods, eco products, bodycare, babycare, toiletries etc.

CUSGARNE ORGANICS

CUSGARNE WOLLAS, CUSGARNE, NR. TRURO TR4 8RL
Tel: 01872 865922 Contact: Teresa & Greg Pascoe
organicbox@btconnect.com
104-acre holding (certified organic for 13 years). Wide range of vegetables, organic free range eggs, Angus beef reared and sold direct from the holding. Box scheme covers Redruth, Falmouth and Truro triangle, Helston, Porthtowan, Portreath, St. Agnes, Roseland peninsula, Grampound, Probus, St. Austell, and Fowey. Wholesale supplies to hotels and restaurants. Polytunnels for winter salads.

EAST PENREST FARM

LEZANT, LAUNCESTON PL15 9NR
Tel: 01579 370186 Contact: J Rider
jrider@lineone.net www.eastpenrest.freeserve.co.uk
Lamb sold from the farm gate as available, please telephone first. Beef sold wholesale.

GEAR FARM SHOP

ST. MARTIN, HELSTON TR12 6DE
Tel: 01326 221150 Fax: 01326 221150 Contact: David Webb
gearfarmshop.hotmail.com
Farm shop selling organic vegetables, fruit, bakery, wholefoods, dairy, fish.

GLUVIAN FARM

MAWGAN PORTH, NEWQUAY TR8 4BG
Tel: 01637 860635 Contact: Mr Sterling
Organic beef and sheep producers.

GOONGILLINGS FARM

GOONGILLINGS FARM, CONSTANTINE, FALMOUTH TR11 5RP
Tel: 01326 340630 Contact: CL Pugh
enquiries@goongillings.co.uk www.goongillings.co.uk
Soil Association G4621. Four attractive holiday cottages and a restored
antique gypsy caravan on a beautiful waterside organic farm, on the
renowned Helford River in West Cornwall. Quay, boats, tennis court. Pets
welcome.

THE GRANARY

NEWHAM ROAD, TRURO TR1 2ST
Tel: 01872 274343 Fax: 01872 223477 Contact: Jill Thomas
sales@granarywholefoods.co.uk www.granarywholefoods.co.uk
Wholesale distributors of healthfoods, natural foods, delicatessen producers
throughout Cornwall, Devon, Somerset, parts of Wiltshire and Dorset.

GREAT GARGUS FARM

TREGONY, TRURO TR2 5SQ
Tel: 01872 530274 Fax: 01872 530274 Contact: Richard Heywood
gargonauts@farming.co.uk
Organic Dorset x Texel lamb, whole or half, sold in freezer packs to caterers
and private customers.

HEART OF DEVON ORGANICS

C/O 37 JUBILEE STREET, NEWQUAY TR7 1LA
Tel: 01647 24894 Fax: 01647 24894 Contact: Geoff Jones
The largest sole wholesaler of quality organic fresh fruit and vegetables in
the south west. Working closely with local and near continent growers.
Deliveries from M4 to Lands End.

HELSETT FARM CORNISH ICE CREAM

HELSETT FARM, LESNEWTH, BOSCASTLE PL35 0HP
Tel: 01840 261207 Contact: Sarah Talbot-Ponsonby
helsett.icecream@lineone.net
Manufacturer of real Cornish ice cream made in small batches, no
stabilisers or emulsifiers, with all added ingredients (e.g. butterscotch, fruit
purée) prepared in the dairy.

HELSETT LAMB

HELSETT FARM, THE BUNGALOW, LESNEWTH, BOSCASTLE PL35 0HP
Tel: 01840 261713 Contact: Nina Talbot-Ponsonby
ntalbotponsonby@aol.com
Seasonal lamb, hoggets, mutton. Will sell privately by arrangement:
telephone first for availability.

KEIGWIN FARMHOUSE

MORVAH, PENZANCE TR19 7TS
Tel: 01736 786425 Contact: Wyatt-Smith
Organic B&B from £20 per person per night with own farmhouse parlour.

KENIDJACK FARM

ST. JUST IN PENWITH TR19 7QW
Tel: 01736 788675 Contact: Mike Bratt
Soil Association symbol holder, Dexter cattle.

KEVERAL FARMERS LTD

KEVERAL FARM, NR SEATON, LOOE PL13 1PA
Tel: 01503 250135 Contact: Gina Cooper
www.keveral.org
Soil Association PK02W. Workers co-op run, organic veg and fruit, sold
through local box scheme. Also available: apple juice and cider, preserves,
Shiitake/oyster mushrooms and fruiting logs, wild magic liquid feed,
organic herb plants, willow cuttings, camping.

LANSALLOS BARTON FARM

LANSALLOS, LOOE PL13 2PU
Tel: 01503 272293 Contact: Mark Russell
Soil Association demonstration Farm. Cream teas and organic meat for sale in tearoom. Open at Easter and June to September.

LESQUITE FARM

LANSALLOS, LOOE PL13 2QE
Tel: 01503 220315 Contact: Richard Tolputt
www.lesquite-polperro.fsnet.net
Organic potatoes and beef. Self-catering cottage for 2.

LITTLE CALLESTOCK FARM

ZELAH, TRURO TR4 9HB
Tel: 01872 540445 Fax: 01872 540445 Contact: Liz & Nick Down
liznick@littlecallestockfarm.co.uk www.littlecallestockfarm.co.uk
Organic Farmers and Growers UKF090940. Delightful spacious barn conversions, ETC 4 and 5 stars, luxuriously equipped. Whirlpool baths, four poster beds, woodburners, on organic dairy farm with Jersey herd. Peaceful location, countryside, coastal walks. Centrally positioned. Brochure available. Organic eggs from farm gate.

LOWER POLGRAIN

ST. WENN, BODMIN PL30 5PS
Tel: 01637 880082 Contact: Jenni Thomson
Organic beef by arrangement, telephone first.

MAKING WAVES VEGAN GUEST HOUSE

3 RICHMOND PLACE, ST IVES TR26 1JN
Tel: 01736 793895 Contact: Simon Money
simon@making-waves.co.uk www.making-waves.co.uk
Beautiful eco-renovated 19th-century house. Ocean views, peaceful, minutes from shop, beaches and harbour. Delicious organic food. Special diets catered for. Children welcome. Voted 'Best Vegan Guest House' (*Vegan* magazine).

MALCHRIS
GRAVESEND GARDENS, TORPOINT PL11 2HN
Tel: 01752 815508 Contact: Whitworth
Top fruit, soft fruit and vegetables.

MANN, J & P
PENWARNE, FALMOUTH TR11 5PH
Tel: 01326 250136 Contact: J & P Mann
Organic beef.

MARSHLAND MANOR
MORWENSTOW, BUDE EX23 9ST
Tel: 01288 331349 Contact: Jane Marsh
Herd of pedigree Aberdeen Angus suckler cows sold to producers.
Traditional organic Cornish apple orchard suitable for cider making and
cooking.

MASSINGALE, STEPHEN CW
HIGH MEADOWS, MORWENSTOW, BUDE EX23 9PH
Tel: 01420 520888 Fax: 01420 22348 Contact: Stephen Massingale
Soil Association G5021. Organic Southdown lamb produced.

MENABURLE FARM
BOCONNOC, LOSTWITHIEL PL22 0RT
Tel: 01208 873703 Contact: Chris Alderman
Beef, sheep, cereals, vegetables for wholesale, apples for cider making,
occasionally eggs.

MEWTON, PG

NANCARROW FARM, MARANZANVOSE, TRURO TR4 9DQ
Tel: 01872 540343 Contact: PG Mewton
pgmewton@talk21.com
Great beef and great lamb, organic, wholesome and delicious. Meat as it should be! Tastes just right.

THE NATURAL STORE

TRENGROUSE WAY, HELSTON TR13 8RT
Tel: 01326 564226 Fax: 01326 564226 Contact: Paul Johnson
A comprehensive range of organic foods, wholefoods and natural remedies including organic fruit and vegetables, organic meat. Natural foods and products of all sorts, including babycare and eco-friendly cleaning products in our newly extended premises.

THE NATURAL STORE

16 HIGH ST., FALMOUTH TR11 2AB
Tel: 01326 311507 Fax: 01326 311507 Contact: Paul Johnson
A comprehensive range of organic foods, wholefoods and natural remedies including organic fruit and vegetables, organic meat. Natural foods and products of all sorts. Eco-friendly babycare and cleaning products.

NICE ORGANICS

THE OLD DAIRY, SANCREED, PENZANCE TR20 8PQ
Tel: 01736 810033 Fax: 01736 810033 Contact: Hugh Lucas
box@niceorganics.co.uk www.niceorganics.co.uk
Soil Association P7752. Box scheme supplying the finest local organic fruit, vegetables & herbs, additional organic foods available, home delivery service, wholesale fruit & vegetables.

OIL IN THE RAW

DILLETTS COTTAGE, ST. DOMINICK PL12 6TE
Tel: 01579 351178 Contact: Dina Iwanski
dina@oilintheraw.co.uk www.oilintheraw.co.uk
Direct supplies to restaurants and private households. Import and distribution of organic olive oil and table olives direct from Greek organic farms—mostly single estates. Greek organic inspection body: DIO 21301930156; 23301980033; 26301980575; 21301940085 and Greek organic inspection body: SOYE 013061.

OLDS, VIVIAN LTD

2 CHAPEL ROAD, ST. JUST, PENZANCE TR19 7HS
Tel: 01736 788520 Fax: 01736 788520 Contact: Randall Olds
mail@vivianolds.co.uk www.vivianolds.co.uk
Soil Association P2997. Butchers with own slaughterhouse offering local and nationwide delivery of locally reared and purchased organic beef, pork and lamb including meat boxes. Why not try our special sausages?

THE ORGANIC BREWHOUSE

UNIT 1, HIGHER BOCHYM RURAL WORKSHOPS, CURY CROSS LANES, HELSTON TR12 7AZ
Tel: 01326 241555 Contact: Andy Hamer
a.hamer@btclick.com
Soil Association registered. Brewery producing solely organic real ales in cask and bottle conditioned form.

OUGHS UNICORN GROCERS

10 MARKET ST., LISKEARD PL14 3JJ
Tel: 01579 343253 Contact: The Manager
www.oughs.co.uk
Delicatessen, stocking some organic goods.

PLANTS FOR A FUTURE
THE FIELD, HIGHER PENPOL, ST. VEEP, LOSTWITHIEL PL22 0NG
Tel: 01208 873554 www.pfaf.org
Day visits and tours, courses on woodland gardening, permaculture, nutrition, research, information, demonstration and supply of edible and otherwise useful plants. Plants for a Future is a registered charity researching and demonstrating ecologically sustainable vegan organic horticulture in the form of woodland gardening and other permacultural practices.

PURE NUFF STUFF
THE EGYPTIAN HOUSE, 6 CHAPEL ST., PENZANCE TR18 6AJ
Tel: 01736 366008 Fax: 01736 366008 Contact: Niky Keane
info@purenuffstuff.co.uk www.purenuffstuff.co.uk
100% natural skincare, toiletries and cosmetics with pure essential oils and organic ingredients. Free of SLS, paraben, synthetic fragrance, synthetic colours.

RENAS-NATURALS
PO BOX 140, PENZANCE TR18 4YW
Tel: 01736 732399 Fax: 01736 732399 Contact: Rena Hine
info@renas-naturals.com www.renas-naturals.com
Very special gifts! Handmade cosmetics including our own big range of over 70 unusual, handmade designer soaps filled with organic Ingredients. Web site also sells organic & fair-traded teas and links to other interesting sites. Wholesale to Europe & New Zealand.

RIDER, J & J
EAST PENREST, LEZANT, LAUNCESTON PL15 9NR
Tel: 01579 370186 Fax: 01579 370477 Contact: Jo Rider
jrider@lineone.net www.eastpenrest.freeserve.co.uk
Soil Association G1897. Organic beef and sheep farm of 120 acres with 5 star self-catering accommodation in converted barn. Children especially welcome. Beautiful countryside. Home-cooked meals available. Lamb sold from the farm gate as available: please telephone first.

ROSEVINNICK ORGANIC FARM
BOFARNEL, LOSTWITHIEL PL22 0LP
Tel: 01208 871122 Contact: Doreen Hassell
Organic beef, pork, ham, bacon, pork sausages and hogs pudding from traditional Large Black pigs, chives, parsley and sage. Telephone first.

ROSUICK ORGANIC FARM
ROSUICK, ST. MARTIN, HELSTON TR12 6DZ
Tel: 01326 231302 Fax: 01326 231302 Contact: Chris Oates
janetoates@btconnect.com www.oatesorganic.co.uk
Family-run organic farm and shop specialising in home-produced meats and organic wool. Beautiful farmhouse, sleeps 10; cottage, sleeps 6—available for holidays. Well worth a visit.

SCILLY ORGANICS
MIDDLE TOWN, ST. MARTINS, ISLES OF SCILLY TR25 0QN
Tel: 01720 423663 Contact: Jonathan Smith
j.smith@scillyorganics.co.uk www.scillyorganics.co.uk
Scilly Organics is a small market garden producing a wide range of vegetables, fruit and herbs for sales to local markets on the islands. We use permaculture principles and grow on permanent raised beds. As a stockless system we rely on seaweed and good compost as fertilisers. Visitors welcome, regular farm walks in the summer and at other times by appointment.

SOUTH PENQUITE FARM
SOUTH PENQUITE, BLISLAND, BODMIN PL30 4LH
Tel: 01208 850491 Fax: 0870 136 7926 Contact: Dominic & Cathy Fairman
thefarm@bodminmoor.co.uk www.southpenquite.co.uk
Soil Association G4771. Camping and field studies on a working organic hill farm high on Bodmin Moor. Interesting farm walk including diverse wildlife habitats, a bronze age hut settlement, a mile of beautiful riverbank and an imposing standing stone. Mongolian yurt available for that 'back to nature' holiday!

SOUTH TORFREY FARM LTD/ORGANIC FARM HOLIDAYS
GOLLANT, FOWEY PL23 1LA
Tel: 01726 833126 Fax: 01726 832625 Contact: Debbie Andrews
southtorfreyfarm@macace.co.uk
Soil Association G2019. A small family farm growing poultry for meat,
Longhorn cattle and mixed arable crops. We offer peaceful breaks in our
award-winning barn conversions—children and pets very welcome.

SPIEZIA ORGANICS LTD
THE BARN WORKSHOP, ROSUICK FARM, ST. MARTIN, HELSTON TR12 6DZ
Tel: 01326 231600 Fax: 01326 231699 Contact: Loredana Spiezia
loredana@spieziaorganics.com www.spieziaorganics.com
Soil Association I7735. Organic body care and ointments handmade in
Cornwall by infusing herbs in food grade oils to extract all the beneficial
properties. Herbs, flowers, oils and nothing else! Water-free, high concen-
tration, very little needed to feel their benefit. For all skin types and ages,
safe in pregnancy unless there is an existing sensitivity to any particular
ingredient. New home range and soaps. See display ad.

STAMPAS FARM
TREAMBLE, ROSE, TRURO TR4 9PR
Tel: 01872 572837 Contact: Michael R Payne
Soil Association GC5081/G2322. Organic vegetables sold at local WI
markets, a farmers' market and from the farm, subject to availability.
Seasonal soft fruit also produced. Supply local box schemes.

STEPHEN GELLY FARM
LANIVET, BODMIN PL30 5AX
Tel: 01208 831213/832557 Contact: Martin Collinge
mhcollinge@aol.com
Organic poultry, lamb and beef.

STONEYBRIDGE ORGANYKS
TYWARDREATH, PAR PL24 2TY
Tel: 01726 813858 Contact: David Pascoe
Vegetables, soft fruit and herbs. Also retail SA certified organic meat. Farm shop open Tuesday to Saturday noon, from Easter to the end of October.

SUNFLOWER WHOLEFOODS
16A CROSS ST., CAMBORNE TR14 8EX
Tel: 01209 715970 Contact: Webb
Organic wholefoods.

TREE OF LIFE ORGANICS
SCALA NIJ, MITHIAN, ST AGNES, TRURO TR5 0QE
Tel: 01872 552661 Contact: Marie Welsh
treeoflife@eurobell.co.uk
Soil Association registered nos. P2068, G2068. We are a small company that is committed to the sustainable organic way of life. We can supply top quality fresh fruit and vegetables and eggs produced locally. Delivery area: Perranporth, St. Agnes, Redruth, Truro and St. Austell.

TRELEASE FARM
ST. KEVERNE TR12 6RT
Tel: 01326 280379 Contact: John Pascoe
john@trelease.biz
Poultry and eggs, beef cattle, sheep, pigs and vegetables. Attends variety of farmers' markets. Holiday cottages to let.

TRENBERTH, WD & BD
TREVALLARD FARM, MOUNT HAWKE, TRURO TR4 8DL
Tel: 01209 890253 Contact: D Trenberth
Soil Association G2763. Producing beef and winter vegetables.

TRETHINNICK FARM
ST. CLEER, LISKEARD PL14 6RR
Tel: 01579 346868 Contact: CM & PT Gregory
Organic lamb and beef supplied to own local client base.

TREVELYAN FARM
ROSUDGEON, PENZANCE TR20 9PP
Tel: 01736 710410 Contact: Tim Jones
Organic seasonal vegetables, meat and other local produce.

WAINGATES FARM
STRATTON, BUDE EX23 9DL
Tel: 01288 356828 Contact: Barbara Mills
barbara.mills2@btopenworld.com
Soil Association G4152. Holiday accommodation: bed & breakfast plus
self-catering on organic holding one and a half miles from sandy beach.

WIDDICOMBE FARE
4 WEST ST., MILLBROOK, TORPOINT PL10 1AA
Tel: 01752 822335 Contact: Jo Widdicombe
Organic fresh fruit and vegetables on Thursdays, wholefoods etc including
wide range of organic products.

WOODA FARM
CRACKINGTON HAVEN EX23 0LF
Tel: 01840 230140 Contact: Max Burrows
max@woodafarm.co.uk www.woodafarm.co.uk
Producer of organic lamb, eggs, apples, juice and vegetables. Self-catering
cottage or catered accommodation with large barn workspace.

CUMBRIA

ALADDIN AROMAS
NENTHEAD, ALSTON CA9 3NP
Tel: 01434 382820 Fax: 01434 382820 Contact: Adam Herdman
alaromas@aol.com www.aladdinaromas.co.uk
Aromatherapy products—essential oils. Available by mail order only.

ALLEGARTH ORGANICS
ALLEGARTH, ROWELTOWN, CARLISLE CA6 6JU
Tel: 01697 748065 Contact: Stuart Boyd
Soil Association G797. A 12-acre smallholding offering unique holiday
accommodation for up to 8 persons in a secluded and unspoilt part of
North Cumbria. A member of Hadrian Organics.

ALSTON WHOLEFOODS LIMITED
FRONT STREET, ALSTON CA9 3HU
Tel: 01434 381588 Contact: Carol Sutton
Workers co-operative shop with range of wholefoods and organic products.
Speciality cheeses, dietary needs, local eggs, bread, cakes, mustards.
Walkers' and cyclists' snacks, delicious ice creams. Mon–Sat 9am–5pm.

BOOTHS SUPERMARKETS
THE OLD STATION, VICTORIA STREET, WINDERMERE LA23 1QA
Tel: 015394 46114 Fax: 015394 88918 Contact: Boothman
www.booths-supermarkets.co.uk
Organic fruit and veg, fresh meat, dairy, frozen burgers, frozen veg, wines,
preserves, flour, bread, cakes.

CASTLETOWN FARM SHOP
FLORISTON RIGG, ROCKLIFFE, CARLISLE CA
Tel: 01228 674400 Fax: 01228 674400 Contact: Hilary Bliss
info@castletownfarmshop.co.uk www.castletownfarmshop.co.uk
Soil Association registered. Retail specialists in locally sourced organic fine foods, including meat, dairy, jams, pickles, fruit and vegetables, and a range of ready meals.

CHILTERN SEEDS
BORTREE STILE, ULVERSTON LA12 7PB
Tel: 01229 581137 Fax: 01229 584549 Contact: D Taylor
info@chilternseeds.co.uk www.chilternseeds.co.uk
Chiltern Seeds catalogue lists over 4,600 items including an organic vegetable section. There are also flowers, trees, shrubs, annuals, houseplants, exotics for your greenhouse, unusual vegetables and herbs.

ECOS PAINTS
UNIT 34, HEYSHAM BUSINESS PARK, MIDDLETON RD., HEYSHAM LA3 3PP
Tel: 01524 852371 Fax: 01524 858978 Contact: Ian West
mail@ecospaints.com www.ecospaints.com
Organic odourless solvent-free paints, varnishes and other related products.

EVA BOTANICALS
MEDBURN, MILTON, BRAMPTON CA8 1HS
Tel: 01697 741906 Fax: 01697 741205 Contact: Debbie Simpson
debbie.simpson@evabotanicals.co.uk www.evabotanicals.co.uk
We offer a wide range of fruit and vegetables in a box scheme with big savings for drop off points. We also grow organic vegetables, culinary and medicinal herbs.

GARDENS & PETS DIRECT

SEAVIEW NURSERIES, NETHERTOWN, EGREMONT CA22 2UQ
Tel: 01946 820412 Fax: 01946 824091 Contact: Keith Singleton
enquiries@cumbriagardensandpetsdirect.co.uk
www.cumbriagardensandpetsdirect.co.uk
Browse through our vast range of products, all available on-line. Organic tomato, plant and lawn food, poultry pellets, organic soil improvers and peat-free composts.

HALLSFORD (AN & HS TOMKINS)

HALLSFORD FARM, HETHERSGILL, CARLISLE CA6 6JD
Tel: 01228 577329 Fax: 01228 577148 Contact: Andrew
thefarm@hallsford.co.uk www.hallsford.co.uk
Soil Association G7042. Beef and lamb producer in North Cumbria. Pedigree beef Shorthorn cattle and one of the largest flocks of rare breed Llanwenog sheep. Top quality marbled Shorthorn beef and rare breed lamb via local farmers' markets, regional food fairs and nationally by mail order. Rare breed pork to be introduced in 2004. Visit the website.

HARLEY FOODS LTD

BLINDCRAKE HALL, BLINDCRAKE, COCKERMOUTH CA13 0QP
Tel: 01900 823037 Fax: 01900 828276 Contact: M Watson
Importer of organic dried fruits, nuts, beans, pulses, herbs, spices, plus a large variety of ingredients for the wholesaler and manufacturer. We also source products on demand.

HOWBARROW ORGANIC FARM

CARTMEL, GRANGE-OVER-SANDS LA11 7SS
Tel: 015395 36330 Fax: 015395 36330 Contact: Paul Hughes
enquiries@howbarroworganic.demon.co.uk
www.howbarroworganic.demon.co.uk
Grow and process medicinal herbs into tinctures and oils. 13-acre small holding producing meat (lamb, beef, turkeys), eggs, vegetables and medicinal herbs. Supply local box scheme, farmers' markets and our award-winning Organic Farm Shop of the year, 2002. Demonstration farm, walks and displays. Soil Association licenced organic B&B and dinner.

KAN FOODS

9 NEW SHAMBLES, OFF MARKET PLACE, KENDAL LA9 4TS
Tel: 01539 721190 Contact: Elizabeth Kan
lizkan@inthelight.info
A wholefood shop with high grade vitamins, herb, oils, organic make-up,
juices, water filters, harmonisers, help and advice.

LADY JANE'S TEA ROOM

CUMBRIAN ANTIQUE CENTRE, ST. MARTIN'S HALL, BRAMPTON CA18 1NT
Tel: 07941 731255 Contact: Victoria Holt
Delicious home-made food prepared with locally grown organic and fair
trade produce where possible. Outside catering a speciality. We are also a
drop-off point for an organic produce box scheme.

LOW SIZERGH BARN FARM SHOP, TEA ROOM & CRAFT GALLERY

LOW SIZERGH FARM, SIZERGH, KENDAL LA8 8AE
Tel: 01539 560426 Fax: 01539 561475 Contact: Alison Park
apark@low-sizergh-barn.co.uk www.low-sizergh-barn.co.uk
Soil Association G5843. Farm trail-part of the Organic Farms Network.
Large farm shop with full range of fine locally produced food; cheese & ice
cream made with the farm's milk; tea room (watch the cows being milked
at 3.45pm); also crafts.

MOTHER EARTH

BIRKROW COTTAGE, BLAWITH, ULVERSTON LA12 8EG
Tel: 01229 885266 Contact: Jane Holroyd
enquiries@motherearth.co,uk www.motherearth.co,uk
The Mother Earth Holistic skin care collection is a range of of 100% natural
cleansers, toners and moisturisers made with organic herbs and essential
oils, hand-made in small batches and formulated by professional therapists.

SUNDANCE WHOLEFOODS

33 MAIN STREET, KESWICK CA12 5BL
Tel: 01768 774712 Contact: Julian Holdsworth
Soil Association member. A wholefood shop with many organic lines.

THE VILLAGE BAKERY

MELMERBY, PENRITH CA10 1HE
Tel: 01768 881811 Fax: 01768 881848 Contact: Chris Curry
info@village-bakery.com www.village-bakery.com
Organic speciality breads, cakes, savoury biscuits, flapjacks, slices,
Christmas goods. Special diet products. Mail order. Nationwide stockists.
Baking courses.

THE WATERMILL

LITTLE SALKELD, PENRITH CA10 1NN
Tel: 01768 881523 Fax: 01768 881047 Contact: Ana Jones
organicflour@aol.com www.organicmill.co.uk
Soil Association (P632) and Biodynamic Agriculture Association registered.
Specialist organic flours, milled by water power in our 18th century watermill to SA and BDAA standards. Mill shop, tea room, mill tours and baking
courses.

WHITEHOLME FARM

WHITEHOLME, ROWELTOWN, CARLISLE CA6 6LJ
Tel: 016977 48058 Contact: Jon and Lynne Perkin
whiteholmefarm@hotmail.com www.whiteholmefarm.co.uk
Whiteholme Farm is an organic livestock farm situated in the north-east of
Cumbria. Home-reared organic beef, lamb and pork is prepared at our on-
farm butchery from traditional breeds and sold to local customers through
direct sales and farmers' markets. Accommodation, education and farm
walks are all available.

DERBYSHIRE

ADAMS, NICK
CRYSTAL SPRINGS FARM, BRAILSFORD, ASHBOURNE DE6 3BG
Tel: 01335 360996 Contact: Nick Adams
Soil Association G5056. Traditional small mixed livestock farm. Beef and lamb from traditional breeds and other organic meats available. Educational visits and informal circular walks to view farm and conservation activities.

ALLSOP, J & D
BROOKFIELDS, BRASSINGTON, MATLOCK DE4 4HL
Tel: 01629 540370 Fax: 01629 540370 Contact: John & Dorothy Allsop
Summer and winter sheep grazing. Second year of organic system.

AMBROSIAN VEGETARIAN FOODS
HIGHFIELDS LODGE, 69 OCCUPATION RD., ALBERT VILLAGE, SWADLINCOTE DE11 8HA
Tel: 01283 225055 Fax: 01283 550536 Contact: Alan Beck
ambrosian@btopenworld.com ambrosianvegetarianfoods.co.uk
Soil Association P6694. Manufacturer of high quality home-made vegan organic food. The range includes pies, pasties, sos rollo, burgers, sosages and sosage and burger mixes. All products are registered with the Vegan Society and produced under organic standards.

ASHBOURNE BISCUITS
BLENHEIM RD., AIRFIELD IND. ESTATE, ASHBOURNE DE6 1HA
Tel: 01335 342373 Fax: 01335 346394 Contact: Roy Johnson
enquiries@ashbournebiscuits.co.uk www.ashbournebiscuits.co.uk
Soil Association registered. An award-winning independent family-run biscuit baker specialising in production of traditional hand-baked biscuits using only the purest natural ingredients, including a developing range of organic sweet and savoury biscuits.

BEANO'S WHOLEFOODS
HOLME ROAD, MATLOCK BATH DE4 3NU
Tel: 01629 57130 Fax: 01629 57143 Contact: Anne Thorne
john@beanos.go-plus.net
Box scheme delivering selection of organic fruit & vegetables.

DOVEDALE CONFECTIONERY LTD
VERNON STREET INDUSTRIAL ESTATE, SHIREBROOK NG20 8SL
Tel: 01623 742277 Fax: 01623 743020 Contact: George Robinson
dovedale@o2.co.uk
Soil Association P3084. We are a private label manufacturer of novelty
chocolate items and biscuits. All our production is own label, therefore all
work is confidential.

ENGLISH ORGANIC FOODS PLC
THE OLD VICARAGE, 226 ASHBOURNE RD., TURNDITCH DE56 2LH
Tel: 01773 550173 Fax: 01773 550855 Contact: Brian Ashby
Organic matching agency.

FRANK WRIGHT LTD
BLENHEIM HOUSE, BLENHEIM RD., ASHBOURNE DE6 1HA
Tel: 01335 341155 Fax: 01335 341171 Contact: Cara Freeston-Smith
cara.freeston-smith@basf-a-n.co.uk
Soil Association P6918. The manufacturers of Soil Association-approved
mineral supplements for organic ruminant livestock, which are essential to
maintain performance, health and welfare. Also available as bespoke
formulations for specific farm needs.

HI PEAK FEEDS LTD
HI PEAK FEEDS MILL, SHEFFIELD RD., KILLAMARSH S21 1ED
Tel: 0114 248 0608 Fax: 0114 247 5189 Contact: P Whitfield
info@hipeak.co.uk www.hipeak.co.uk
Manufacturers and distributors of organic and UKROFS permitted animal
feeds for all farm livestock, horses and dogs. Nationwide delivery and mail
order. Soil Association licence no. P2486, OF&G licence no. 11UKP090258.
We supply farmers and smallholders.

JEFFERY, H & SON

ASTON HOUSE FARM, SUDBURY, NR. ASHBOURNE DE6 5AG
Tel: 01283 585410 Contact: Robert Jeffery
r.jeffery@farmline.com www.newlandowner.co.uk
Beef from longhorn cattle born and reared on this organic farm is available fresh or frozen by appointment from the farmhouse (mobile: 07971 566907). The farm is conveniently situated just off the A50 on Lichfield Rd, Sudbury.

LOWER HURST FARM

LOWER HURST FARM, HARTINGTON, NR. BUXTON SK17 0HJ
Tel: 01298 84900 Fax: 01298 84732 Contact: Catherine Pyne
sales@lowerhurstfarm.co.uk www.lowerhurstfarm.co.uk
Soil Association G7616, P7654. A small farm in Derbyshire producing exclusive organic beef from its own herd of pure bred Hereford cattle. Awarded 'Best Beef/Sheep Farm' in the 2003 Organic Food Awards and also the winner of the Waitrose Small Producer Awards 2002. Full range of products is available through mail order or secure on-line shop. A 'Monthly' shop is held at the farm on the 1st Friday in every month, and also Open Days where visitors can walk the farm trail, take a tractor tour around the Herefords or simply relax in the stunning surroundings whilst enjoying a delicious steak and a glass of wine.

MEYNELL LANGLEY ORGANIC FOOD

MEYNELL LANGLEY, KIRK LANGLEY, ASHBORNE DE6 4NX
Tel: 01332 824815 Contact: Helen Meynell
Beef from our suckler herd of pedigree Welsh blacks, lamb, chicken, eggs and vegetables. Turkey and geese to order for Christmas, all produced on the farm. Also locally produced pork. Farm shop Fri 1–6.30pm, Sat 10am–2pm, other times (phone). Local deliveries possible, not box scheme. All meat products except turkeys and geese for Christmas are frozen; fresh meats can be available to order.

MIMMO'S
1 ST. MARY'S GATE, WIRKSWORTH, MATLOCK DE4 4DQ
Tel: 01629 826724 Contact: Melanie Glendinning
Soil Association member (personal, not business). Home-made Sicilian
dishes using seasonal organic meat and vegetables, pasta, rice and herbs.

NATURAL CHOICE
24 ST. JOHN ST., ASHBOURNE DE6 1GH
Tel: 01335 346096 Fax: 01335 346096 Contact: Steve Parker
naturalchoice@tiscali.co.uk www.naturalchoicehealth.co.uk
Health foods, wholefoods, natural supplements. Natural therapy centre.

NEW HOUSE ORGANIC FARM
KNIVETON, ASHBOURNE DE6 1JL
Tel: 01335 342429 Contact: RA Smail
bob@newhouse.farm.co.uk
OF&G 11UK F030109. Hill farm producing beef, lamb, eggs, veg and fruit.
Farm shop. School visits. Waymarked archaeological farm trail.
Accommodation in converted barn with solar panel and wind turbine. Plus
large organised camping.

NORTHERN TEA MERCHANTS
CROWN HOUSE, 193 CHATSWORTH RD., CHESTERFIELD S40 2BA
Tel: 01246 232600 Fax: 01246 555991 Contact: James Pogson
enquiries@northern-tea.com www.northern-tea.com
Soil Association P1719. Tea bag manufacturers, coffee roasters. Packers of
fine teas and gourmet coffees.

ORGANIC PUMPKIN
KINGFISHER COTTAGE, KING ST., DUFFIELD, DERBY DE56 4EU
Tel: 01332 370254 Fax: 01332 370254 Contact: David Yolshina-Cash
www.organicpumpkin.co.uk
Organic Food Federation 00461. Fresh seasonal organic vegetables picked
and delivered the same day. Evening delivery Wednesday and Thursday.

THE ORGANIC SHOP
3 SETT CLOSE, NEW MILLS SK22 4AQ
Tel: 01663 747550 Fax: 01663 747550 Contact: D Carroll
theorganicshop@aol.com
Complete range of organic products.

SUNFLOWER HEALTH STORE
20 MARKET PLACE, ILKESTON DE7 5QA
Tel: 0115 930 4750 Contact: P Leach
We sell a wide range of groceries, supplements and cosmetics, stocking as
many organic and ethically produced goods as possible. We are pleased to
order items not stocked if available.

WELEDA (UK) LTD
HEANOR ROAD, ILKESTON DE7 8DR
Tel: 0115 944 8222 Fax: 0115 944 8210 Contact: Roger Barsby
info@weleda.co.uk www.weleda.co.uk
Demeter certified. Weleda produces natural medicines and body care
products, using ingredients from our Demeter-certified gardens.

WILD CARROT
5 BRIDGE ST., BUXTON SK17 6BS
Tel: 01298 22843 Contact: Julian Grant
shop@wildcarrot.freeserve.co.uk www.wildcarrot.freeserve.co.uk
Soil Association GC5018, R7228. We are a wholefood workers co-op
specialising in organic foods and alcohol, fair-traded goods and
environmentally friendly products. We support local and UK growers and
prepare organic veg boxes. We are a member of Organic 2000.

DEVON

ACLAND ORGANIC MEATS
EAST ACLAND FARM, LANDKEY, BARNSTAPLE EX32 0LD
Tel: 01271 830216 Contact: Charles Morrish
Soil Association M12W. Beef and lamb.

AGROFORESTRY RESEARCH TRUST
46 HUNTERS MOON, DARTINGTON, TOTNES TQ9 6JT
Tel: 01803 840776 Contact: M Crawford
mail@agroforestry.co.uk www.agroforestry.co.uk
Research charity producing books and information on fruits, nuts and
agroforestry; also plants, seeds and rootrainers.

ALAN'S APPLE
26 FORE STREET, KINGSBRIDGE TQ7 1NY
Tel: 01548 852308 Contact: Alan Knight
Traditional greengrocer stocking organic vegetables, organic dairy produce,
organic ice cream and organic meat and poultry.

THE ARK WHOLEFOODS SHOP
38 EAST STREET, ASHBURTON TQ13 7AX
Tel: 01364 653020 Contact: Kennedy
the-ark@clara.co.uk
Small is beautiful: this shop is crammed full of a huge variety of lines
including many organic ones. Vegetables are sourced from Heart of Devon
and Woodlands Organics. Baked goods are home-made or come from a
local vegetarian bakery. Organic lines are represented in most dry goods
and dairy sectors too.

THE BARTON

THE BARTON, POUGHILL, CREDITON EX17 4LE
Tel: 01363 866349 Contact: Anne Wander
a.wander@btinternet.com
Luxury on-farm self-catering holiday accommodation with indoor pool
(from summer 2004).

BEAMING BABY

UNIT 1, PLACE BARTON FARM, MORELEIGH, TOTNES TQ9 7JN
Tel: 0800 0345 672 Fax: 01548 821 589 Contact: Charlie Wynne
charlie@beamingbaby.com www.beamingbaby.com
Beautiful organic baby clothes, the best choice of washable nappies,
eco-disposable nappies, natural wipes, organic and natural baby toiletries.
Eco-friendly toys, natural bedding. Essentials for mother, and many treats.
too.

BEDPORT FARM

BEDPORT FARM, BURRINGTON, UMBERLEIGH EX37 9LE
Tel: 01769 560592 Fax: 01769 560592 Contact: S Tyler-Upfield
12,000 organic laying hens producing eggs.

BEE ORGANIC

MOOTHILL CROSS, STAVERTON TQ9
Tel: 07817 467936 Contact: Paul Hutchings
Soil Association G6389. A small-scale operation growing a huge range of
vegetables and herbs and fruit. We particularly specialise in heritage
varieties to conserve genetic diversity, and grow for flavour.

BISHOPS FARM

STAPLEDON, ANVIL CORNER, HOLSWORTHY EX22 6NR
Tel: 07812 756430 Contact: Tom & Sue Barnes
Soil Association G7841. Producing free range organic eggs for supermarket
outlets.

BRAGG, MC

THE GATEHOUSE, SHILLINGFORD ABBOTT, EXETER EX2 9QU
Tel: 01392 833040 Contact: Martyn Bragg
martyn.bragg@virgin.net
Soil Association G2572. We grow fresh vegetables and herbs for our box
scheme, delivering to the Exeter area. We also grow cereals: wheat, barley,
triticale and protein crops.

BUCKFAST ORGANIC BAKERY

HAMLYN HOUSE, MARDLE WAY, BUCKFASTLEIGH TQ11 0NR
Tel: 01364 642279 Fax: 01364 642279 Contact: Sally Carson
sallycarson@buckfastleighbakery.com www.buckfastleighbakery.com
Soil Association P2974. Manufacturers of savoury vegetarian and organic
pies, gluten-free pies and cakes, high-fruit organic flapjacks. Products also
available from www.theorganicfarmersmarket.co.uk.

BUCKLAND FILLEIGH ORGANIC PRODUCE

BRAMLEY WOOD, BUCKLAND FILLEIGH, BEAWORTHY EX21 5JD
Tel: 01409 281693 Contact: Jane Bartlett
bramleywood@tiscali.co.uk
Sustainable woodland organic enterprise deriving main income from
organic free range eggs, horticulture, plant raising and forest fruits.
Forestry products include charcoal, logs, timber, mushrooms, self-building
log/timber home.

CERIDWEN HERBS

CERIDWEN, OLD RECTORY LANE, PYWORTHY EX22 6SW
Tel: 01409 254450 Contact: Rob Meredith
cdt-dlee@supanet.com
Soil Association G2255/P7995. Organic veg, fruit, herbs, plants, jams,
chutneys, eggs. Part of Holsworthy Organics veg box scheme. Farmers'
markets and Tavistock pannier market (Fridays).

CHIMAN'S
CLEAVE FARM, EAST DOWN, BARNSTAPLE EX31 4NX
Tel: 01271 883864 Fax: 01271 882843 Contact: Sally Agarwal
sallyagarwal@yahoo.co.uk
Soil Association P5692. Dried spice blends for home-cooked Indian meals—
recipes on the back of the packs. Catering packs also available.

COTONS CONTINENTAL CHOCOLATES
UNIT 1 ISLAND SQUARE, ISLAND STREET, SALCOMBE TQ8 8DP
Tel: 01584 844004 Fax: 01458 844345 Contact: Robin Coton
robin@cotonschocolates.co.uk www.cotonschocolates.co.uk
Hand-made chocolates using Belgian organic chocolate. Cotons brands
include award-winning plain and milk chocolate 100g bars, we also make
truffles, Easter egg and Christmas models.

THE CAFE AND SHOP
THE SQUARE, CHAGFORD TQ13 8AE
Tel: 01647 432571 Fax: 01647 432985 Contact: Ruth Olley
compost@properjob.eclipse.co.uk www.properjob.ik.com
Café, wholefood and greengrocery shop. All goods are organic, fair
traded or local—or all three.

COWLING, MR & MRS NR
DOCKWELL FARM, WIDECOMBE IN THE MOOR, NEWTON ABBOT TQ
Tel: 01364 621268 Contact: NR Cowling
vennorm@btinternet.com
Soil Association P5549. Organic beef, single suckler herd raised on
Dartmoor. Simmental cross calves for sale in the autumn.

DARTINGTON TECH—THE REGIONAL CENTRE FOR ORGANIC HORTICULTURE

WESTMINSTER HOUSE, 38/40 PALACE AVENUE, PAIGNTON TQ3 3HB
Tel: 01803 867693 Fax: 01803 867693 Contact: Cherry Lyons
clyons@dartingtontech.co.uk www.dartingtontechco.uk
The Regional Centre for Organic Horticulture is an education and resource centre for the promotion of organic gardening and horticulture. We offer courses for professionals and amateurs at our Soil Association-certified site.

DARTMOOR DIRECT CO-OPERATIVE LTD

MITCHELCOMBE FARM, HOLNE, NEWTON ABBOT TQ13 7SP
Tel: 01364 631528 Contact: Roger Mitchell
Home delivery service: bottled water, local produce and organic foods.

DEVON FOODS LTD

KNIGHTSWOOD FARM, BLUEBELL LANE, CULLOMPTON EX15 1RW
Tel: 01884 32816 Fax: 01884 32806 Contact: Graham Frankpitt
sales@devonfood.co.uk www.devonfood.co.uk
Specialise in production of Soil Association organic day-old chicks, table birds, duck, guinea fowl, hatching eggs and point of lay pullets.

DITTISHAM FARM

CAPTON, DARTMOUTH TQ6 0JE
Tel: 01803 712452 Contact: Sue Fildes
sue@self-cater.co.uk www.self-cater.co.uk/dff
Organic beef: 'Red Ruby Devon' breed. Organic rare-breed pork: 'Berkshire' breed. See our pigs at the Devon, Cornwall, Bath & West & Royal Shows—ring me for confirmation. Organic hen & duck eggs. Self-catering accommodation in rural bungalow for 2 adults (+ cot).

DRAGONFLY FOODS

2A MARDLE WAY, BUCKFASTLEIGH TQ11 0NR
Tel: 01364 642700 Fax: 01364 642700 Contact: Simon Boreham
info@beany.co.uk www.beany.co.uk
Manufacturer of organic chilled soya bean products, including tofu, Beanys, Soysage and Tatty, an organic chilled potato product. Sold to independent health food shops in the UK.

DROUGHTWELL FARM

SHELDON, HONITON EX14 4QW
Tel: 01404 841349 Contact: Ian & Sue Cochrane
droughtwellfarm@aol.com
Organic sheep and beef. Self-catering for 2 plus a cot in one end of the farmhouse, dog welcome.

EARTHSTAR, LITTLE EAST LAKE FARM

EAST CHILLA, BEAWORTHY EX21 5XF
Tel: 01409 221417 Contact: M Robley
EARTHSTAR@myactiveware.co.uk
Producers and sellers direct to the consumer of Soil Association symbol standard eggs, vegetables, preserves and soft fruit. Produce delivered locally. Members of Holsworthy Organics veg box scheme.

ECO SCI—WEST COUNTRY COMPOST

WOLFSON LABORATORIES, HIGHER HOOPERN LANE, EXETER EX4 4SG
Tel: 01392 424846 Fax: 01392 425302 Contact: Steve Bullock
mail@ecosci.co.uk www.ecosci.co.uk
Soil Association I1848. Eco Sci compost over 40,000 tons of recycled green waste to produce West Country Compost, quality compost that both nourishes and conditions the soil. Available in bags, on pallets and bulk, throughout the South-west.

ELDER, D
LOWER CHITTERLEY FARM, SILVERTON, EXETER EX5 4BP
Tel: 01392 860856 Fax: 01392 860856 Contact: D Elder
darren1963landie@aol.com
Direct sales to the public of beef, lamb, poultry and eggs produced to Soil
Association standards.

ENDACOTT, WA LTD
21 EAST ST., OKEHAMPTON EX20 1AT
Tel: 01837 52888 Fax: 01837 54381 Contact: Michael Finucane
Soil Association P4830. Wholesale and retail bakers and confectioners:
organic bread and rolls.

FERRYMAN POLYTUNNELS LTD
BRIDGE RD., LAPFORD, CREDITON EX17 6AE
Tel: 01363 83444 Fax: 01363 83050 Contact: Hugh Briant-Evans
info@ferryman.uk.com www.ferryman.uk.com
Manufacturers of polytunnel greenhouse kits for private and commercial
growers.

FISHLEIGH ESTATE
FISHLEIGH HOUSE, OKEHAMPTON EX20 3QA
Tel: 01837 810124 Fax: 01837 810124 Contact: Victoria Sargent
enqiries@fishleighestate.com www.fishleighestate.com
We sell fully traceable, well hung organic beef and lamb. We have won
many prestigious conservation awards including the Bronze Otter Award.
We are members of CLA, NFU, Soil Association.

FORD BARTON LTD
FORD BARTON, STOODLEIGH, TIVERTON EX16 9PP
Tel: 01398 351139 Fax: 01398 351157 Contact: Sally
sales@fordbarton.co.uk www.fordbarton.co.uk
Soil Association G5659. Naturally dyed, organic Wensleydale wool from our
own sheep, using mainly dyes from the farm. Producing an exclusive range
of knitted and woven household goods and garments.

FOUNTAIN VIOLET FARM

MOUNT RIDLEY RD., KINGSWEAR TQ6 0DU
Tel: 01803 752363 Fax: 01803 752885 Contact: Emma Jones
ed@fvfarm.freeserve.co.uk
Soil Association registered. Organic beef from pure breed South Devon
herd available via convenient mail order and box scheme.

GREAT CUMMINS FARM

TEDBURN ST. MARY, EXETER EX6 6BJ
Tel: 01647 61278 Fax: 01647 61278 Contact: David Garaway
davidgaraway@yahoo.co.uk
Soil Association G5570. Production and sale of organic vegetables, soft
fruit, lamb and eggs.

THE GREEN HOUSE

2A LOWER PANNIER MARKET, CREDITON EX17 2BL
Tel: 01363 775580 Contact: Loo Brown
Comprehensively stocked friendly wholefood shop—mostly organic. Dried,
chilled, frozen foods, fresh local fruit and veg. Environmentally friendly
cleaning products, cosmetics. Natural remedies, Fairtrade, gifts. We source
anything on request!

GREENACRES ORGANIC PRODUCE

COOMBE BANK, TIPTON ST. JOHN, SIDMOUTH EX10 0AX
Tel: 01404 815829 Fax: 01404 815829 Contact: Roger Cozens
roger@greenacres-consultancy.co.uk
Herbs (culinary and medicinal), vegetables, lamb and eggs. Consultancy in
arable and horticulture, overseas aid and relief consultancy.

GREENFIBRES

99 HIGH ST., TOTNES TQ9 5PF
Tel: 01803 868001 Fax: 01803 868002 Contact: William Lana
mail@greenfibres.com www.greenfibres.com
Organic clothing, bedding, fabrics, household linen and mattresses made
from organic raw materials (organic cotton, organic linen, organic wool)
under fair and safe working conditions. Feel and look good while
supporting organic agriculture and ethical work practices. See display ad.

GREENLIFE DIRECT

11 THE PADDOCKS, TOTNES IND. PARK, TOTNES TQ9 5XT
Tel: 01803 868733 Fax: 01803 864948 Contact: Liz and Penny
enquiries@greenlife.co.uk www.greenlife.co.uk
Greenlife Direct retail a wide range of nutritional supplements including
competitively priced own label and hard-to-find products. Practitioner
discounts. Established 1989. Now the largest independent health/whole-
food shop in the West Country.

GRIFFIN'S YARD

NORTH RD., SOUTH MOLTON EX36 3AZ
Tel: 01769 572372 Contact: Graeme Wilkinson
Tea, coffee, fruit, veg, dairy, fresh meat, dried foods, grains, cereals,
pasta, sauces, seeds, honey, eggs, eco products, frozen foods, vegetarian
foods, ice cream, wines, beers, ciders, everything organic!

THE HEALTH FOOD STORE

GAMMON WALK, BARNSTAPLE EX31 1DJ
Tel: 01271 345624 Contact: Pat Jackman
Organic spreads, oats, flakes, oils and much more, with a friendly
information service.

HEALTHWISE
81 FORE STREET, KINGSBRIDGE TQ7 1AB
Tel: 01548 857707 Contact: Irene Jeeninga
Large range of organic dried fruits, nuts, grains, beans, breakfast cereals, honeys, dairy and non-dairy chilled, soya and rice milks, fruit juices, herbal remedies and medicines. Also Ecover products.

HEART OF DEVON ORGANICS
LANGRIDGE FARM, CREDITON EX17 5HH
Tel: 01647 24894 Fax: 01647 24894 Contact: Geoff Jones
The largest sole wholesaler of organic fresh fruit and vegetables in the South-west. Working closely with local and near continent growers. Deliveries from M4 to Lands End.

HEAVEN SCENT HERBS
UNIT 9, GIDLEYS MEADOW, CHRISTOW, EXETER EX6 7QB
Tel: 01647 252847 Fax: 01647 252847 Contact: Anne Tarrant
anne@heavenscentherbs.co.uk www.heavenscentherbs.co.uk
Twelve varieties of hand-made herb and spice mustards available in standard jars, gift packs and catering sizes. Retail, mail order, wholesale and available through The Organic Farmers Market website.

HEIDI'S HOMEMADE
1 BOSSELL PARK, BUCKFASTLEIGH TQ11 0DX
Tel: 01364 644256 Fax: 01364 644256 Contact: Heidi Acland
charles@bossellpark.fsnet.co.uk
An ethical business hand-producing organic ready meals and gratins: delicious, nutritionally wholesome and wheat-free. Available through farm shops, health food stores, delis, National Trust outlets and home delivery.

HERBIE'S WHOLE FOOD VEGETARIAN RESTAURANT
15 NORTH ST., EXETER EX4 6Q
Tel: 01392 258473 Contact: Tony Mudge
Vegetarian restaurant using organic ingredients where available and local produce in season.

HERON VALLEY CIDER AND ORGANIC JUICE

CRANNACOMBE FARM, HAZELWOOD, LODDISWELL, KINGSBRIDGE TQ7 4DX
Tel: 01548 550256 Fax: 01548 550256 Contact: Shirley & Stephen Bradley
National award-winning producers of organic apple based fruit juices and
sparkling and traditional still organic ciders, pressed from hand-selected
fruit at our farm based in the stunning River Avon valley.

HIGHDOWN ORGANIC FARM

HIGHDOWN FARM, BRADNINCH, EXETER EX5 4LJ
Tel: 01392 881028 Fax: 01392 881272 Contact: Sandra Vallis
svallis@highdownfarm.co.uk www.highdownfarm.co.uk
Soil Association G2121. We offer quality self-catering accommodation on
our organic dairy farm. Peacefully situated in the heart of Devon with
breathtaking views of the surrounding countryside.

HIGHER CROP

'PYNES', BRIDFORD, NR. EXETER EX6 7JA
Tel: 01647 252470 Contact: Chris Towell
Soil Association G6688. Much of the vegetables and fruit we grow is either
unobtainable in supermarkets or of very old origin—from Italy, France and
Britain. Also salad potatoes such as Ratte etc. Strictly by appointment,
visitors can arrange to visit to buy in-season produce.

HIGHER HACKNELL ORGANIC MEAT

HIGHER HACKNELL FARM, BURRINGTON, UMBERLEIGH EX37 9LX
Tel: 01769 560909 Fax: 01769 560909 Contact: Jo Budden
enquiries@higherhacknell.co.uk www.higherhacknell.co.uk
Producer and retailer of quality tasty organic meat. Our 350-acre family
farm in Devon has been organic since 1988 and won numerous awards for
conservation and for our produce. Nationwide weekly deliveries and local
delivery. Also available from Exeter and Exmouth farmers' markets.

HIGHER SHARPHAM BARTON FARM

COACHYARD COTTAGE, SHARPHAM, ASHPRINGTON, TOTNES TQ9 7UT
Tel: 01803 732324 Contact: Richard Smith
Annual on-farm family camp, 1st week in August.

HILL COTTAGE & SOUTH BEER

BEER MILL FARM, CLAWTON, NR. HOLSWORTHY EX22 6PF
Tel: 01409 253093 Contact: Elaine Green
lgsg@supanet.com www.selfcateringcottagesdevon.co.uk
Self-catering cottages; we grow our own organic veg and eggs (not
certified) and supply guests from local certified sources (veg box scheme
and Providence Farm). Soil Association members as individuals.

HILLMEAD FARM

UGBOROUGH, IVYBRIDGE PL21 0HQ
Tel: 01752 892674 Fax: 01752 690111 Contact: Jane Johns
info@hillhead-farm.co.uk www.hillhead-farm.co.uk
Traditional partly organic working farm, with cattle, sheep, vegetables and
poultry. Offer welcoming and well appointed accommodation. Delicious
breakfasts using home-grown, local and organic produce.

HOLSWORTHY ORGANICS

c/o LITTLE EAST LAKE FARM, EAST CHILLA, BEAWORTHY EX21 5XF
Tel: 01409 221417 Contact: Mo Robley
moyra@holsworthyorganics.co.uk www.holsworthyorganics.co.uk
Marketing co-op selling organic veg, fruit, herbs, eggs, preserves and other
produce. Producer member of Soil Association (no. PR30W).

HURFORD, T & J

WIXON FARM, CHULMLEIGH EX18 7DS
Tel: 01769 580438 Contact: T & J Hurford
Soil Association G1747. Organic Aberdeen Angus beef and chicken
produced to Soil Association standards, sold from farm or from Bristol
Farmers' market every Wednesday 9am–2pm, Corn Street, Bristol.

KEENOR, CJ & ME

MOUNTICOMBE FARM, CHULMLEIGH EX18 7EQ
Tel: 01769 580305 Contact: Colin Keenor
ckeenor@uks.net
Organic milk production.

KILWORTHY KAPERS
11 KING ST., TAVISTOCK PL19 0DS
Tel: 01822 615039 Contact: Mr&Mrs Kiely
We stock a wide range of organically grown foods including fruit, vegetables and eggs. Also supplements, herbal remedies etc.

KINGDOM, RUTH
GIBBETT MOOR FARM, RACKENFORD, TIVERTON EX16 8DJ
Tel: 01884 881457 Contact: Ruth Kingdom
Soil Association G2438. Small suckler herd of Devon cattle on rare Culm grassland. Their meat is well hung, of excellent flavour.

KITTOW, JD & SE
ELBURY FARM, BROADCLYST, EXETER EX5 3BH
Tel: 01392 462817 Fax: 01392 462817 Contact: Jon Kittow
Soil Association G7302. Traditional Devon mixed farm: farm trail and opportunity to see how the dairy, beef, sheep and arable enterprises integrate into a sustainable farming system. Visitors by appointment, occasional open days.

LEAFCYCLE
COOMBE FARM, COVE, TIVERTON EX16 7RU
Tel: 01398 331808 Fax: 01398 331808 Contact: Michael Cole
www.leafcycle.co.uk
Soil Association C37W. Leafu, a highly nutritious vegan organic food ingredient made from leaves. Leafcycle camps—a green space for green camps. The Occasional Café, an outdoor organic experience.

LINSCOMBE FARM
NEWBUILDINGS, SANDFORD, CREDITON EX17 4PS
Tel: 01363 84291 Contact: Phil Thomas
farmers@linscombe.fsnet.co.uk
Soil Association G2047. Box scheme within 10-mile radius of farm. 300 varieties of vegetable grown. Joint Box Scheme of the Year Award winner 2001. Farmers' markets: Crediton 1st Sat of month, Exmouth 2nd Wed, Cullompton 2nd Sat, Exeter every Thursday.

LITTLE COMFORT FARM

LITTLE COMFORT FARM, BRAUNTON EX33 2NJ
Tel: 01271 812414 Fax: 01271 812414 Contact: Jackie Milsom
jackie.milsom@btclick.com www.littlecomfortfarm.co.uk
Soil Association G7089. Organic mixed farm of 70 acres producing Devon
cattle, Lleyn x Texel sheep, poultry and pigs, farm gate and mail order
sales. Self-catering holidays in four barn conversions. School visits for farm
and wildlife. Coarse fishing.

LUGG SMALLHOLDING, SUE

ORSWELL COTTAGE ORGANIC GARDEN, STOKE RIVERS,
BARNSTAPLE EX32 7LW
Tel: 01598 710558 Contact: Sue & John Lugg
Soil Association G7413; Henry Doubleday Organic Research Association.
Small organic holding: sheep, goats and poultry are part of the ecosystem
of vegetable production. Eggs from free range roaming hens and ducks.
Guinea fowl, lamb, vegetables and herb plants. Barnstaple Pannier market
on Fridays.

LUSCOMBE ORGANIC DRINKS

LUSCOMBE FARM, COLSTON ROAD, BUCKFASTLEIGH TQ11 0LP
Tel: 01364 64 30 36 Fax: 01364 64 44 98 Contact: Gabriel David
g@luscombe.co.uk www.luscombe.co.uk
Soil Association P2222. Produce and bottle the most genuine soft drinks
using all organic ingredients and great attention to detail. From apple juice
through ginger beer, elderflower to Sicilian lemonade.

MARSHFORD ORGANIC PRODUCE

11 BUTCHERS ROW, BARNSTAPLE EX31 1BW
Tel: 01271 322855 Contact: Vanessa Ebdon
enquiries@marshford.co.uk www.marshford.co.uk
Soil Association E19W, PE19W. Award-winning growers and retailers, 100%
organic. Our own vegetables, salads and herbs. Other local Devon meat,
poultry, eggs, dairy etc. Selection of groceries. Best Small Organic Shop
2001/2002. Customer service 01237 477160.

MARSHFORD ORGANIC PRODUCE

CHURCHILL WAY, NORTHAM, NR. BIDEFORD EX39 1NG
Tel: 01237 477160 Contact: Vanessa Ebdon
enquiries@marshford.co.uk www.marshford.co.uk
Soil Association E19W, PE19W. Award-winning growers and retailers, 100%
organic. Our own vegetables, salads and herbs. Other local Devon meat,
poultry, eggs, dairy etc. Selection of groceries. Best Small Organic Shop
2001/2002.

MAUNDER LTD, LLOYD

WILLAND, CULLOMPTON EX15 2PJ
Tel: 01884 820534 Fax: 01884 821404 Contact: Adrian Blyth
adrian.blyth@lloydmaunder.co.uk www.lloydmaunder.co.uk
Lloyd Maunder supply organic lamb and organic chicken to the major
multiples to Soil Association standards.

THE MEAT JOINT

HILLSBOROUGH HOUSE, LOXHORE, BARNSTAPLE EX31 4SU
Tel: 01271 850335 Fax: 01271 850335 Contact: Kim Seggons
themeat.joint@care4free.net
Soil Association G4331. From our small farm in Loxhore, North Devon, we
supply beef, pork, lamb, chicken, bacon, sausages and Christmas turkeys.
Contact Kim Seggons for price list and delivery arrangements.

MIDDLE CAMPSCOTT FARM

MIDDLE CAMPSCOTT FARM, LEE, ILFRACOMBE EX34 8LS
Tel: 01271 864621 Contact: Karen Wright
middle.campscott@farmersweekly.net www.middlecampscott.co.uk
Soil Association G1923, P1923. We produce hard pressed ewe's and goat's
milk cheeses using milk from our own farm; wool and woollen products
from our naturally coloured Shetland sheep and milking flock; lamb; Ruby
Devon beef.

MILK LINK LTD
PLYM HOUSE, 3 LONGBRIDGE RD., PLYMOUTH PL6 8LY
Tel: 01752 331800 Fax: 01752 331812 Contact: Lee Richards
lee.richards@milklink.com www.milklink.com
Dairy co-operative.

NATURAL WAY
28 HYDE RD., PAIGNTON TQ4 5BY
Tel: 01803 665529 Fax: 01803 665529 Contact: Michael Jull
info@naturalwayhealth.co.uk www.naturalwayhealth.co.uk
Organic drinks, fruits, nuts, pulses and cereals. Range of organic herbal
supplements and body care products. Mail order service available.

NATURE'S PLATE—ORGANIC VEGETARIAN CATERERS
8 TADDIFORD RD., EXETER EX4 4AY
Tel: 01392 413578 Fax: naturesplate@yahoo.com Contact: Rob Barker
www.naturesplate.co.uk
Nature's Plate—organic vegetarian wholefood experience. Event and private function caterers. Locally sourced, freshly prepared, delicioous and
nutricious cuisine. Soil Association, Vegetarian and Vegan Society certified
and also carbon balanced.

NATURE'S ROUND
DART MILLS, OLD TOTNES RD, BUCKFASTLEIGH, NEWTON ABBOT TQ11 0NF
Tel: 07810 127376 Contact: Brent Tebbutt
naturesround@beeb.net
Bulk fruit and vegetable enquiries. Year round home delivery of vegetables,
fruit, eggs, Dartmoor water (still & sparkling), fruit juices, tofu and
wholefoods. Three sizes of vegetable boxes; you can modify or choose
from a weekly price list. Wholesome Food Association.

NATUREMADE OASIS
EAST JOHNSTONE, BISH MILL, SOUTH MOLTON EX36 3QE
Tel: 01769 573571 Fax: 01769 573571 Contact: Esme Brown
sales@naturemade.co.uk www.naturemade.co.uk
Soil Association P1741. Vegetarian food manufacturers. Small family
business manufacturing and distributing vegetarian foods. Mail order
available. Also producing cow's milk yoghurts, drinking yoghurts and
cream. Goat milk and products in organic conversion, complete Spring
2004.

NICHOLSONS WHOLEFOOD & HEALTH SHOP LTD
12 FORE ST., KINGSBRIDGE TQ7 1DQ
Tel: 01548 854347 Fax: 01548 854335 Contact: Frances Stathers
An Aladdin's cave packed with a vast selection of wholefoods including
gluten-free and eco-friendly products, wide choice of supplements and
toiletries.

NORWEGIAN WOOD/ORGANIC B&B
NORWEGIAN WOOD, BERRY POMEROY, TOTNES TQ9 6LE
Tel: 01803 867462 Contact: Heather Nicholson
heather@norwegianwood.eclipse.co. ok www.organicbedandbreakfast.info
We offer a healthy holiday: no microwaves, no GMOs, organic food of the
best quality. Non-smoking, children welcome. Also clinical workshops for
iridology and nutrition, and in-house consultations.

O'HANLONS BREWING CO LTD
GREAT BARTON FARM, WHIMPLE EX5 2NY
Tel: 01404 822412 Fax: 01404 823700 Contact: Liz O'Hanlon
info@ohanloons.co.uk www.ohanlons.co.uk
Brewer of organic beer.

OLD CUMMING ORGANIC FARM

COLSTON ROAD, BUCKFASTLEIGH TQ11 0LP
Tel: 01364 642672 Contact: The Manager
Soil Association G2495. Family-run organic farm producing high quality fresh pre-packed organic produce. Salad packs, leaf vegetables and fruit juice. Highly commended fruit juice in 2003 Soil Association awards.

ORCHARD WHOLEFOODS

16 HIGH ST., BUDLEIGH SALTERTON EX9 6LQ
Tel: 01395 442508 Contact: Jane Long
janelong@gmx.net
We are a well-stocked health shop with an ever-growing organic section. It includes almost all vegetarian foods except for fresh fruit and vegetables.

THE ORGANIC FARMERS MARKET LTD

DARTS FARM, CLYST ST. GEORGE, EXETER EX3 0QH
Tel: 01392 875678 Fax: 01392 879461 Contact: Fennella Reeves
mail@theorganicfarmersmarket.co.uk www.theorganicfarmersmarket.co.uk
On-line home delivery service offering nationwide home delivery of organic products from the finest West Country farms. The on-line market is packed with a variety of wonderful seasonal products including vegetables, meat, dairy, textiles and much more. See display ad.

ORGANIC POULTRY EQUIPMENT LTD

PETERHALES HOUSE, TRINITY, CULLOMPTON EX15 1PE
Tel: 07974 353073 Fax: 01884 35004 Contact: Peter Crowe
organicpoultryequipment@yahoo.co.uk
www.organicpoultryequipment.co.uk
Suppliers of well insulated, low cost, modular poultry housing, developed by organic table bird producers. Features include a highly efficient feeding system, excellent welfare standards and a very durable structure. Secondary telephone number: 01884 33218.

ORIGINAL ORGANICS LTD

UNIT 9 LANGLANDS BUSINESS PARK, UFFCULME EX15 3DA
Tel: 01884 841515 Fax: 01884 841717 Contact: Clive Roberts
Manufacturer of the world famous 'Original Wormery' and Rotol Composter.

OTTER VALLEY POULTRY

SPURTHAM FARM, UPOTTERY, HONITON EX14 9QD
Tel: 01404 861209 Fax: 01404 861715 Contact: RG Gardner
Soil Association P5599. Family-run poultry abattoir, offering a personal
service to customers, specialising in the processing of all aspects of organic
poultry.

OTTERY WHOLEFOODS

5A MILL ST., OTTERY ST. MARY EX11 1AB
Tel: 01404 812109 Fax: 01404 815020 Contact: Vanessa Terry
ottery.wholefoods@vigin.net
We sell an extensive selection of fresh, local, organic produce: dried fruit,
cereals, grains, pasta, flour, wines, beers, and ecological cleaning and
sanitary products.

PALMER, MS KATE

WEST YEO FARM, WITHERIDGE, TIVERTON EX16 8PY
Tel: 01884 861269 Contact: Kate Palmer
Soil Association G7284. Historic farm with Red Devon beef, rare breed
coloured sheep and arable production. Culm grassland borders the Little
Dart River, featuring otters and kingfishers. Old orchard restoration.

THE PANTRY

13 STATION RD, SOUTH BRENT TQ10 9BE
Tel: 01364 73308 Contact: Jill Cruz
thepantry@btinternet.com
Local sausages & bacon (some organic), organic vegetables, bread, milk,
yoghurt.

PERCY'S COUNTRY HOTEL & RESTAURANT

COOMBESHEAD ESTATE, VIRGINSTOW, NR. OKEHAMPTON EX21 5EA
Tel: 01409 211236 Fax: 01409 211460 Contact: Ross Hayward
info@percys.co.uk www.percys.co.uk
Percy's are the 2003 Organic Restaurant of the Year and a showcase for
the West Country's expansive larder of superlative organic produce. A
tremendous amount of the menu, including a bespoke breed of lamb,
vegetables, herbs and dazzling eggs, is home grown. Exmoor duck and
chicken, too, set on a stunning 130-acre estate. Eight deluxe bedrooms
with jacuzzis and king size beds, relaxation and rejuvenation.

PILGRIM ORGANICS

HIGHER CARLEY FARM, LIFTON PL16 0EB
Tel: 01566 784944 Contact: Jilly Thompson
jilly@pilgrimorganics.co.uk
Producers of organic day-old Aylesbury ducklings and finished birds.

PROPER JOB

CRANNAFORDS IND PARK, CHAGFORD TQ13 8DJ
Tel: 01647 432985 Fax: 01647 432985 Contact: Jo Hodges
compost@properjob.eclipse.co.uk www.properjob.ik.com
Community business. Holistic co-op. Developing from waste to resource
issues, especially composting, collecting compostables, education/con-
sciousness raising. Organic veg production and sale in our community
shop/café. Setting up training in related issues. Organic collection round.

PROVIDENCE FARM ORGANIC MEATS

PROVIDENCE FARM, CROSSPARK CROSS, HOLSWORTHY EX22 6JW
Tel: 01409 254421 Fax: 01409 254421 Contact: Pammy Riggs
info@providencefarm.co.uk www.providencefarm.co.uk
Winners of Organic Food Awards 2000, 2001, 2002 and 2003. Producing
quality chicken, duck, guinea fowl, goose, pork, bacon, sausages, lamb,
beef and eggs. Farm shop selling whole range of local organic fayre.

REAPERS

18 BAMPTON ST., TIVERTON EX16 6AA
Tel: 01884 255310 Contact: Carol Peard
Reapers is a wholefood health food store, featuring a wide range of organic goods, including fresh fruit and vegetables.

RICHARD'S

64 FORE ST., TOPSHAM, EXETER EX3 0HL
Tel: 01392 873116 Fax: 01392 873116 Contact: Richard Tucker
r4richard@aol.com
Fruit and vegetables, eggs and fruit juices.

RIVERFORD FARM FOOD SHOP AT KITLEY

KITLEY, YEALMPTON, PLYMOUTH PL8 2LT
Tel: 01752 880925 Fax: 01752 880263 Contact: Peter Marr
office@riverfordfarmshop.co.uk www.riverford.co.uk
Organic Farmers and Growers registered. Farm shop and café offering a wide range of organic food (vegetables, meat, dairy, wine, dry goods and plant seeds etc.). Emphasis on quality food from local producers.

RIVERFORD FARM SHOP

RIVERFORD, STAVERTON, TOTNES TQ9 6AF
Tel: 01803 762523 Fax: 01803 762571 Contact: Deborah Nash
riverfordfarmshop@riverford.co.uk www.riverford.co.uk
Organic Farmers and Growers cert no. UKP100357. Organic and locally produced beef, lamb, chicken, pork, free range eggs, cheese, wine & beer, bread and pies, dry goods and Riverford Organic Milk.

RIVERFORD FARM SHOP

38 HIGH STREET, TOTNES TQ9 5RY
Tel: 01803 863959
riverfordfarmshop@riverford.co.uk www.riverford.co.uk
Opening in June 2004, selling organic and locally produced beef, lamb, chicken, pork, free range eggs, cheese, wine & beer, bread and pies, dry goods and Riverford Organic Milk.

RIVERFORD ORGANIC VEGETABLES
WASH BARN, BUCKFASTLEIGH TQ11 0LD
Tel: 01803 762720 Fax: 01803 762718 Contact: Tieneka Drew
mail@riverford.co.uk www.riverford.co.uk
Soil Association W24W. Award-winning organic vegetable box scheme,
delivering to houses across the South and South West of England. One of
the founding members of the South Devon Organic Producers, a producer
group of 13 family-run farms who grow 85 different varieties for the box
scheme, making Riverford one of the largest producer's of organic vegetables in the UK.

ROBERT OWEN COMMUNITIES
LOWER SHARPHAM BARTON FARM, ASHPRINGTON, TOTNES TQ9 7DX
Tel: 01803 732502 Fax: 01803 732502 Contact: B Roodenburg-Vermaat
sharphamfarm@roc-uk.org
Day centre for people with learning disabilities. Dairy, beef, sheep, laying
birds and vegetables. Produce milk, meats, eggs and veg.

ROCOMBE FARM FRESH ICE CREAM LTD
OLD NEWTON RD., HEATHFIELD, NEWTON ABBOT TQ12 6RA
Tel: 01626 834545 Fax: 01626 835777 Contact: Peter Redstone (M.D.)
info@rocombefarm.co.uk www.rocombefarm.co.uk
Luxury organic dairy ice cream, organic frozen yoghurt and organic fruit
sorbet. Soil Association P1006.

RODANDBENS
BICKHAM FARM, KENN, EXETER EX6 7XL
Tel: 01392 833833 Fax: 01392 833832 Contact: Rodney Hall
rod@rodandbens.com www.rodandbens.com
Mixed farm supplying vegetables locally and nationwide by mail order.
Highly commended Organic Food Awards 2002 and 2003. Rick Stein's food
superheroes.

ROSE COTTAGE ORGANICS
RUMLEIGH, BERE ALSTON PL20 7HN
Tel: 01822 840297 Contact: Pete Mayston
pmayston@fish.co.uk
Soil Association G5300. Seasonal vegetables, apples, soft fruit and herbs, grown in Tamar Valley. Box scheme, free delivery in Bere Alston, Tavistock, Yelverton areas.

SACKS
80 HIGH ST., TOTNES TQ9 5SN
Tel: 01803 863263 Contact: Michael White
Soil Association R1907. We sell a comprehensive range of organic vegetarian food. A wide range of fresh organic fruit and vegetables always in stock.

SEASONS
8 WELL ST., EXETER EX4 6QR
Tel: 01392 201282 Contact: Parviz Kargar
Organic vegetables, grains, beans, pulses, dried fruit and natural groceries.

SEEDS BAKERY & HEALTH STORE
35 HIGH ST, TOTNES TQ9 5NP
Tel: 01803 862526 Contact: Barry Pope
Bakery baking organic bread and non-organic cakes and savouries.

SEEDS BAKERY & HEALTH STORE
22 DUKE ST., DARTMOUTH TQ6 9TZ
Tel: 01803 833200 Contact: Barry Pope
Bakery baking organic bread and non-organic cakes and savouries.

SEEDS BAKERY & HEALTH STORE
19 HIGH ST, EXMOUTH EX8
Tel: 01395 265741 Contact: Barry Pope
Bakery baking organic bread and non-organic cakes and savouries.

SHARPHAM PARTNERSHIP LTD

SHARPHAM ESTATE, ASHPRINGTON, TOTNES TQ9 7UT
Tel: 01803 732203 Fax: 01803 732122 Contact: M Sharman
info@sharpham.com www.sharpham.com
Soil Association G2483. A 200-acre tenancy on a 500 acre estate that is
almost all organic (and biodynamic). Producing organic milk, organic
cheeses. Non-organic estate grown and bottled wines.

SHILLINGFORD ORGANICS

THE GATEHOUSE, SHILLINGFORD ABBOTT, EXETER EX2 9QU
Tel: 01392 833040 Contact: Martyn Bragg
martyn.bragg@virgin.net
We grow fresh vegetables and herbs for our box scheme, delivering to the
Exeter area. We also grow cereals: wheat, barley, triticale and protein crops.
We are developing an organic kitchen and bakery to produce ready-made
meals, salads and bread products.

SKYSPROUTS

GOSWORTHY COTTAGE, HARBERTON, TOTNES TQ9 7LP
Tel: 01364 72404 Fax: 01364 72404 Contact: Brett Kellett
skysprouts@ic24.net
Growers of organic beansprouts, alfalfa sprouts, alfalfa and broccoli sprouts,
alfalfa and fenugreek sprouts, mung, aduki, lentil, chickpea, sunflower and
sunflower salads. Supplying wholesalers, shops and veggie box schemes
throughout the UK.

SMALE, PM &ME

THE BARTON, BURRINGTON, UMBERLEIGH EX37 9JQ
Tel: 01769 520216 Contact: Peter & Marilyn Smale
bartonfarm@yahoo.com www.burrington-barton.co.uk
Soil Association G4554. An organic farm with an abundance of wildlife
raising cattle and sheep. Also providing quality B&B accommodation using
organic or local produce where ever possible. En suite rooms. Prices from
£25.00 per person per night.

SOUTH DEVON ORGANIC PRODUCERS LTD
C/O WASH BARN, BUCKFASTLEIGH, DEVON TQ11 0LD
Contact: Ian Noble
Tel: 01803 762100 Fax: 01803 762100
sdop@farmersweekly.net www.sdopltd.co.uk
Co-operative of growers producing organic vegetables.

TAMAR ORGANICS
THE ORGANIC GARDEN CENTRE, GULWORTHY, TAVISTOCK PL19 8JE
Tel: 01822 834887 Fax: 01822 834284 Contact: Cathy or Neil Guilfoy
tamarorganics@aol.com www.tamarorganics.co.uk
Soil Association G1823, P1823. Seed and organic mail order company
specialising in organic seeds for gardeners and growers. Organic garden
centre, seeds, plants and soft fruit, open Tuesday–Friday 9.30am–5pm,
Saturday 10.30am–3pm; Closed Sundays and Bank Holidays. See display ad.

TOMS, R & M
PARKHILL FARM, SHIRWELL, BARNSTAPLE EX31 4JN
Tel: 01271 850323 Fax: 01271 850323 Contact: The Manager
Soil Association G2959. Organic beef and sheep. Non-organic free range
chicken. Camping. Residential caravan for holiday let.

TUCKER, EDWIN & SONS
BREWERY MEADOW, STONEPARK, ASHBURTON, NEWTON ABBOT TQ13 7DG
Tel: 01364 652233 Fax: 01364 654211 Contact: Chrissie Gregory
seeds@edwintucker.com www.edwintuckers.com
Mail order and retail shop: seeds, organic seeds and potatoes. We have
retail outlets which carry stocks of feed, saddlery, gardening equipment
and agricultural fertilisers. Our mail order department sells seeds, organic
seeds, potatoes including some unusual varieties.

URSELL, DJ & SJ
ALLER FARM, DOLTON, WINKLEIGH EX19 8PP
Tel: 01805 804414 Contact: David Ursell
ursell@farmersweekly.net
Soil Association G791. Beef and cereals.

WARD, GR & RJ
PARSONAGE FARM, IDDESLEIGH, WINKLEIGH EX19 8SN
Tel: 01837 810318 Contact: The Manager
Soil Association G6241. Organic dairy.

WATERGATE MUSHROOM FARM
UMBERLEIGH EX37 9AG
Tel: 01769 540502 Fax: 01769 540502 Contact: Marie Flanagan
Soil Association P5255. Situated in North Devon, we only produce organic mushrooms.

WELL HUNG MEAT
CARSWELL FARM, HOLBETON, PLYMOUTH PL8 1HH
Tel: 01752 830494 Fax: 01752 830565 Contact: Graeme Roy
sales@wellhungmeat.com www.wellhungmeat.com
Winners of the Soil Association Organic Food Awards in both 2001 and 2002, Well Hung Meat supplies the very best organic lamb, beef and poultry direct to your door.

WEST CHILLA FARM
WEST CHILLA, BEAWORTHY EX21 5XQ
Tel: 01409 221256 Contact: Tim Ramsay
Soil Association G5225. West Chilla Farm is a 13-hectare organic mixed holding currently producing beef, sheep, pork, fruit and veg with holiday cottage to let.

WEST EMLETT FARM
BLACK DOG, CREDITON EX17 4QB
Tel: 01363 877689 Fax: 01363 877468 Contact: Olly Curtis
Soil Association G4950. On our 240-acre farm we grow cereals and keep cattle and sheep. We also produce Soil Association standard eggs which we distribute to retailers and wholesalers throughout southern England.

WEST FORDE ORGANICS

THE BARTON, POUGHILL, CREDITON EX17 4LE
Tel: 01363 866349 Contact: Anne Wander
westfordeorganics@btopenworld.com
Direct sales of top quality home-produced organic lamb.

WEST HILL FARM

WEST DOWN, ILFRACOMBE EX34 8NF
Tel: 01271 815477 Fax: 01271 813316 Contact: Susannah Batstone
info@westhillfarm.org www.westhillfarm.org
Bottling and distributing non-homogenised milk, creams, yoghurts and
butter from our own herd. Dairy products for those who care about taste,
goodness and the countryside.

WEST ILKERTON FARM

WEST ILKERTON FARM, LYNTON EX35 6QA
Tel: 01598 752310 Fax: 01598 752310 Contact: Victoria Eveleigh
eveleigh@westilkerton.co.uk www.westilkerton.co.uk
Hill livestock farm: store and breeding stock for sale at certain times of the
year. Organic Devon cattle and Exmoor Horn and Exmoor Horn x sheep
(breeding stock and young stock) will be for sale in autumn. See
www.westilkerton.co.uk. Self-catering holiday cottage, ETC 4 star, to let.
Horse-drawn tours over Exmoor using Shire horses.

WEST LAKE FARM

CHILLA, BEAWORTHY EX21 5XF
Tel: 01409 221991 Fax: 01409 221991 Contact: Linda Davis & Georgia Travis
westlakefarm@lineone.net www.theorganicfarmersmarket.co.uk
Production of award-winning single variety apple juices and traditionally
fermented ciders, cider vinegar, development of soft drinks, Christmas
geese, self-catering studio barn, group demonstrations in season by
appointment.

WESTCOUNTRY ORGANICS
NATSON FARM, TEDBURN ST. MARY, EXETER EX6 6ET
Tel: 0164 724724 Fax: 0164 724031 Contact: Bruce Burton
enquiries@westcountryorganics.co.uk www.westcountryorganics.co.uk
National mail order of organic foods including a range of vegetables and
fruit, dairy products, drinks and vegetarian products.

WILLOW VEGETARIAN GARDEN RESTAURANT
87 HIGH STREET, TOTNES TQ9 5PB
Tel: 01803 862605 Contact: Maha Roberts
A popular fully vegetarian restaurant selling delicious food, hand-prepared
from natural, largely organic ingredients. 65% of all purchases are organic
including all wines, beers, juices, teas and coffees.

WINSLADE, LB
BEECH GROVE FARM, KNOWSTONE, SOUTH MOLTON EX36 4RS
Tel: 01398 341551 Contact: LB Winslade
Organic beef producer.

WOODLAND ORGANICS
MOORFOOT CROSS, WOODLAND, NR. DENBURY,
NEWTON ABBOT TQ12 6EQ
Tel: 01803 813760 Contact: Mike Jones
Wholesome Food Association member. 7-acre holding ethically producing
over 80 varieties of fruit and vegetables plus free range eggs. Operating
direct delivery veg boxes plus supplying trade locally.

 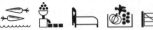

YARNER
BOVEY TRACEY TQ13 9LN
Tel: 01364 661503 Fax: 01364 661504 Contact: Patrick & Maja Holman
mail@yarner.com
Soil Association G7555. Organic farm and function venue. High quality
bulk spring water supplied to Yeo Valley as an ingredient for Rocombe Farm
and Marks & Spencer organic sorbet product ranges.

DORSET

BARTON MEADOWS

BARTON MEADOWS FARM, DORCHESTER RD., CERNE ABBAS DT2 7JS
Tel: 01300 341336 Fax: 01300 341336 Contact: DG Gourley
bartonmeadows@tiscali.co.uk
Soil Association G956. We sell prime Angus beef, pork, lamb and mutton.
Both fresh and frozen, plus honey and Romney fleece for spinners. Also
available are organic watercolours and prints by Elizabeth Bairstow.

BECKLANDS FARM

WHITCHURCH CANONICORUM, BRIDPORT DT6 6RG
Tel: 01297 560298 Contact: Hilary and Francis Joyce
becklandsorganicfarm@btopenworld.com www.becklandsorganicfarm.com
Small farm shop with farm produce, organic groceries and Ecover cleaning
products, eco-environmental information and crafts. Sells own Red Ruby
Devon X beef, geese, eggs, cheese and vegetables in season. Lemon curd
and other home-made preserves using farm fruit. Logs, planked poplar to
order, comfrey rootcuttings and plant fertiliser. Nettle juice. One of Rick
Stein's Food Heroes and recommended by Delia Smith's website. Comfrey
roots and plant fertiliser. Sometimes en suite B&B with full organic breakfast. During July & August, organic lunches and teas outside plus Thursday
afternoon guided farm walks at 2pm (also bank holiday Sunday afternoons). Adults £3.50 children £2 or family ticket £10. Groups any time by
arrangement.Two-hour guided walks include badger sett, wildlife ponds
and egg collection—start again 2004 late May bank holiday.

BIBBY, R & E

WHITE SHEET FARM, BEAMINSTER DT8 3SF
Tel: 01308 862066 Contact: Elaine Bibby
Soil Association G4325. Produce quality, grass-fed beef from an organic
farm. Ring first for availability.

BOTHEN HILL PRODUCE

7 GREEN LANE, BOTHENHAMPTON, BRIDPORT DT6 4ED
Tel: 01308 424271 Fax: 01308 424271 Contact: ML De Greeff
sales@bothenhillproduce.co.uk www.bothenhillproduce.co.uk
Family-run smallholding producing wide range of quality vegetables
throughout the year, alongside beef and lamb from our closed pedigree
flock of Hampshire Down sheep. Local deliveries. Wholesale available.

BOURNE ORGANIC

39 ST. CLEMENTS RD., BOURNEMOUTH BH1 4DX
Tel: 01202 778516 Contact: Lisa Northover
mail@bourneorganic.co.uk www.bourneorganic.co.uk
Bourne Organic delivers organic fresh produce, grocery products, Ecover
products and natural toiletries to homes and businesses throughout the
Bournemouth area.

CAKE, JE, M & R

WALLIS FARM, CATTISTOCK, DORCHESTER DT2 0JL
Tel: 01300 320653 Contact: Rupert Cake
rupert@wallisfarm.com www.wallisfarm.com
Organic hay.

CANNINGS COURT ORGANIC FARM SHOP

CANNINGS COURT, PULHAM, DORCHESTER DT2 7EA
Tel: 01258 818035 Contact: John Dennison
john.cannings-court@care4free.net
Soil Association G4511. Eight acres of organic land growing a full range of
seasonal vegetables, salads and organic free range eggs. All produce is sold
direct to local consumers via the year round box-scheme, independent
retailers and restaurants. The farm shop and local delivery service also
supplies local organic bread, milk, cream and fruit.

CHILDHAY MANOR ORGANICS

CHILDHAY MANOR, BLACKDOWN, BEAMINSTER DT8 3LQ
Tel: 01308 868709 Fax: 01308 868119 Contact: Lucy Blackburn
lucy@childhaymanor.com www.childhaymanor.com
We produce our own organic pork, bacon and beef, which we supply, as
well as organic lamb and chickens from other local farmers. We deliver to
butchers throughout the South of England, and operate an overnight
hamper delivery scheme to the general public, nationwide.

CLIPPER TEAS LTD

BROADWINDSOR RD., BEAMINSTER DT8 3PR
Tel: 01308 863344 Fax: 01308 863847 Contact: Paul Machin
enquiries@clipper-teas.com www.clipper-teas.com
Award-winning organic and Fairtrade tea, coffee, hot chocolate and
infusions. Available worldwide, and direct from Clipper at
www.clipper-teas.com.

COWDEN HOUSE BED & BREAKFAST

COWDEN HOUSE, GODMANSTONE, DORCHESTER DT2 7AG
Tel: 01300 341377 Contact: Tim Mills
www.cowdenhouse.co.uk
A rural retreat serving locally produced organic vegetarian food.

DORSET FARMS

LITTLEWINDSOR, BEAMINSTER DT8 3QU
Tel: 01308 868822 Fax: 01308 868973 Contact: Sarah Chaffey
admin@dorset farms.co.uk www.dorsetfarms.co.uk
Soil Association P2595. Producers of quality organic ham and bacon. Ham
available on or off the bone and pre-packed. Bacon sliced in packs of
2.27kg or pre-packed.

DORSET PASTRY

UNIT 8D HYBRIS BUSINESS PARK, WARMWELL RD., CROSSWAYS,
DORCHESTER DT2 8BF
Tel: 01305 854860 Fax: 01305 854870 Contact: Moira Blake
enquiries@dorsetpastry.com www.dorsetpastry.com
Small Producer of the Year 2003/4. Produces fine organic pure butter
frozen, ready rolled puff, sweet and flavoured pastry. Local ingredients
hand folded and rested in the traditional manner.

DORSET WILDLIFE TRUST

45 HIGH ST., TOLLER PORCORUM, DORCHESTER DT2 0DN
Tel: 01300 320573 Contact: Paul Comer
paul@paulcomer.f9.co.uk
Soil Association G898. We run as a farmed nature reserve, producing fat
and store lambs and suckled calves/store cattle.

DOWN TO EARTH

18 PRINCES ST., DORCHESTER DT1 1TW
Tel: 01305 268325 Contact: A Bowley
Retailers of a wide range of organic produce including butter, cheese, eggs,
fruits and vegetables, bread, dried foods, frozen and chilled produce.
Specialists in British cheeses.

EWELEAZE FARM

THE CARTSHED, CHURCH LANE, OSMINGTON, WEYMOUTH DT3 6EW
Tel: 01305 833690 Contact: Peter Broatch
peter@eweleaze.co.uk www.eweleaze.co.uk
Soil Association G6652. Small organic farm producing Aberdeen Angus
beef, lamb and eggs. Direct sales of eggs and meat from the door.
Camping is available during August, with access to a private beach. A
holiday cottage is available for weekly lets, in nearby Osmington village
(see website).

FOOTS EGGS
STONEY FARM, BISHOPS CAUNDLE, SHERBORNE DT9 5ND
Tel: 01963 23033 Fax: 01963 23093 Contact: Bill Foot
emmafoot@hotmail.com
Wholesale other producers' eggs to hotels, shops etc.

FORD FARM, ASHLEY CHASE ESTATES
PARKS FARM, LITTON CHENEY, DORCHESTER DT2 9AZ
Tel: 01308 482580 Fax: 01308 482608 Contact: Claire Pike
cheese@fordfarm.com www.fordfarm.com
Soil Association P4414. Traditional West Country farmhouse cheese
producers. Organic, kosher and flavoured cheeses are our speciality
including traditional cloth-wrapped cheddar.

FOX, JH
WEST CLIFF FARM, WEST BAY, BRIDPORT DT6 4HS
Tel: 01308 425316 Contact: Shaun Fox
shaunfox@farmersweekly.net or shaun.fox@fwi.co.uk
We specialise in fruit and veg together with lamb and potatoes, supply
some box schemes but sell through local farm shop or Sunday markets.
Orders by phone welcome.

FRUITS OF THE EARTH
2A VICTORIA GROVE, BRIDPORT DT6 3AA
Tel: 01308 425827 Contact: The Manager
Organic vegetables, milk, cereals, wine, teas, rice, coffees, pulses, bread,
chocolate, yoghurts, dried fruit, herbs, spices, and lots more.

GOLD HILL ORGANIC FARM
CHILD OKEFORD, NR. BLANDFORD FORUM DT11 8HB
Tel: 01258 861413 Fax: 01258 861413 Contact: Sara Cross
From May until March we sell up to 35 varieties of vegetables, fruit, organic
beef, milk and bread through our farm shop, at weekends only: Fri & Sat
9–1, 2–5.30 Sun 9–1. Veg box scheme. Also at Castle Cary Market
(Tuesdays). Deliver to Blandford and Shaftesbury.

GREEN VALLEY FARM SHOP
LONGMEADOW, GODMANSTONE, DORCHESTER DT2 7AE
Tel: 01300 342164 Fax: 01300 342164 Contact: David Nesling
We are a farm shop selling principally organic products including organic
vegetables, local organic meat, eggs, milk, bread, cheese, wines,
wholefoods, groceries, Ecover products and refill systems.

THE HEALTH MINISTRY
16 HIGH ST., CHRISTCHURCH BH23 1AY
Tel: 01202 471152 Fax: 01202 471152 Contact: Hilary Bateman
Wide range of organic dried goods e.g. nuts, pulses, flour, drinks, ice
cream, spreads, etc.

HERITAGE PRIME—EARNESTLY BRITISH MEATS OF RARE QUALITY
SHEDBUSH FARM, MUDDY FORD LANE, STANTON ST. GABRIEL,
BRIDPORT DT6 6DR
Tel: 01297 489304 Fax: 01297 489531 Contact: Denise Bell
heritageprime@aol.com
Biodynamic farming—food more carefully produced than the highest
organic standard. All animals and land treated homoeopathically, pork,
sausage, bacon and ham, lamb, beef and occasionally poultry—seasonally.
Domestic boxes, all joints and cuts butchered, with Slow Food recipes. Mail
order only. Nationwide. Favourite of the finest chefs in England, where
Nigella buys her meat!

JUICE CAFE LTD
9 BURLINGTON ARCADE, OLD CHRISTCHURCH RD., BOURNEMOUTH BH1 2HZ
Tel: 01202 314143 Contact: M De Wal'esch
Café using some organic ingredients.

THE KINGCOMBE CENTRE
LOWER KINGCOMBE, TOLLER PORCORUM, DORCHESTER DT2 0EQ
Tel: 01300 320684 Fax: 01300 321409 Contact: Nigel Spring
nspring@kingcombe-centre.demon.co.uk
www.kingcombe-centre.demon.co.uk
Residential study centre in converted farm buildings beside the river Hooke:
offers courses and holidays in a wide range of subjects for adults and
children, fit and disabled. Day visits for schools and guided walks.
Organically reared pork and lamb.

LEAKERS BAKERY
29 EAST ST, BRIDPORT DT6 3JX
Tel: 01308 423296 Contact: The Manager
Organic milk, eggs, cream, and we use many organic ingredients in our
products.

LONG CRICHEL BAKERY
LONG CRICHEL, WIMBORNE BH21 5JU
Tel: 01258 830852 Fax: 01258 830855
Contact: Jamie Campbell & Kathy Davies
info@longcrichelbakery.co.uk www.longcrichelbakery.co.uk
Soil Association P6534. Organic bakery including handcrafted bread and
cakes baked in a wood fired brick oven. Open Thurs, Friday afternoons to
Saturday all day; phone first as times vary. Fresh organic vegetables from
walled garden in season.

LONG CRICHEL ORGANIC WALLED GARDEN
LONG CRICHEL, OPPOSITE LONG CRICHEL ORGANIC BAKERY,
WIMBORNE BH21 5JU
Tel: 01258 830295 Contact: Anni Sax
Soil Association G7461. Organic fruit and vegetables growers comprising of
2.5 acres with walled garden using permaculture/forest garden methods,
specialising in oriental salad and herb production. Registered for WOOFERS.

LONGMEADOW ORGANIC VEGETABLES

GODMANSTONE, DORCHESTER DT2 7AE
Tel: 01300 341779 Fax: 01300 341779 Contact: Patsy Chapman
chapmans.longmeadow@virgin.com
Soil Association C60W. We are an organic market garden, established 1987,
growing a variety of vegetables and some fruit, available through our own
box scheme and Green Valley Farm Shop.

MANOR FARM

GODMANSTONE, DORCHESTER DT2 7AH
Tel: 01300 341415 Fax: 01300 341170 Contact: Will Best
will@manor-farm-organic.co.uk www.manor-farm-organic.co.uk
Mixed farm, organic since 1986. Pasteurised whole and semi-skimmed milk
and cream. Lamb and mince prepared for the freezer. Also wheat, combed
wheat reed and rearing calves. Day visits for schools, etc. Accommodation—
self-catering or partially catered, economic. Occasional open days.

MANOR FARM ORGANIC MILK LTD

MANOR FARM, GODMANSTONE, DORCHESTER DT2 7AH
Tel: 01300 341415 Fax: 01300 341170 Contact: Pam Best
pam@manor-farm-organic.co.uk www.manor-farm-organic.co.uk
Producers of organic cartonned, pasteurised whole milk, semi-skimmed
milk and cream. Distribution over the South of England.

MILLS, TIM

COWDEN HOUSE, FRYS LANE, GODMANSTONE, DORCHESTER DT2 7AG
Tel: 01300 341377 Contact: Tim Mills
www.cowdenhouse.co.uk
Vegetarian B&B. Spacious, comfortable house in beautiful Dorset countryside. Local organic produce (evening meal available). Local therapies
arranged. Warm, professional hospitality in a peaceful environment.

MODBURY FARM
BURTON BRADSTOCK, BRIDPORT DT6 4NE
Tel: 01308 897193 Fax: 01308 897193 Contact: Tim & Julie Garry
timgarry@btinternet.com
Soil Association P7552, G7551. Organic Jersey herd with farm shop selling
our own milk, cream and summer vegetables. Also locally sourced organic
and non-organic produce (meat, eggs, cheese, ice cream, preserves, etc).

NATURAL DYE COMPANY
STANBRIDGE, WIMBORNE BH21 4JD
Tel: 01258 840549 Fax: 01258 840958 Contact: Sarah Burnett
naturaldyecompany@boltblue.com www.naturaldyecompany.com
The Natural Dye Company offers hand-knitted jackets, coats and cardigans
in silk, wool and cashmere, coloured with our famous natural, organic dyes.

ORGANIX BRANDS
KNAPP MILL, MILL RD., CHRISTCHURCH BH23 2LU
Tel: 01202 479701 Fax: 01202 479712 Contact: Marie Van-Hagen
marie.vanhagen@organixbrands.com www.organixbrands.com
Organix has over 50 organic recipes in its range including baby and
toddler meals in jars for babies from 4 months, 7 months and 12 months,
infant cereals, breadsticks, cereal bars, rice cakes, savoury snacks and
raisins.

PAMPERED PIGS
2 THE GREEN, TOLPUDDLE, DORCHESTER DT2 7EX
Tel: 01305 848107 Fax: 01305 848107 Contact: Amanda Crocker
pamperedpigs@fsmail.net www.organic.pork.co.uk
Small family-run farm producing organic pork and beef. We sell direct
to the public via our own farm shop and farmers' markets. Mail order
available, UK only.

REAL MEALS
64 ARNEWOOD RD., BOURNEMOUTH BH6 5DL
Tel: 01202 418381 Contact: J De Comyn
Caterer, delivery of hot organic lunches. Nice, friendly people, will do gluten-free, dairy-free, wheat-free.

RECTORY FARM
EAST CHALDON ROAD, WINFRITH NEWBURGH, NR. DORCHESTER DT2 8DJ
Tel: 01305 852835 Contact: Annette Evans
Organic eggs. Soil Association G2057. The farm lies approx 2.5 miles from Lulworth Cove. Open, free of charge to visitors.

RESPECT ORGANICS
31 BELL ST., SHAFTESBURY SP7 8AR
Tel: 01747 851561 Fax: 01747 851715 Contact: Vince Adams
info@respectorganics.com www.respectorganics
Soil Association P5888. Owner of the Respect brand, specialising in the ambient cake market. We license other manufacturers to produce our cake for us.

SLEPE FARM LTD
SLEPE FARM, SLEPE, NR. POOLE BH16 6HS
Tel: 01202 622737 Fax: 01202 620844 Contact: James Selby Bennett
j.selbybennett@virgin.net
Soil Association G7085. Beef and corn farm with wild heath grazed beef and wild game, wildlife and large barn available for exhibitions and craftsmen's workshops (furniture design and restoration).

SPETCH, LEONARD
THORNCOMBE FARM, HIGHER BOCKHAMPTON, DORCHESTER DT2 8QH
Tel: 01305 251695 Contact: Leonard Spetch
Small family farm specialising in high quality beef reared on well managed grassland. Some cereals also grown.

STOATE, NR AND SONS

CANN MILLS, SHAFTESBURY SP7 0BL
Tel: 01747 852475 Fax: 01747 851936 Contact: Michael Stoate
michaelstoate@lineone.net
Traditional stoneground flour millers since 1832 producing a full range of
organic flour for all your baking requirements.

STURTS FARM COMMUNITY

SHEILING TRUST, THREE CROSS ROAD, WEST MOORS, FERNDOWN BH22 0NF
Tel: 01202 870572 (farm) Fax: 01202 854763 Contact: Markus Konig (Farmer)
office@sturtsfarm.com www.sturtsfarm.com
Fully biodynamic certified large market garden, farm includes dairy, beef,
poultry, pigs, 90 acres. Farm shop includes full range of fruit and veg, dry
goods, health products. Shop tel: 01202 894292. Garden tel: 01202 875275.

SUNNYSIDE ORGANIC FARM

SUNNYSIDE FARM, LOWER KINGCOMBE, TOLLER PORCORUM, DORCH-
ESTER DT2 0EQ
Tel: 01300 321537 Fax: 01300 321537 Contact: Mandie Fletcher
mandiefletcher@sunnyside95.fsnet.co.uk www.sunnysideorganicfarm.co.uk
Soil Association G875, P7913. Mixed organic farm with luxury holiday
cottage, farm shop for seasonal vegetables, lamb, beef, eggs and local
artist exhibiting in the middle of the Dorset Wildlife Trust Reserve.

TAMARISK FARM

WEST BEXINGTON, DORCHESTER DT2 9DF
Tel: 01308 897781/897784 Contact: Adam Simon
farm@tamariskfarm.co.uk www.tamariskfarm.co.uk
All home grown on family farm by the sea. Order direct from the farm:
beef, lamb, mutton, sausages, wholemeal wheat and rye flours and vegetables all year round (Soil Association no. P07W). Deliver to DT6. Farm shop
open every Friday morning between 8.30 and 10.30 for meat and flour or
at any other time by arrangement.

THE WATERCRESS COMPANY
MAEN, CULLIFORD RD., DORCHESTER DT1 1QQ
Tel: 01929 401400 Fax: 01929 462693 Contact: Tom Amery
tom.amery@thewatercresscompany.com
Soil Association G4732. Growers of organic watercress from our farms in
UK, Spain and Florida.

WEST HEMBURY FARM
WEST HEMBURY FARM, ASKERSWELL, DORCHESTER DT2 9EN
Tel: 01308 485289 Fax: 01308 485041 Contact: Andy & Chris Hunt
farm@westhembury.com www.westhembury.com
Soil Association G2097. A mixed organic farm with self-catering accommodation for 2 to 6 people in converted stone barns (4 star). Farm gate sales
of organic beef. Rare breed White Park cattle and Sussex chickens.

WOODLANDS PARK DAIRY
WOODLANDS, WIMBORNE BH21 8LX
Tel: 01202 822687 Fax: 01202 826051 Contact: Richard Murray
sales@woodlands-park.co.uk www.woodlands-park.co.uk
Soil Association P5037. Producers of live sheep's and goat's milk yoghurts
and fromage frais in natural and four fruit flavours; goat's milk butter and
organic sheep's milk yoghurts. No GMOs.

YOUNG, ES & SON
STONEY DOWN FARM, RUSHALL LANE, CORFE MULLEN, WIMBOURNE
BH21 3RS
Tel: 01202 650303 Contact: Julia Van-Boven
Soil Association G5426. Selling eggs and lamb from gate, male ram lambs,
Suffolks.

ACORN DAIRY

ARCHDEACON NEWTON, DARLINGTON DL2 2YB
Tel: 01325 466999 Fax: 464567 Contact: Graham Tweddle
organic@acorndairy.co.uk www.
Process organic milk from own farm, delivering to doorsteps in and around
the Darlington area with organic bread, eggs, cheeses, yoghurts, butter,
fruit juices and clotted cream. Poultry once a month.

HARBOUR HOUSE FARMS

HARBOUR HOUSE FARMS, PLAWSWORTH, CHESTER-LE-STREET DH3 4EJ
Tel: 0191 388 3184 Fax: 07092308473 Contact: The Manager
hhf@hhfarms.fsnet.co.uk
Soil Association G5832. Cereals, lamb, beef and top fruit.

THE HEALTH WAREHOUSE

15 POST HOUSE WYND, DARLINGTON DL3 7LU
Tel: 01325 468570 Contact: Michael Barker
mjbarker2@hotmail.com
Large independent health store specialising in home-baked products and
organic chilled and ambient foods. Also herbal and natural remedies and
supplements.

PIERCEBRIDGE FARM

PIERCEBRIDGE, DARLINGTON DL2 3SE
Tel: 01325 374251 Contact: Chris Hodgson
piercebridgefarm@zoom.co.uk
A 280-acre organic farm by the river Tees built on a Roman site, producing
dried plucked chickens, eggs, potatoes, meat. Retailing a vast range of
100% organic products, including bread and fruit juices from Botton
Village, and special dietary products. Coffee shop.

ADM MILLING
KINGSGATE, 1 KING EDWARD RD., BRENTWOOD CM14 4HG
Tel: 01277 262525 Fax: 200320 Contact: Jason Hall
jason-hall@admworld.com www.admmilling.co.uk
Manufacturer of high quality flours, improvers, premixes and concentrates, including organic flours.

ALLAN, PP & PARTNERS
LANGFORD BRIDGE FARM, KELVEDON HATCH, BRENTWOOD CM15 0LB
Tel: 01277 362012 Contact: Juliet Moore
Producer of combinable crops: milling wheat, feed wheat, barley, beans, oats, rye.

ASHLYNS ORGANIC FARM
HIGH LAVER HALL, HIGH LAVER, ONGAR CM5 0DU
Tel: 01277 890188/9 Fax: 01277 890188 Contact: Jim Collins
info@ashlyns.co.uk www.ashlyns.co.uk
Soil Association G2401, P5815. Home grown produce delivered direct to your door through our box scheme or available in our new Organic Farm Shop, offering home-grown vegetables, fruit, meat and home-made delicatessen.

AURO ORGANIC PAINT SUPPLIES
UNIT 2, PAMPHILLIONS FARM, DEBDEN, SAFFRON WALDEN CB11 3JT
Tel: 01799 543077 Fax: 01799 542187 Contact: Richard Hadfield
sales@auroorganic.co.uk www.auroorganic.co.uk
Importers of natural organic paints 100% free from petrochemicals and their derivatives. The range includes emulsions, glosses, eggshells, woodstains, floor finishes, waxes, varnishes and adhesives, all of which are uncompromising in their use of natural ingredients.

BROWNING, ROBERT & SON

TEY BROOK FARM, GREAT TEY, COLCHESTER CO6 1JE
Tel: 01206 210320 Fax: 01206 212597 Contact: Richard Browning
teybrook@aol.com www.cleanearth.co.uk
Arable, vegetable, herb producer.

BUNTINGS

89 HIGH STREET, MALDON CM9 5EP
Tel: 01621 853271 Fax: 01376 561233 Contact: Stephen Bunting
www.buntingfoods.co.uk
Retail fine food shop specialising in butchery, delicatessen, home-made
pies, cooked meats, patés. Delivery areas CM8, CM9, CO6.

DALGETY

MORETON MILL, ONGAR CM5 0DP
Tel: 01277 899700 Fax: 01277 898206 Contact: Organic Seed Department
seed.marketing@dalgety.co.uk www.dalgety.co.uk
Organic seed producers.

DIATOMACEOUS EARTH EUROPE LTD

CREEK VIEW, MALDON RD., GREAT WIGBOROUGH, COLCHESTER CO5 7SB
Tel: 01206 735732 Fax: 01206 735704 Contact: Mark Newman
sales@d-earth.co.uk www.d-earth.co.uk
Feed Grade Diatomaceous Earth Products for use in grain storage. Our
granules can be added to the bulk of the grain to control insects and
protect against infestation. Our powder can be used as a surface treatment
to control grain insects. Diatomaceous Earth Powder for use in poultry
houses to control Red Mite.

DOUBLE DRAGON CO

4 TRING CLOSE, BARKINGSIDE, ILFORD IG2 7LQ
Tel: 020 8554 3838 Fax: 020 8554 3883 Contact: Alice Chiu
info@doubledragon.co.uk www.doubledragon.co.uk
Soil Association P6143. Importer of organic Green Tea, China Green Tea, Pure Ginseng Tea, Pure Ginkgo Biloba Tea, Jasmine Tea, Green Tea with Ginkgo Biloba Tea. We are a wholesaler of Ginseng, Royal Jelly, essential balm etc. Beautiful packaging, reasonable prices.

FARMER KIT ORGANICS

LITTLE BOWSERS FARM, BOWSERS LANE, LITTLE WALDEN, SAFFRON WALDEN CB10 1XQ
Tel: 01799 527315 Fax: 01799 527315 Contact: The Manager
sales@farmerkit.co.uk www.farmerkit.co.uk
Soil Association G2143. Little Bowsers Farm produces organic free range eggs and organic top fruit, apples, pears, plums. Also organic soft fruits. We deliver regularly to London wholesalers.

FUERST DAY LAWSON LTD

UNIT 4, FOURTH AVENUE, BLUEBRIDGE IND. ESTATE, HALSTEAD CO9 2SY
Tel: 01787 473826 Fax: 01787 475029 Contact: Mark Clarke
mclarke.halstead@fdl.co.uk www.fdl.co.uk
We are a processor of dried cereals, fruit and seeds.

HALSTEAD FOOD SERVICES LTD

UNIT 1, 1ST AVENUE, BLUEBRIDGE, HALSTEAD CO9 2EX
Tel: 01787 473222 Fax: 01787 479026 Contact: Nick Galley
halsteadfoods@hotmail.com
Soil Association registered. We clean, dice and pack organic nuts, dried fruits, seeds and cereals.

HART WORLDWIDE LTD
MILL HOUSE, RIVERWAY, HARLOW CM20 2DW
Tel: 01279 639669 Fax: 01279 635257 Contact: Andrew Howe
ahowe@hartww.com
Soil Association P6778. Importer of organic top fruit.

HDRA, HENRY DOUBLEDAY RESEARCH ASSOCIATION, THE ORGANIC KITCHEN GARDEN
AUDLEY END HOUSE, SAFFRON WALDEN CB11 4JF
Tel: 024 7630 3517 Fax: 024 7663 9229 Contact: Susan Kay-Williams
enquiry@hdra.org.uk www.hdra.org.uk
HDRA, the organic organisation, runs the walled kitchen garden at Audley End House, an English Heritage property. The 2-acre walled garden include heritage vegetables, vinery and fruit house. For opening hours please contact English Heritage 01799 522399.

HEPBURNS OF MOUNTNESSING
269 ROMAN ROAD, MOUNTNESSING, BRENTWOOD CM15 0UH
Tel: 01277 353289 Fax: 01277 355589 Contact: Gordon Hepburn
Traditional butcher and grazier with a reputation for quality and service. Established 1932. Highgrove organic beef, lamb and pork when available. Deliver locally and to London (over £50 free).

ILFORD FARMERS' MARKET
PEDESTRIANISED ILFORD HIGH RD., NR. TOWN HALL, ILFORD
Tel: 020 7704 9659 Contact: Cheryl Cohen
info@lfm.org.uk www.lfm.org.uk
First and third Saturdays of the month 9am to 2pm. Here farmers sell home-grown foods grown or made within 100 miles of the M25, including fruit, veg, meat, dairy, eggs, honey, juice, bread, preserves and plants. Note: some, but not all, producers are organic. Run by London Farmers' Markets, PO Box 37363, London N1 7WB.

IPSWICH ORGANIC GARDENERS GROUP
BABOUSHKA, 223 MERSEA ROAD, COLCHESTER CO2 8PN
Tel: 01206 570859 Contact: Jill Carter
tetley@macunlimited.net www.irene.org.uk
Gardening group affiliated to the HDRA, meeting once a month from
September to May, speaker each month. Bi-monthly newsletter, discount
seeds and bulk purchasing scheme. Also attend local events to promote
organic gardening.

KINGS SEEDS
MONKS FARM, PANTLINES LANE, COGGESHALL RD., KELVEDON CO5 0PG
Tel: 01376 570000 Fax: 01376 571189 Contact: Tony Ward
sales@kingsseeds.com www.kingsseeds.com
Soil Association P5847. Organic seeds supplier to grower and home
gardener, large range of organic seeds, both flowers and vegetables. Also
untreated standard seed available.

LEGG, RG
HEARDS FARM, HEARDS LANE, SHENFIELD, BRENTWOOD CM15 0SF
Tel: 01277 211883 Contact: Roger Legg
Soil Association G4499. Home-produced vegetables, fruit, plants, cut
flowers etc; seasonal box scheme, local delivery and WI market.

MANNINGTREE ORGANIC GROWERS
83 HUNGERDOWN LANE, LAWFORD, MANNINGTREE CO11 2LY
Tel: 01206 231399 Contact: Marina O'Connell
nina@rspopuk.com
We are a group of 4 growers producing top fruit and soft fruit, salads and
eggs, lavender oils and associated cosmetic products in the Stour valley.
Wholesale and Stoke Newington farmers' market.

ORGANIC CHOICE
60 HIGH ST., HALSTEAD CO9 2JG
Tel: 01787 478471 Fax: 01787 478457 Contact: Peter & Nathalie Coleby
info@organicchoice.net www.organicchoice.net
Organic delicatessen offering fresh fruit & vegetables, traditional & speciality cheeses, paté, hand-carved ham, award-winning breads, wine, groceries, dairy, chilled & frozen foods, environmentally friendly products. Free home delivery throughout Essex and Suffolk borders. Price list available. Credit cards accepted.

OXLEY HILL FARM
LAYER RD., ABBERTON, COLCHESTER CO5 7NH
Tel: 01206 735522 Fax: 01206 561622 Contact: Steve Miller
Soil Association G7658. Farm producer of cattle and sheep, timber, sloes and blackberries.

PILGRIM'S NATURAL
4 KING GEORGES PLACE, HIGH ST., MALDON CM9 5BZ
Tel: 01621 858605 Contact: Mary Chimba
Retailer and packer of a wide range of organic food including butter and yoghurts, ice cream, bread and cakes.

SAWDON, J M
PELDON HALL, PELDON, NR. COLCHESTER CO5 7PU
Tel: 07973 750367 Fax: 01206 735791 Contact: J Sawdon
j.sawdon@farmline.com www.peldonhall.com
Store/bag/dress/clean/dry/blend wheat, barley, triticale, oats, beans, peas, maize, lucerne and bran.

SOYA FRESH!

3 CORONATION HILL, EPPING CM16 5DT
Tel: 0845 330 6781 Fax: 0870 706 2744 Contact: James Summers
office@soyafresh.co.uk www.soyafresh.co.uk
We sell soya milk-making machines, tofu-making kits, UK grown organic
soya beans, natural nigari and associated ingredients & products including
vegan GM-free supplements. See display ad.

SUFFOLK HERBS

COGGESHILL RD., KELVEDON CO5 9PG
Tel: 01376 572456 Fax: 01376 571189 Contact: Tony Ward
sales@suffolkherbs.com www.suffolkherbs.com
Organic seed supplying for the home gardener, large produce. Also
untreated standard varieties of seeds available.

SUNRISE HEALTHFOODS LTD

31 SPA RD., HOCKLEY SS5 4AZ
Tel: 01702 207017 Contact: Richard
Modern healthfood shop offering 2,000 products including many organic
lines, frozen and chilled foods, special dietfoods and supplements. Friendly
service and competent advice always available.

UNILEVER BESTFOODS

LONDON RD., PURFLEET RM19 1SD
Tel: 01708 684533 Fax: 01708 684544 Contact: RM Livingston
bob.livingston@unilever.com
Soil Association P7592. Food manufacturers: principally vegetables, fruit,
spreads and savoury products.

USHER, JENNY
GREEN OAKS, THRESHERS BUSH, NR. HARLOW CM17 0NS
Tel: 01279 444663 Contact: Jenny Usher
Soil Association U02E. Organic fruit and veg.

WATER LANE NURSERIES
NAYLAND, COLCHESTER CO6 4JS
Tel: 01206 262880 Fax: 01206 262880 Contact: Simon Faithfull
Soil Association G3059. Soil Association licensed mixed vegetable and fruit growers.

THE WHOLEFOOD STORE
26 HIGH ST., MANNINGTREE CO11 1AJ
Tel: 01206 391200 Contact: Jon or Sarah
jondyvig@hotmail.com
We are an independent and friendly wholefood store selling an extensive range of organic dried foods, fresh fruit and vegetables, dairy products, drinks, bread and pastries.

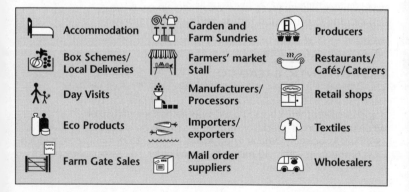

Accommodation	Garden and Farm Sundries	Producers
Box Schemes/ Local Deliveries	Farmers' market Stall	Restaurants/ Cafés/Caterers
Day Visits	Manufacturers/ Processors	Retail shops
Eco Products	Importers/ exporters	Textiles
Farm Gate Sales	Mail order suppliers	Wholesalers

ADEYS FARM ORGANIC MEATS

ADEYS FARM, BREADSTONE, BERKELEY GL13 9HF
Tel: 01453 511218 Fax: 01453 511218 Contact: Caroline Wilson
cwilson@adeysfarm.fsnet.co.uk
Organic beef, lamb, pork, bacon, burgers, speciality sausages. Traditional breeds including Aberdeen Angus, Gloucester Old Spot, well hung and traditionally butchered.

ALDERTON NURSERIES

STOW RD., ALDERTON, NR. TEWKESBURY GL20 8NH
Tel: 01242 620394 Fax: 01242 620261 Contact: Stephen Haslum
Soil Association G5705. Small family business growing protected glasshouse crops: tomatoes, cucumbers, beans, courgettes, peppers.

ALLIED GRAIN LTD

103 CIRENCESTER BUSINESS PARK, LOVE LANE, CIRENCESTER GL7 1XD
Tel: 01285 6491430 Contact: David Whyte
david.whyte@alliedgrain.co.uk www.alliedgrain.co.uk
Organic and in conversion, wheat, barley, oats and brans.

THE AUTHENTIC BREAD CO

STRAWBERRY HILL FARM, STRAWBERRY HILL, NEWENT GL18 1LH
Tel: 01531 828181 Fax: 01531 828151 Contact: Jane Davis
breadbaron@authenticbread.co.uk www.authenticbread.co.uk
Wholesale bakers of speciality organic bread, cakes, croissants, pasties, etc. 1996 Soil Association Organic Food Award Winner, 1998 highly commended. Own distribution within 60 mile radius; mail order. Soil Association symbol no. P1912. See display ad.

BETTER FOR ORGANICS
36 SILVER STREET, DURSLEY GL11 4ND
Tel: 01453 545090 Fax: 01453 548895 Contact: Kathryn Francis
info@betterfororganics.co.uk www.betterfororganics.co.uk
High quality organic food store stocking fresh fruit and vegetables, fresh
meat and poultry, eggs, milk, freshly baked craft bread and much more.
Free home delivery service available.

BOWLDOWN FARMS LTD
BOWLDOWN FARMS LTD, TETBURY GL8 8UD
Tel: 01666 890224 Fax: 01666 890433 Contact: GEM or JFG Vernon
admin@bowldownfarmsltd.co.uk
Soil Association G4157. We seek to retain the traditional Cotswold farm,
specialising in organic North Devon beef, lamb and arable products.
Conservation and amenity issues are uppermost in our priorities. Box scheme
for lamb in autumn and developing box scheme for beef from March to May.

CAMPHILL VILLAGE TRUST—OAKLANDS PARK
OAKLANDS PARK, NEWNHAM ON SEVERN GL14 1EF
Tel: 01594 516550 Fax: 01594 516550 Contact: Kai Lange
wholesale: kaigarden@onetel.com www.oaklandspark.org.uk
box scheme: anna@bergamot.basil.freeuk.com www.bergamot.basil.freeuk.com
box scheme tel: 01594 516344/510365.
Biodynamic Agricultural Association (Demeter) 101, Soil Association V01M.
Working community with people with special needs. Involved with regional
biodynamic land training (2 years), vegetables, herbs and fruit for wholesaling
and box scheme. Some meat available for box scheme customers.

CORBETT, JDR & JL
NEW HOUSE FARM, HIGHLEADON, NEWENT GL18 1HQ
Tel: 01452 790209 Fax: 01452 790209 Contact: Janet Corbett
cjojan@aol.com
Farm shop selling beef, lamb, pork, bacon, gammon, sausages and burgers.
Free range eggs. Trafitional beef breeds. Open weekdays 10am–5pm, week-
ends 10am–12noon. Three self contained holiday cottages—sleeps 2 to 6.
One suitable for disabled. Not suitable for children. CL Touring caravan site.
Adults only. electric hook-ups. Flat, mowed site.

COTSWOLD HEALTH PRODUCTS LTD
UNIT 5/8 TABERNACLE RD., WOTTON-UNDER-EDGE GL12 7EF
Tel: 01453 843694 Fax: 01453 521375 Contact: Keidrich Davies
sales@cotsherb.co.uk www.cotsherb.co.uk
Soil Association no. P1926. Importers of herbs and spices.

COTSWOLD SEEDS LTD
THE COTSWOLD BUSINESS VILLAGE, LONDON RD.,
MORETON IN MARSH GL56 0JQ
Tel: 01608 652552 Fax: 01608 652256 Contact: Ian Wilkinson
info@cotswoldseeds.com www.cotswoldseeds.com
Soil Association P5985. Seed merchants: Cotswold Seeds is a very specialist
supplier of forage and green manure seeds mixtures for organic farms. We
offer impartial advice and a next day delivery service. Call 0800 252211 for
a catalogue or visit our website www.cotswoldseeds.com/organic.

CROOKED END FARM ORGANICS
RUARDEAN, FOREST OF DEAN GL17 9XF
Tel: 01594 544482 Contact: Morag Norman
crooked.end@talk21.com
Soil Association (G2393) and HDRA. Small mixed organic farm, close to
forest and Wye Valley, producing free range eggs, fruit & vegetables in
season, lamb, beef, pork, cider, perry. Self-catering holiday cottage.
Stunning views to Welsh mountains.

DAIRY CREST LTD
OLDENDS LANE, STONEHOUSE GL10 2DG
Tel: 01453 435543 Fax: 01453 435812 Contact: John Middleton
john.middleton@dairycrest.co.uk www.dairycrest.co.uk
Dairy Crest process organic dairy products, produced from raw milk, to suit
market requirements, including organic cream and butter.

DAYLESFORD CREAMERY

NEW FARM, DAYLESFORD, MORETON IN MARSH GL56 0YG
Tel: 01608 658005 Fax: 01608 658009 Contact: Joe Schneider
j.schneider@daylesfordcreamery.com www.daylesfordcreamery.com
Soil Association P7707. Makers of speciality farmhouse cheeses, produced
from our own supply of organic milk, made and ripened on the farm by
traditional methods.

DAYLESFORD ORGANIC FARMSHOP

DAYLESFORD, NR KINGHAM, MORETON IN MARSH GL56 0YG
Tel: 01608 731700 Fax: 01608 658009 Contact: Tamsin Borlase
enquiries@daylesfordfarmshop.com www.daylesfordorganic.com
At Daylesford, we offer the freshest seasonal produce from our fully organic
estates, with a passionate commitment to quality. We practise compassionate
farming and sustainability: organic beef, lamb, venison and poultry; heritage
variety vegetables and fruits; top award-winning hand-made organic cheeses;
organic breads, pastries, and much more. Discover the taste of the finest
food from Daylesford—to take away, or in our restaurant. See display ad.

ECOTRICITY

AXIOM HOUSE, STATION ROAD, STROUD GL5 3AP
Tel: 01453 756111 Fax: 01453 756222 Contact: Customer Services
info@ecotricity.co.uk www.ecotricity.co.uk
Green electricity supplier. Dedicated to building clean new energy sources
that won't contribute to global warming. Ecotricity matches the standard
price of your local electricity supplier so it shouldn't cost you more than
'normal' polluting electricity.

FUTURA FOODS UK LTD

WYNCHFIELD HOUSE, CALCOT, NR. TETBURY GL8 8YJ
Tel: 01666 890500 Fax: 01666 890522 Contact: Ellen Svensson
info@futura-foods.com www.futura-foods.com
Soil Association P1642. Danish manufacturing and dairy trading organisation. Selling and developing organic dairy products for UK retail/wholesale
sectors. Marketed under 'Futura Organic' label.

GLOBAL ORGANIC MARKETS

UNIT 5, CANAL IRONWORKS, HOPE MILL LANE, LONDON ROAD,
BRIMSCOMBE, STROUD GL5 2SH
Tel: 01453 884123 Fax: 01453 884123 Contact: Andie Soutar
globalorganicmarkets@fsmail.net
Fresh fruit, vegetables and eggs: wholesale delivery and collection for box
schemes, shops, restaurants and growers. Retail sales from our stalls in
Stroud (Gloucestershire) Shambles Market (Friday 8.30–5pm) and Old
Spitalfields, London (Sunday 9.30–6pm).

GRAINFARMERS PLC

UNIT 3, COMPTON BUSINESS CENTRE, COMPTON ABDALE,
CHELTENHAM GL54 4DL
Tel: 01242 890003 Fax: 01242 890516 Contact: David King
david.king@grainfarmers.co.uk www.grainfarmers.co.uk
Soil Association P6901. Wholesaling organic cereals and pulses.

THE GREEN SHOP

BISLEY GL6 7BX
Tel: 01452 770629 Fax: 01452 770104 Contact: Jane Powell
enquiries@greenshop.co.uk www.greenshop.co.uk
Natural paints, renewable energy installations, rain harvesting, organic
bodycare, jams, preserves and chocolate, books, and plenty more! Visit our
shop or website.

HEALTH-WISE

27 NORTH WALK, YATE BS37 4AP
Tel: 01454 322168 Fax: 01454 322168 Contact: W Round
Open 9–5.30 Mon-Sat supplying organic cereal, nuts, seeds, jam, flour,
vegetarian food, margarines, sheep and goat's milk products.

HOBBS HOUSE BAKERY

UNIT 6, CHIPPING EDGE ESTATE, HATTERS LANE,
CHIPPING SODBURY BS37 6AA
Tel: 01454 321629 Fax: 01454 329757
Contact: Clive Wells & Trevor Herbert
admin@hobbshousebakery.co.uk www.hobbshousebakery.co.uk
Soil Association P1632. A traditional craft bakery producing award-winning breads. Three retail outlets, and supplies to outlets within 50-mile radius.

HOBBS HOUSE BAKERY

39 HIGH ST, CHIPPING SODBURY BS37 6BA
Tel: 01454 317525 Fax: 01454 329757
Contact: Clive Wells & Trevor Herbert
admin@hobbshousebakery.co.uk www.hobbshousebakery.co.uk
We are licensed by the Soil Association (P1632), producing organic white and wholemeal bread for our own shops and wholesale outlets.

JAMES' GOURMET COFFEE CO LTD

YARTLETON FARM, MAY HILL, LONGHOPE GL17 0RF
Tel: 0870 787 0233 Fax: 01432 831003 Contact: Peter James
enquiries@jamesgourmetcoffee.com www.jamesgourmetcoffee.com
Discerning, ethical, passionate coffee specialists. Great coffee! Traditional service. See display ad.

JUST WHOLEFOODS

UNIT 16 CIRENCESTER BUSINESS EST., ELLIOTT ROAD, LOVE LANE,
CIRENCESTER GL7 1YS
Tel: 01285 651910 Fax: 01285 650266 Contact: Anne Madden
info@justwholefoods.co.uk www.justwholefoods.co.uk
Just Wholefoods have been manufacturing organic products for over 10 years. The product range includes dried soup mixes, ready meals and confectionery lines. They proudly accepted a Certificate of Excellence for their product Organic VegeBears at The Soil Association Organic Awards 2000 as overall winners in the category of confectionery and snacks. The company now has sufficient capacity to manufacture gum-based confectionery products and our other dry products under private labels.

KITCHEN GARDEN PRESERVES

UNIT 15, SALMON SPRINGS TRADING ESTATE, CHELTENHAM ROAD, STROUD GL6 6NU
Tel: 01453 759612 Fax: 01453 755899 Contact: Barbara Moinet
info@kitchengardenpreserves.co.uk www.kitchengardenpreserves.co.uk
Soil Association P2409. We make top quality hand-made preserves including our Award-Winning Seville Orange Marmalade (1999 Organic Food Awards: Category Winner) and Organic Beetroot Chutney (Category Winner 2003) Sold through independent retailers, box schemes and by mail order.

LA BODEGA

TAURUS CRAFTS, THE OLD PARK, LYDNEY GL15 6BU
Tel: 01594 844841 Fax: 01594 845636 Contact: Dirk Rohwedder
bodega@tauruscrafts.co.uk www.tauruscrafts.co.uk
La Bodega stocks local produce and organic foods, specialising in organic wines, chocolates, coffees and deli foods. We are part of the Taurus Crafts Centre, celebrating healthy living and creative design by bringing together wholesome food, fine arts and handmade crafts. The centre is open to the public from 10am to 5.30pm every day.

LIVING EARTH PRODUCE

RUSKIN MILL, OLD BRISTOL RD, NAILSWORTH GL6 0LA
Tel: 01453 837510 Fax: 01453 835029 Contact: Andy Horton
Organic and biodynamic food store. Vegetables, fruit, frozen meat, milk, cheese, yoghurts, herbs and spices, eggs and a wide range of groceries.

MAD HATTERS ORGANIC RESTAURANT

3 COSSACK SQUARE, NAILSWORTH GL6 0DB
Tel: 01453 832615 Fax: 01453 832615 Contact: Carolyn Findlay
mafindlay@waitrose.com
Since there are GMOs in animal feeds we use totally organic meat, milk, butter, cream and cheese. Non-smoking. Wheelchair access. Local seasonal organic produce cooked classically without additives or cheap substitutes by four enthusiastic and idealistic chefs. Organic wines, beers and soft drinks. Bright informal décor.

MELCOURT INDUSTRIES LTD

BOLDRIDGE BRAKE, LONG NEWTON, TETBURY GL8 8RT
Tel: 01666 502711 Fax: 01666 504398 Contact: Catherine Dawson
mail@melcourt.co.uk www.melcourt.co.uk
Soil Association I1222. Melcourt are specialist manufacturers of growing
media products derived from sustainable forest residues. We supply
professional growers and the landscape industry with bark and wood-
derived mulches, soil ameliorants and play surfaces.

MOTHER NATURE

2 BEDFORD ST., STROUD GL5 1AY
Tel: 01453 758202 Fax: 01453 752595 Contact: Kurt Hilder
mnstroud@aol.com
Food on three floors. Organic wine, meat, bread, dairy products,
champagne and perry. Specialist in water filtration filters, purifiers and
systems.

THE NATURAL GROCERY STORE LTD

150 – 156, BATH ROAD, CHELTENHAM GL53 7NG
Tel: 01242 243737 Fax: 01242 238872 Contact: Paul Lewis
triple8.trading@virgin.net
Organic fresh fruit and vegetables, dairy, meat, poultry, fish, bread, cakes,
wine, beer, spirits, cider, canned, dried and bottled groceries and provisions. All under one roof of 2,000 square feet. Open daily 8am–10pm.

NEAL'S YARD REMEDIES

9 ROTUNDA TERRACE, MONTPELLIER ST., CHELTENHAM GL50 1SW
Tel: 01242 522136 Fax: 01242 522136 Contact: Sally Lorman
nyr@chelt.net www.nealsyardremedies.com
Neal's Yard Remedies manufacture and sell natural skincare products, and
stock an extensive range of herbs, essential oils, homoeopathic remedies
and books. We also have therapy rooms.

NEWARK FARM

OZLEWORTH, WOOTON-UNDER-EDGE GL12 7PZ
Tel: 01453 842144 Fax: 01453 521432 Contact: Steve Redman
We produce beef, lamb, multicoloured free range hens' eggs, Ministry-approved seed potatoes, ware potatoes and vegetables.

NUTRITION CENTRE

98 HIGH ST., TEWKESBURY GL20 5JZ
Tel: 01684 299620 Fax: 01684 274462 Contact: V BALE
sales @nutritioncentre.co.uk www.nutritioncentre.co.uk
Retail and mail order health food store with large range of organic foods and related products. Experienced and friendly trained staff. New internet shop.

NUTRITION CENTRE

133 BATH RD., CHELTENHAM GL53 7LT
Tel: 01242 514150 Fax: 01242 580509 Contact: Anne Mitchell
sales @nutritioncentre.co.uk www.nutritioncentre.co.uk
Retail and mail order health food store with large range of organic foods and related products. Experienced and friendly trained staff. New internet shop.

NUTRITION CENTRE

28 WINCHCOMBE ST., CHELTENHAM GL52 1LX
Tel: 01242 529934 Fax: 01242 528700 Contact: Vicky Calderone
sales@nutrition centre.co.uk www.nutritioncentre.co.uk
Retail and mail order health food store with large range of organic foods and related products. Experienced and friendly trained staff. New internet shop.

THE ORANGE TREE

317 HIGH STREET, CHELTENHAM GL50 3HW
Tel: 01242 234232 Contact: Khan
Vegetarian/vegan restaurant offering world cuisine in relaxed atmosphere. Special diets catered for. Small patio open in summer.

THE ORGANIC FARM SHOP

ABBEY HOME FARM, BURFORD ROAD, CIRENCESTER GL7 5HF
Tel: 01285 640441 Fax: 01285 644827 Contact: Hilary Chester-Master
info@theorganicfarmshop.co.uk www.theorganicfarmshop.co.uk
Soil Association G1715, R5253. 100% organic, award-winning farm, shop
and café with garden. Courses, educational visits, trailer rides, woodland
walk. Our own vegetables, meat, eggs and frozen meals, also general
groceries. Greenfield camping.

THE ORGANIC SHOP

THE SQUARE, STOW-ON-THE-WOLD GL54 1AB
Tel: 01451 831004 Contact: Sheila Wye
The first independently owned retail shop in the UK specialising in the sale
of Soil Association symbol produce, including meat. Open 9.00am to
5.30pm every day except Christmas and Boxing Day.

PARK CORNER FARMS

PARK CORNER, CIRENCESTER GL7 6LS
Tel: 01285 760850 Fax: 01285 760850 Contact: J Hoskins
jeremy.hoskins@ukonline.co.uk
Soil Association G5440, OLMC. We breed and feed top beef (Shorthorn &
Angus cows) by a Charolais. We also sell high index Charolais bulls,
selected for calving and natural fleshing. Weight pays.

PHILLIPS, CG & JF

MACARONI FARM, EASTLEACH, CIRENCESTER GL7 3NG
Tel: 01367 850237 Fax: 01367 850526 Contact: Charles Phillips
cphillips@macaroni-farm.co.uk
Soil Association G6372. Pedigree South Devon beef herd, Aberdeen Angus
beef herd, Lleyn x Texel lambs, wheat, barley, peas, beans, forage crops.

PINETUM PRODUCTS
PINETUM LODGE, CHURCHAM GL2 8AD
Tel: 01452 750402 Fax: 01452 750402 Contact: David Wilkin
Associated with Good Gardeners Association. We run a B&B with excellent accommodation. Natural products and food used and a lecture on organics if required. Organic products for sale by mail order.

RUSKIN MILL COLLEGE
THE FISHERIES, HORSLEY GL6 1PL
Tel: 01453 837500 Fax: 01453 837506 Contact: Julian Pyzer
www.ruskin-mill.org.uk
Biodynamic Agricultural Association 245. Part of special needs further education college with biodynamic market garden and mixed farm, and fish farm. Café and shop; crafts, exhibitions, workshops, concerts, story-telling and talks.

SEVERN BANK ORGANICS
CAMAROY FARM, BROADOAK, NEWHAM-ON-SEVERN,
GLOUCESTER GL14 1JB
Tel: 01594 516367 Contact: J Babij
An organic smallholding specialising in seasonal vegetables and all year round production of mixed salad leaves. We also produce organic eggs and a limited amount of organic pork. We have a farm shop open Thursday to Sunday in summer months.

SHIPTON MILL LTD
LONG NEWNTON, TETBURY GL8 8RP
Tel: 01666 505050 Fax: 01666 504666 Contact: John Lister
enquiries@shipton-mill.com www.shipton-mill.com
We are a small flour mill in the heart of the Cotswolds, producing stone-ground organic flours for the craft baker as well as supplying the home baker through our friendly mail order service. Members of the Soil Association.

SLIPSTREAM ORGANICS

34A LANGDON RD., CHELTENHAM GL53 7NZ
Tel: 01242 227273 Fax: 01242 227798 Contact: Nick McCordall
info@slipstream-organics.co.uk www.slipstream-organics.co.uk
Soil Association R1732. Award-winning box scheme, established June 1994,
supplying locally grown organic food to over 500 households in
Cheltenham, Gloucester and Stroud. Good local supplier links.

SMILECHILD

PO BOX 274, CHELTENHAM GL53 7YP
Tel: 0800 195 6982 Fax: 01242 269635 Contact: Rebecca Cambridge
info@smilechild.co.uk www.smilechild.co.uk
On-line shopping for the planet conscious parent. Smilechild offers a full
range of Fair Trade and organic clothes, wooden toys, natural toiletries,
eco-nappies and more.

STROUD COMMUNITY AGRICULTURE LTD

HAWKWOOD COLLEGE, PAINSWICK OLD ROAD, STROUD GL
Tel: 0845 458 0814 Contact: The Members
info@stroudcommunityagriculture.org
www.stroudcommunityagriculture.org
A community co-operative which runs a farm business. The farm grows
vegetables and has pigs and cattle. Anyone can become a member: get a
weekly veg bag with an option to buy meat also. Membership tel: 01453
840037.

ST. AUGUSTINES FARM

ARLINGHAM, GLOUCESTER GL2 7JN
Tel: 01452 740277 Fax: 01452 740277 Contact: Robert Jewell
staugustines@btconnect.com
Dairy Farm. School and family visits from 2004.

SUNSHINE CRAFT BAKERY

THE BRITISH SCHOOL, SLAD ROAD, STROUD GL5 1QW
Tel: 01453 752592 Contact: Michael Hill
Bake and supply organic bread, cakes and savouries (vegetarian) for our
own shop (see below) and Cheltenham Nutrition Centres.

SUNSHINE HEALTH SHOP & ORGANIC BAKERY

25 CHURCH ST., STROUD GL5 1JL
Tel: 01453 763923 Contact: Ray Hill
Over 3,000 organic and health food products including dietary
supplements, herbal and homoeopathic medicines, cosmetics and toiletries.
Hand-crafted bread using nature's organic ingredients. Manufacturers of
Thompson's Slippery Elm foods.

THORNBURY ORGANIC CO-OP

9 CROSSWAYS RD., THORNBURY BS35 2YL
Tel: 01454 415345 Contact: Judith Dale
judithdale@blueyonder.co.uk
Local buying co-op. We provide a wide range of organic groceries, fruit,
vegetables, dairy, bread, wines, beers, fish and meat, which are locally
sourced where possible. Local delivery only.

WHITFIELD FARM ORGANICS

WHITFIELD FARM, FALFIELD, WOTTON UNDER EDGE,
GLOUCESTERSHIRE GL12 8DR
Tel: 0845 283 0232 Fax: 0845 283 0232 Contact: Mr Blair (Manager)
jfb@whitfieldfarmorganics.co.uk www.whitfieldfarmorganics.co.uk
We produce beef that is grass-fed and organic beef, sold on farm and at
local farmers' markets, and organic soft fruit. We grow strawberries,
raspberries, tayberries, gooseberries, redcurrants & blackcurrants.

WYEDEAN WHOLEFOODS
15 MARKET PLACE, COLEFORD GL16 8AW
Tel: 01594 810303 Contact: Barry Cocker
Hundreds of organic lines. Wholefoods, gluten- and dairy-free, cruelty-free cosmetics; SLS-free toiletries. Excellent range of vitamins, minerals and herbals. Wide range of chilled and frozen products.

WYEDEAN WHOLEFOODS
13 MARKET STREET, CINDERFORD GL14 2RT
Tel: 01594 825455 Contact: Barry Cocker
Hundreds of organic lines. Wholefoods, gluten- and dairy-free, cruelty-free cosmetics; SLS-free toiletries. Excellent range of vitamins, minerals and herbals. Wide range of chilled and frozen products.

WYEDEAN WHOLEFOODS
2 HARE LANE, GLOUCESTER GL1 2BB
Tel: 01452 423577 Contact: Barry Cocker
Hundreds of organic lines. Wholefoods, gluten- and dairy-free, cruelty-free cosmetics; SLS-free toiletries. Excellent range of vitamins, minerals and herbals. Wide range of chilled and frozen products.

WYEDEAN WHOLEFOODS
MARKET SQUARE, NEWENT GL18 1PS
Tel: 01531 821922 Contact: Barry Cocker
Hundreds of organic lines. Wholefoods, gluten- and dairy-free, cruelty-free cosmetics; SLS-free toiletries. Excellent range of vitamins, minerals and herbals. Wide range of chilled and frozen products.

WYEDEAN WHOLEFOODS
18 NEWERNE STREET, LYDNEY GL15 5RF
Tel: 01594 841907 Contact: Barry Crocker
Hundreds of organic lines. Wholefoods, gluten- and dairy-free, cruelty-free cosmetics; SLS-free toiletries. Excellent range of vitamins, minerals and herbals. Wide range of chilled and frozen products.

ABSOLUTE AROMAS LTD
2 GROVE PARK, MILL LANE, ALTON GU34 2QC
Tel: 01420 540400 Fax: 01420 540401 Contact: David Tomlinson
relax@absolute-aromas.com
Aromatherapy products. Available by mail order and from health food stores.

BRIDGEGUILD LTD
BUDBRIDGE MANOR NURSERY, MERSTONE, NEWPORT PO30 3DH
Tel: 01983 840623 Fax: 01983 840225 Contact: JPH Verey
piers.verey@wightsalads.com
Organic glasshouse-grown cherry and beef tomatoes, sold through our marketing company 'Wight Salads Ltd' to UK supermarkets.

BROUGHTON ORGANICS
THE ANCHORAGE, SALISBURY RD., BROUGHTON,
NR. STOCKBRIDGE SO20 8BX
Tel: 01794 301234 Contact: SL Tidy
Soil Association T07S and ECEAT (European Centre for Eco-Agro Tourism). Broughton Organics grow and supply organic produce (specialising in vegetables, eggs and poultry meat). We aim to provide an alternative to globalisation by supplying local food to local people. Camping available.

CHEEKY RASCALS
STONE BARN, 1 BROWS FARM, FARNHAM RD, LISS GU33 6JG
Tel: 0870 873 2600 Fax: 0870 873 2800 Contact: Selina Russell
sales@cheekyrascals.co.uk www.cheekyrascals.co.uk
Importers of baby and toddler nursery equipment. In particular, washable nappies and kiddy and buggy boards. Member of the Real Nappy Association. National delivery.

COLLINS, MJ & LK

PARK FARM, HECKFIELD, HOOK RG27 0LD
Tel: 0118 932 6535 Fax: 0870 167 4860 Contact: Martin Collins
martin@parkfarm.fsnet.co.uk
Organic beef, pork and lamb produced with traditional breeds, also fresh
fruit and veg and dairy products. Visitors to the shop are welcome to walk
around the farm—bring your wellies. Open Tuesday, Wednesday a.m.,
Thursday, Friday & Saturday. Shop tel: 0118 932 6650.

FUNDAMENTALLY FUNGUS

MYCOMARKETING LTD, MEON HILL FARM, STOCKBRIDGE SO23 0QD
Tel: 01264 811170 Fax: 01264 811170 Contact: Jane Dick
jdfungus@mycomarketing.fsnet.co.uk www.fundamentallyfungus.co.uk
Soil Association P5809. Speciality mushrooms. Growers and sellers of fresh
speciality mushrooms to catering and restaurant trade. Retail packs of
mixed and single variety speciality mushrooms for shops.

GODSHILL ORGANICS

NEWPORT RD., GODSHILL, ISLE OF WIGHT PO38 3LY
Tel: 01983 840723 Fax: 01983 840723 Contact: R Illman (Partner)
godshill.organics@virgin.net www.godshillorganics.com
Soil Association G1724, P5015. Wide range of fresh produce grown on-site.
Weekly deliveries and seasonal box scheme. On-site shop selling very wide
range of groceries and fresh veg. Local farmers' market each Friday.

HARROWAY ORGANIC GARDENS

KINGSCLERE RD., WHITCHURCH RG28 7QB
Tel: 01256 895346 Fax: 01256 895346 Contact: Steve Forster
hogveg@hotmail.com
Soil Association G971, P971. Organic farm and farm shop, selling organic
vegetables, fruit, eggs and cheese.

LAVERSTOKE PARK PRODUCE

HOME FARM, LAVERSTOKE PARK, WHITCHURCH RG28 7NT
Tel: 01256 890900 Fax: 01256 890900 Contact: Mike Fisher
mike@laverstokepark.co.uk
Soil Association G2740. Box scheme delivering vegetables, fruit and eggs in
Basingstoke and Winchester areas. Wholesale supplies to local independent
retailers.

LYME REGIS FINE FOODS LTD

STATION IND. ESTATE, LIPHOOK GU30 7DR
Tel: 01428 722900 Fax: 01428 727222 Contact: The Manager
info@lymeregisfoods.com www.lymeregisfoods.com
Soil Association P4348. Manufacturers of natural and organic healthy snack
bars, particularly fruit, cereal and marzipan bars. Found in health food
shops and major supermarkets.

MATSOFRESH LTD

FENWICK HARRISON BUILDING, 16–20 CAMP RD.,
FARNBOROUGH GU14 6EW
Tel: 08702 405420 Fax: 01252 669009 Contact: Matt Rogers
sales@matsofresh.co.uk www.matsofresh.co.uk
Soil Association P6392. Growers, importers and distributors to processors,
catering, retail and packers.

MILL FARM ORGANIC SHOP

MILL FARM, ISINGTON, NR. ALTON GU34 4PN
Tel: 01420 22331 Fax: 01420 22331 Contact: James Mayhew
info@millfarmorganic.co.uk www.millfarmorganic.co.uk
Soil Association G6840. Fully organic farm. Status achieved Dec 2002.
Producer of pedigree beef and lamb. Farm Open Days at certain times of
the year. Shop open Thursday, Friday & Saturday 9am to 5pm. Shop stocks
own as well as other organic and local produce. Farm trails open all year
with maps available in the shop.

NATURALLY HEALTH FOODS
5 WATERLOO COURT, SHAWS WALK, ANDOVER SP10 1QJ
Tel: 01264 332375 Contact: Karen Harmer
pookieharmer@btopenworld.com
Independent NAHS registered health store with full range of VMS, herbals, supplements and homoeopathic products. Health notes on-line computer programme. Specialist dietary needs a priority.

NATURALLY ORGANIC
ELM COTTAGE, POND LANE, CLANFIELD PO8 0RG
Tel: 023 9236 0196 Fax: 023 9236 0196 Contact: Alex Handford
Wholesale distribution of certified organic fruit and vegetables. Also organic fruit and vegetable box home delivery service.

PARK FARM ORGANICS
HECKFIELD, HOOK RG27 0LD
Tel: 0118 932 6650 Contact: Roger David & Mandy Tarrant
mandy@parkfarmorganics.co.uk www.parkfarmorganics.co.uk
Organic beef, pork and lamb produced with traditional breeds, also fresh fruit and veg and dairy products. Open Tuesday, Wednesday, Thursday, Friday and Saturday. Local box scheme.

PEMBERTON, DAVID
MOULSHAY FARM BUILDINGS, WILDMOOR, SHERFIELD ON LODDON, HOOK RG27 0HH
Tel: 01256 882171 Fax: 01256 882171 Contact: David Pemberton
david@tukt.co.uk
Organic grazing available for sheep.

PETTY, WOOD & CO

PO BOX 66, LIVINGSTONE RD., ANDOVER SP10 5LA
Tel: 01264 345500 Fax: 01264 332025
info@pettywood.co.uk www.pettywood.co.uk
Petty Wood sells, distributes and markets speciality ambient food products
to the retail and wholesale sectors. Portfolio includes Duchy Originals,
Yarrah Pet Food, Sacla, Baxters and our own 'Epicure Organics'.

POLLEN ORGANICS LIMITED

THREE FIRS HOUSE, BRAMSHOTT CHASE GU26 6DG
Tel: 01428 608870 Fax: 01428 608890 Contact: Richard Pollen
organics@pollenorganics.com www.pollenorganics.com
Soil Association registered. Organic sauces, relishes, dressings, nuts and
nibbles. Pollen Organics has established a strong brand identity in organic
grocery foods such as Soil Association award-winning pesto sauces, mayonnaise and hollandaise sauces, pasta sauce, red onion marmalade and Seville
orange marmalade with exceptional taste, dressings, nuts and nibbles.

THE PUREWINE COMPANY

51 ALCANTARA CRESCENT, OCEAN VILLAGE, SOUTHAMPTON SO14 3HR
Tel: 023 8023 8214 Fax: 023 8023 8186 Contact: Barry Martin
service@purewine.co.uk www.purewine.co.uk
Importers of organic, vegetarian, vegan and biodynamic wines. Wholesale
trade distributors to the on and off licence trade. Also retail through mail
order. Orderline 023 8022 7760 or sales@purewine.co.uk.

RASANCO LTD

THE ESTATE OFFICE, SUTTON SCOTNEY SO21 3JW
Tel: 01962 761935 Fax: 01962 761860 Contact: Russell Smart
ras@rasanco.com www.rasanco.com
Soil Association P2960. Rasanco is a specialist organic ingredients supplier
offering the food and drink manufacturer a one-stop shop for their organic
raw materials. We subscribe to a 'from field to finished foods' ethic.

SCOLTOCKS HEALTH FOODS

1 MARKET PLACE, RINGWOOD BH24 1AN
Tel: 01425 473787 Contact: Yvonne Tilley
Member of National Association of Health Stores, member of Institute of
Health Food Retailing. Jams, pulses etc. Dietary foods, vegetarian specialist.

SUNNYFIELDS ORGANIC

JACOBS GUTTER LANE, TOTTON, SOUTHAMPTON SO40 9FX
Tel: 023 8087 1408 Fax: 023 8087 1146 Contact: Louise
info@sunnyfields.co.uk www.sunnyfields.co.uk
Sunnyfields grows a large range of organic vegetables and sells a full range
of organic products through our shop (open 7 days) and home delivery
service to Hampshire and London.

TIMBER!

5 STAR LANE, RINGWOOD BH24 1AL
Tel: 01425 483505 Contact: Sana Stephens
sanastephens@yahoo.co.uk www.loveorganic.com
Organic clothing from well established organic companies such as People
Tree, Bishopston trading and many more. All the companies we use have
their own certified cotton. We also sell Green Baby clothing and other
organic products such as bedding.

TURF CROFT ORGANIC HERBS

TURF CROFT COTTAGE, BURLEY, RINGWOOD BH24 4DF
Tel: 01425 403502 Fax: 01425 403502 Contact: Simon Weir
Soil Association W165 and BDAA member. Wholesale specialists in fresh
culinary herbs all year round. Extensive range, home-produced in season,
imported out of season. A range of packet sizes and styles available.

UPTON HOUSE FARM

UPTON HOUSE FARM, WONSTON, WINCHESTER SO21 3LR
Tel: 01962 760219 Fax: 01962 761419 Contact: Robin Readhead
Producing British chickens that taste like those that granny produced
before chemicals were intruded. Supplier of organic poultry compost.

WARBORNE ORGANIC FARM

WARBORNE FARM, WARBORNE LANE, BOLDRE, LYMINGTON SO41 5QD
Tel: 01590 688488 Fax: 01590 688096 Contact: George Heathcote
Soil Association G2404. We deliver boxes of organic vegetables, grown on
our farm, to local households. Free range eggs and organic meat also
available. Farm shop. 'Buy local—eat organic'.

WEEK FARM/AVON ORGANICS

WATTONS LANE, MATCHAM, RINGWOOD BH24 2DG
Tel: 01202 484628 Contact: CJ Snow
csnow-weekfarm@btinternet.com
Organic beef/sheep farmer/producer, together with vegetable box scheme,
supplying Bournemouth to Ringwood and surrounding areas.

THE WINCHESTER BAKERY

51 HATHERLEY RD., WINCHESTER SO22 6RR
Tel: 01962 861477 Contact: Alison Reid
Soil Association P5584. Organic home-made bread, available through local
shops and farmers' markets.

ABUNDANCE PRODUCE

GLENTHORPE, LITTLE BIRCH, HEREFORD HR2 8BD
Tel: 01981 540181 Fax: 01981 540181 Contact: Tim Headley
Biodynamic Agricultural Association (Demeter) no. 260. Box scheme and
local delivery in Herefordshire.

ARKSTONE MILL PRODUCE

ARKSTONE MILL, KINGSTONE HR2 9HU
Tel: 01981 251135 Contact: Paul Izod
arkstone@arkstonemill.ndirect.co.uk
Soil Association G7119. Boxes of seasonal vegetables and fruit delivered
weekly, throughout south Herefordshire and Hereford. Every box made up
individually to suit customer's preferences.

BIOSPHERE ORGANICS

2 WYNNS GREEN COTTAGES, BURLEY GATE, HEREFORD HR1 3QT
Tel: 01432 820082 Fax: 01432 820088 Contact: Paul Burgess
biosphere-organics@supanet.com www.biosphere-organics.supanet.com
Growers, importers and wholesalers of fresh fruit, vegetables, herbs and
spices. We can supply frozen products in bulk. Suppliers to packers,
processors, box schemes, restaurants, shops, caterers throughout the UK.

BUTFORD ORGANICS

BUTFORD FARM, BOWLEY LANE, BODENHAM HR1 3LG
Tel: 01586 797195 Fax: 01568 797885 Contact: Janet & Martin Harris
tuolomne@aol.com
We are certified with the Soil Association (no. G5368). We are small scale
producers of award-winning cider and perry, organic pork, geese, eggs,
seasonal vegetables, soft and top fruit.

DUNKERTONS CIDER CO LTD & THE CIDER HOUSE RESTAURANT

LUNTLEY, PEMBRIDGE, NR. LEOMINSTER HR6 9ED
Tel: 01544 388653 Fax: 01544 388654 Contact: Ivor Dunkerton
dunkertons@pembridge.kc3.co.uk www.dunkertons.co.uk
Ciders and perry, still and sparkling. Draught and bottled. Traditional local varieties of cider apples pressed, fermented and bottled at the mill. The Cider House Restaurant, using organic produce as available, Tel 01544 388161, contact Susie Dunkerton.

FIELD FAYRE

18–19 BROAD ST., ROSS-ON-WYE HR9 7EA
Tel: 01989 566683 Fax: 01989 566924 Contact: Denise Hunt
denise@field-fayre.co.uk www.field-fayre.co.uk
Friendly shop in town centre. Specialising in organic produce including local fruit and vegetables, bread, dairy products, meat and fish, chocolate, wine, beer and local cider.

FODDER THE HEALTH STORE

26–27 CHURCH ST., HEREFORD HR1 2LR
Tel: 01432 358171 Fax: 01432 277861 Contact: Sue Jordan
The largest range of organic wholefood, veg, bread, yoghurts, wines, cider in the area, plus herbal and homoeopathic remedies. Also Ecover products, essential oils.

GEORGE'S DELICATESSEN

25 HIGH ST., KINGTON HR5 3AX
Tel: 01544 231400 Contact: Clive & Kathryn Genders
A wide selection of cheeses, local and organic goods, wines, beers, ciders, loose herbs, tea and coffee.

GREEN ACRES ORGANIC GROWERS

GREEN ACRES FARM SHOP, DINMORE, HEREFORD HR4 8ED
Tel: 01568 797045 Contact: S Jenkins
Soil Association J14M. Organic produce including meat, vegetables, fruit, ice cream, cider, wine, preserves etc. Open Tuesday–Saturday 9am–5.30pm. Sunday and Monday by arrangement. Local delivery service.

GREEN CUISINE LTD

PENRHOS COURT, KINGTON HR5 3LH
Tel: 01544 230720 Fax: 01544 230754 Contact: Daphne Lambert
daphne@greencuisine.org www.greencuisine.org
Soil Association E2051. Green Cuisine runs courses on food and health and offers consultations and natural therapies. The company also produces books and educational material. See also Penrhos Ltd and The Penrhos Trust.

HANDLEY ORGANICS

HARDWICKE ORGANICS FARM, UPPER HARDWICKE LANE, WINSLOW, BROMYARD HR7 4SX
Tel: 01885 483364 Contact: Horace Handley
Soil Association G2141. Organic growers for wholesalers.

HAY WHOLEFOODS AND DELICATESSEN

41 LION ST., HAY-ON-WYE HR3 5AA
Tel: 01497 820708 Contact: Mandy
Large and comprehensive wholefood shop with wide range of organic goods including wine, cheese, vegetables and groceries. Good delicatessen with organic choice where possible.

HAYGROVE FRUIT

REDBANK, LEDBURY HR8 2JL
Tel: 01531 631797 Fax: 01531 634069 Contact: Alan Hale
packhouse@haygrove.co.uk www.haygrove.co.uk
Soil Association Grower code G6412, Producers code P5435. Fresh fruit and frozen bulk juice sales from organic fruits. Haygrove Organic production in UK, South Africa and Hungary.

HELME, EBM AND SONS

POOL HULLOCK, LLANDINABO HR
Tel: 01989 730632 Fax: 01989 730632 Contact: Jeremy Helme
Soil Association G613. General veg and Pool Hullock extra delicious organic chickens.

HENCLOSE ORGANIC FARM PRODUCE

LITTLE DEWCHURCH, HEREFORD HR2 6PP
Tel: 01432 840826 Contact: Karen Tibbetts
Demeter organic certification no. 394. Home-produced lamb, pork, kid, bacon, sausages and goat's milk from old and semi-rare breeds. 22 years organic status. Phone for availability and collection. Self-catering converted barn for holidays or long lets.

HOPES OF LONGTOWN

THE FARMERS BARN, LONGTOWN HR2 0LT
Tel: 01873 860444 Contact: Christine Hope
info@hopesoflongtown.co.uk www.hopesoflongtown.co.uk
An independent village shop and post office retailing local products, fair trade teas and coffees, organic and vegan supplies, fresh fruit and veg and home-made cakes.

LEDBURY WHOLEFOODS

82 THE HOMEND, LEDBURY HR8 1BX
Tel: 01531 632889 Contact: Nelson & Alice Shield
ledbury.wholefoods@virgin.net
Natural food and medicine store. Speciality and diet foods, gluten-free, organic and fair trade products. Vitamins and remedies, therapists, allergy testing, homoeopathy, therapy rooms.

THE MEADOW CHEESE CO LTD

HAZEL PARK, DYMOCK RD., LEDBURY HR8 2JQ
Tel: 01531 631300 Fax: 01531 631170 Contact: C Bennett
clive@meadowcheese.co.uk www.meadowcheese.co.uk
Soil Association P4698. Grated and dried, chilled and frozen cheese ingredients for food manufacturers, including formulated cheese products.

MEE, J R

SPRINGFIELD FARM, STEENSBRIDGE, LEOMINSTER HR6 0LU
Tel: 01568 760270 Fax: 01568 760418 Contact: R. Mee
Farmers and packers of high grade table birds (chickens and turkeys) for
sale to wholesalers and retailers—also at our farm gate.

NATURE'S CHOICE RESTAURANT & GUESTHOUSE

RAGLAN HOUSE, 17 BROAD ST., ROSS-ON-WYE HR9 7EA
Tel: 01989 763454 Fax: 01989 763064 Contact: Kathryn Roberts
nature@roberts9535.freeserve.co.uk
Delicious organic food with an American influence. Smoke-free,
eco-friendly environment. Monday to Saturday 10am to 5pm, Thursday
to Saturday evenings 6pm to 9pm. Vegan, vegetarian, children's menus.
B&B downtown Ross-on-Wye.

NITTY GRITTY WHOLEFOODS

24 WEST ST., LEOMINSTER HR6 8ES
Tel: 01568 611600 Contact: Pamela Horsley
Traditional wholefood shop. Free range eggs and dairy produce, trees and
herbaceous.

ORGANIC OPTIONS

15A BROAD ST., LEOMINSTER HR6 8BT
Tel: 01568 612154 Fax: 01568 617510 Contact: Richard Sharpham
Specialist organic shop. Everything you need: meat and fish, dairy, bakery,
fruit & vegetables, frozen meals, dairy and dairy-free ices, wine and beer.
Living Nature and Green People bodycare range. Ecover with refills, organic
clothing. Fresh juice bar using organic produce.

PAUL RICHARDS HERBAL SUPPLIES

THE FIELD, EARDISLEY HR3 6NB
Tel: 01544 327360 Fax: 01544 327360 Contact: Paul Richards
paul.herbs@ntlworld.com
Soil Association PR10M. Fresh herbal tinctures (echinacea and many others), herbal oils and ointments (comfrey, calendula/hypericum, chickweed, horse chestnut). Wholesale, retail, mail order, own label. Contract herb grower and herbal product supplier.

PENRHOS

PENRHOS COURT, KINGTON HR5 3LH
Tel: 01544 230720 Fax: 01544 230754 Contact: Martin Griffiths
info@penrhos.co.uk www.penrhos.co.uk
700-year-old farmstead—now the most delightful hotel anywhere. Millennium Marque award for environmental excellence. Voted Best Organic Restaurant of the Year 2002. See also Green Cuisine Ltd and The Penrhos Trust.

POSTLETHWAITE'S HERBAL PRODUCTS

THE FIELD, EARDISLEY HR3 6NB
Tel: 0870 240 3379 Fax: 0870 240 3379 Contact: Paul Richards
paul.herbs@ntlworld.com
Soil Association PR10M. We supply a wide range of tinctures and other herbal products in retail sizes with the familiar gold label. Most are fresh tinctures made using home-grown herbs and we offer an own label service for large and small runs. Mail order also available.

THE RICE CAKE

THE HOMEND MEWS, THE HOMEND, LEDBURY HR8 1BN
Tel: 01531 635860 Fax: 01531 631892 Contact: Clio Lever
help@thericecake.co.uk www.thericecake.co.uk
Top-quality organic and wholefood groceries, natural products and homoeopathic remedies at discount prices. Resource website. Helping you in some way.

THE SEPTEMBER ORGANIC DAIRY

WHITEHILL PARK, WEOBLEY HR4 8QE
Tel: 01544 312910 Fax: 01544 312911 Contact: Adam Glyn-Jones
sales@september-organic.co.uk www.september-organic.co.uk
Soil Association P4691. Producers of 100% organic dairy ice cream.
Delicious range of original flavours using fairly traded ingredients.
Wholesale and retail suppliers.

SNELL, AJ & CI

PENCOYD COURT FARM, ST. OWENS CROSS, HEREFORD HR2 8JY
Tel: 01989 730229 Fax: 01989 730603 Contact: A Snell
a.snell@pcf.u-net.com
Soft fruit farm producing amongst other crops, organic blackcurrants.
Available fresh, frozen or processed.

STEPHENS, TP

NEWTON COURT, NEWTON, LEOMINSTER HR6 0PF
Tel: 01568 611721 Contact: T Stephens
tps1@dialstart.net
Soil Association G7479. Organic cider makers.

STEVENSON, PEGGY ANNE

WINDLE PARK, CLIFFORD, HAY-ON-WYE HR3 5HA
Tel: 01497 831666 Contact: P Stevenson
Soil Association G5055. Small organic holding producing Hereford beef,
Portland lamb and Tamworth pork, all reared outside. Accommodation for
riders and their horses, caravan site.

SUNNYBANK VINE NURSERY

JOURNEY'S END, KING STREET, EWYAS HAROLD, HEREFORD HR2 0EE
Tel: 01981 240256 Contact: BR Edwards
vinenursery@hotmail.com www.vinenursery.netfirms.com
Specialist producer of vines for both eating and wine. Plants grown without
sprays or artificial fertilisers. Growing collection of seedless and
disease-resistant varieties.

SURVIVAL WHOLEFOODS

UNIT 1, PRINCE OF WALES BUSINESS PARK, BRIDGE ST., LEOMINSTER HR6 8EA
Tel: 01568 614147 Fax: 01568 612678 Contact: Mark & Mary Hatt
'A unique wholefoods experience'. Shop with delivery service to the
Midlands, Wales, Herefordshire, Shropshire, Worcestershire, Gloucestershire.
Survival Wholefoods is run by Mark and Mary Hatt. We are dedicated to
the organic ethos.

WELSH FRUIT STOCKS

LLANERCHIR, BRYNGWYN, VIA KINGTON HR5 3QZ
Tel: 01497 851209 Contact: Sian Fromant
sian@welshfruitstocks.co.uk www.welshfruitstocks.co.uk
Propagators of top quality soft fruit plants, including organic strawberry
plants, raspberry canes, black/red/white currant bushes, gooseberry bushes,
jostaberry bushes. Mail order gardeners list and growers list available.

WESTON'S CIDER

THE BOUNDS, MUCH MARCLE, LEDBURY HR8 2NQ
Tel: 01531 660233 Fax: 01531 660619 Contact: Jules Schad
marketing@westons-cider.co.uk www.westons-cider.co.uk
Soil Association P1776. Westons have been producing cider since 1880.
The organic cider was winner at the Organic Food Awards in 1998 and
2003. Producers of Organic Vintage Cider and Organize, the non-alcoholic
nutrient drink. See display ad.

WIGGLY WIGGLERS

LOWER BLAKEMERE FARM, BLAKEMERE HR2 9PX
Tel: 01981 500391 Fax: 01981 500108 Contact: David Pitman
david@wigglywigglers.co.uk www.wigglywigglers.co.uk
Wiggly Wigglers supply natural gardening products including worm and
conventional composters, garden bird food and feeders including live feed,
insect and mammal habitats and wild flowers.

WILLEY WINKLE PURE WOOL BEDDING MANUFACTURERS
OFFA HOUSE, OFFA ST., HEREFORD HR1 2LH
Tel: 01432 268018 Fax: 01432 268018 Contact: Jeff Wilkes
www.willeywinkle.co.uk
Traditional mattress makers using organic wool filling and organic outer cover ticking. Also suppliers of organic bedding sheets, duvets, pillows, towelling etc.

WYEDEAN WHOLEFOODS
4 GLOUCESTER ROAD, ROSS-ON-WYE HR9 5BU
Tel: 01989 562340 Contact: Barry Crocker
Hundreds of organic lines. Wholefoods, gluten- and dairy-free, cruelty-free cosmetics; SLS-free toiletries. Excellent range of vitamins, minerals and herbals. Wide range of chilled and frozen products.

Herefordshire

It was a time for fast learning. I did not know anything about growing corn or sugar beet. The world of pedigree Hereford cattle was a mystery. The countryside all around me seemed to burst with an almost tropical growth. Each field seemed to have a different crop, and they all had to be managed to keep on top of them. The work was very varied, and was done without tractors or pick-up trucks, just horses and manpower. It was also good fun, with time to go to the village hop and also the Three Counties Agricultural Show and the local plough-ing match. And I must have been growing up, because I went out with a girl for the first time—at the age of eighteen!

My settling in period was smooth, but I was very homesick for my dogs and the high moor, and I had some difficulty with the different dialect. The very first morning I was asked to clean out the pigs, and being unable to find a wheelbarrow I asked Tom, "Where's wheel bara?" Tom asked me three times what I wanted. He finally went off and came back ten min-utes later with the required wheelbarrow. Two months later Tom told me that he could not understand a word I had said, so he had gone to ask Mr Downing what I was supposed to be doing, they had worked out that I must need a wheelbarrow. I for my part had difficulty in understanding their sing-song accent. The words 'thee', 'thou' and 'yonder' were not used at all, and they did not understand my morning greeting of "Now then". It is a shortened version of "Now then, how are you today?" Sometimes I used to go as far as "Now then, how is ta", but it still brought blank looks.

From *Working with the Curlew: A Farmhand's Life* by Trevor Robinson, Green Books, £7.95

HERTFORDSHIRE

ALCOHOLS LTD

CHARRINGTONS HOUSE, THE CAUSEWAY, BISHOP'S STORTFORD CM23 2EW
Tel: 01279 658464 Fax: 01279 757613 Contact: Peter McKay
peter.mckay@alcohols.co.uk www.alcohols.co.uk
Alcohols Ltd. produce organic gin and vodka and market organic alcohol,
supplying in bulk and packed.

BROUGHTON PASTURES ORGANIC FRUIT WINE CO

THE SILK MILL, BROOK STREET., TRING HP23 5EF
Tel: 01442 823993 Fax: 01442 823993 Contact: Brian Reid
organicfruitwine@aol.com www.BroughtonPastures.Co.uk
The UK's foremost producer of organic fruit wines. Available in several
delicious flavours including mead, ginger wine and a sparkling elderflower
wine made in the traditional 'Methode Champenoise'. Look out for our
new range of Fairtrade Organic Wines in 2004. Soil Association no. P1652.
See display ad.

CEREAL PARTNERS

2 ALBANY PLACE, 28 BRIDGE ROAD EAST, WELWYN GARDEN CITY AL7 1RR
Tel: 01707 824400 Fax: 01707 824569 Contact: Aline Spittal
aline.spittal@uk.nestle.com www.cerealpartners.co.uk
Cereal Partners UK manufacture a wide range of ready-to-eat breakfast
cereals and include organic within the portfolio.

CLARE JAMES HEALTH FOODS

13A HEMPSTEAD RD., KINGS LANGLEY WD4 8BJ
Tel: 01923 263195 Contact: Bridget Johnstone
A high street shop selling organic dairy produce, bread, grains, flour, nuts,
dried fruit, sugar, honey, jams, cereals, juices, tea, toiletries and much more
besides.

COOKS DELIGHT

360–364 HIGH STREET, BERKHAMSTED HP4 1HU
Tel: 01442 863584 Fax: 01442 863702 Contact: Rex Tyler
rex@cooksdelight.co.uk www.organiccooksdelight.co.uk
Queens Award 2001/Business in the Community. National Training Award
Champion. Certified organic and biodynamic shop buying ethically from
UK where available, otherwise trading in an environmentally and socially
responsible way, and recycling. Fresh fruit and vegetables, grains, flours,
4,500 organic foods.

EASTWOODS OF BERKHAMSTED

15 GRAVEL PATH, BERKHAMSTED HP4 2EF
Tel: 01442 865012 Fax: 01442 877212 Contact: Joe Collier
joe.collier@btinternet.com www.eastwoodsofberkhamsted.co.uk
Organic meat specialist, national winners of 8 Soil Association Awards.
Order on-line, mail order, fax, phone. 'Highgrove' meats, many products.

EQ WASTE MANAGEMENT

APPSPOND LANE, POTTERS CROUCH, ST. ALBANS AL2 3NL
Tel: 0870 560 2060 Fax: 01727 867866 Contact: Jo Fitzpatrick
jo.fitzpatrick@eqwaste.com www.organeq.co.uk
OrganEQ's peat-free range of composts and soil blends are produced from
a sustainable botanical source providing a high quality supplement for the
horticultural and agricultural markets. Delivery available nationwide.

EVERYBODY ORGANIC LTD

6 HILL RISE, POTTERS BAR EN6 2RR
Tel: 01707 651243 Fax: 01707 652235 Contact: George Harvey
enquiries@everybodyorganic.com www.everybodyorganic.com
Soil Association P7703. Delivering fresh organic fruit and vegetables direct
to your door every week. We also offer an excellent range of organic
groceries, champagne, wine & beer. Gift hampers available. Delivering all
over the UK with boxes from £9.

FAIRHAVEN WHOLEFOODS

27 JUBILEE TRADE CENTRE, OFF JUBILEE ROAD, OFF BALDOCK ROAD,
LETCHWORTH SG6 1SP
Tel: 01462 675300 Fax: 01462 483008 Contact: Robin Sternberg
sales@fairhaven.co.uk www.fairhaven.co.uk
Large store, easy parking, personal service. Ring for directions. Deliveries
throughout N.Herts/S.Beds. Huge range of organics, diet foods,
supplements, bodycare and more.

FARM2DOOR.ORG

PO BOX 2067, WATFORD WD17 4ZH
Tel: 01923 490526 Fax: 01923 490659 Contact: Barry Couldridge
www.farm2door.org
Check the website or ring for details—delivery to local collection points
(approximately 30 miles radius of Watford). Fruit and vegetables: seasonal.
Delivery areas covered: AL1–10, HA2–8, HP1–27, SG1–18 and WD1–7. All
produce sourced from Soil Association suppliers.

HARMONY

53 HIGH STREET, TRING HP23 5AG
Tel: 01442 822 311 Contact: Susan Gould
Dried goods, tinned goods and other foodstuffs. No fresh vegetables or
meat produce. Household cleaners, beauty products etc.

ORGANIC KOSHER FOODS LTD

PO BOX 3079, HIGH BARNET EN5 4ZD
Tel: 0709 280 7344 Fax: 0709 280 7343 Contact: Leon Pein
info@organickosher.co.uk www.organickosher.co.uk
Organically-reared Kosher (suitable for halal consumers) meat, poultry and
fish (plus other products in due course). Every animal is sourced from
organic farms. See www.organickosher.co.uk, or call 0800 458 K-O-S-H-E-R
(0800 458 5-6-7-4-3-7) for a list of stockists.

PLANT HEALTH CARE
121 HIGH ST., BERKHAMSTED HP4 2DJ
Tel: 01442 864431 Fax: 01442 870148 Contact: Jason Holohan
info@planthealthcare.co.uk www.planthealthcare.co.uk
Manufacturers and suppliers of Soil Association approved liquid organic fertilizers, based on all plant extracts. We supply 5 different analyses; 9:2:2, 9:2:7, 8:3:3, 6:5:6 and 4:2:8. We also supply bacterial and fungal products.

REDBOURNBURY WATERMILL
REDBOURN RD., ST. ALBANS AL3 6RS
Tel: 01582 792874 Fax: 01582 792874 Contact: Mandy James
redbrymill@aol.com www.redbournmill.co.uk
Soil Association P4343. Working 18th century watermill museum producing organic wholemeal, white, brown, semolina & rye flour. Open to public, Sunday 2.00–5.30pm, Easter–October. Group visits, schools, etc.

WELWYN HATFIELD MUSEUM SERVICE
MILL GREEN MUSEUM & MILL, MILL GREEN, HATFIELD AL9 5PD
Tel: 01707 271362 Fax: 01707 272511 Contact: Carol Rigby
museum@welhat.gov.uk
Soil Association P1470. Working water mill producing organic stoneground wholemeal flour.

Scientific Objectivity

Research in the Journal of the American Medical Association revealed that studies of cancer drugs funded by non-profit groups were eight times more likely to reach unfavourable conclusions as the studies funded by the pharmaceutical companies. Or consider the case of the genetically modified artificial sweetener aspartame: About 165 peer-reviewed studies were conducted on it by 1995. They were divided almost evenly between those that found no problem and those that raised questions about the sweetener's safety. Of those studies that found no problem, 100 percent were paid for by the manufacturer of the sweetener. All of the studies paid for by non-industry and non-government sources raised questions.

From *Seeds of Deception: Exposing Corporate and Government Lies about the Safety of Genetically Engineered Food* **by Jeffrey M. Smith, Green Books, £9.95**

ALMANZORA LTD
NORTH WING, NETTLESTEAD OAST, MAIDSTONE RD., PADDOCK WOOD
Tel: 01892 836992 Fax: 01892 836933 Contact: Simon Bilecki
simon.bilecki@almanzorauk.co.uk www.almanzorauk.co.uk
Suppliers of high quality organic olive oil and fresh, frozen and prepared
produce to packers, processors and wholesalers.

ASSOCIATION KOKOPELLI (TERRE DE SEMENCES)
RIPPLE FARM, CRUNDALE, NR. CANTERBURY CT4 7EB
Fax: 01227 730790 Contact: Chris Baur
comments@organicseedsonline.com www.organicseedsonline.com
Organic vegetable and flower seed suppliers. Over 1,000 varieties available.

BARKER LTD, JJ
HOOK PLACE FARM, SOUTHFLEET, GRAVESEND DA13 9NH
Tel: 01474 833555 Fax: 01474 834364 Contact: Lawrence Frohn
sales@jjbarker.co.uk
UK-based grower and importer, packer and distributor of organic pro-
duce—mainly salads and legumes primarily for the UK multiples. Soil
Association no. P2380.

BROCKMAN, AG & CO
PERRY COURT FARM, GARLINGE GREEN, CANTERBURY CT4 5RU
Tel: 01227 732001 Fax: 01227 732001 Contact: Patrick Brockman
agbrockmanco@farmersweekly.net
Producers of Demeter certified organic foods since 1953. Beef, milling
wheat, oats, wheat flour, vegetables, salads and herbs. Sales through farm
shop, box scheme, farmers' markets, local shops and wholesalers.

BURSCOMBE CLIFF FARM
EGERTON, ASHFORD TN77 5RB
Tel: 01233 756468 Fax: 01233 756468 Contact: Ben Garratt & Hilary Jones
Soil Association symbol no. G683. Organic livestock farm offering beef, lamb, pork, bacon, sausages. Occasionally fleece, top fruit, eggs. WWOOF host open farm. Telephone us.

CANON GARTH LTD
ALEXANDER HOUSE, 31–39 LONDON RD., SEVENOAKS TN13 1AR
Tel: 01732 743434 Fax: 01732 743444 Contact: The Manager
Peanuts and treenuts.

CANTERBURY WHOLEFOODS
1 & 2 JEWRY LANE, CANTERBURY CT1 2RP
Tel: 01227 464623 Fax: 01227 764838 Contact: Jason Robbins
info@canterbury-wholefoods.co.uk www.
Soil Association R1676. We are a large, traditional wholefood store specialising in organics, fresh fruit and vegetables, bulk sales and discounts, county-wide delivery service.

CHURCH VIEW FARM
SEVENOAKS RD., IGHTHAM TN15 9AZ
Tel: 01732 886680 Contact: The Manager
Soil Association G6051. Organic box delivery scheme including vegetables, fruit, eggs and juice. Some farm gate sales.

Wisdom of the Rats

The Washington Post reported that rodents, usually happy to munch on tomatoes, turned their noses up at the genetically modified FlavrSavr tomato that scientists were so anxious to test on them. Calgene CEO Roger Salquist said of his tomato, "I gotta tell you, you can be Chef Boyardee and . . . [they] are still not going to like them." Rats were eventually force fed the tomato through gastric tubes and stomach washes. Several developed stomach lesions; seven of forty died within two weeks. The tomato was approved.

From *Seeds of Deception: Exposing Corporate and Government Lies about the Safety of Genetically Engineered Food* by Jeffrey M. Smith, Green Books, £9.95

COMMONWORK
BORE PLACE, CHIDDINGSTONE TN8 7AR
Tel: 01732 463255 x229 Fax: 01732 740264 Contact: Lyn Kelly
info@commonwork.org www.commonwork.org
Conference and study centre with organic, wildlife and permaculture gardens on commercial organic farm. Residential accommodation for groups undertaking their own training and development work. Environmental education programme and organic farm/food study days offered by Commonwork. Focus in 2004-05 on hands-on vocational training in organic farming for people of all abilities. New focus on food and health (growing, cooking and eating) from 2004 as part of 'The Big Stir' campaign. Seasonal open days for the public. Development education centre (global education) in Maidstone.

COMMONWORK ORGANIC FARMS LTD
BORE PLACE, CHIDDINGSTONE, EDENBRIDGE TN8 7AR
Tel: 01732 463255 Fax: 01732 740264 Contact: Michael Cottrell
www.commonwork.org
Approved milk producer selling to OMSCo.

COUCHMAN, RF
CHUN FARM, CHURN LANE, HORSMONDEN, TONBRIDGE TN12 8HL
Tel: 01892 722547 Contact: Roger Couchman
Soil Association G4567. Organic vegetables and salads including tomatoes, cucumbers, peppers, lettuce, aubergines, carrots, beetroot, spinach, calabrese, pak-choi, melons, cobnuts, French and runner beans, kale, courgettes, kohl-rabi, strawberries.

DABBS PLACE ORGANIC FARM
COBHAM, GRAVESEND DA13 9BL
Tel: 07712 439304 Contact: J Fermor
mail@organicveg.net www.organicveg.net
Soil Association F165. Local box scheme, vegetables, arable farm.

DAVIES & DAVIES, JEFFREY LTD

ARCTIC HOUSE, RYE LANE, DUNTON GREEN, SEVENOAKS TN24 5HL
Tel: 01732 450948 Fax: 01732 452012 Contact: Dominic Wright
info@ www.davies-davies.co.uk
Jeffrey Davies & Davies Ltd are a pork processing and export company.
Trading in a wide variety of meats, throughout Great Britain, Europe and
the Far East.

DEFENDERS LTD

OCCUPATION RD., WYE, ASHFORD TN25 5EN
Tel: 01233 813121 Fax: 01233 813633 Contact: The Manager
help@defenders.co.uk www.defenders.co.uk
Defenders supplies a comprehensive range of biological controls and
integrated control products to gardeners by mail order.

EAST MALLING RESEARCH

NEW RD, EAST, MALLING ME19 6BJ
Tel: 01732 843833 Fax: 01732 849067 Contact: Jean Fitzgerald
jean.fitzgerald@emr.ac.uk www.eastmallingresearch.com
We carry out research projects on organic apples and strawberries and plan
to include more top and soft fruits in our organic demonstration area.

ESPECIALLY HEALTH

119 HIGH STREET, SEVENOAKS TN13 1UP
Tel: 01732 741181 Fax: 01732 740719 Contact: Wendy Kent
wendy.kent@totalise.co.uk www.especiallyhealth.co.uk
Wholefoods and healthfoods including sprouted wheat (essene), spelt and
other non-wheat breads. Dietary consultations, blood group advice, allergy
testing, vitamin and mineral testing, massage, flower therapy and medical
herbalism.

FOOD FOR LIVING
1 BANKS PLACE, MARKET PLACE, DARTFORD DA1 1EX
Tel: 01322 278790 Fax: 01322 278790 Contact: John Frisby
info@foodforliving.co.uk www.foodforliving.co.uk
Health food shop with a wide range of organic foods.

GALA COFFEE & TEA LIMITED
MILL HOUSE, RIVERSIDE WAY, DARTFORD DA1 5BS
Tel: 01322 272411 Fax: 01322 278600 Contact: Louise Lloyd-Rossi
gala@gala-coffee-tea.co.uk www.gala-coffee-tea.co.uk
Gala is a unique company focused on the special requirements of both
retailers and food service companies producing coffee and tea under
private label.

GOOD FOOD WINES LTD
NO. 3 WAREHOUSE, WHITEWALL RD., STROOD ME2 4EW
Tel: 01634 290592 Fax: 01634 716617 Contact: Heather Bennett
info@goodfoodwines.com www.goodfoodwines.com
Suppliers of ingredients to the food industry for wines, beers, spirits and
vinegars: organic and non-organic.

GRANARY HERBS
THE GRANARY, MILGATE PARK, ASHFORD ROAD, BEARSTED ME14 4NN
Tel: 01622 737314 Fax: 01622 739781 Contact: Christine Brown
Mail order only (no callers). Tinctures, fluid extracts and creams made from
fresh organic home grown herbs. Swedish bitters.

GREENCELL LTD
ST. JOHNS HOUSE, 37–41 SPITAL ST., DARTFORD DA1 2DR
Tel: 01322 425555 Fax: 01322 425500 Contact: Jeff Geary
info@greencell.com www.greencell.com
Fresh imported organic fruit sourced to give 12 month continuity. We
store, condition, pack and distribute to retailers, wholesalers, food service
providers and processors through the UK.

HDRA, HENRY DOUBLEDAY RESEARCH ASSOCIATION, YALDING ORGANIC GARDENS

BENOVER RD., YALDING, NR. MAIDSTONE ME18 6EX
Tel: 01622 814650 Fax: 01622 814650 Contact: Susan Kay-Williams
chiefexecutive@hdra.org.uk www.hdra.org.uk
Yalding Organic Gardens trace the course of garden history through 16 landscaped displays, illustrating the organic techniques used to maintain them. Shop for browsing and organic café for refreshments.

HEALTH MATTERS

28 ROYAL STAR ARCADE, MAIDSTONE ME14 1SL
Tel: 01622 691179 Fax: 01622 691179 Contact: Marion Allen
www.maidstonehealthfoods.co.uk
We offer a wide range of organic wholefoods and also offer food intolerance testing.

HERBAL HEALTH LTD

PO BOX 114, SISSINGHURST, CRANBROOK TN17 2XQ
Tel: 01580 713613 Fax: 01580 712714 Contact: Jo d'Armenia
joe.d@qi-teas.com www.qi-teas.com
Supplier of top quality organic China tea under the Qi (chee) label, including traditional loose leaf teas and green tea blends with abundant organic fruit and herbs.

HERBS, GARDENS & HEALTH

27 NORTHDOWN RD., ST. PETER'S, BROADSTAIRS CT10 2UW
Tel: 01843 600201 Fax: 01843 863134 Contact: Juliet Seeley
juliet@herbsgardenshealth.com www.herbsgardenshealth.com
Mostly organic health foods, special diet foods, natural and organic toiletries, Ecover, herbal remedies, vitamins, minerals and supplements, organic veg-in-a-box from Wingham, etc.

HIGHFIELD FARM
BETSHAM RD., SOUTHFLEET DA13 9PD
Tel: 01474 832850 Fax: 01474 832850 Contact: The Manager
Beef and hay producer.

HORTON PARK FARM
THE PENT, POSTLING, HYTHE CT21 4EY
Tel: 01303 862436 Fax: 01303 863723 Contact: Chris Reynolds
cr.reynolds@farmline.com
Soil Association G4082. 900 acre mixed farm, 100 sucklers, 160+ ewes.
Angus x South Devon beef freezer packs available by prior booking, also
whole or half lambs during the summer months. Arable crops grown for
seed.

INTERNATIONAL PRODUCE LTD
SHEERNESS PRODUCE TERMINAL, SPADE LANE, SITTINGBOURNE ME9 7TT
Tel: 01634 269200 Fax: 01634 269269 Contact: Bruce Bell
info@internationalproduce.com www.internationalproduce.com
International importers of organic and non-organic produce.

IVY HOUSE FARM
IVY HOUSE, SANDHILLS, ASH, NR. CANTERBURY CT3 2NG
Tel: 01304 812437 Fax: 01304 812437 Contact: Andrew Ward
Our farm, registered with the Soil Association, produces a range of organi-
cally grown vegetables for wholesale and retail. Our farm shop also sells
organically grown produce from other certified producers.

JUBILEE FARM
RHODES MINNIS, NR. CANTERBURY CT4 6YA
Tel: 01303 862317 Fax: 01303 864257 Contact: Wilf Missing
jubilee@farmline.com
Soil Association G7668. Mixed farm, livestock including Aberdeen Angus
herd, sheep, poultry, free range eggs, vegetables, cereals, top fruit and soft
fruit.

LUDDESDOWN ORGANIC FARMS LTD

COURT LODGE, LUDDESDOWN, NR. COBHAM DA13 0XE
Tel: 01474 813376 Fax: 01474 815044 Contact: Gerry Minister
organic@luddesdown.u-net.com www.luddesdownorganicfarms.co.uk
Soil Association S38S. 950 acres producing cereals, beans, red clover for
seed, forage, beef and vegetables. All grown to Soil Association standards.
Wholesaler and retailer—including vegetable box scheme delivery scheme
and home-produced beef.

MACK MULTIPLES DIVISION

TRANSEESA ROAD, PADDOCK WOOD TN12 6UT
Tel: 01892 835577 Fax: 01892 836401 Contact: Elliot Mantle
elliot.mantle@mackmultiplesco
Importers and ripeners of organic bananas and organic coconuts. Minimum
order 25 cartons. Distribution England and Wales.

MICHAELS WHOLEFOODS

UNITS 1, 5 & 7, NORTHDOWN IND. PARK, ST. PETERS, BROADSTAIRS
CT10 3JP
Tel: 08451 306307 Fax: 01843 604603 Contact: Michael Pile
enquiries@michael-wholefoods.co.uk
Dried foods hand packed to order. Own label available.

NASH NURSERY LTD

NASH, NR. ASH, CANTERBURY CT3 2JU
Tel: 01304 812250 Contact: Paul Dovey
paul@nashnursery.co.uk www.nashnursery.co.uk
Soil Association G2528. Organic farm producing chicken, turkey, ducks and
geese, fruit and vegetables. Abattoir and processing room on-site.

NEAL'S YARD REMEDIES
8 EAST ST., BROMLEY BR1 1QX
Tel: 020 8313 9898 Fax: 020 8313 9898 Contact: Anja Lange
mail@nealsyardremedies.com www.nealsyardremedies.com
Retail store specialising in natural remedies and cosmetics including herbs,
homoeopathy, aromatherapy, nutrition and flower remedies.

PIZZA ORGANIC LTD
3C DORSET ST., SEVENOAKS TN13 1LL
Tel: 01732 454664 Contact: Mike Traszko
info@pizzapiazza.co.uk www.pizzapiazza.co.uk
Expanding range of Soil Association accredited restaurants featuring a
menu packed full of organic stonebaked pizza, sautéed pasta, gourmet
burgers, grilled fish and fabulous desserts to die for.

PIZZA ORGANIC LTD
76 MOUNT PLEASANT RD., TUNBRIDGE WELLS TN1 1RJ
Tel: 01892 547124 Contact: Mike Traszko
info@pizzapiazza.co.uk www.pizzapiazza.co.uk
Expanding range of Soil Association accredited restaurants featuring a
menu packed full of organic stonebaked pizza, sautéed pasta, gourmet
burgers, grilled fish and fabulous desserts to die for.

THE REAL ICE COMPANY
LODGE RD., STAPLEHURST, KENT, TN12 0QY
Tel: 01580 892200 Fax: 01580 893414 Contact: Carl Whitewood
carl@realiceco.co.uk
Manufacturer of private label organic ice cream for major retailers and food
service.

REGENT HEALTH

12 ALBERT ROAD, BELVEDERE DA17 5LJ
Tel: 01322 446244 Contact: Derek Rogers (Owner)
Large range organic gluten-free, dairy-free, diabetic, chilled and frozen foods available. Local deliveries (minimum order). Friendly advice, mail service. If we haven't got it, we will get it!

RIPPLE FARM ORGANICS

CRUNDALE, CANTERBURY CT4 7EB
Tel: 01227 730898 Contact: Martin Mackey
main@iplefarmorganics.co.uk www.ripplefarmorganics.co.uk
Soil Association G737. Growers of organic vegetables, salad and soft fruit to supply own local, year-round, box scheme, farmers' markets and London organic shops.

ROWCLIFFE, ANTHONY & SON LTD

UNIT B, PADDOCK WOOD DISTRIBUTION CENTRE, PADDOCK WOOD TN12 6UU
Tel: 01892 838999 Fax: 01892 836585 Contact: Steve Smith
arowcliffeinfo@aol.com www.rowcliffe.com
Nationwide distributors of dairy products.

SIMPLY WILD FOOD COMPANY

84–86 GROSVENOR RD., TUNBRIDGE WELLS TN1 2AS
Tel: 08456 586140 Fax: 08456 586148 Contact: Ian Nuttall
enquiries@simplywildorganics.co.uk www.simplywild.biz
Simply Wild is a retail outlet for organic fruit, vegetables, eggs, home-produced meat and freshly baked bread. A large selection of other organic products are also available, and a café.

SIMPLY WILD FOOD COMPANY

BOURNES STORES, HIGH ST., BRENCHLEY TN12 7NQ
Tel: 01892 722066 Contact: Ian Nuttall
enquiries@simplywildorganics.co.uk www.simplywild.biz
Simply Wild at Bournes Stores is a retail outlet for organic fruit, vegetables, eggs, home-produced meat and freshly baked bread. A large selection of other organic products is also available.

SIMPLY WILD FOOD COMPANY

PULLENS FARM, LAMBERHURST RD., HORSMONDEN TN12 8ED
Tel: 08456 586141 Fax: 08456 586141 Contact: Emily Reiss
enquiries@simplywildorganics.co.uk www.simplywild.biz
Simply Wild is a family-run business which offers a range of home-delivery boxes, each containing fresh locally produced organic vegetables, fruit, eggs, bread and meat to your doorstep.

TERRA MIA

37E CAMBRIDGE RD, BROMLEY BR1 4EB
Tel: 07816 419055 Contact: Guido Traverso
info@terramiaorganic.net www.terramiaorganic.net
Registered under Organic Farming—EC Control System No 2092/91.
Terra Mia is a small business dedicated to import organic Italian food directly from Italy to the London area. Our products are made by small handcraft companies producing typical regional organic delicatessen goods.

TINY SPROUT

LITTLE BOURNE, FURZEFIELD AVE., SPELDHURST TN3 0LD
Tel: 01892 863646 Contact: Sian van Zyl
sian.vanzyl@tinysprout.co.uk www.tinysprout.co.uk
Organic baby gift hampers: mail order and web delivery service, featuring award-winning ethically produced, eco-friendly products and organic cotton clothing to welcome new baby and pamper new parents.

WILLOW FARM B&B
STONE CROSS, BILSINGTON, ASHFORD TN25 7JJ
Tel: 01233 721700 Fax: 01233 720484 Contact: Renee Kemp Hopper
renee@willow-farm.freeserve.co.uk www.willowfarmenterprises.co.uk
B&B on an organic smallholding in peaceful rural area. Close to Yalding
Gardens. Easy access M20, Channel ports and Tunnel. From £25 per person
per night.

WINGHAM COUNTRY MARKET
SHATTERLING, CANTERBURY CT3 1JW
Tel: 01227 720567 Fax: 01227 720567 Contact: Andrew Ward
We sell an extensive range of organic produce at our farm shop, including
fresh vegetables grown on our Soil Association registered (G977) farm.

WINTERWOOD FARMS
CHARTWAY ST., EAST SUTTON, MAIDSTONE ME17 3DN
Tel: 01622 844286 Fax: 01622 844274 Contact: Stephen Taylor
organics@winterwood.co.uk www.winterwood.co.uk
Soft fruit grower/ packer. Main customers are UK multiples. Also actively
growing in Poland, France, Spain and South Africa.

Accommodation | Garden and Farm Sundries | Producers
Box Schemes/ Local Deliveries | Farmers' market Stall | Restaurants/ Cafés/Caterers
Day Visits | Manufacturers/ Processors | Retail shops
Eco Products | Importers/ exporters | Textiles
Farm Gate Sales | Mail order suppliers | Wholesalers

BLAIRS NURSERIES LTD
LOW CARR NURSERY, HEAD DYKE LANE, PILLING, PRESTON PR3 6SJ
Tel: 01253 790471 Fax: 01253 790099 Contact: Nev Dunne
blairs_nursery@hotmail.com
We are a 2-acre organic tomato nursery established for 25 years. Our fruit is of supermarket quality, fully graded and we are able to supply supermarkets, wholesalers, box schemes, retailers, caterers etc. Salad tomato, vine tomato, cocktail vine tomato, baby plum tomato and peppers available from April to November.

BOOTHS SUPERMARKETS
4–6 FISHERGATE, PRESTON PR1 3LJ
Tel: 01772 251701 Fax: 01772 204316 Contact: The Manager
admin@booths-supermarkets.co.uk www.booths-supermarkets.co.uk
Regional supermarket chain.

CHORLEY HEALTH FOOD STORE LTD
18 NEW MARKET ST., CHORLEY PR7 1DB
Tel: 01257 276146 Fax: 01257 276146 Contact: J Clark (Owner)
Adjacent to main car park, taxi rank and bus station. We stock a good range of organic foods, drinks and supplements, and are always happy to supply any non-stock line either over the counter or by mail order.

COMMERCIAL FREEZE DRY LTD
45 ROMAN WAY, LONGRIDGE RD., RIBBLETON, PRESTON PR2 5BD
Tel: 01772 654441 Fax: 01772 655004 Contact: Garry Hincks
gh@commercialfreezedry.co.uk www.commercialfreezedry.co.uk
Soil Association P2697. Freeze drying on a commission dry or product sourced basis of any organic products. Meat, dairy, fruit, vegetables, all handled.

FLINTOFF, LIBBY

BROOK HOUSE FARM, TARNACRE LANE, ST MICHAEL'S ON WYRE, PRESTON PR3 0TB
Tel: 01995 679728 Fax: 01995 679728 Contact: Libby Flintoff
lib@theflintoffs.fsnet.co.uk
Soil Association G1898. Grower: mainly protected cropping including cucumbers, aubergines, French beans, celery and onions. Also some field vegetables.

FOLD HOUSE FARM

HEAD DYKE LANE, PILLING, PRESTON PR3 6SJ
Tel: 01253 790541 Fax: 01253 790541 Contact: R Harrison
Soil Association G2176. Growers of field vegetables for sale to box schemes, market stalls, shops, supermarkets and wholesalers plus organic beef suckler herd with store cattle available for sale.

FREE RANGE KIDS

GARSTANG RD. EAST, POULTON-LE-FYLDE FY6 8HJ
Tel: 01253 896290 Contact: Lynda Howard
info@freerangekids.co.uk www.freerangekids.co.uk
One stop shop for baby slings, carriers, real washable nappies, organic and fair trade clothing and toys from around the world. Family-run business. Carefully researched products, thoroughly tested, beautiful and practical.

GIELTY, A & D

LYNCROFT FARM, BUTCHERS LANE, AUGHTON GREEN, ORMSKIRK L39 6SY
Tel: 01695 421712 Fax: 01695 422117 Contact: Alf Gielty
Organic Farmers and Growers. Organic vegetables grown for wholesale. Also farm shop open Thursdays 10am–3pm and local box delivery scheme on Thursday and Friday evenings.

GROWING WITH NATURE

BRADSHAW LANE NURSERY, PILLING, NR. PRESTON PR3 6AX
Tel: 01253 790046 Fax: 01253 790046 Contact: Alan Schofield
Soil Association S44N, RS44N. Growers' box scheme with seasonal vegetables and salads.

KEER FALLS FOREST FARM
ARKHOLME, CARNFORTH LA6 1AP
Tel: 015242 21019 Fax: 015242 21730 Contact: PJ Onions
philip@keerfalls.co.uk www.keerfalls.co.uk
Soil Association G7569. Producers of delicious organic lamb and beef, rare breed lamb, forest ducklings, herbs, hardwood timber and firewood. See our website for more details www.keerfalls.co.uk.

LEHMANN SFI LTD, GUY
ALSTON HOUSE, WHITE CROSS, SOUTH ROAD, LANCASTER LA1 4QX
Tel: 01524 581560 Fax: 01524 581562 Contact: Mark Lehmann
sales@guylehmann.com www.guylehmann.com
Specialists in supply of organic bulk dry mustard ingredients. Bulk organic wine, spirit and speciality vinegar. Organic sunflower, millet, linseed, caraway, pumpkin. All UK and Europe—minimum delivery: dry goods 25kg, liquids 1,000ltrs.

McKINSEY HEALTHY HERBS
ORRELL RD., ORRELL, WIGAN WN5 8QZ
Tel: 01695 632825 Fax: 01942 736286 Contact: Mandy Welland-Bray
Organic herb nursery. We specialise in pot-grown and fresh-cut culinary and medicinal herbs. Browse our extensive stock, talk to our knowledgeable staff or relax in our tea room. Open Monday, Wednesday, Friday & Saturday 10 till 4.

OLVERSON LTD, NORMAN
KERSHAW'S FARM, SMITHY LANE, SCARISBRICK, ORMSKIRK L40 8HL
Tel: 01704 840392 Fax: 01704 841096 Contact: Brian Olverson
sales@redvelvet.co.uk www.redvelvet.co.uk
Farming. Prepacking and beetroot processing. Soil Association P2631. Vegetables.

ONLY NATURAL
64 STANDISHGATE, WIGAN WN1 1UW
Tel: 01942 236239 Contact: B Arrowsmith
Health food shop stocking a large selection of organic products: teas, juices, pasta, cereals, rice cakes, etc. Orders taken for organic vegetables.

PORTER, ROY
9 BRIDGE RD., CHATBURN, CLITHEROE BB7 4AW
Tel: 01200 441392 Fax: 01200 441096 Contact: Roy Porter
Soil Association R4342. A very traditional butchers shop, whose products include organic meat and poultry. All meat is hung for 7–10 days depending on species and butchered to customers' individual requirements.

ROYAL OAK FARM ORGANICS
ROYAL OAK FARM, BICKERSTAFFE, NR. ORMSKIRK L39 0EE
Tel: 01695 423259 Fax: 01695 423259 Contact: Peter Lydiate
Soil Association G5301. Potatoes, vegetables and other horticultural produce.

SAKER VEGETARIAN FOODS LTD
CANTEEN MILL, BURNLEY RD., TODMORDEN OL14 7DR
Tel: 01706 818189 Fax: 01706 818189 Contact: Karl Badger
Long established wholesale bakers, specialising in organic breads and cakes. We also produce vegan and vegetarian pastries, and confectionery including sugar and gluten-free products.

SINGLE STEP CO-OPERATIVE LTD
78A PENNY ST, LANCASTER LA1 1NN
Tel: 01524 63021 Contact: Linda
Wholefood co-op selling a wide range of organic and Fairtrade products, including fresh fruit and vegetables. Vegetarian and sugar-free policies.

STAVELEY'S EGGS LTD

COPPULL MOOR FARM, PRESTON ROAD, COPPULL, NR. CHORLEY PR7 5EB
Tel: 01257 791595 Fax: 01257 794700 Contact: KT Staveley
eggs@staveleys.sagehost.co.uk www.staveleyseggs.co.uk
Organic egg production and distribution, Lion quality standards and RSPCA
Freedom Food standards, wholesale deliveries, most places to shops etc.
Eggs in pre-packs to Organic Food Federation standards.

TASTE CONNECTION

76 BRIDGE ST., RAMSBOTTOM, BURY BL0 9AG
Tel: 01706 822175 Fax: 01706 822941 Contact: Iseult or Adrian Richards
tasteconnection@aol.com www.tasteconnection.com
Speciality and organic food shop (two storey). First floor is almost entirely
organic: veg, meats, dairy, general grocery. Basement has deli counter with
huge cheese selection. Speciality: olive oils from around the world.

VICTORIA FOODS

BRIGHT ST., LEIGH WN7 RQH
Tel: 01942 686800 Fax: 01942 680814 Contact: Dan Ross
dan.ross@victoriafoods.co.uk www.victoriafoods.co.uk
Dry mixes, dessert mixes for the food industry.

WARD & THOMPSON

THE MARKET GARDEN, GREEN LANE, PREESALL, POULTON-LE-FYLDE FY6 0NS
Tel: 01253 811644 Fax: 01253 811644 Contact: Y Thompson
Soil Association W15N. Salad and vegetable crops.

WHALE TAIL CAFE

78A PENNY ST, LANCASTER LA1 1XN
Tel: 01524 845133 Contact: Tricia Rawlinson
Spacious and friendly café offering home-made veggie and vegan food and
on Fridays an organic main meal option.

BAMBURY ORGANIC FARM

BAMBURY FARM, BAMBURY LANE, PEATLING MAGNA LE8 5UE
Tel: 0116 247 8907 Fax: 0116 247 8907 Contact: Nick, Sue, Anthony Staines
bamburyfarm@btinternet.com
Soil Association G1104. Bambury Organic Farm is a small family-run farm
providing fresh organic vegetables to the local community. There is a range
of box sizes, plus a wide selection of fruit and free range eggs. Free delivery
is included in the service.

BETH'S KITCHEN & GROWING CONCERN

HOME FARM, WOODHOUSE LANE, NANPANTAN,
LOUGHBOROUGH LE11 3YG
Tel: 01509 268984 Contact: The Manager
www.growingconcern.co.uk
OF&G 31UKF100035. Rapidly expanding farm café/restaurant, serving
Growing Concern's unique rare breed meat, organic bakery, organic pies,
cakes etc. Delightful small animal playbarn and ancient woodland walk

BROCKLEBY FARM

SWAN LODGE BUNGALOW, UPPER BROUGHTON,
MELTON MOWBRAY LE14 3BH
Tel: 01664 820030 Contact: Ian Jalland
ian.jalland@farmline.com www.brocklebyfarm.co.uk
Soil Association G5920. Specialist suppliers of rare breed meats, including
Hebridean Lamb, Jacob Lamb and Portland Lamb.

CHEVELSWARDE ORGANIC GROWERS

THE BELT, SOUTH KILWORTH, LUTTERWORTH LE17 6DX
Tel: 01858 575309 Contact: Ruth Daltry
john@chevel.freeserve.co.uk www.chevelswardeorganics.co.uk
Soil Association D03M, P5595; HDRA. Off licence. Growers to Soil
Association standards: vines for white and red wine, vegetables for local
box scheme and farm shop supplies. Shop open daily for veg, fruit, wines
and organic groceries.

CLAYBROOKE MILL

FROLESWORTH LANE, CLAYBROOKE MAGNA LE17 5DB
Tel: 01455 202443 Contact: Sally Eales
claybrookemill@yahoo.co.uk
Soil Association P1578. We are a 300-year-old working watermill,
producing 40 different varieties of flours, plus many other products.

CORNER PLOT VEGETABLES

NB REYNARDINE AND URE, c/o THE BOATYARD, MILL LANE,
THURMASTON LE4 8AF
Tel: 0116 269 7920 Contact: Francesca Beamish
cesca@cornerplotvegetables.co.uk www.cornerplotvegetables.co.uk
Bag scheme, with total customer choice from a weekly emailed list.
Produce from 3/4-acre organic smallholding and other organic producers.
Requests encouraged. Free delivery to Leicester.

CURRANT AFFAIRS

9A LOSEBY LANE, LEICESTER LE1 5DR
Tel: 0116 251 0887 Contact: Kevin Taylor
www.currantaffairs.co.uk
Currant Affairs is a natural food store selling a wide range of organic produce. We also have an on-site bakery producing freshly prepared take-away.

EVERARDS BREWERY

CASTLE ACRES, NARBOROUGH LE19 1BY
Tel: 0116 201 4100 Fax: 0116 282 7164 Contact: Graham Giblett
mail@everards.co.uk www.everards.co.uk
Public house. Beer production, wholesaling and public house retailing.

FARMCARE

OADBY LODGE FARM, GARTREET RD., LEICESTER LE2 2FG
Tel: 0116 259 2342 Fax: 0116 259 2352 Contact: Nick Padwick
nick.padwick@letsco-operate.com
Organic dairy and arable producer based on Farmcare's Stoughton Estate.

GNC

18 SILVER ST., LEICESTER LE1 5ET
Tel: 0116 262 4859 Contact: L Baker
www.gnc.co.uk
Organic dried fruits, nuts, pastas etc.

GRIFFITHS, DT & PM

PIPER FARM, LONG WHATTON, LOUGHBOROUGH LE12 5BE
Tel: 01509 650291 Contact: DT & PM Griffiths
davidgriffiths1@amserve.com
7.4 hectare holding running 60 breeding ewes. Contract hedging and
stone walling. Lamb producers.

GROWING CONCERN

HOME FARM, WOODHOUSE LANE, NANPANTAN, LOUGHBOROUGH,
LEICESTERSHIRE LE11 3YG
Tel: 01509 239228 Fax: 01509 239228 Contact: M. Bell
Redevelopment since winning Organic Food Award includes visitors' rare
breed centre, on-farm bakery/restaurant, ready-made meals. Mail order.

LONG CLAWSON DAIRY LTD
WEST END, LONG CLAWSON, MELTON MOWBRAY LE14 4PJ
Tel: 01664 821732 Fax: 01664 823236 Contact: John Burdett
enquiries@clawson.co.uk www.clawson.co.uk
Stilton-blended cheese manufacturers (dairy).

MANOR FARM
LONG WHATTON, LOUGHBOROUGH LE12 5DF
Tel: 01509 646413 Fax: 01509 843344 Contact: V Matravers
vw@manororganicfarm.co.uk www.manororganicfarm.co.uk
Soil Association G1778, shop licence P4948, Elm Farm Research Centre
Demonstration Farm. Award-winning mixed organic family farm producing
cereals, vegetables, potatoes, meat and eggs. All sold through our farm
shop and at local farmers' markets, including home-made sausages and
burgers. Farm trail open. Farm shop open Thursday, Friday & Saturday.

THE NATURALLY GOOD FOOD DELIVERY SERVICE
THE STABLE YARD, COTESBACH HALL, MAIN STREET, COTESBACH,
LUTTERWORTH LE17 4HX
Tel: 01455 556878 Fax: 01455 550855 Contact: Sue McGrath
orders@goodfooddelivery.co.uk www.goodfooddelivery.co.uk
Soil Association P6641. Shop plus home delivery and mail order for huge
range of organic wholefoods, fruit & veg, plus gluten-free and dairy-free
foods, toiletries and household cleaners. Hard to find foods found! Also the
Keeper, an alternative to tampons.

NEWCOMBE, PC & KJ
LUBCLOUD FARM, OAKS IN CHARNWOOD, LOUGHBOROUGH LE12 9YA
Tel: 01509 503204 Fax: 01509 651267 Contact: Phil & Kay Newcombe
Soil Association G2934. Organic dairy farm with 120 milking cows. Bed
and breakfast accommodation in the beautiful Charnwood Forest within
the National Forest area.

OSBASTON KITCHEN GARDEN
OSBASTON HALL, OSBASTON, NR. NUNEATON CV13 0DR
Tel: 01455 440811 Contact: Flick Rohde
Soil Association G1523. Walled kitchen garden (1 acre) growing organic fruit, vegetables and herbs.

PAUL'S TOFU
66–68 SNOW HILL, MELTON MOWBRAY LE13 1PD
Tel: 01664 560572 Fax: 01664 410345 Contact: I Brammer
paul@soyfoods.co.uk
Wholesale supplier of organic fruit and vegetables and baked goods.

PICKS ORGANIC FARM SHOP
THE COTTAGE, HAMILTON GROUNDS, KING ST., BARKBY THORPE LE4 3QF
Tel: 0116 269 3548 Fax: 0116 269 3548 Contact: Nicola Chambers
Home-produced organic pork, beef, lamb, chicken, turkey, guinea fowl, duck and eggs. Seasonal fruit and vegetables, free local delivery and box scheme available. Farm shop selling organic meats, vegetables, wines, beers, ales, breads, ice creams, dairy produce, jams, chutneys, etc.

QUENBY HALL ORGANIC FOODS
QUENBY HALL, HUNGARTON LE7 9JF
Tel: 0116 259 5224 Fax: 0116 259 5224 Contact: Aubyn de Lisle
enquiries@quenbyhall.co.uk www.quenbybeef.co.uk
Soil Association G2914. Organic English Longhorn beef, born and raised on the ancient natural grassland, sold to order, free local delivery; mail order throughout UK mainland.

RUTLAND ORGANIC POULTRY
CUCKOO FARM, KETTON, NR. STAMFORD PE9 3UU
Tel: 01780 722009 Fax: 01780 722488 Contact: Pat Taylor
cuckoofarm@farmersweekly.net www.rutlandorganicpoultry.co.uk
Soil Association G5618, P7892. Chickens, chicken portions, guinea fowl, year-round Norfolk Black turkeys, barbary ducks and Christmas geese.

SEEDS OF CHANGE
FREEBY LANE, WALTHAM ON THE WOLDS LE14 4RS
Tel: 0800 952 0000 www.seedsofchange.co.uk
Seeds of Change offer accessible day to day products, all 100% certified organic. The range includes dried pasta, pasta sauces, ethnic sauces, stir-in sauces, soups and cereal bars.

WATTS, DA
THE BUNGALOW, SPRINGFIELD FARM, SAPCOTE LE9 4LD
Tel: 01455 272840 Contact: DA Watts
watts.donkeylane@btinternet.com
Soil Association G1251 P5631. Organic vegetable producer/own box scheme around Hinckley and surrounding area (50% own or local). Also fruit, eggs and bread. Small beef herd.

WHISSENDINE WINDMILL
MELTON ROAD, WHISSENDINE LE15 7EU
Tel: 01664 474172 Contact: Nigel Moon
OF&G P080027. 19th century windmill (4 pairs of millstones) producing bread and pastry flours: rye, spelt, oats, barley meals.

WOOD – FAMILY BUTCHER, MICHAEL F
51 HARTOPP RD., LEICESTER LE2 1WG
Tel: 0116 270 5194 Fax: 0116 270 5194 Contact: Richard Wood
www.mfwood.co.uk
Soil Association R1979. Retailing of beef, lamb, pork, chicken, turkey, cheese, eggs and butter from a traditional butcher's shop established in 1968.

ALFORD FIVE SAILED WINDMILL

EAST STREET, ALFORD LN13 9EQ
Tel: 01507 462136 Contact: Geoff Dees
enquiries@fivesailed.co.uk www.fivesailed.co.uk
Working windmill producing stoneground flours from certified organic grain and cereals of high nutritional value and flavour. Mill, shop and tea room open all year. Open as follows: Jan–Mar on Tues, Sat & Sun; Apr, May, June on Tues, Fri, Sat & Sun; July, Aug, Sep, daily; Oct on Tues, Fri, Sat & Sun; Nov & Dec on Tues, Sat & Sun. Opening Times 10am–5pm (Sun 11am–5pm) Winter closing 4pm. Additional opening for school and bank holidays.

BARKSTON HEATH MUSHROOMS

HEATH LANE, BARKSTON HEATH, GRANTHAM NG32 2DE
Tel: 01400 230845 Fax: 01400 230901 Contact: Robert & Linda Ranshaw
barkstonheath@aol.com
Growing organic mushrooms.

BRIDGE FARM ORGANIC FOODS

BRIDGE FARM, SNITTERBY CARR, GAINSBOROUGH DN21 4UU
Tel: 01673 818272 Fax: 01673 818477 Contact: Patty Phillips
Soil Association G2283, P7071. Producers of organic goat's milk and cheese, seasonal organic vegetables, free range eggs. Customers join our conservation group, receive newsletters, attend farm open days, and undertake conservation tasks.

BROXHOLME FARM SHOP

GRANGE FARM, BROXHOLME, NR. SAXILBY LN1 2NG
Tel: 01522 704212 Contact: Carl Sutcliffe
Lincolnshire Organic Producers, Soil Association G4752. Soil Association eggs, potatoes and Christmas turkeys. Turkeys available mail order or collected from farm shop.

CHEERS NURSERIES
ELEVEN ACRE LANE, KIRTON, BOSTON PE20 1LS
Tel: 01205 724258 Fax: 01205 724259 Contact: Henry Cheer
henry@cheersnurseries.co.uk
Raise organic vegetable transplants.

ECOLODGE
ROSE COTTAGE, STATION RD., OLD LEAKE, BOSTON PE22 9RF
Tel: 01205 871396 Contact: Geri Clarke
gclarke@internationalbusinessschool.net
www.internationalbusinessschool.net/ecolodge
Ecolodge built from Lincolnshire wood, powered by wood and wind.
Filtered rainwater for washing. Self-catering. Sleeps 4. Spacious, secluded in
8 acres of wood/meadowland. Walking, cycling and birding. £150 short
breaks, £300 per week. 10% discount for bookings 3 months or more in
advance.

EDEN FARMS
OLD BOLINGBROKE, SPILSBY PE23 4EY
Tel: 01790 763582 Fax: 01790 763582 Contact: Marjorie Stein
info@edenfarms.co.uk www.edenfarms.co.uk
Soil Association S31M. Organic salads and vegetables. Eden Farms has
been growing organic vegetables for 23 years, and delivers to homes
and shops in Lincolnshire, Nottinghamshire and the East Midlands. Also
farmers' markets in these areas.

ENTERPRISE SEEDS LTD
CLOVER HOUSE, BOSTON RD., SLEAFORD NG34 7HD
Tel: 01529 415555 Fax: 01529 413333 Contact: The Manager
dennis.pell@entseeds.co.uk www.entseeds.co.uk
Soil Association P5679. Agricultural seed producers for cereals, peas, beans,
grass and forage crops for resale direct to farmers and grounds throughout
England and Wales.

GLEADELL AGRICULTURE LTD

LINDSEY HOUSE, HEMSWELL CLIFF, GAINSBOROUGH DN21 5TH
Tel: 01427 421223 Fax: 01427 421230 Contact: Brian Wilburn
Organic grain marketing specialists. Soil Association no. P596. Organic
marketing company committed to serving and promoting organic farming
since 1986. Market specialists for all types and grades of certified organic
cereals and pulses. See display ad.

GOODACRE, JM & A

OLD MANOR FARM, SEWSTERN, GRANTHAM NG33 5RF
Tel: 01476 860228 Fax: 01476 860228 Contact: Andrew Goodacre
Soil Association G4146. Potato specialist business offering several different
varieties for sale and contract growing and grading services.

HOLBEACH WHOLEFOODS

32 HIGH ST., HOLBEACH, SPALDING PE12 7DY
Tel: 01406 422149 Fax: 01406 362939 Contact: D.R. West
springsunshine@aol.com
Natural food store: loose wholefoods, vegetarian and vegan foods, natural
healthcare, organic bread, fruit and veg to order. Bulk discounts. Owners
vegan, ethical business.

JACK BUCK GROWERS

OAK HOUSE, HOLBEACH BANK, SPALDING PE12 8BL
Tel: 01406 422615 Fax: 01406 426173 Contact: Tony Ruigrok
sales@jackbuck.co.uk www.jackbuck.co.uk
Soil Association P5546. Growers, packers and processors of speciality
vegetables.

KEEP YOURSELF RIGHT 2

4 RAVENDALE STREET, SCUNTHORPE DN15 6NE
Tel: 01724 854236 Contact: Mary Moss
Health food shop selling a wide range of pre-packed organic foods.

LINCOLNSHIRE ORGANICS
HOLME HALL, HOLME, SCUNTHORPE DN16 3RE
Tel: 01724 866493 Fax: 01724 866493 Contact: Sally Jackson
enquiries@lincolnshireorganics.com www.lincolnshireorganics.com
A welcoming farm shop stocking home-grown pork, eggs and vegetables.
Supplemented by a wide range of organic products. Children's play area.
Organic café serving home-grown (organic where possible) snacks, cakes,
drinks and ice cream. Opening hours are Wed to Sat 9.30–5.30 and Sun
10–4.

LOUTH WHOLEFOOD CO-OP
7–9 EASTGATE, LOUTH LN11 9NB
Tel: 01507 602411 Contact: John Hough
Wholefood shop selling wide range of organic products including fresh fruit
and vegetables, dried fruit, nuts, cereals, tea, coffee, wine, cheese, yoghurt,
other chilled and frozen products, toiletries, essential oils, and much more.

MAUD FOSTER MILL
WILLOUGHBY RD., BOSTON PE21 9EG
Tel: 01205 352188 Contact: James Waterfield
The tallest working windmill in Britain producing stoneground organic
flours to Organic Food Federation symbol standard for the wholesale and
retail trade.

McARD (SEEDS), SM
39 WEST RD, POINTON, SLEAFORD NG34 0NA
Tel: 01529 240765 Fax: 01529 240765 Contact: Susan McArd (Manager)
seeds@smmcard.com www.smmcard.com
Organic seeds, vegetables, flowers and herbs. Unusual vegetables.

MOUNT PLEASANT WINDMILL & TRUE LOAF BAKERY
NORTH CLIFF ROAD, KIRTON-IN-LINDSEY DN21 4NH
Tel: 01652 640177 Fax: 01652 640177
Contact: Mervin & Marie-Christine Austin
trueloafbakery@aol.com www.trueloafbakery.co.uk
and www.mountpleasantwindmill.co.uk
Four-sailed windmill, restored 1991, producing a range of 10 Soil
Association (no. P1497) organic stoneground flours solely by windpower.
Mill, flour sales, tea room, open Tuesday to Sunday all year. Organic bakery
with traditional wood-fired oven producing good selection of organic
breads. Open all year. School & Group visits welcome. Evening tours also
available. Coaches must book prior to visit.

NATURAL REMEDY WAREHOUSE
4 BROADGATE HOUSE, WESTLODE ST., SPALDING PE11 2AF
Tel: 01775 724994 Fax: 01775 761104 Contact: H Girdlestone
nrw@enzymepro.com www.spalding.org.uk/nrw
We stock a variety of organic foods, e.g. bread, flour, honey, yoghurts.
Special requests taken. 10% discount on case orders.

NEWFARM ORGANICS
JF & J EDWARDS & SONS, SOULBY LANE, WRANGLE, BOSTON PE22 9BT
Tel: 01205 870500 Fax: 01205 871001 Contact: Jane Edwards
newfarmorganics@zoom.co.uk www.newfarmorganics.co.uk
Organic Farmers and Growers 31UKF120010.We produce food that is
organic and truly traceable. We specialise in growing potatoes, cauliflowers,
cabbage, cereals and beans. We also produce quality beef from our Lincoln
Red x suckler herd.

NU-TREL PRODUCTS LTD
PARK FARM, KETTLETHORPE, LINCOLN LN1 2LD
Tel: 01522 704747 Fax: 01522 704748 Contact: Brian Aconley
www.nutrelgroup.co.uk
Soil Association I3022. Manufacturers of speciality fertilisers for use in
organic crop production.

OLIVER SEEDS

THE OLD WOOD, SKELLINGTHORPE, LINCOLN LN6 5UA
Tel: 01522 507300 Fax: 01522 507319 Contact: Francis Dunne
info@oliverseeds.co.uk www.oliverseeds.co.uk
Soil Association P7038. Seed merchants. Grass mixtures, maize, fodder crops, green manure, amenity grass, wild flowers to farmers, and landscaping. Own production, mixing, warehousing, supported by technical team on phone and on-site.

OMEX AGRICULTURE

BARDNEY AIRFIELD, TUPHOLME, LINCOLN LN3 5TP
Tel: 01526 396000 Fax: 01526 396011 Contact: Andy Eccles
andye@omex.com www.omex.com
Manufacture and application of tailor-made liquid suspension fertilisers based on supplementary nutrients listed in the SA standards. Omex also supply a range of crop trace elements and plant health promoters certified by SA. Organomex Biomex (based on Trichoderma) stimulates crop emergence and competes with soil borne plant pathogens. Organomex Rootboost is an optional additive to suspension fertilisers and stimulates crop rooting, aiding establishment and nutrient uptake. Organomex Kelpak is a seaweed-based growth stimulator for application to emerged crops. Organomex Gard-S is a garlic concentrate, used to boost crop's natural defences and Organomex 6-2-4 is a foliar feed, used to maintain crop growth during periods of nutrient stress.

SADD, B M

BIRCHWOOD FARM, DRAWDYKE, SUTTON ST. JAMES, SPALDING PE12 0HP
Tel: 01945 440388 Contact: BM Sadd
Soil Association S34M. Field and glasshouse crops.

SINCLAIR HORTICULTURE LTD, WILLIAM

FIRTH RD, LINCOLN LN6 7AH
Tel: 01522 537561 Fax: 01522 513609 Contact: The manager
info@william-sinclair.co.uk www.william-sinclair.co.uk
Manufacturers of compost, lawn care, fertilisers, bark and mulches.

SPICE OF LIFE
4 BURGHLEY CENTRE, BOURNE PE10 9EG
Tel: 01778 394735 Contact: DR West
david.west@kcl.ac.uk
Retailer of wholefoods (not pre-packed), many organic lines, bulk, Ecover, fresh org bread and veg. 1,000 sq ft walk-around shop.

STRAWBERRY FIELDS
SCARBOROUGH BANK, STICKFORD, BOSTON PE22 8DR
Tel: 01205 480490 Fax: 01205 480490 Contact: Pam Bowers
pam@strawberryfields75.freeserve.co.uk
www.strawberryfieldsorganics.co.uk
Soil Association B40M. Growing organically since 1975, we specialise in salads, herbs, strawberries and the more unusual vegetables, with attention on high quality and reliability. Wholesale, multiple and retail outlets supplied.

SWEDEPONIC UK LTD
SPALDING RD., BOURNE PE10 0AT
Tel: 01778 424224 Fax: 01778 421200 Contact: Mark Powell
mark@swedeponic.co.uk
The UK's first certified organic potted herb specialist. We supply box schemes, wholesalers and retailers.

UTOPIA UK
ENTERPRISE WAY, PINCHBECK, SPALDING PE11 3YR
Tel: 01775 716800 Fax: 01775 716808 Contact: Lucy Crawford
lcrawford@utopiauk.com www.utopiauk.com
Importation and supply of fresh exotic/tropical fruit and vegetables to the UK multiple retailers. Organic products include pineapple, papaya, mango, citrus, sweet potato, asparagus and other exotics.

WATTS, PN
VINE HOUSE FARM, DEEPING ST. NICHOLAS, SPALDING PE11 3DG
Tel: 01775 630208 Fax: 01775 630244 Contact: Nicholas Watts
p.n.watts@farming.co.uk
Soil Association G2618. Growing and selling potatoes, French beans,
courgettes and sweetcorn.

WHEELBARROW FOODS
3 THORNGARTH LANE, BARROW ON HUMBER DN19 7AW
Tel: 01469 530721 Contact: Andrew Spacey (Coordinator)
Wheelbarrow Foods produces vegetables, fruit and herbs to Soil Association
standard. Farm gate sales. Local delivery to shops. Vegetable box scheme.
Small shop. Distribution point.

WILSFORD ORGANICS
11 MAIN ST., WILSFORD, GRANTHAM NG32 3NS
Tel: 01400 230224 Contact: John Scott
Soil Association licensed G1708. Produce for sale: organic free range eggs
and vegetables. Phone first.

WOODLANDS
KIRTON HOUSE, KIRTON, NR. BOSTON PE20 1JD
Tel: 01205 722491 Fax: 01205 722905 Contact: Andrew Dennis
info@woodlandsfarm.co.uk www.woodlandsfarm.co.uk
Soil Association G2224, P5094. Mixed organic farm, producing vegetables,
beef and lamb for local, regional and multiple outlets. Organic bronze
turkeys available Christmas and Easter. Box scheme delivering to LN, PE,
NN & LE postcodes.

WORLDWIDE FRUIT LTD
WEST MARSH RD., SPALDING PE11 2BB
Tel: 01775 717000 Fax: 01775 717001 Contact: Mark Everett
mark.everett@worldwidefruit.co.uk www.worldwidefruit.co.uk
Major fruit importer and UK pip/soft fruit producer servicing all of the
major multiple retailers; specialists in fruit ripening. Year-round supply of
apple, pear, kiwi, avocado and dates.

Wisdom of the Geese

There's a farmer in Illinois who's been planting soybeans on his 50-acre field for years.
Unfortunately, he also had a flock of soybean-eating geese that took up residence in a pond
nearby. Geese, being creatures of habit, returned to the same spot the next year to again
feast on his soybeans. But this time, the geese ate only from a specific part of his field. There,
as a result of their feasting, the beans grew only ankle high. The geese, it seemed, were boy-
cotting the other part of the same field where the beans were able to grow waist-high. The
reason: this year, the farmer had tried the new, genetically engineered soybeans. And you can
see exactly where they were planted, for there is a line right down the middle of his field with
the natural beans on one side and the genetically engineered beans, untouched by the geese,
on the other. Visiting that Illinois farm, veteran agricultural writer C.F. Marley said, "I've never
seen anything like it. What's amazing is that the field with Roundup Ready [genetically engi-
neered] beans had been planted to conventional beans the previous year, and the geese ate
them. This year, they won't go near that field."

From *Seeds of Deception: Exposing Corporate and Government Lies about the Safety of
Genetically Engineered Food* by Jeffrey M. Smith, Green Books, £9.95

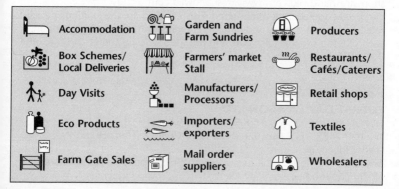

Accommodation	Garden and Farm Sundries	Producers
Box Schemes/ Local Deliveries	Farmers' market Stall	Restaurants/ Cafés/Caterers
Day Visits	Manufacturers/ Processors	Retail shops
Eco Products	Importers/ exporters	Textiles
Farm Gate Sales	Mail order suppliers	Wholesalers

CLEAN BEAN
170 BRICK LANE E1 6RU
Tel: 020 7247 1639 Fax: 020 7247 1639 Contact: Neil McLennan
cleanbean@ssba.info
Soil Association P2200. Clean Bean manufactures fresh organic tofu which is supplied to restaurants and wholefood stores in the London area, and directly from our stalls at Borough Market every Saturday and Spitalfields Organic Market every Sunday.

THE CROWN
223 GROVE RD. E3 5SN
Tel: 020 8981 9998 Fax: 020 8983 2336 Contact: Jon Smart
crown@singhboulton.co.uk www.singhboulton.co.uk
Soil Association certified. Organic gastro pub opposite Victoria Park. Beautiful listed building with balconies overlooking the park. Serving high quality food and drink, twice daily changing menu, 40 wines, real ales. No-smoking restaurant area. Bookings in advance.

FRESH & WILD
194 OLD STREET EC1V 9FR
Tel: 020 7250 1708 Contact: The Manager
shop@freshandwild.com www.freshandwild.com
Organic Food Federation registered. Fresh & Wild are the leading specialist retailer of organic foods and natural remedies, with six stores in London, each offering organic juice bars and hot food deli. Customer careline: 0800 917 5175.

FUERST DAY LAWSON LTD
DEVON HOUSE, 58–60 ST. KATHERINE'S WAY E1 9LB
Tel: 020 7488 0777 Fax: 020 7702 3200 Contact: Frank Horan
seeds@fdl.co.uk
Seeds, pulses, honey, fruit juices, essential oils suppliers and processors of all dry commodities in a Soil Association approved facility.

NAPIER BROWN & CO LTD
1 ST. KATHARINE'S WAY E1W 1XB
Tel: 020 7335 2500 Fax: 020 7335 2502 Contact: C Sergeant
sales@napierbrown.co.uk www.napierbrown.co.uk
Napier Brown are the largest independent sugar distributor in the UK. We offer a wide range of organic sugars and syrups in both industrial and retail packs from factories approved by the Soil Association. Deliver nationally.

OLD SPITALFIELDS ORGANIC MARKET
65 BRUSHFIELD ST. E1 6AA
Tel: 01243 779716 Contact: Bart Ives
Every Sunday, covered market from 10am–5pm. Established 1993. The alternative to supermarkets and cheaper. Largest range certified organic fresh fruit, veg, breads, dairy, meat, wine etc from producers and traders.

THE ORGANIC DELIVERY COMPANY
70 RIVINGTON ST. EC2A 3AY
Tel: 020 7739 8181 Fax: 020 7613 5656 Contact: John Barrow
info@organicdelivery.co.uk www.organicdelivery.co.uk
Soil Association R2443. Large range of organic vegetarian and vegan groceries of the highest quality delivered to you, throughout London. Affordable and convenient. Order by telephone or securely on-line. Highly commended in the Soil Association awards, and registered with them.

TWIN TRADING LTD
THIRD FLOOR, 1 CURTAIN ROAD EC2A 3LT
Tel: 020 7375 1221 Fax: 020 7375 1337 Contact: Marc Monsarrat
info@twin.org.uk
Soil Association Licensed. Fairtrade importer of coffee, cocoa, nuts etc.

VERTUE GREEN CARPET CLEANING
60–64 UPPER CLAPTON RD, HACKNEY E5 9JP
Tel: 020 8806 7294 Contact: S Girardi vertueltd@hotmail.com
Vertue have developed and supply the leading technology in cleaning products. Liquids are kelp seaweed-derived, non-toxic and not tested on animals. Competitive range of 100% recycled paper products. Products extract toxic chemicals whilst cleaning.

LONDON NORTH

ALARA WHOLEFOODS LTD
110–112 CAMLEY ST. NW1 0PF
Tel: 020 7387 9303 Fax: 020 7388 6077 Contact: Alex Smith
alexsmith@alara.co.uk www.alara.co.uk
Soil Association P1301. Alara are specialist manufacturers and packers of cereals especially muesli with over 40 different types of organic muesli currently produced in our BRC higher level accredited factory. Branded and own label available catering to over twenty-five international markets.

ALTERNATIVES HEALTH CENTRE
1369 HIGH ST., WHETSTONE N20 9LN
Tel: 020 8445 2675 Contact: D Thankey
www.naturesalternative.co.uk
Health food shop with clinic. Organic, tinned, packets, frozen and chilled products, supplements, homoeopathic and herbal remedies, tinctures, cosmetics, books and magazines.

BUMBLEBEE
30–33 BRECKNOCK RD. N7 0DD
Tel: 020 7607 1936 Fax: 020 7607 1936 Contact: Gillian Haslop
info@bumblebee.co.uk www.bumblebee.co.uk
A huge range of organic and vegetarian foods, specialising in organic fruit
and vegetables, cheeses, olive oils and mediterranean foods, organic wines
and beers, gluten- and wheat-free products, as well as fairtraded and macrobiotic ranges. Deliveries in London, Oxford and Greater London. Local
box scheme. Carrier deliveries cost £10 to anywhere in the UK mainland.

THE CELTIC BAKERS
42B WATERLOO RD., CRICKLEWOOD NW2 7UH
Tel: 020 8452 4390 Fax: 020 8452 8235 Contact: Syd Aston
info@thecelticbakers.co.uk www.thecelticbakers.co.uk
A dedicated organic vegetarian bakery specialising in most aspects of hand-
made bread production (including 100% ryes and sourdough methods),
cakes, pastries and savouries.

CHAPEL FARMERS' MARKET
CHAPEL MARKET, PENTON ST. END, ISLINGTON N1
Tel: 020 7704 9659 Fax: 020 7359 1938 Contact: London Farmers' Markets
info@lfm.org.uk www.lfm.org.uk
Wednesdays 9am–3pm. Here farmers sell home-grown foods grown or
made within 100 miles of the M25, including fruit, veg, meat, dairy, eggs,
honey, juice, bread, preserves, plants. Note: some, but not all, producers
are organic.

COMMUNITY FOODS LTD
BRENT TERRACE NW2 1LT
Tel: 020 8450 9419/9411 Fax: 020 8208 1551/1803 Contact: Dave Price
info@communityfoods.co.uk www.communityfoods.co.uk
Soil Association no. P1422. We are an importer and distributor of a large
range of natural products including several hundred organic lines. Bulk
dried fruit, nuts, pulses etc. plus brands like Sanchi, Crazy Jack, Nature's
Path, Eunature, Emile Noel, Monki, Shady Maple, Rebar and many more.

DAY PLUS ONE LTD
UNIT 11A&B, CRUSADER IND. ESTATE, 167 HERMITAGE RD.,
LONDON N4 1LZ
Tel: 020 8802 1088 Fax: 020 8802 3862 Contact: A Lauchlan
plus1@gotadsl.co.uk
Soil Association P1469. Packer of organic wholefoods under the Organic
Day's brand and customers own label. Supplier of a large range of organic
pre-packs in a wide variety of sizes. Product range includes, amongst
others, nuts, dried fruit, rice, pulses, grains, cereals and snacks.

THE DUKE OF CAMBRIDGE
30 ST. PETER'S STREET, ISLINGTON N1 8JT
Tel: 020 7359 9450 Fax: 020 7359 1877 Contact: Geetie Singh
duke@singhboulton.demon.co.uk www.singhboulton.co.uk
Soil Association certified. Organic gastro pub serving high quality organic
food and drink, twice daily changing menu, choice of 40 wines, real ales.
No-smoking restaurant area where bookings can be made in advance. Won
Time Out Gastro Pub of the Year 2000.

ECO-CUISINE.CO.UK
4 HEDGE LANE, PALMERS GREEN N13 5SH
Tel: 020 8882 0350 Contact: Sonya Meagor
enquiries@eco-cuisine.co.uk www.eco-cuisine.co.uk
Catering business. We use organic, free range products in our catering, using
the freshest produce available and supporting British farmers/producers.

FRESH & WILD
49 PARKWAY, CAMDEN TOWN NW1 7PN
Tel: 020 7428 7575 Contact: The Manager
shop@freshandwild.com www.freshandwild.com
Organic Food Federation registered. Fresh & Wild are the leading specialist
retailer of organic foods and natural remedies, with six stores in London,
each offering organic juice bars and hot food deli. Customer careline: 0800
917 5175.

FRESH & WILD

32–40 STOKE NEWINGTON CHURCH ST. N16 0LU
Tel: 020 7254 2332 Contact: The Manager
shop@freshandwild.com www.freshandwild.com
Organic Food Federation registered. Fresh & Wild are the leading specialist retailer of organic foods and natural remedies, with six stores in London, each offering organic juice bars and hot food deli. Customer careline: 0800 917 5175.

GREEN BABY CO LTD

345 UPPER STREET, ISLINGTON N1 0PD
Tel: 020 7226 4345 Fax: 020 7226 9244 Contact: Jill Barker
info@greenbaby.co.uk www.greenbaby.co.uk
A mail order and retail outlet for planet-friendly parents. Green Baby sells washable nappies, organic cotton clothing, gel-free disposable nappies and natural toiletries for mother and baby.

GROUNDED

139B CHURCH WALK, UNIT 6, STOKE NEWINGTON N16 7QX
Tel: 020 7503 0279 Contact: Samuel Yeung
organic@blueyonder.co.uk www.dressorganic.co.nr
Stylish and funky organic clothing design label. We also offer to measure service and high end designs.

HAELAN CENTRE

41 THE BROADWAY, CROUCH END N8 8DT
Tel: 020 8340 4258 Fax: 020 8292 2232 Contact: John Krahn
www.haelan.co.uk
One of Britain's original wholefood and herbal stores, offering a complete range of vegetarian and vegan organic food, organic skin care, also eco cleaning products, an on-site complementary health clinic, herbal dispensary and homoeopathic pharmacy.

THE HAMPSTEAD TEA & COFFEE COMPANY
PO BOX 2448 NW11 7DR
Tel: 020 8731 9833 Fax: 020 8458 3947 Contact: Kiran Tawadey
info@hampsteadtea.com www.hampsteadtea.com
Organic Food Award winners 98 & 99 for our high quality range of biodynamic and fair trade teas. Certified by BDAA. Products at health food stores
and by mail order.

HEALTHQUEST LTD
7 BRAMPTON RD. NW9 9BX
Tel: 020 8206 2066 Fax: 020 8206 2022 Contact: Ashwin Mehta
info@healthquest.co.uk www.healthquest.co.uk
HealthQuest supplies the stylish Organic Blue range of wellbeing products
(aromatherapy, bodycare and herbal supplement ranges), the award
winning Earth Friendly Baby range (natural baby toiletries) and Natalia
aromatherapy range (pregnancy).

HONEY ROSE BAKERY
6 FORTUNE WAY NW10 6UF
Tel: 020 8960 5567 Fax: 020 8960 5598 Contact: Lise Madsen
cakes@honeyrosebakery.com www.honeyrosebakery.com
Dedicated organic operation hand-baking award-winning muffins,
brownies, cookies, and cakes. Beautifully packaged for retail and to go, or
unwrapped for foodservice. We derive great satisfaction in preserving time
honoured baking crafts.

HUGO'S CAFÉ
23–25 LONSDALE ROAD NW6 6RA
Tel: 020 7372 1232 Fax: 020 7328 8097 Contact: Carol Jones
We serve organic vegetarian and meat dishes.

ISLINGTON FARMERS' MARKET
ESSEX ROAD, OPPOSITE ISLINGTON GREEN, ISLINGTON N1
Tel: 020 7704 9659 Contact: London Farmers' Markets
info@lfm.org.uk www.lfm.org.uk

JUST ORGANIC
113 WILBERFORCE RD. N4 2SP
Tel: 020 7704 2566 Fax: 020 7704 2566 Contact: Mike Adams
Mike_veg@hotmail.com
Soil Association P2042. Fresh organic fruit and vegetables, delivered to your
door. £10 or £15 mixed boxes, free delivery.

MARIGOLD HEALTH FOODS
102 CAMLEY ST. NW1 0PF
Tel: 020 7388 4515 Fax: 020 7388 4516 Contact: David Swinstead
sales@marigoldhealthfoods.co.uk
Soil Association P2604, OF&G UK2 P0015. Wholesaler of vegetarian food,
drinks, nutritional supplements and animal-free products particularly strong
in organic and chilled. Distribute to South-East England; Marigold
Bouillon Powder and Yogi Teas stocked by wholesalers throughout UK.

NATURAL HEALTH
339 BALLARDS LANE, N. FINCHLEY N12 8LJ
Tel: 020 8445 4397 Fax: 020 8445 4397 Contact: D Thankey
www.naturesalternative.co.uk
Health food store with clinic for alternative therapies. Organic foods,
supplements, tinctures, homoeopathic and herbal remedies, cosmetics,
books, tapes and CDs.

NEAL'S YARD REMEDIES
68 CHALK FARM RD., CAMDEN NW1 8AN
Tel: 020 7284 2039 Fax: 020 7428 0390 Contact: A Rodriguez
mail@nealsyardremedies.com www.nealsyardremedies.com
Natural remedies: medicinal herbs and tinctures, homoeopathic remedies,
flower essences, essential oils, books.

PITFIELD BEER SHOP & BREWERY

14 PITFIELD ST. N1 6EY
Tel: 020 7739 3701 Fax: 020 7729 9636 Contact: Martin Kemp
sales@pitfieldbeershop.co.uk www.pitfieldbeershop.co.uk
Organic Farmers & Growers registered. Award-winning organic brewery
and shop offering over 600 beers and ciders, many organic. Self-brew wine
and beer supplies. Wholesale and mail order across UK.

PLOT 21 PERMACULTURE ALLOTMENTS

ALEXANDRA PALACE ALLOTMENTS, OFF ALEXANDRA PALACE WAY N17
Tel: 020 7916 7390 Contact: S Girardi
A loose non-profit-making organisation running courses on permaculture
and producing home-grown crops using permaculture principles.

REVITAL HEALTHSHOP

35 HIGH RD, WILLESDEN GREEN NW10 2TE
Tel: 020 8459 3382 Fax: 020 8459 3722 Contact: Bakhat Khadka
enquire@revital.com www.revital.com
Health shop.

SAN AMVROSIA HEALTH FOODS

UNIT 8, THE STONEBRIDGE CENTRE, RANGEMOOR RD. N15 4LP
Tel: 020 8801 2180 Fax: 020 8801 8558 Contact: D Georgiou
Soil Association P4139. Manufacturers of fresh dips (vegetarian).

SIMPLY BREAD

BUILDING E, THE CHOCOLATE FACTORY, WESTERN ROAD N22 6UY
Tel: 020 8889 7159 Fax: 020 8889 2428 Contact: Jack Flatter
info@simply-bread.co.uk
Soil Association P2628. Wholesale bakery specialising in organic rye bread,
organic wholemeal, organic white and organic croissants.

SKOULIKAS, GEORGE LTD

UNIT 5, 998 NORTH CIRCULAR RD, COLES GREEN RD. NW2 7JR
Tel: 020 8452 8465 Fax: 020 8452 8273 Contact: Colin Morrison
gskoul1@aol.com
Imports and distribution of mediterranean organic foods including olives,
olive oil, tahini, halva, sesame bars, orange and lemon juice, pesto and
polenta.

SOUTH LONDON BAKERS & NATURAL RISE FOODS

21 BERNARD RD. N15 4NE
Tel: 020 8808 2007 Fax: 020 8808 2007 Contact: Mana/Inder
inder333@aol.com
Organic craft bakers since 1981, specialising in hand-moulded organic
yeasted and sourdough breads produced without additives, flour improvers
and preservatives. Deliveries available throughout the Greater London area.

SWISS COTTAGE FARMERS' MARKET

02 CENTRE CAR PARK, FINCHLEY ROAD NW3
Tel: 020 7704 9659 Contact: London Farmers' Markets
info@lfm.org.uk www.lfm.org.uk
Wednesdays 10am–3pm. Here farmers sell home-grown foods grown or
made within 100 miles of the M25, including fruit, veg, meat, dairy, eggs,
honey, juice, bread, preserves, plants. Note: some, but not all, producers are
organic. Run by London Farmers' Markets, PO Box 37363, London N1 7WB.

TASTE MATTERS LTD

PO BOX 43845 NW6 6WH
Tel: 020 7328 2885 Fax: 020 7328 9228
Contact: Alex Morritt / Patricia Collins
info@tastematters.co.uk www.tastematters.co.uk
Taste Matters Ltd. produces a premium range of chilled 'food to go' products sold under the Taste Matters brand through leading independent
organic food retailers, health food stores, food halls and delicatessens.

TEACRATE
151 SCRUBS LANE NW10 6RH
Tel: 020 8282 0000 Fax: 020 8282 0061 Contact: Kate Barrett
kateb@teacrate.com www.teacrate.com
Tray rental, purchase and washing company. We offer food tray washing
services to Soil Association organic standard, tray rental and purchase as
well as full logistic and financial packages for anyone in the food industry.
Diverse range of crates and also plastic pallets.

TEMPLE HEALTH FOODS
17 TEMPLE FORTUNE PARADE NW11 0QS
Tel: 020 8458 6087 Fax: 020 8905 0800 Contact: M Dadia
Complete range of wholefoods with many organic alternatives, books and
information leaflets. Delivery service, free newsletter and samples.

TEXTURE
84 STOKE NEWINGTON CHURCH STREET N16 0AP
Tel: 020 7241 0990 Fax: 020 7241 1991 Contact: Jeff Gilbert
jag@textilesfromnature.com www.textilesfromnature.com
Eco textiles, mail order, retail, wholesale and manufacturer of pillows,
cushions, bed linen, curtains and fabric by the metre.

UK5 ORGANICS
60–64 UPPER CLAPTON RD., HACKNEY E5 9JP
Tel: 020 7237 7277 Fax: 020 7237 7277 Contact: Kevin Harrison
uk5organics@hotmail.com www.uk5.info
Enquiries line 07799 790279. Deliveries to east, south east and north
London of organic veg, fruit and groceries on Mondays, Tuesdays and
Wednesdays, dependent on post code.

ABEL & COLE

8–15 MGI ESTATE, MILKWOOD ROAD SE24 0JF
Tel: 020 7737 3648 Fax: 020 7737 7785 Contact: Matthew Harwood
organics@abel-cole.co.uk www.abel-cole.co.uk
Abel and Cole offer seasonal organic fruit and vegetable boxes, meats, fish, dairy, breads, beers, wines, juices and pantry goods. Soil Association Best Home Delivery Service award winner 2002.

G. BALDWIN & CO

171–173 WALWORTH RD SE17 1RW
Tel: 020 7703 5550 Fax: 020 7252 6264 Contact: Stephen Dagnell
sales@baldwins.co.uk www.baldwins.co.uk
Herbalist and essential oils. Complementary and alternative product supplier.

BLACKHEATH FARMERS' MARKET

BLACKHEATH RAIL STATION CAR PARK, 2 BLACKHEATH VILLAGE SE3
Tel: 020 7704 9659 Contact: London Farmers' Markets
info@lfm.org.uk www.lfm.org.uk

CAPRICORN ORGANICS

15, SEDGEHILL RD., CATFORD SE6 3QU
Tel: 020 8306 2786 Contact: Alison Wise
alison@capricornorganics.co.uk www.capricornorganics.co.uk
Local home delivery service. Individual orders or boxes. Mostly UK fruit and veg, bread, eggs and cheese.

DANDELION

120 NORTHCOTT ROAD SW11 6QU
Tel: 020 7350 0902 Contact: Hilel Friedman
Wide range of organic fresh and dried foods including take-away foods, vitamins, supplements, etc.

FARM-A-ROUND

OFFICES B143, NEW COVENT GARDEN MARKET, NINE ELMS LANE, LONDON SW8 5PA
Tel: 020 7627 8066 Fax: 01748 822007 Contact: Isobel Davies
info@farmaround.co.uk www.farmaround.co.uk
Organic Farmers and Growers UKP08009. Home delivery service of assorted bags of fresh organic produce. Prices from £4 for a mini fruit box, also organic grocery range. Delivery charge: £1 throughout Greater London.

FOOD BRANDS GROUP LTD

9–10 CALICO HOUSE, PLANTATION WHARF, BATTERSEA SW11 3TN
Tel: 020 7978 5300 Fax: 020 7924 2732 Contact: Edward Chapman
www.fbg.co.uk
Food Brands Group Ltd trades in teas and coffees (Percol), soft drinks (Santa Cruz Organic) and wines.

THE FOOD FERRY COMPANY

UNIT B24–27, NEW COVENT GARDEN MARKET, NINE ELMS LANE SW8 5HH
Tel: 020 7498 0827 Fax: 020 7498 8009 Contact: Jonathan Hartnell-Beavis
e@foodferry.com www.foodferry.com
Grocery delivery to homes and businesses in central London. Full range of organic fruit and vegetables (including boxes), meat, poultry, larder foods, drinks and eco-friendly cleaning products.

FRESH & WILD
305–311 LAVENDER HILL SW11 1LN
Tel: 020 7585 1488 Contact: The Manager
shop@freshandwild.com www.freshandwild.com
Organic Food Federation registered. Fresh & Wild are the leading specialist retailer of organic foods and natural remedies, with six stores in London, each offering organic juice bars and hot food deli. Customer careline 0800 917 5175.

FROM GREENWICH
17 ANCHORAGE POINT, ANCHOR & HOPE LANE SE7 7SQ
Tel: 020 8269 0409 Fax: 020 8269 0417 Contact: John Herbert
office@fromgreenwich.co.uk www.fromgreenwich.co.uk
Delicious cakes.

GREEN & BLACK'S
2 VALENTINE PLACE SE1 8QH
Tel: 020 7633 5900 Fax: 020 7633 5901 Contact: Neil Turpin
enquiries@greenandblacks.com www.greenandblacks.com
Green & Black's make award-winning, quality organic chocolate combining the highest environmental and ethical standards. Their delicious range of organic chocolate products includes chocolate bars, hot chocolate, cocoa, ice creams, chocolate covered almonds and chocolate hazelnut spread. Certified by the Soil Association and available nationwide at supermarkets, good health food stores and delicatessens.

GREENWICH ORGANICS
86 ROYAL HILL, GREENWICH SE10 8RT
Tel: 020 8488 6764 Fax: 020 8488 0136 Contact: Fred Tyler
office@greenwichorganics.co.uk www.greenwichorganics.co.uk
Soil Association R6610. Organic shop and delivery service to south and east London, wide range of produce and groceries, including freshly baked bread, beer and wine, and dairy.

HERE
CHELSEA FARMERS' MARKET, 125 SYDNEY ST, CHELSEA SW3 6NR
Tel: 020 7351 4321 Fax: 020 7351 2211 Contact: Michelle Smith
organicwarehouse@onetel.net.uk www.herestores.co.uk
The most comprehensive supermarket in the UK, stocking only 100% organic
foods/drink. Natural supplements and bodycare. Café area/take-out.
Deliveries in London. Mail Order.

LANGRIDGE ORGANIC PRODUCTS LTD
UNIT A55–57, NEW COVENT GARDEN MARKET, NINE ELMS LANE SW8 5EE
Tel: 020 7622 7440 Fax: 020 7622 7441 Contact: Alex Pearce
sales@langridgeorganic.com www.langridgeorganic.com
Soil Association P7570. Langridge specialise in the wholesale supply of
organic fruit, vegetables and dairy products to independent retailers, box
schemes, restaurants, schools and hospitals. Our produce is sourced from
our network of growers throughout the UK, Europe and the rest of the
world. Langridge operates a policy of buying the most locally available
organic produce at all times.

MATERIA AROMATICA
7 PENRHYN CRESCENT SW14 7PF
Tel: 020 8392 9868 Fax: 020 8255 7126 Contact: Isabelle Poignart
info@materia-aromatica.com www.materia-aromatica.com
Soil Association registered. Aromatherapy, essential oils and skin care
products. Certified organic essential oils and vegetable oils, 100% natural
skin and body care made with organic ingredients, free from chemicals and
preservatives.

MONMOUTH COFFEE COMPANY
2 PARK ST SE1 9AB
Tel: 020 7645 3561 Fax: 020 7645 3565 Contact: Sophie Deguillaume
beans@monmouthcoffee.co.uk www.monmouthcoffee.co.uk
Coffee roasters, wholesalers and retailers.

NATURISIMO.COM
UNIT 10, 28 OLD BROMPTON RD. SW7 3SS
Tel: 020 7584 7815 Contact: Cristina Manas
info@naturisimo.com www.naturisimo.com
Beauty/skin care products. 100% natural and organic skin care products
from exceptional brands: Living Nature, Organic Blue, Green People,
Spiezia Organics, Weleda etc. No synthetic chemicals or preservatives, artifi-
cial colours or fragrances. No animal testing.

NEAL'S YARD REMEDIES
32 BLACKHEATH VILLAGE, BLACKHEATH SE3 9SY
Tel: 020 8318 6655 Contact: Alina Frymorgan
mail@nealsyardremedies.com www.nealsyardremedies.com
Retail shop selling Neal's Yard Remedies products.

NEAL'S YARD REMEDIES
6 NORTHCOTE ROAD, CLAPHAM JUNCTION SW11 1NT
Tel: 020 7223 7141 Fax: 020 7223 7174 Contact: Pamela Loch
mail@nealsyardremedies.com www.nealsyardremedies.com
Natural health shop with a therapy centre attached.

NEAL'S YARD REMEDIES
12–14 CHELSEA FARMERS MARKET, SYDNEY ST. SW3 6NR
Tel: 020 7351 6380 Contact: Bodhi Hunt
mail@nealsyardremedies.com www.nealsyardremedies.com
Neal's Yard Remedies manufactures and retails natural cosmetics in addition
to stocking an extensive range of herbs, essential oils, homoeopathic
remedies and reference material.

NEAL'S YARD REMEDIES (HEAD OFFICE)

8–10 INGATE PLACE, BATTERSEA SW8 3NS
Tel: 020 7498 1686 Fax: 020 7498 2505 Contact: The Manager
mail@nealsyardremedies.com www.nealsyardremedies.com
Neal's Yard Remedies manufactures and retails natural cosmetics in addition
to stocking an extensive range of herbs, essential oils, homoeopathic
remedies and reference material. Customer Services: 020 7627 1949,
cservices@nealsyardremedies.com.

THE OLD POST OFFICE BAKERY

76 LANDOR RD., CLAPHAM SW9 9PH
Tel: 020 7326 4408 Fax: 020 7326 4408 Contact: John Dungavel
www.oldpostofficebakery.co.uk
Organic craft bakery, hand-made yeasted and sourdough bread including
100% rye sourdough. Soil Association licence no. P5506.

ORGANIC EXPRESS LTD – CATERERS WHO CARE

17 ANSDELL RD, PECKHAM SE15 2DT
Tel: 020 7277 6147 Fax: 020 7277 6147 Contact: John Kavaliauskas
info@organic-express.co.uk www.organic-express.co.uk
Event Caterers. Organic Express–Caterers Who Care supply only accredited
organic catering for conferences, events and special occasions. We support
local producers and Fairtrade products whenever possible. Enjoy eating
your ethics.

ORGANIC TRADE LTD

PREMIER HOUSE, 325 STREATHAM HIGH ROAD, STREATHAM SW16 3NT
Tel: 020 8679 8226 Fax: 020 8679 8823 Contact: Raj Shah
rshah@organictrade.co.uk www.organictrade.co.uk
Import wholesalers of all organic edible nuts, dried fruits, pulses, seeds and
cereals. Delivery to all of UK.

PECKHAM FARMERS' MARKET
PECKHAM SQUARE, PECKHAM HIGH STREET SE15
Tel: 020 7704 9659 Contact: London Farmers' Markets
info@lfm.org.uk www.lfm.org.uk
Sundays 9.30am–1.30pm. Here farmers sell home-grown foods grown or
made within 100 miles of the M25, including fruit, veg, meat, dairy, eggs,
honey, juice, bread, preserves, plants. Note: some, but not all, producers
are organic. Run by London Farmers' Markets, PO Box 37363, London N1
7WB.

PIMLICO ROAD FARMERS' MARKET
ORANGE SQUARE, CORNER OF PIMLICO RD. AND EBURY STREET SW1
Tel: 020 7704 9659 Contact: Cheryl Cohen
cheryl@lfm.org.uk www.lfm.org.uk

PIZZA ORGANIC LTD
75 GLOUCESTER RD. SW7 4SS
Tel: 020 7370 6575 Contact: Mike Traszko
info@pizzapiazza.co.uk www.pizzapiazza.co.uk
Expanding range of Soil Association accredited restaurants featuring a
menu packed full of organic stonebaked pizza, sautéed pasta, gourmet
burgers, grilled fish and fabulous desserts to die for.

PIZZA ORGANIC LTD
20 OLD BROMPTON RD. SW7 3DL
Tel: 020 7589 9613 Contact: Mike Traszko
info@pizzapiazza.co.uk www.pizzapiazza.co.uk
Expanding range of Soil Association accredited restaurants featuring a
menu packed full of organic stonebaked pizza, sautéed pasta, gourmet
burgers, grilled fish and fabulous desserts to die for.

PLANET ORGANIC
25 EFFIE RD, FULHAM SW6
Contact: Renée J. Elliott
deliveries@planetorganic.com www.planetorganic.com
Planet Organic is about good food. We are the original one-stop organic and natural food supermarket with an in-house juice bar and freshly cooked organic food to go. We are the modern mecca for those seeking everything for a healthy lifestyle.

POTS FOR TOTS
UNIT WHE, WANDSWORTH BUSINESS VILLAGE, 3–9 BROOMHILL RD., WANDSWORTH SW18 4JQ
Tel: 0845 450 0875 Fax: 020 8870 4466 Contact: Jo Semple Piggot
info@potsfortots.co.uk www.potsfortots.co.uk
Pots For Tots is a 100% organic baby and toddler food producer. No salt, sugar or additives. Some are gluten-, milk- and lactose-free. You can order on-line, we deliver nationally and to homes and offices, and are at Borough Market on Saturdays.

PROVENDER
103 DARTMOUTH ROAD, FOREST HILL SE23 3HT
Tel: 020 8699 4046 Fax: 020 8699 4046 Contact: Ali Megahead
Wholefoods, organic bakers, café, healthy food, organic croissants and pastries, quiches, organic meals.

RAVENSBOURNE WINE
UNIT 602, BELL HOUSE, 49 GREENWICH HIGH RD. SE10 8JL
Tel: 020 8692 9655 Fax: 020 8692 9655 Contact: Terry Short (Director)
sales@ravensbournewine.co.uk
Wine merchant. Retail/wholesale, delivery and mail order of select range of organic wines and beers. Free delivery of mixed cases of wine and beers and Decantae bottled mineral water to London addresses.

RDA ORGANIC
PO BOX 31750 SW15 2YQ
Tel: 020 8875 4770 Fax: 020 8875 0370 Contact: Patrick O'Flaherty
juice@rdaorganic.com www.rdaorganic.com
RDA Organic is an awarding-winning range of fresh, pure, organic juices
and smoothies. The range consists of 7 delicious flavours, including the
UK's Best Organic Soft Drink (Organic Food Awards 2003).

REVITAL HEALTHPLACE
3A THE COLONNADES, 123–151 BUCKINGHAM PALACE RD SW1W 9SH
Tel: 020 7976 6615 Contact: The Manager
enqire@revital.com www.revital.com
Health shop, over 80% organic foods and cosmetics.

SCAN FOODS UK LTD
1A AMIES ST. SW11 2JL
Tel: 020 7228 4046 Fax: 020 7223 4534 Contact: Paul Aston
www.swedishkitchen.co.uk
Soil Association P6027. Supplier of Swedish organic meat and processed
products including organic Swedish meatballs.

TODAY'S LIVING
92 CLAPHAM HIGH STREET SW4 7UL
Tel: 020 7622 1772 Fax: 020 7720 2851 Contact: H Soor
Health food shop.

WELL BEAN
9 OLD DOVER ROAD, BLACKHEATH SE3 7BT
Tel: 020 8858 6854 Contact: Derek Rogers
Large range of organic foods, wholefoods, gluten-free, diabetic, dairy-free.
Nutritional advice, mail order, local deliveries. If we haven't got it, we'll get it!

WESTFALIA MARKETING (UK) LTD
MARKET TOWERS, 1 NINE ELMS LANE SW8 5NQ
Tel: 020 7720 8544 Fax: 020 7720 4209 Contact: Simon Curry
simon@westfaliauk.co.uk www.westfaliauk.co.uk
Soil Association registered. Importation of conventional and organic
avocados and mangos, primarily from parent company in South Africa, but
also other sources. Newly added Fairtrade ranges introduced.

WIMBLEDON PARK FARMERS' MARKET
WIMBLEDON PARK FIRST SCHOOL, HAVANA ROAD, WIMBLEDON SW19
Tel: 020 7704 9659 Contact: London Farmers' Markets
info@lfm.org.uk www.lfm.org.uk

WINDMILL ORGANICS LTD
UNIT 4, ATLAS TRANSPORT ESTATE, BRIDGES COURT SW11 3QS
Tel: 020 7294 2300 Fax: 020 7223 8370 Contact: Noel McDonald
sales@windmillorganics.fsnet.co.uk
Organic Food Federation registered. Production and distribution of organic
foods—dairy products, tofu, margarine, bakery goods, pasta, canned
pulses, juices etc. Main brand: Biona.

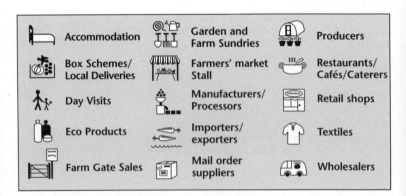

Accommodation	Garden and Farm Sundries	Producers
Box Schemes/ Local Deliveries	Farmers' market Stall	Restaurants/ Cafés/Caterers
Day Visits	Manufacturers/ Processors	Retail shops
Eco Products	Importers/ exporters	Textiles
Farm Gate Sales	Mail order suppliers	Wholesalers

AINSWORTHS HOMOEOPATHIC PHARMACY

36 NEW CAVENDISH ST. W1G 8UF
Tel: 020 7935 5330 Fax: 01883 344602 Contact: Tony Pinkus
ainsworth01@btconnect.com www.ainsworths.com
Homoeopathic remedies for prevention and treatment of all your livestock.
Books and courses on homoeopathy. All animals can be treated without
residues. Help and advice in implementing homoeopathic regimes on the
farm. Lectures and seminars by arrangement.

ALARA

58–60 MARCHMONT STREET WC1N 1AB
Tel: 020 7837 1172 Fax: 020 7833 8089 Contact: Xavier Kara
xavier@bio-terra.com
All organic products. Vitamins, beauty, fresh veg, fruit and dairy.

ANONA

THE HOGARTH CENTRE, HOGARTH LANE, CHISWICK W4 2QN
Tel: 020 8987 8337 Fax: 020 8747 0511 Contact: Richard Taylor
richard@anona.co.uk
Anona import organic fresh produce, including asparagus, Brussels sprouts,
blueberries, cherries and raspberries, supplying predominantly European
supermarkets and wholesale outlets. For more information contact
richard@anona.co.uk.

AUSTRALIS DISTRIBUTION LTD

12 TOWNSEND HOUSE, 22 DEAN ST. W1D 3RY
Tel: 0845 456 0639 Fax: 020 7504 8099 Contact: Lara Smith
lara@australisdistribution.com www.australisdistribution.com
We import Australian personal care products that are naturally based,
organic, free from harmful additives and free from harmful by-products in
manufacture.

BABYLICIOUS LTD

PO BOX 32265, EALING W5 1XP
Tel: 020 8231 8847 Fax: 020 8231 8841 Contact: Sally Preston
info@babylicious.co.uk www.babylicious.co.uk

At last there is a real alternative to jars or making babyfood yourself:
Babylicious. A brand new concept in frozen babyfood, promising your baby
delicious meals that are highly nutritious, ready to eat in seconds, and
virtually waste-free: it is sold in small frozen portions, so you use what
your baby wants, when they want. It is as good as home-made, without
the guilt.

BONTERRA VINEYARDS

REGENT ARCADE HOUSE, 19–25 ARGYLL ST. W1F 7TS
Tel: 020 7478 1300 Fax: 020 7287 4661 Contact: Kate Sweet
www.bonterra.com

Bonterra Vineyards are one of the world's leaders in organic viticulture
producing a range of premium wines from organically grown grapes.

BUSHWACKER WHOLEFOODS

132 KING STREET, HAMMERSMITH W6 0QU
Tel: 020 8748 2061 Contact: Chris Shipton (Partner)

Everything you would expect in a good wholefood shop, with the emphasis on organically grown products including fresh fruit and vegetables, free
range eggs and baby foods. We veto genetically modified foods. We pack
down organic foods. Soil Association no. R1566. We have been Soil
Association members since the early 1980s.

BUXTON FOODS LTD/STAMP COLLECTION/PETER RABBIT ORGANICS

12 HARLEY STREET W1G 9PG
Tel: 020 7637 5505 Fax: 020 7436 0979 Contact: Elizabeth Buxton
sales@buxtonfoods.com www.buxtonfoods.com

We produce the Stamp Collection range of award-winning organic, wheat-
free, dairy-free products including flour, confectionery, bread, sheep's cheeses.
Also Peter Rabbit Organics, an award-winning range of children's foods with
no added salt or sucrose, for age 12 months plus. Products include store cup-
board staples such as pasta, sauces and cereals as well as wholesome snacks.

CAVIPUK LTD
2 SHERATON ST., SOHO W1F 8BH
Tel: 0870 366 6145 Fax: 0870 140 0377 Contact: Peter Kattinis
cavipuk@cavipuk.co.uk www.cavipuk.co.uk
Cavipuk Ltd is a leading company in its field. Our product line ranges from basic T shirt, sweatshirt and polo shirt to fashionable sports wear and casual clothing. All of our organic cotton products are certified by Societé Generale de Surveillance SA, Geneva, Switzerland.

CLEARSPRING LTD
19A ACTON PARK ESTATE W3 7QE
Tel: 020 8749 1781 Fax: 020 8746 2259 Contact: Maria Furugori
info@clearspring.co.uk www.clearspring.co.uk
Soil Association P1474. Extensive range of organic and traditional whole-food products from around the world. Specialise in authentic Japanese foods. All vegan, free of added sugar and artificial additives. Mail order available.

COFFEE PLANT
180 PORTOBELLO ROAD W11 2EB
Tel: 020 7221 8137 Contact: Ian Henshall
coffee@pro-net.co.uk www.coffee.uk.com
Coffee roaster: supplies coffee, cocoa, tea, herb tea for retail, retail mail order, caterers and own label packs for retailers. Coffee can be beans or ground, 1kg or 250g packs. See display ad.

EALING FARMERS' MARKET
LEELAND RD, WEST EALING W13
Tel: 020 7704 9659 Contact: Cheryl Cohen
info@lfm.org.uk www.lfm.org.uk
Saturdays 9am to 1pm. Here farmers sell home-grown foods grown or made within 100 miles of the M25, including fruit, veg, meat, dairy, eggs, honey, juice, bread, preserves, plants. Note: some, but not all, producers are organic. Run by London Farmers' Markets, PO Box 37363, London N1 7WB.

FARM W5

19 THE GREEN, EALING W5 5DA
Tel: 020 8566 1965 Contact: Tom Beeston
tom@farmw5.co.uk www.farmw5.co.uk
Our organic and artisan food market supplies fresh, seasonal, locally
sourced food, produced properly and ethically. You will find organic and
artisan breads, cakes, vegetables, wines, meat and poultry, preserves, British
cheeses, hand-made chocolates and much more.

FRESH & WILD

210 WESTBOURNE GROVE W11 2RH
Tel: 020 7229 1063 Contact: The Manager
shop@freshandwild.com www.freshandwild.com
Organic Food Federation registered. Fresh & Wild are the leading specialist
retailer of organic foods and natural remedies, with six stores in London,
each offering organic juice bars and hot food deli. Customer careline: 0800
917 5175.

FRESH & WILD

69–75 BREWER ST., SOHO W1F 9US
Tel: 020 7434 3179 Contact: The Manager
shop@freshandwild.com www.freshandwild.com
Organic Food Federation registered. Fresh & Wild are the leading specialist
retailer of organic foods and natural remedies, with six stores in London,
each offering organic juice bars and hot food deli. Customer careline: 0800
917 5175.

FRESH & WILD (HEAD OFFICE)

208–210 WESTBOURNE GROVE W11 2RH
Tel: 020 7792 9020 Fax: 020 7792 1341 Contact: The Manager
shop@freshandwild.com www.freshandwild.com
Organic Food Federation registered. Fresh & Wild are the leading specialist
retailer of organic foods and natural remedies, with six stores in London,
each offering organic juice bars and hot food deli.

THE FRESH FOOD CO

THE ORCHARD, 50 WORMHOLT RD. W12 0LS
Tel: 020 8749 8778 / 07939 326616 Fax: 020 8749 5936
Contact: Thoby Young
organics@freshfood.co.uk www.freshfood.co.uk
The UK's longest established (1989) nationwide home delivery service of
fresh organic and wild harvested foods. We are special because our products
are grown, packed and shipped to our customers in the area where they are
produced. We give free advice to our customers and offer consultancy services to businesses. Free catalogue on request. Too many prizes to mention!

FRESH! ORGANICS

3 PRINCES STREET W1B 2LD
Tel: 020 7493 8727 Fax: 020 7493 8729 Contact: Chantelle Ludski
info@fresh-go-organic.com www.fresh-go-organic.com
The complete organic 'food to go' company: manufacturing, to wholesaling and retailing of sandwiches, salads, soups and so on. A truly organic
experience!

JENKIM UK LTD

48 BOSTON RD., HANWELL W7 3TR
Tel: 020 8840 8687 Fax: 020 8840 8687
Contact: Ron Salim & Jennifer Quay
jenkim@onetel.com www.agrologistic.com
Distributor and supplier of Agroneem organic insecticide emulsifiable
concentrate and Agroneem organic fertiliser. Product extracted from the
neem tree. Organic Material Review Institute (OMRI) listed and US EPA
approved.

LIDGATE, C

110 HOLLAND PARK AVENUE W11 4UA
Tel: 020 7727 8243 Fax: 020 7229 7160 Contact: David Lidgate
Organic beef and lamb from Highgrove, home of HRH Prince Charles.
Deliveries to City and West London daily. Eros award for Top Twenty
London food shops, National Pie Championships in 1993 & 1996, Utrecht
European Championship Gold Medal awards 1998, *Tatler* magazine Best
UK Butchers 1998/99.

LUPPOLO LTD
42 WESTBOURNE TERRACE WC2 6QE
Tel: 020 7262 4562 Fax: 020 7262 9078 Contact: Claudio Bincoletto
ccluppolo@netscapeonline.co.uk
Soil Association P6921. Importing products for the catering industry, day
walks on organic farms, cookery and dietetic courses. Teaching in Tuscany
on local wild herbs, expert on ECC 2092/91.

MARYLEBONE FARMERS' MARKET
CRAMER ST. CAR PARK, CORNER MOXTON ST.,
OFF MARYLEBONE HIGH ST. W1
Tel: 020 7704 9659 Contact: Cheryl Cohen
info@lfm.org.uk www.lfm.org.uk
Sundays 10am to 2pm. Here farmers sell home-grown foods grown or made
within 100 miles of the M25, including fruit, veg, meat, dairy, eggs, honey,
juice, bread, preserves, plants. Note: some, but not all, producers are organic. Run by London Farmers' Markets, PO Box 37363, London N1 7WB.

MILLER OF KENSINGTON
14 STRATFORD ROAD, KENSINGTON W8 6QD
Tel: 020 7937 1777 Contact: Mohamed El Banna
millerofkensington@email.com
Soil Association organic meat specialist; catering service up to 100 people.
Delicatessen and traiteur.

NEAL'S YARD BAKERY
6 NEALS YARD WC2H 9DP
Tel: 020 7836 5199 Fax: 020 7379 7291 Contact: John Loffler
nealsyardbakery@wwmail.co.uk www.nealsyardbakery.co.uk
Bakers of a wide range of organic breads, cakes and pastries. Everything is
baked on the premises, extensive variety of vegetarian savouries and sweets
to take away and to eat in upstairs café. Soil Association registered.

NEAL'S YARD REMEDIES

15 NEAL'S YARD, COVENT GARDEN WC2H 9DP
Tel: 020 7379 7222 Contact: Clare Madison
mail@nealsyardremedies.com www.nealsyardremedies.com
Soil Association certified products. Toiletries, herbs, aromatherapy products.

NEAL'S YARD REMEDIES

9 ELGIN CRESCENT W11 2JA
Tel: 020 7727 3998 Contact: The Manager
mail@nealsyardremedies.com www.nealsyardremedies.com
Neal's Yard Remedies manufactures and retails natural cosmetics in addition
to stocking an extensive range of herbs, essential oils, homoeopathic
remedies and reference material.

NOTTING HILL FARMERS' MARKET

CAR PARK BEHIND WATERSTONES, ACCESS VIA KENSINGTON PLACE W8
Tel: 020 7704 9659 Contact: London Farmers' Markets
info@lfm.org.uk www.lfm.org.uk
Saturdays 9am–1pm. Here farmers sell home-grown foods grown or made
within 100 miles of the M25, including fruit, veg, meat, dairy, eggs, honey,
juice, bread, preserves, plants. Note: some, but not all, producers are organic. Run by London Farmers' Markets, PO Box 37363, London N1 7WB.

PIZZA ORGANIC LTD

100 PITSHANGER LANE W5 1QX
Tel: 020 8998 6878 Contact: Mike Traszko
info@pizzapiazza.co.uk www.pizzapiazza.co.uk
Expanding range of Soil Association accredited restaurants featuring a
menu packed full of organic stonebaked pizza, sautéed pasta, gourmet
burgers, grilled fish and fabulous desserts to die for.

PLANET ORGANIC
42 WESTBOURNE GROVE W2 5SH
Tel: 020 7727 2227 Fax: 020 7221 1923 Contact: Renée J. Elliott
deliveries@planetorganic.com www.planetorganic.com
Planet Organic is about good food. We are the original one-stop organic
and natural food supermarket with an in-house juice bar and freshly
cooked organic food to go. We are the modern mecca for those seeking
everything for a healthy lifestyle.

PLANET ORGANIC
22 TORRINGTON PLACE WC1E 7HJ
Tel: 020 7436 1929 Fax: 020 7436 1992 Contact: Renée J Elliott
deliveries@planetorganic.com www.planetorganic.com
Planet Organic is the original one-stop organic and natural food
supermarket with Juice Bar, Food to Go and café. We have 9,000 products
in grocery, fruit & veg, meat & fish, and health & bodycare. We are the
modern mecca for those seeking everything for a healthy lifestyle.

PORTOBELLO WHOLEFOODS
266 PORTOBELLO ROAD W10 5TY
Tel: 020 8968 9133 Fax: 020 8960 1840 Contact: Kate Dafter
Portobello Wholefoods stocks an ever-increasing range of healthfood
products, including natural remedies, vitamins and minerals, organic
produce and gluten-free. Regular special offers and friendly service provides
everything you need in a healthfood shop, and more. Open 7 days a week.

THE RITZ
150 PICCADILLY W1J 9BR
Tel: 020 7493 8181 Fax: 020 7493 2687 Contact: Trevor Burke
tburke@theritzlondon.com
Restaurant.

THOROGOODS OF EALING
113 NORTHFIELDS AVE, EALING W13 9QR
Tel: 020 8567 0339 Fax: 020 8566 3033 Contact: Paul Thorogood
Beef, lamb, pork, chicken, turkeys, bacon, cooked ham. Local delivery.

ISLE OF MAN

MANN SPECIALITY FOODS
KERE-VOLLEY, CORDEMAN SAINT MARKS, BALLASALLA IM9 3AJ
Tel: 01624 851971 Fax: 01624 852418 Contact: Robin Ratcliffe
raratcliffe.honey@manxnet.com
Import and distribution of organic honey.

	Accommodation		Garden and Farm Sundries		Producers
	Box Schemes/ Local Deliveries		Farmers' market Stall		Restaurants/ Cafés/Caterers
	Day Visits		Manufacturers/ Processors		Retail shops
	Eco Products		Importers/ exporters		Textiles
	Farm Gate Sales		Mail order suppliers		Wholesalers

ANTONELLI BROTHERS LTD
THE BAKERY, WEYMOUTH RD., ECCLES M30 8FB
Tel: 0161 789 4485 Fax: 0161 789 5592 Contact: Mark Antonelli
info@antonelli.co.uk www.antonelli.co.uk
Soil Association P6011. The UK specialist maker of ice cream cones.
Organic sugar and Smoothy Waffle cones stocked. Other cones could be
made to order with eight weeks notice. Main stockists are Yeo Valley in
Devon (home of Rocombe Ice Cream) and September Dairy Ice Cream in
Herefordshire. Direct deliveries can be arranged.

CHORLTON WHOLEFOODS
64 BEECH RD., CHORLTON-CUM-HARDY, MANCHESTER M21 9EG
Tel: 0161 881 6399 Fax: 0161 881 6399 Contact: Annie Lazenby
Established in 1982, we sell organic fruit and veg, dairy produce, dried
goods, herbal supplements etc. Home delivery within Greater Manchester.
Practitioner visits and consultations.

CORNMELL, R.M. ORGANIC FOOD SPECIALIST
459 HALLIWELL RD., BOLTON BL1 8DE
Tel: 01204 846844 Contact: RM Cornmell
Meat products, poultry, cheese, eggs, bread, dry cured bacon and ham,
wholefoods. Open Mon, Tues, Weds half day. Thurs, Altrincham Farmers'
market 9am–4pm. Friday 9am–5pm, Saturday 9am–5pm.

ECO-INTERIORS OF CHORLTON
9 HAZEL COURT, DUDLEY RD., WHALLEY RANGE, MANCHESTER M16 8DS
Tel: 0161 861 8219 Contact: Simon Corble
scorble@yahoo.co.uk
Painters, decorators and floor sanders. We provide a high quality painting
and decorating service using only organic, solvent-free products from
recognised sources. We also sand floors and varnish and treat garden
fences/sheds.

The Organic Works

Are you:

An organic producer who:

- Wants to spend less time and money on paperwork and more time on organic production?
- Wants to add value to your organic product?
- Wants to reduce costs by improving the efficiency of your business?
- Wants to expand or diversify your business?

If the answer is yes we would like to meet you.

We are a friendly team of experts with many years experience in organic business management

Telephone: 01392 875678
email: mail@theorganicworks.co.uk

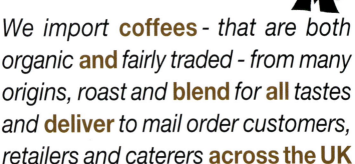

woottonorganic

food at its finest – direct to your table

The historic estate of Wootton in Staffordshire is preserved by the Bamford family as a model of excellence in organic farming. We care deeply about animal welfare and sustainability; our animals are reared in the passionate belief that our future must lie in finer food, reared with care. We have fully organic venison, lamb, Aberdeen Angus beef and poultry, and can offer retail and mail order to our customers.

Wootton Organic
Ramshorn Farley Oakamoor
Staffordshire ST10 3BZ
Telephone 0800 652 9469
Fax 01538 709900
mailorder@woottonorganic.com
www.woottonorganic.com

*daylesford*organic

FARMSHOP

ORGANIC: A BEAUTIFUL WAY TO SELL FOOD

AT DAYLESFORD, WE OFFER THE FRESHEST SEASONAL FOOD FROM OUR FULLY ORGANIC ESTATES, WITH A PASSIONATE COMMITMENT TO QUALITY. WE PRACTICE COMPASSIONATE FARMING AND SUSTAINABILITY: ORGANIC BEEF, LAMB, VENISON, AND POULTRY; HERITAGE VARIETY VEGETABLES, AND FRUITS; TOP AWARD-WINNING HANDMADE ORGANIC CHEESES; ORGANIC BREADS, PASTRIES...AND MUCH MORE. OUR STORE OFFERS CUSTOMERS AN EXCEPTIONAL RANGE OF FINE FOODS. DISCOVER THE TASTE OF THE FINEST FOOD FROM DAYLESFORD.

DAYLESFORD ORGANIC FARMSHOP DAYLESFORD NEAR KINGHAM
GLOUCESTERSHIRE GL56 0YG www.daylesfordorganic.com
TELEPHONE 01608 731 700 EMAIL enquiries@daylesfordfarmshop.com
TO AVOID DISAPPOINTMENT PLEASE CALL THE FARMSHOP TO CHECK OPENING HOURS

ORGANIC CIDER
Alc 6.5% Vol

Produced using organically grown cider apples and matured in old oak vats. Easy to drink with a ripe apple aroma and a well balanced taste

ORGANIC VINTAGE CIDER
Alc 7.3% Vol

Produced using organically grown cider apples from a single year's crop and matured in old oak vats. A full bodied, rich, well balanced cider

Tel:01531 660233
www.westons-cider.co.uk

Support the
Soil Association

The heart of organic food and farming > Keep food GM-free
> Ban the misuse of antibiotics in farming > Reduce pesticide residues
in food > Enhance animal welfare > Support wildlife. See the website
www.soilassociation.org/support or ☏ **0117 914 2447**. For just
£3 a month you get updates on our work plus...

Free book
The Truth About Food is a fascinating read revealing the
often hidden story about what we eat and how it is produced.

Regular magazine
Living Earth is our thought-provoking
magazine, with contributions from
Monty Don and Sophie Grigson.

Fridge magnet
If you give £5 a month or more
we'll also send you our new fridge
magnet (offer expires 1 April 2005).

Also available from Green Books . . .

GREEN HOLIDAY GUIDE
Great Britain & Ireland 2002/3

The European Centre for Ecological and Agricultural Tourism promotes sustainable tourism on organic farms and other small-scale, eco-friendly places to stay, many of them well off the beaten track. Includes 180 places to stay, many on working organic farms, offering a homely, informal atmosphere, tasty meals, and often farm trails and an abundance of animals both wild and domesticated. **Green Books/ECEAT 224pp in full colour 210 x 148mm ISBN 1 903998 08 5 £9.95 pb**

GREEN HOLIDAY GUIDE
Spain & Portugal 2002/3

ordering details overleaf

This companion publication gives details of 120 places to stay in Spain and 40 in Portugal: *Campsites:* 27 in Spain and 25 in Portugal; *B&B and guesthouses:* 73 in Spain in 20 in Portugal; *Self-catering cottages/apartments:* 59 in Spain and 20 in Portugal; *Hostels and group accommodation:* 6 in Spain. **Green Books/ECEAT 144pp in full colour 210 x 148mm ISBN 1 903998 15 8 £7.95 pb**

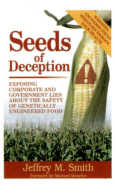

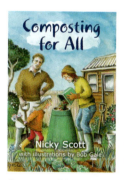

EIGHTH DAY

111 OXFORD RD., MANCHESTER M1 7DU
Tel: 0161 273 4878 Fax: 0161 273 4869 Contact: Tim Gausden
mail@eighth-day.co.uk www.eighth-day.co.uk
Vegetarian health food shop: over 1,000 organic lines including foods and
complementary remedies, vegetarian café and catering with some organic
food.

GLEBELANDS MARKET GARDEN LTD

c/o 24 ATHOL RD., WHALLEY RANGE M16 8QN
Tel: 0161 718 5328 Contact: Lesley Bryson
glebelands@ntlworld.com
Growers. Horticultural enterprise linked to Unicorn Grocery Ltd, local food
campaigning and educational work.

HEALTH & VEGETARIAN STORE

33 OLD CHURCH STREET, NEWTON HEATH, MANCHESTER M40 2JN
Tel: 0161 683 4456 Contact: Pamela Fynan
Herbal and homoeopathic remedies, all foods are vegetarian, chilled and
frozen. Large selection of organic foods and fruit and vegetables. Helpful
friendly advice, local deliveries.

LEES, JW & CO (BREWERS) LTD

GREENGATE BREWERY, MIDDLETON JUNCTION M24 2AX
Tel: 0161 643 2487 Fax: 0161 655 3731 Contact: CG Dennis
giles.dennis@jwlees.co.uk www.jwlees.co.uk
Soil Association P7505. Brewers.

LIMITED RESOURCES

UNIT 3, BROOK ST, HIGHER HILLGATE, STOCKPORT SK1 3HS
Tel: 0161 477 2040 Fax: 0161 226 3777 Contact: Barbara Eadie
info@limited-resources.co.uk www.limited-resources.co.uk
Soil Association R1738. Free delivery service: organic fruit, veg, dairy, meat,
fish, wholefoods, beers, wines, gardening and pet supplies, toiletries and
cleaning products. Also mail order: ring for details.

MARBLE BEERS LTD
73 ROCHDALE RD., MANCHESTER M4 4HY
Tel: 0161 819 2694 Contact: James Campell
Production of organic/vegan real ale, sold at outlets in the northern quarter, Deansgate and Chorlton-cum-Hardy. Products include Northern Quarter, Cloudy Marble, Manchester Bitter, Ginger Marble, Lagonda IPA.

MOSSLEY ORGANIC AND FINE FOODS
11–13 ARUNDEL STREET, MOSSLEY OL5 0NY
Tel: 01457 837743 Fax: 01457 837542 Contact: Pauline Proctor
shop@mossleyorganicandfinefoods.co.uk
www.mossleyorganicandfinefoods.co.uk
Huge range of natural food, many organic.Wide range fresh, quality organic fruit and vegetables available. Chilled, frozen, dairy produce, deli-counter. Many organic wines and beers. Specialist, individual friendly service. Fair Trade products supported. Soil Association member. Free delivery/box scheme.

NEAL'S YARD REMEDIES
29 JOHN DALTON ST., MANCHESTER M2 6DS
Tel: 0161 835 1713 Fax: 0161 835 9322 Contact: The Manager
mail@nealsyardremedies.com www.nealsyardremedies.com
Neal's Yard Remedies manufactures and retails natural cosmetics in addition to stocking an extensive range of herbs, essential oils, homoeopathic remedies and reference material.

ORGANIC 2000 LTD
UNIT B23, NEW SMITHFIELD MARKET, OPENSHAW M11 2WJ
Tel: 0161 223 4944 Fax: 0161 223 4955 Contact: Petra Dalton
O2thousand@tiscali.co.uk
Umbrella co-operative. Largest and longest established organic fruit and vegetable wholesaler in the north-west and beyond. We supply box schemes and retail outlets, sourcing extensively from local producers. We offer an extensive list of fruit, veg, dairy products and more, including imported goods. Fair Trade goods are supported. Deliveries available.

ORIGINAL ORGANICS

A18 NEW SMITHFIELD MARKET, GORTON, MANCHESTER M11 2WJ
Tel: 0161 220 7788 Fax: 0161 220 9906 Contact: Nev Dunn or Stuart
originalorganics@hotmail.com www.original-organics.co.uk
We work with local producers of fresh organic food and import when
necessary to generate a comprehensive list of fruit, veg, milk, cheese, eggs,
butter and sprouted seeds offered to shops, box schemes, caterers. Delivery
possible.

UNICORN GROCERY

89 ALBANY RD., CHORLTON, MANCHESTER M21 0BN
Tel: 0161 861 0010 Fax: 0161 861 7675 Contact: Kellie Bubble
office@unicorn-grocery.co.uk www.unicorn-grocery.co.uk
Soil Association GC5018, R2957. We are a large, friendly wholesome
foodstore specialising in fresh and organic produce. Over 2,000 good value
lines. We also cater for people with more specialised dietary needs.

Wisdom of the Cows and Pigs

*Bill Lashmett watched as two or three cows were let into a feeding area at a time. The first
trough they came to contained fifty pounds of shelled Bt maize. The cows sniffed it, withdrew
and walked over to the next trough, which contained fifty pounds of natural shelled maize.
The cows finished it off. When they were done and released from the pen, the next group
came in and did the same thing. Lashmett said the same experiment was conducted on
about six or seven farms in Northwest Iowa, in 1998 and again in 1999. Identical trials with
pigs yielded the same results, also for two years in a row.*

*Lashmett, who has a background in biochemistry and agriculture, says that animals have a
natural sense to eat what is good for them and avoid what isn't. He witnessed this first-hand
in another experiment conducted by a feed store in Walnut Grove, Iowa. They put twenty-
three separate vitamins and minerals, each in their own bin, out where cows could eat them.
The cows would alternate their choice of bins in such a way, according to Lashmett, that they
received a balanced, healthy diet. Moreover, their preferences changed with the seasons and
climate, demonstrating a natural inclination to follow the dictates of their bodies' needs.*

From *Seeds of Deception: Exposing Corporate and Government Lies about the Safety of
Genetically Engineered Food* by Jeffrey M. Smith, Green Books, £9.95

THE BILLINGTON FOOD GROUP LIMITED

CUNARD BUILDING, LIVERPOOL L3 1EL
Tel: 0151 243 9001 Fax: 0151 243 9011 Contact: Nick Eastwood
(Industrial Sales), Keith Scarlett (Export Sales)
bfg@billingtons.co.uk www.billingtons.co.uk
Billington's supplies a range of organic cane sugars to retail and
manufacturing sectors, both within UK and worldwide. All products are
certified by the Soil Association.

CHURCH FARM ORGANICS

CHURCH FARM, CHURCH LANE, THURSTASTON, WIRRAL CH61 0HW
Tel: 0151 648 7838 Fax: 0151 648 9644 Contact: Steve & Brenda Ledsham
sales@churchfarm.org.uk www.churchfarm.org.uk
Soil Association G5381 & R2617. Picturesque farm with beautiful views,
producing most vegetables for award-winning shop. 'Best Farm Shop'
Organic Food Awards 2001 and second in the Radio 4 Food and Farming
Awards 2004. Includes coffee bar. Bed and Breakfast Accommodation and
holiday cottage. Wide range of seasons and events—see website for details.

FORSTER ORGANIC MEATS

SHOOTS DELPH FARM, BIRCHLEY VIEW, MOSS BANK, ST. HELENS WA11 7NU
Tel: 01942 831058 Fax: 01942 831867 Contact: Anne or Chris Forster
j&jforster@farmline.com www.forsterorganicmeats.co.uk
We produce our own beef and lamb, sell and deliver locally fresh packs
labelled and ready for eating or freezing. Farmers' Markets at Liverpool 1st
and 3rd Saturdays every month and now Bootle. We have our own butchery on the farm (very close to Carr Mill off the East Lancs Road).
Customers are welcome to call by arrangement, or Thursdays when the
butchery is open until 6.00pm.

MOLYNEUX ORGANIC MEDICINAL AND AROMATIC PLANT FARM AND RESEARCH CENTRE

MILL HOUSE FARM, EAGER LANE, LYDIATE L31 4HS
Tel: 0151 526 0139 Fax: 0151 526 0139 Contact: David Molyneux
sales@phytobotanica.com www.phytobotanica.com
Producers of the first certified organic essential oils in the UK (lavender, peppermint, roman chamomile, german chamomile) and organic hydrosols. On-farm commercial hydrodistillation facilities, dispensary and conference centre for educational days (e.g. aromatherapy and holistic therapies).

ONLY NATURAL

48 WESTFIELD ST., ST. HELENS WA10 1QF
Tel: 01744 759797 Contact: B. Arrowsmith
Healthfood shop stocking a range of organic foods, but not fresh fruit and veg.

ORGANIC DIRECT

57 BLUNDELL ST., LIVERPOOL L1 0AJ
Tel: 0151 707 6949 Fax: 0151 707 6949 Contact: Ruth Weston
Fresh organic fruit and vegetables, weekly deliveries direct to your door from £6. Also vegan organic wholefood deliveries, many organic lines.

SEASONED PIONEERS LTD

UNIT 101, SUMMERS RD., BRUNSWICK BUSINESS PARK, LIVERPOOL L3 4BJ
Tel: 0151 709 9330 Fax: 0151 709 9330 Contact: Mark Steene
info@seasonedpioneers.co.uk www.seasonedpioneers.co.uk
Seasonings, over 50 organically certified. Spice blends: dry roasted to traditional recipes maximising flavour and ensuring genuine results in the kitchen.

WINDMILL WHOLEFOOD CO-OP
337 SMITHDOWN RD., LIVERPOOL L15 3JJ
Tel: 0151 734 1919 Contact: Brian Rider
windmill@windmill.abelgratis.co.uk www.merseyworld.com/windmill
Wide range of vegetarian and vegan organic wholefoods, fruit, vegetables, wines and beers. Ethical bodycare and cleaning products. Magazines and books. Soil Association Licensed (no. GCS018/R1736). Deliver to post code areas L1–L8, L11–L18, L20–L23.

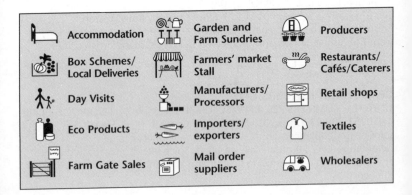

MIDDLESEX

BOMBAY HALWA LTD
23 MERRICK RD., SOUTHALL UB2 4AW
Tel: 020 8574 6275 Fax: 020 8813 8310 Contact: T Elyas
taibelyas@bombayhalwa.com www.
Soil Association P2936. Meat-free site for organic and conventional ready meals, snacks, chutneys, desserts and speciality ethnic foods; Indian, Asian, Mexican, Italian.

BRENT COUNCIL PARKS SERVICE
660 HARROW ROAD, WEMBLEY HA0 2HB
Tel: 020 8937 5619 Fax: 020 8903 3799 Contact: Leslie Williams
leslie.williams@brent.gov.uk
Organic hay: approximately 60 hectares available for harvest.

GAIA WHOLEFOODS
123 ST. MARGARET'S RD., TWICKENHAM TW1 2LH
Tel: 020 8892 2262 Contact: David Kennington
Soil Association R1562. Small, traditional, friendly, helpful wholefood shop. Wide organic range: fruit, vegetables, bread, eggs, chilled, macrobiotic, convenience, toiletries. Mon–Fri 9.30am–7pm, Sat 9.30am–5pm.

HORIZON FOOD LTD.
UNIT 21 & 25, REDBURN IND. ESTATE, WOODALL ROAD, ENFIELD EN3 4LE
Tel: 020 8443 3455 Fax: 020 8443 5040 Contact: Constantine Azar
cos@horizonfood.co.uk www.horizonfood.co.uk
Organic dried fruit including organic stuffed dried fruit. Packers for major distributors.

NATURE SECRETS
145A WEMBLEY PARK DRIVE, WEMBLEY HA9 8HQ
Tel: 020 8903 7517 Contact: Marco Kurek
uk@naturesecrets.com www.naturesecrets.com
100% certified organic virgin coconut oil. Retail, wholesale, mail order.

PIZZA ORGANIC LTD
3–5 HIGH ST., RUISLIP HA4 7AU
Tel: 01895 633567 Contact: Mike Traszko
info@pizzapiazza.co.uk www.pizzapiazza.co.uk
Expanding range of Soil Association accredited restaurants featuring a
menu packed full of organic stonebaked pizza, sautéed pasta, gourmet
burgers, grilled fish and fabulous desserts to die for.

REVITAL HEALTH CENTRE (HEAD OFFICE)
78 HIGH ST, RUISLIP HA4 7AA
Tel: 01895 629950 Fax: 01895 630869 Contact: The Directors
enquire@revital.com www.revital.com
Revital has everything you need for optimum nutrition and health care. We
are the largest independent health food retailer in the UK and offer a quick,
efficient mail order service.

TWICKENHAM FARMERS' MARKET
HOLLY ROAD CAR PARK, HOLLY ROAD, OFF KING STREET, TWICKENHAM TW1
Tel: 020 7704 9659 Contact: London Farmers' Markets
info@lfm.org.uk www.lfm.org.uk
Saturdays 9am–1pm. Here farmers sell home-grown foods grown or made
within 100 miles of the M25, including fruit, veg, meat, dairy, eggs, honey,
juice, bread, preserves, plants. Note: some, but not all, producers are
organic. Run by London Farmers' Markets, PO Box 37363, London N1
7WB.

NORFOLK

ABBEY FARM ORGANICS

ABBEY FARM, ABBEY RD, FLITCHAM, KING'S LYNN PE31 6BT
Tel: 01485 609094 Fax: 01485 609094 Contact: Edward Cross
xxflitcham@eidosnet.co.uk www.abbeyfarm.co.uk
Producers of fresh vegetables for box delivery scheme around north and
west Norfolk and local markets. Also organic fruit, wild bird seed, bird hide
and occasional farm walks.

ARTHUR'S ORGANIC DELIVERIES

2 NEW BARN COTTAGES, OLD BUCKENHAM, ATTLEBOROUGH NR17 1PF
Tel: 01953 887582 Contact: Tony & Donna Park
arthurs@limpets.freeserve.co.uk www.eostreorganics.co.uk
Box scheme, central southern Norfolk including Dereham, Watton,
Wymondham and Attleborough. Boxes provided by local co-operative
Eostre Organics. Also local organic apple juice, flour from Garboldisham
Windmill, monthly wholefoods.

ASH FARM ORGANICS

ASH FARM, STONE LANE, BINTREE, DEREHAM NR20 5NA
Tel: 01362 683228 Fax: 01362 683710 Contact: C. and W. van Beuningen
csvb@btinternet.com www.ashfarmorganics.co.uk
In our farm shop we sell pork, beef, poultry and vegetables (when available), all organically produced on our 370-acre family farm. We also sell
lamb and free range eggs, organically produced within Norfolk. We make
our own pork sausages, including a gluten-free variety and cure and oak-
smoke bacon and gammon. Our farmshop is open Fridays
10.30am–3.00pm and Saturdays 9.30am–12.00noon; any other time by
appointment. You can also find us each 2nd Saturday of the month on
Dereham farmers' market. (The first two weekends after Christmas we'll be
closed). We organise occasional farm tours.

AU NATUREL

GROVE FARM, HOLT RD., AYLMERTON, NORWICH NR11 8QA
Tel: 01263 837255 Contact: Nick Amis
nicksherryamis@yahoo.co.uk
PYO or delivered strawberries, raspberries, blackberries, eating/cooking apples and plums, plus soon to arrive: eggs.

BARKER ORGANICS

THE WALLED GARDEN, WOLTERTON HALL, NORWICH NR11 7LY
Tel: 01263 768966 Contact: David Barker
Biodynamic Agricultural Association (Demeter) 370. Historic walled garden, a real live working kitchen garden growing vegetables and fruit using bio-dynamic methods. Selling all produce direct to the local community via a box scheme.

BARRIER ANIMAL HEALTHCARE

36–37 HAVESCROFT IND. ESTATE, NEW RD., ATTLEBOROUGH NR17 1YE
Tel: 01953 456363 Fax: 01953 455594 Contact: Sandy Morris
sales@barrier-biotech.com www.footrot.co.uk
Soil Association I2656. Manufacturer of animal health products and agricultural healthcare products. Specialist manufacturers of high quality non-toxic, non-irritant healthcare products. Our effective range of agricultural products are designed for intensive farming and also Soil Association certified, and so suitable for organic farming systems. Call 01953 456363 or visit www.ragwort.com.

THE BOOJA BOOJA COMPANY

HOWE PITS, NORWICH RD., BROOKE NR15 1HJ
Tel: 01508 558888 Fax: 01508 557844 Contact: Colin Mace
Soil Association P4181. Manufacturers of organic dairy-free, vegetarian, vegan, wheat- and gluten-free chocolates.

CATTERMOLE QUALITY BUTCHERS, SIMON
KING ST., NEW BUCKENHAM, NR. NORWICH NR16 2AF
Tel: 01953 860264 Fax: 01953 860024 Contact: Sue Cattermole
simon@scatty.co.uk www.scatty.co.uk
Soil Association P6154. Butcher selling a large range of fresh organic meat
and poultry products. Beef, pork, lamb, chicken, own sausages and bacon
from our own smoke house.

CHOLMONDELEY ESTATES
THE ESTATE OFFICE, HOUGHTON, KING'S LYNN PE31 6UE
Tel: 01485 528167 Fax: 01485 528167 Contact: RJS Miller
organic@houghtonhall.com www.houghtonhall.com
Soil Association G5603. Organic arable, beef (Longhorn) and sheep
(Norfolk Horn and Southdown).

CRONE'S
FAIRVIEW, FERSFIELD RD., KENNINGHALL NR16 2DP
Tel: 01379 687687 Fax: 01379 688323 Contact: Robert Crone
info@crones.co.uk www.crones.co.uk
Soil Association P1587. Makers of a range of award-winning apple juices
and ciders. Also organic cider vinegar, apple cherry, pear and apple.
Contact us for our full range. Sales ex-gate by prior appointment.

DIANE'S PANTRY
8 MARKET PLACE, REEPHAM, NORWICH NR10 4JJ
Tel: 01603 871075 Contact: Diane Turner (Owner)
Wholefood, healthfoods, supplements and small bakery with coffee shop
attached. Organic bread baked to order.

DOMINI QUALITY FOODS
VILLAGE FARM, MARKET WESTON, DISS IP22 2NZ
Tel: 01359 221333 Fax: 01359 221835 Contact: Jane Capon
jcapon@dominifoods.fnset.co.uk
Small traditional farm selling top quality home-produced fare, dairy products (untreated milk, cream, butter) from the Domini Jersey herd, Aberdeen Angus beef, lamb, pork and chicken.

EOSTRE ORGANICS
WALNUT TREE FARM, BUNWELL ST., ATTLEBOROUGH NR16 1NA
Tel: 01953 789639 Fax: 01953 789000 Contact: Grahame Hughes & Dot Bain
info@eostreorganics.co.uk www.eostreorganics.co.uk
Mainly wholesale plus farmers' markets and packing for box schemes.

GARBOLDISHAM WINDMILL
DISS IP22 2RJ
Tel: 01953 681593 Contact: Adrian Colman
Soil Association P4546. Bread flours, oat products, gluten-free flours available from mill or through shops in Norfolk and Suffolk. Please telephone for details (may get answering machine).

GERMAIN'S TECHNOLOGY GROUP UK
HANSA RD., HARDWICK IND. ESTATE, KING'S LYNN PE30 4LG
Tel: 01553 774012 Fax: 01553 773145 Contact: Mark Butler
info@germains.com www.germains.com
Soil Association P7187. High performance seed technology products for organic use under the brand 'ProBio', including coatings, pellets, steeping, priming and non-chemical disinfection. Wide range of agricultural and horticultural seeds handled.

THE GREENHOUSE

42–46 BETHEL ST., NORWICH NR2 1NR
Tel: 01603 631007 Contact: The Coordinator
www.greenhousetrust.co.uk
The Greenhouse is an educational charity providing solutions to
environmental problems. The building houses an organic, vegetarian/vegan
licensed café and shop plus meeting rooms and herb garden. The shop
acts as a contact point for local veg box scheme and is stockist of a wide
range of organic and GMO-free foods. A resource centre offering meeting
space, offices and other facilities to local and regional voluntary groups.

HARVEYS PUREMEAT

63 GROVE RD., NORWICH NR1 3RL
Tel: 01603 621930 Fax: 01603 621908 Contact: Nigel Harvey
info@puremeat.org.uk www.puremeat.org.uk
Established in 1924, Harveys is Norwich's only certified (O.F.F.) organic
butcher and game dealer. Retail shop, wholesale supplies to restaurants,
hotels, etc. by arrangement. Local game including venison. See website.

THE HERBARY

CHURCH FARM, MIDDLE RD., SHOULDHAM THORPE, KING'S LYNN PE32 1TF
Tel: 01366 348175 Fax: 01366 348176 Contact: K Vallance
theherbary@btcponnect.com
Soil Association G6463. Salads, growers of organic leafy herb and speciality
salad crops.

J & C FARMS

ESTATE OFFICE, GAYTON HALL, KING'S LYNN PE32 1PL
Tel: 01553 636292 Fax: 01553 636292 Contact: The Manager
marshamgaytonhall@farming.co.uk
Arable farm producing cereals, potatoes, sugar beet with organic pig
enterprise managed by others.

KENT, JR
CHURCH BARN FARM, ARMINGHALL NR14 8SG
Tel: 01508 495574 Contact: JR Kent
Soil Association G1819. Farm gate sales of top fruit, roots and squash. PYO blackcurrants, broad beans and other produce—rabbits and pigeons permitting.

KETTLE FOODS LTD
BARNARD ROAD, BOWTHORPE, NORWICH NR5 9JB
Tel: 01603 744788 Fax: 01603 740375 Contact: Louisa Grant
info@kettlefoods.co.uk www.kettlefoods.co.uk
Soil Association P2662. Our all natural potato chips are made from selected organically grown potatoes, hand cooked in organic sunflower oil. Two seasonings are available: Lightly Salted, and Sea Salt with Crushed Black Peppercorns.

LETHERINGSETT WATER MILL
RIVERSIDE RD., LETHERINGSETT, HOLT NR25 7YD
Tel: Tel:01263 713153 Contact: Mike Thurlow
Water Mill (1798) restored to working order producing organic 100% wholewheat flour. Demeter BDAA member (no. 262). Working demonstrations when we make flour (varies between winter and summer). Mail order sales; deliveries to NR25 & all Norfolk.

THE METFIELD ORGANIC BAKERY LTD
THE STORES, THE STREET, METFIELD, HARLESTON IP20 0LB
Tel: 01379 586798 Fax: 01379 586798 Contact: Phil Smith
Soil Association R1531. Bakery. Producers of hand crafted organic bread, cakes and savouries.

MORTONS TRADITIONAL TASTE LTD
GROVE FARM, SWANTON ABBOTT, NORWICH NR10 5DL
Tel: 01692 538067 Fax: 01692 538478 Contact: Rob Morton
mortons@whitwellhall.co.uk www.mortonstraditionaltaste.co.uk
Specialist poultry producers supplying large processors.

NATIONWIDE FOOD PACKING LTD
13 NORWICH ROAD IND. ESTATE, WATTON, THETFORD IP25 6DR
Tel: 01953 885735 Contact: B Henderson
Soil Association P2619. Contract packers, bulk to retail. Mostly dry canning of bouillon gravy granules.

NATURAL FOODSTORE
NORFOLK HOUSE YARD, ST. NICHOLAS ST., DISS IP22 4LB
Tel: 01379 651832 Contact: M Meiracker
Soil Association R1547. Vegetarian wholefood shop concentrating on real organic foods. Local organic dairy, vegetables, bread and cakes. We stock a full range of dried organic wholefoods and have a well stocked deli counter.

NATURAL SURROUNDINGS
BAYFIELD ESTATE, HOLT NR25 7JN
Tel: 01263 711091 Fax: 01263 711091 Contact: Peter Loosley
loosley@farmersweekly.net www.naturalsurroundings.org.uk
Wildflower and countryside centre specialising in plants for the wildlife garden. Wildflower and herb nursery growing in peat-free, organic composts.

NEAL'S YARD REMEDIES
26 LOWER GOAT LANE, NORWICH NR2 1EL
Tel: 01603 766681 Contact: The Manager
mail@nealsyardremedies.com www.nealsyardremedies.com
Neal's Yard Remedies manufactures and retails natural cosmetics in addition to stocking an extensive range of herbs, essential oils, homoeopathic remedies and reference material.

NORFOLK ORGANIC GARDENERS
25 ST. MILDRED'S RD., NORWICH NR5 8RS
Tel: 01603 504468 Contact: Jan Hunt
info@norfolkorganic.org.uk www.norfolkorganic.org.uk
Local group of Soil Association and HDRA. We aim to promote the organic movement in Norfolk by increasing public awareness of organic methods of farming and gardening.

ORGANIC FARMING (CASTLE ACRE) LTD

MANOR FARM, CASTLE ACRE, KING'S LYNN PE32 2BJ
Tel: 01760 755380 Fax: 01760 755548 Contact: Catherine Sands
organicfarming@farmersweekly.net www.organicfarmingcastleacre.co.uk
Supplying the local public and restaurants with poultry, including chicken,
seasonal turkey and goose, also Aberdeen Angus beef, Poll Dorset and
Lleyn lamb. All produce direct from the farm. Vegetables available soon.

THE ORGANIC FEED COMPANY

NORFOLK MILL, SHIPDHAM, THETFORD IP25 7SD
Tel: 01362 822903 Fax: 01362 822910 Contact: Sophie Edwards
sales@organicfeed.co.uk www.organicfeed.co.uk
Soil Association registered. Organic feed for layers, poultry, pigs, sheep,
goats and cattle. Vegetarian Society Approved. Available nationally through
retail outlets in 20kg sacks.

ORGANICS-ON-LINE LTD

PARK HOUSE, GUNTHORPE HALL, MELTON CONSTABLE NR24 2PA
Tel: 0845 052 0777 Contact: Annette Ward (MD)
annette.ward@organics-on-line.com www.organics-on-line.com
Business to business internet trading site. Organics-on-line offers a large
range of organic products. The site acts as a means of facilitating trade
direct from the producer to the buyer and is targeting business to business
trade in organics.

PARADISE ORGANICS

64 GLENN RD., PORINGLAND, NORWICH NR14 7LU
Tel: 01508 494260 Contact: Debbie Paradise
deb@paradised.fsnet.co.uk www.paradiseorganics.co.uk
Member of Soil Association. Home delivery service of local (as much as
possible) organic vegetables, fruit and wholefoods.

PEARCE LTD, ALFRED G

GARAGE LANE IND. ESTATE, COMMON LANE, SETCHEY,
KING'S LYNN PE33 0BE
Tel: 01553 810456 Fax: 01553 811464 Contact: Simon Pearce
info@alfredgpearce.co.uk www.alfredgpearce.co.uk
Soil Association P5559. Suppliers of prepared and semi-prepared root
vegetables, and a selection of IQF vegetables to the manufacturing and
food service industry. We process products giving full traceability by using
dedicated growers to ensure the continuity of supply.

PLACE UK (R & JM PLACE LTD)

CHURCH FARM, TUNSTEAD NR12 8RQ
Tel: 01692 536225 Fax: 01692 536928 Contact: SF Shaw
admin@placeuk.com www.placeuk.com
Soil Association P1734. Growers and processors of soft fruit, vegetables,
beansprouts and carbohydrate products. Processing facility for IQF, bulk
freezing, rehydrated, blanching, puréeing, cutting and slicing.

RAINBOW WHOLEFOODS

OLD FIRE STATION STABLES, LABOUR IN VAIN YARD, NORWICH NR2 1JD
Tel: 01603 630484 Fax: 01603 664066 Contact: Richard Austin
info@rainbowwholefoods.co.uk www.rainbowwholefoods.co.uk
A sensational traditional wholefood shop with fresh organic vegetables,
fresh organic bread daily and 14 types of seaweed. All our goods are
guaranteed GM-free.

SALLE MOOR HALL FARM

SALLE MOOR HALL FARM, SALLE, REEPHAM, NORWICH NR10 4SB
Tel: 01603 879046 Fax: 01603 879047 Contact: Douglas Whitelaw
douglas@salleorganics.com www.salleorganics.com
Soil Association G1883. Soil Association registered organic farm selling
lamb, beef, eggs and vegetables direct to the door, through vegetable box
scheme and wholesale. Also self-catering cottage.

SAVORY EGGS, J

HIGHFIELD FARM, GREAT RYBURGH, FAKENHAM NR21 7AL
Tel: 01328 829249 Fax: 01328 829422 Contact: Elizabeth Savory
jegshighfield@onet.co.uk www.broadland.com/highfield
J. Savory Eggs laying flock, converting June 2000. Soil Association No
G2947. Speciality egg production. Mrs E. Savory, farmhouse B&B, member
FHB, Four Diamonds ETB.

STABLE ORGANICS

THE STABLES, GRESHAM, NORWICH NR11 8RW
Tel: 01263 577468 Contact: Anne Hood
Soil Association G1112. All vegetables and fruit freshly picked to order from
organic walled garden. Eggs. Caravan, cabin, in area of outstanding natural
beauty. Three miles from north Norfolk coast; nearest town is Sheringham.

STONEHOUSE ORGANIC FARM

STONEHOUSE FARM, WEST HARLING, NORWICH NR16 2SD
Tel: 01953 717258 Fax: 01953 717333 Contact: Richard Evans
stonehouse.farm@farming.co.uk
Organic farm producing cattle, sheep and pigs.

THECAFE AT WHALEBONE HOUSE

WHALEBONE HOUSE, HIGH STREET, CLEY NEXT THE SEA NR25 7RN
Tel: 01263 740336 Contact: Kalba Meadows
whalebone.house@virgin.net www.thecafe.org.uk
Unique, award-winning vegetarian restaurant with rooms. Modern British
seasonal cooking using home-grown and local organic produce; daily
changing menu; organic wine list. Open for dinner from Tuesday to Saturday
plus lunch on Sunday: booking essential. Two guest bedrooms for dinner-
based breaks of two or more nights. A green/climate-neutral restaurant.

THE TREEHOUSE
14–16 DOVE ST., NORWICH NR2 1DE
Tel: 01603 763258 Contact: Slogg
The Treehouse sells freshly made meals, salads and home-made cakes at lunchtimes and Thurs–Sat evenings. We use a wide range of ingredients from local suppliers where possible.

TRADITIONAL NORFOLK POULTRY
GARAGE FARM, HARGHAM ROAD, SHROPHAM NR17 1DS
Tel: 01953 498434 Fax: 01953 498962 Contact: Mark Gorton
enquiries@tnpltd.com
We are producers and processors of organic chicken and turkeys all year round. We are members of Organic Farmers and Growers, no. 31UKF120071.

WEBSTER, TWC
EDGE GREEN FARM, KENNINGHALL, NORWICH NR16 2DR
Tel: 01953 887724 Contact: TWC Webster
Soil Association G7018. Farming mixed arable and livestock, beef cattle, all cereals and pulses etc, sugar beet. All fully organic.

YETMAN'S
37 NORWICH RD., HOLT NR25 6SA
Tel: 01263 713320 Contact: The Manager
Restaurant using in-season local organic produce.

Missing Chickens
According to BBC News, April 27, 2002:

"Safety tests on genetically modified maize currently growing in Britain were flawed, it has emerged. The crop, T-25 GM maize, was tested in laboratory experiments on chickens. During the tests, twice as many chickens died when fed on T-25 GM maize, compared with those fed on conventional maize. This research was apparently overlooked when the crop was given marketing approval in 1996."

From *Seeds of Deception: Exposing Corporate and Government Lies about the Safety of Genetically Engineered Food* by Jeffrey M. Smith, Green Books, £9.95

NORTHAMPTONSHIRE

ALPRO UK
ALTENDIEZ WAY, LATIMER BUSINESS PARK, BURTON LATIMER NN15 5YT
Tel: 01536 720600 Fax: 01536 725793 Contact: Laura Colabuono
commercialuk@alpro.be www.alprosoya.co.uk
Europe's leading manufacturer of dairy-free alternatives to milk, cream,
yoghurt and desserts.

ARCADIA ORGANICS
MOORFIELD , WARKTON, KETTERING NN16 9XJ
Tel: 01536 525298 Fax: 01536 373609 Contact: Wayne Davis
enquiries@arcadiaorganics.co.uk www.arcadiaorganics.co.uk
Soil Association P7637. Retail farm shop—fresh fruit and veg, meats from
Graig Farm Organics, box scheme delivery locally (10 miles). Also
composts, grow bags, books, wines, beers etc. Opening times: Friday
10am–6pm, Saturday 9am–1pm.

DAILY BREAD CO-OPERATIVE LTD
THE OLD LAUNDRY, BEDFORD RD., NORTHAMPTON NN4 7AD
Tel: 01604 621531 Fax: 01604 603725 Contact: John Clarke
northampton@dailybread.co.uk www.dailybread.co.uk
Soil Association P1498. We retail wholefoods, with an increasing range of
organic flours, grains, nuts, fruits, etc. Also organic soya milk, fruit and
veg, yoghurts and cheeses.

GOODNESS FOODS
SOUTH MARCH, DAVENTRY NN11 4PH
Tel: 01327 706611 Fax: 01327 300436 Contact: Lesley Cutts
lesley.cutts@goodness.co.uk www.goodness.co.uk
Soil Association P1636. We carry a fantastic range of organic foods,
thousands of products including frozen and chilled foods. We deliver
throughout the the UK. Phone for details or look at our websites—trade:
www.goodness.co.uk, or retail: www.GoodnessDirect.co.uk.

GRANOVITA UK LTD

5 STANTON CLOSE, FINEDON RD. INDUSTRIAL ESTATE,
WELLINGBOROUGH NN8 4HN
Tel: 01933 273717 Fax: 01933 273729 Contact: Kate Percival
kate.percival@granovita.co.uk www.granovita.co.uk
GranoVita UK manufactures a wide range of vegetarian products, many of
which are organic. Our range includes the following organic products;
breakfast cereals, sauces, soya drinks, patés, desserts—and a great deal
more. Our organic certifying bodies are: QC&I, Organic Farmers &
Growers (UK2), and the Soil Assn (UK5).

LEAFCYCLES

24 ST MICHAELS AVENUE, NORTHAMPTON NN1 4JQ
Tel: 01604 628956 Contact: Jenny Vaughan
Fruit and veg supplied by Eden Farms. Fruit and vegetable boxes can be
collected from us (near town centre) or Daily Bread. Deliveries during day-
time, and evening to Abington only. Delivery areas NN1, NN2, NN3, NN4.

MARTLET NATURAL FOODS

10–14 MEADOW CLOSE, ISE VALLEY, WELLINGBOROUGH NN8 4BH
Tel: 01933 442022 Fax: 01933 440815 Contact: The Manager
Producers and suppliers of retail and bulk organic products. Preserves,
chutneys, cider and wine vinegars, honey, molasses, malt, sugar syrups,
mincemeat, sauces. Also seaweed extract, biostimulants and fertilisers. Soil
Association approved.

ONE (ORGANIC, NATURAL & ETHICAL) FOOD LTD

19 AUSTIN WAY, ROYAL OAK TRADING ESTATE, DAVENTRY NN11 5QY
Tel: 0870 871 1112 Fax: 0870 871 1113 Contact: Neil A Stansfield
info@onefood.co.uk www.onefood.co.uk
Marketer and producer of organic meat, poultry, dairy, fruit and vegetables.
Naturally reared fish and game, a broad range of wholefoods, grains and
pulses. All our growers benefit from our ethical trading policy.

ORGANIC TRAIL

18 DISWELL BROOKWAY, DEANSHANGER, MILTON KEYNES MK19 6GB
Tel: 01908 568952 Fax: 01908 568952 Contact: Jim Lawlor
jimlawlor@tiscali.co.uk www.organictrail.co.uk
Local delivery of English organic vegetables to your door (seasonal
produce): Milton Keynes, Towcester, Olney and surrounding villages.

PHOENIX FOODS

BRAKEY RD., CORBY NN17 5LU
Tel: 01536 200101 Fax: 01536 202218 Contact: C Wilding
sales@phoenixfoods.co.uk
Soil Association P3068. Manufacturer of dry powdered food stuffs: hot
chocolate, drinks, custard powder etc.

RUSSELLS OF EVENLEY

23 THE GREEN, EVENLEY, BRACKLEY NN13 5SQ
Tel: 01280 702452 Fax: 01280 840274 Contact: Nick Russell
nicks40@v21.me.uk www.evenley.net
Village delicatessen offers some organic lines. Organic bread daily, organic
produce occasionally. Other products available to order.

SAVE THE BACON

5 CASTLE ASBY RD., YARDLEY HASTINGS NN7 1EL
Tel: 01604 696859 Fax: 01604 696859 Contact: Douglas & Carol Austin
doug@savethebacon.com www.savethebacon.com
We source British organic foods: meat, poultry, fish, cheese and farmhouse
cooking. We take orders over the telephone and internet. Deliveries locally
(Northants, Milton Keynes, Beds) and nationally.

THE SONORA FOOD COMPANY LTD

STEPHENSON CLOSE, DRAYTON FIELDS IND. ESTATE, DAVENTRY NN11 5RF
Tel: 01327 705733 Fax: 01327 703592 Contact: Janet Marnewick
janetm@sonora.co.uk www.discoveryfoods.co.uk
Manufacturers of flour tortillas and corn chips to major high street retailers.

BURNLAW CENTRE

BURNLAW, WHITFIELD, HEXHAM NE47 8HF

Contact: Garry Villiers-Stuart

gvs38@hotmail.com

Smallholding, we also run retreats; courses in dance, painting, healing and mysticism and Baha'i wisdom. Good place for time out, come and stay, organic beef (very scrumptious!), fabulous setting and lots of (natural) enlightenment on tap!

CROPPED UP

DILSTON COLLEGE, CORBRIDGE NE45 5RJ

Tel: 07947 856641 Fax: 01434 633721 Contact: Sue Hick

Soil Association G4553. Organic fruit and veg box scheme operating June 1st to Christmas only. All produce except potatoes grown on-site. Local deliveries to Hexham, Haydon Bridge and Allendale.

THE GOOD LIFE SHOP

50 HIGH ST., WOOLER NE71 6BG

Tel: 01668 281700 Contact: Liz Girdwood

goodlife_wooler@hotmail.com

Ours is a family-run business specialising in local and continental cheeses, wholefoods, organic ranges. Herbs and spices are weighed to order.

THE GREEN SHOP

30 BRIDGE ST., BERWICK UPON TWEED TD15 1AQ

Tel: 01289 305566 Fax: 01289 305566 Contact: Ross & Pauline Boston

shop@thegreenshop.go-plus.net

Complete and only green shopping since 1993. Organic seeds, clothing, toiletries, alcohol. Nearly 2,000 prepacked foods, plus breads, chilled, frozen, fruit'n'veg & meat. 24 mile delivery. Fair trade too. A very warm welcome.

THE MARKET SHOP

48 BRIDGE STREET, BERWICK-UPON-TWEED TD15 1AQ
Tel: 01289 307749 Fax: 01289 307749 Contact: Jill Spence
Health food shop, wholefoods, herbs and spices.

MATFEN HOME FARM

C/O CLUTTONS, BLACKETT HOWE, MATFEN NE20 0RP
Tel: 01661 886888 Fax: 01661 886777 Contact: Jonathan Shepherd
Soil Association registered. Production of quality finished lamb and beef.

NOAH'S PLACE

31 MAIN ST, SPITTAL, BERWICK-UPON-TWEED TD15 1QY
Tel: 01289 332141 Contact: Humphrey & Nathalie Gudgeon
info@noahsplace.co.uk www.noahsplace.co.uk
Family run B&B and tearoom close to sandy beach, historic town of
Berwick-upon-Tweed, Holy Island, Scottish Borders. Organic food, natural
bedclothes. English, French, German spoken. Children welcome, bicycle
storage.

NORTH EAST ORGANIC GROWERS

EARTH BALANCE, WEST SLEEKBURN FARM, BOMARSUND,
BEDLINGTON NE22 7AD
Tel: 01670 821070 Fax: 01670 821026 Contact: Alasdair Wilson
neog@care4free.net www.neog.co.uk
Soil Association GCS015, P1779. NEOG Ltd, a workers co-operative, has
been running a box scheme since 1996 for vegetables, fruit and eggs
serving Tyneside and Northumberland and more recently Durham. We
grow a wide range of vegetables throughout the year including salads and
brassicas and source also from the increasing number of local organic
growers. We were Commended in the Organic Box Scheme of the Year
Awards 2003.

NORTHUMBRIAN QUALITY MEATS
MONKRIDGE HILL FARM, WEST WOODBURN, HEXHAM NE48 2TU
Tel: 01434 270184 Fax: 01434 270320 Contact: Steve Ramshaw
enqs@northumbrian-organic-meat.co.uk
www.northumbrian-organic-meat.co.uk
Distributor of organic beef, lamb and pork.

ROCK MIDSTEAD ORGANIC FARM
ROCK MIDSTEAD, ROCK, ALNWICK NE66 2TH
Tel: 01665 579225 Contact: Beth Sutherland
ian@rockmidstead.freeserve.co.uk

SMALES, LC & SON
THORNTON FARM, BERWICK-UPON-TWEED TD15 2LP
Tel: 01289 382223 Fax: 01289 382018 Contact: Jane Smales
janesmales@lcsmales-son.co.uk www.lcsmales-son.co.uk
Organic Farmers and Growers UKF040517. Produce, store and dry organic
cereals. Registered organic seed producer. Cater for all orders large and
small.

STAKEFORD NURSERIES
EAST VIEW, STAKEFORD NE62 5TR
Tel: 01670 855130 Fax: 01670 855130 Contact: Derek Easton
Soil Association G2080. Producer of organic vegetables, herbs and
tomatoes in modules and pots.

NOTTINGHAMSHIRE

FARMSHOP HOME DELIVERY
SHACKERDALE, FOSSE RD., CAR COLSTON, NR. BINGHAM NG13 8JB
Tel: 0800 169 7009 Fax: 01949 829124 Contact: David Rose
order@farmshop.net www.farmshop.net
Soil Association licence applied for. The complete home delivery service for
people living in the East Midlands.

HAYWOOD OAKS ORGANICS
HAYWOOD OAKS, BLIDWORTH, MANSFIELD NG21 0PE
Tel: 01623 795000 Fax: 01623 792268 Contact: Jamie Speed-Andrews
enquiries@haywoodoaks.com www.haywoodoaks.com
Soil Association G4551; P9058. Organic vegetable growers with nearly 500
acres of certified organic land. We aim to supply our produce locally where
possible. Suppliers to wholesalers, retailers, box schemes, packers. Washing
and packing facilities available. Delivery possible throughout the UK.

THE NATURAL FOOD CO
37 MANSFIELD ROAD, NOTTINGHAM NG1 3FB
Tel: 0115 955 9914 Fax: 0115 955 9914 Contact: Oren Harkavi
oren@naturalfoodcompany.net
We are a well stocked wholefoods shop, organic lines expanding all the
time: cereals, honeys, pulses, grains, condiments, teas, coffee, chocolate,
baby foods, etc.

THE NATURAL FOOD CO
31 LONG ACRE, BINGHAM NG13 8AF
Tel: 01949 876483 Fax: 01949 876483 Contact: Oren Harkavi
oren@naturalfoodcompany.net
We are a well stocked wholefoods shop, organic lines expanding all the
time: cereals, honeys, pulses, grains, condiments, teas, coffee, chocolate,
baby foods, etc.

NOTTINGHAM CITY COUNCIL

GREEN'S MILL & SCIENCE CENTRE, WINDMILL LANE, SNEINTON,
NOTTINGHAM NG2 4QB
Tel: 0115 915 6878 Fax: 0115 915 6875 Contact: David Bent
enquiries@greensmill.org.uk www.greensmill.org.uk
Soil Association P4518. Museum: a working tower windmill built in 1807,
once operated by the mathematician George Green (1793–1841) Now
producing organic stoneground flours, including Organic Food
Award-winning wholemeal and white spelt flour.

ONIONS (FARMS), PJ

SHELTON LODGE, NR. NEWARK NG23 5JJ
Tel: 01949 850268 Fax: 01949 850714 Contact: Peter Onions
Organic cereal and pulse storage, drying and cleaning. TASCC registered.
Food standards bagging line available to bag out of bulk storage.

OUT OF THIS WORLD

VILLA ST., BEESTON, NOTTINGHAM NG9 2NY
Tel: 0115 943 1311 Contact: Nigel Clifton
info@ootw.co.uk www.outofthisworld.coop
Small chain of ethical and organic supermarkets in Newcastle-upon-Tyne
and Nottingham. Selling over 4,000 products, most food products certified
organic, plus fairly traded crafts, recycled paper and bodycare products etc.
Consumer co-op with over 17,500 members.

ROOTS NATURAL FOODS

526 MANSFIELD RD., SHERWOOD, NOTTINGHAM NG5 2FR
Tel: 0115 960 9014 Contact: Ken Dyke
Pure vegetarian, organic retailer, box scheme and delivery service.

ROSEMARY'S HEALTH FOODS

6 LINCOLN STREET, NOTTINGHAM NG1 3DJ
Tel: 0115 950 5072 Fax: 0115 950 5072
Contact: Tracey Marshall (Manageress)
enquiries@rosemaryshealthfoods.co.uk www.rosemaryshealthfoods.co.uk
We sell an extensive range of organic healthy, dried, fresh, chilled, frozen
foods and herbal remedies.

SHOULS, DI

BARN FARM COTTAGE, KNEETON ROAD, EAST BRIDGFORD NG13 8PJ
Tel: 01949 20196 Contact: Di Shouls
B&B £20 per person per night. A warm welcome awaits you here in this
delightful cottage overlooking the Trent Valley. Three large bedrooms, two
sitting rooms, two bathrooms, garden, good off-road parking. Soil
Association member of long standing.

TRINITY FARM

AWSWORTH LANE, COSSALL NG16 2RZ
Tel: 0115 944 2545 Fax: 0115 944 2545 Contact: LR Winter
orders@trinityfarm.co.uk www.trinityfarm.co.uk
Meat, veg, salad, fruit. Farm shop with full range of dairy and dried goods
including nursery stock.

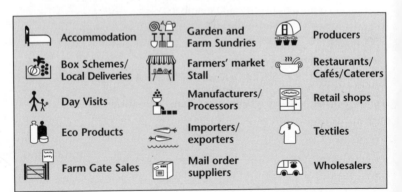

Accommodation	Garden and Farm Sundries	Producers
Box Schemes/ Local Deliveries	Farmers' market Stall	Restaurants/ Cafés/Caterers
Day Visits	Manufacturers/ Processors	Retail shops
Eco Products	Importers/ exporters	Textiles
Farm Gate Sales	Mail order suppliers	Wholesalers

OXFORDSHIRE

BEANBAG NATURAL HEALTH
2 WESLEY WALK, WITNEY OX28 6ZJ
Tel: 01993 773922 Fax: 01993 708689 Contact: John Bright
john@beanbag-health.co.uk www.beanbag-health.co.uk
Vegetarian health food shop with over 250 organic products. Meat-free, dairy-free, gluten-free, wheat-free. Pick-up point for Coleshill Organics box scheme.

BRITISH BAKELS
GRANVILLE WAY, OFF LAUNTON RD., BICESTER OX26 4JT
Tel: 01869 247098 Fax: 01869 242979 Contact: PJ Hemson
phemson@bakels.com www.bakels.com
Ingredient supplier. Manufacturers of organic cake mixes, scone mixes, muffin mixes, bread improvers, crumb softeners and baking powders. National distribution.

CHIPPING NORTON ORGANICS
UNIT 11, ELMSFIELD INDUSTRIAL ESTATE, CHIPPING NORTON OX7 5XL
Tel: 01608 642973 Fax: 01608 642973 Contact: Serena Howard
sales@chippingnortonorganics.co.uk www.chippingnortonorganics.co.uk
Soil Association registered no. R1816. Wide range of local, UK and imported veg and fruit. Boxes made up to suit individual requirements. Also bread, eggs, milk, all organic. Weekly deliveries within 15 mile radius of Chipping Norton.

COTSWOLD HONEY LTD
AVENUE 3, STATION LANE, WITNEY OX28 4HZ
Tel: 01993 703294 Fax: 01993 774227 Contact: N Dixon
neil@cotswoldhoney.co.uk www.cotswoldhoney.co.uk
Processor and bottler of organic honey for retail and industrial use.

ELLIOTT, R & S
RECTORY CLOSE &, BOW FARMS, c/o 21–23 HIGH ST.,
STANFOLD IN THE VALE SN7 8LH
Tel: 01367 710595 Fax: 01367710640 Contact: Robert Elliott
relliott@btconnect.com
Soil Association G4141. Old Gloucester (rare breed) herd; organic
certification; breeding and fattening/finishing stock available periodically.
Please ring to discuss.

M. FELLER, SON & DAUGHTER
54/55 COVERED MARKET, OXFORD OX1 3DY
Tel: 01865 251164 Fax: 01865 200553 Contact: Mitzi Feller
www.mfeller.co.uk
Soil Association P4455. Family organic butcher shop. Local delivery service
available.

FINE LADY BAKERIES LTD
SOUTHAM ROAD, BANBURY OX16 7RR
Tel: 01295 227600 Fax: 01295 271430 Contact: David Howlett
info@finelady.co.uk
Fine Lady Bakeries Ltd produce a range of organic bread and rolls for both
the retail and sandwich making industries. Soil Association licence no.
P1543.

FRUGAL FOOD
17 WEST SAINT HELEN STREET, ABINGDON OX14 5BL
Tel: 01235 522239 Contact: Val Stoner
Wholefood grocer specialising in organics, special diets (i.e. gluten-free/
vegan), wines, cheese, supplements, cleansing products and much more,
with friendly knowledgeable staff.

GLUTTONS DELICATESSEN
110 WALTON STREET, OXFORD OX2 6AJ
Tel: 01865 553748 Contact: Adrian Tennissen
Friendly family-run delicatessen specialising in excellent home-cooked foods. Comprehensive range of local and organic produce, large selection of organic wines.

IVY COTTAGE CAMPING
SULGRAVE ROAD, CULWORTH, BANBURY OX17 2AP
Tel: 01295 768131 Contact: J McKenzie (Proprietor)
Seasonal organic fruit and veg, free range eggs, geese, ducks, chickens, cats. Many attractions nearby, easy distance to Oxford, Stratford and Warwick. Garden flat for minimum of 6 monthly let. Camping field available: £6 per tent per night plus £1 per person.

MATTHEWS LTD, FWP – THE COTSWOLD FLOUR MILLERS
STATION RD., SHIPTON UNDER WYCHWOOD, CHIPPING NORTON OX7 6BH
Tel: 01993 830342 Fax: 01993 831615 Contact: Joy McCarthy
sales@fwpmatthews.co.uk www.fwpmatthews.co.uk
Soil Association P1521. Flour millers. An independent, family-owned flour mill. Producing high quality organic flours, supplying all markets from the home breadmaker to bakers shops to large food production companies.

MEAT MATTERS
BLANDYS FARMHOUSE, LETCOMBE REGIS, WANTAGE OX12 9LJ
Tel: 01235 762461 Fax: 01235 772526 Contact: Diane Glass
diane@meatmatters.uk.com www.meatmatters.uk.com
Meat Matters delivers fresh organic meat, poultry, eggs, fruit, vegetables and groceries as well as fresh fish direct to your door with no delivery charge throughout the UK. Call Freephone 08080 067426 for a catalogue.

MUTCHMEATS LTD
NEWCLOSE LANE, WITNEY OX29 7GX
Tel: 01993 772972 Fax: 01993 776239 Contact: Andrew Mutch
Abattoir. Private kill facility.

NEAL'S YARD REMEDIES
56 HIGH ST., OXFORD OX1 4AS
Tel: 01865 245436 Fax: 01865 245436 Contact: Mark Higgins
mark.higgins@lineone.net www.nelsyardremedies.com
Supplier of organic natural medicines and natural cosmetics.

NEW SEASONS
THE OLD POST OFFICE, LOCKINGE, WANTAGE OX12 8QD
Tel: 01235 821110 Fax: 01235 834294 Contact: John Breakspear
jb@newseasons.co.uk www.newseasons.co.uk
Essential oils, vegetable oils, flower waters, massage oils, bath oils, bath
milk, bath salts, face & body spritzers, room sprays, creams and lotions.

NORTH ASTON ORGANICS
3 SOMERTON RD., NORTH ASTON OX25 6HP
Tel: 01869 347702 Contact: Mark Stay
We grow and supply a wide range of seasonal vegetables and herbs to
surrounding villages and Oxford city. Also Deddington market, 4th
Saturday each month and Wolvercote Farmers' Market every other Sunday.

PICKLES
8 UPPER HIGH ST., THAME OX9 3ER
Tel: 01844 212056 Contact: Heather Brown
www.picklesdeli.co.uk
Delicatessen specialising in fine food, with café area and special diet
products.

RED KITE FARMS
SOUTHEND FARM, TURVILLE HEATH, HENLEY ON THAMES RG9 6JR
Tel: 01491 638155 Fax: 01491 638633 Contact: Clare Pool
clare@redkitefarms.com www.redkitefarms.com
Mixed organic farm with 400 dairy cows and 1,650 acres. Small on-farm
milk processing unit.

ROWSE HONEY LTD

MORETON AVENUE, WALLINGFORD OX10 9DE
Tel: 01491 827400 Fax: 01491 827434 Contact: Stuart Bailey (MD)
rowse.honey@rowsehoney.co.uk www.rowsehoney.co.uk
Importer and processor of organic honey from Argentina, New Zealand,
Australia, Mexico, Turkey and Brazil. Also importer and processor of organic
pure Canadian maple syrup. Soil Association no. P2375.

SARSDEN ORGANICS

WALLED GARDEN, SARSDEN ESTATE, CHIPPING NORTON OX7 6PW
Tel: 01608 659670 Fax: 01608 659670 Contact: Rachel Siegfried
sarsdenorganics@btopenworld.com
Two-acre walled garden producing a variety of vegetables and fruit for sale
locally on regular farmers' market in Oxford. Veg box including fruit, herbs
and flowers for collection from the walled garden one day a week (Friday)
by pre-arranged order form.

SAUNDERS, M

STEP FARM, LECHLADE ROAD, FARINGDON SN7 8BH
Tel: 01367 240558 Fax: 01367 244324 Contact: Miles Saunders
miles@stepfarm.fsnet.co.uk
Sell organic lamb, beef. Jointed and frozen. Opening times by arrangement.

TOLHURST ORGANIC PRODUCE

WEST LODGE, HARDWICK, WHITCHURCH-ON-THAMES, PANGBOURNE,
READING RG8 7RA
Tel: 0118 984 3428 Fax: 0118 984 3428 Contact: Iain Tolhurst
tolhurstorganic@yahoo.co.uk
Organic growers since 1976. Box scheme deliveries to Reading and Oxford
drop-off points. We produce over 90% of the vegetables that we sell.
Organic fruit also available. Alternative phone/fax: 01865 556151.

UHURU WHOLEFOODS
48 COWLEY ROAD, OXFORD OX4 1HZ
Tel: 01865 248249 Contact: Annette Mngxitama
Specialise in the sale of organic wholefoods, macrobiotics and gluten-free foods. Organic fruit and vegetables (local where possible) and local box scheme. Monthly local home deliveries.

Wisdom of Squirrels

For years, a retired Iowa farmer fed squirrels on his farm through the winter months by placing corncobs on feeders. One year, just for the heck of it, he decided to see if the squirrels had a preference for Bt maize or natural maize. He put natural maize in one feeder and Bt maize in another about twenty feet away. The squirrels ate all the maize off the natural cobs but didn't touch the Bt. The farmer dutifully refilled the feeder with more natural maize and sure enough, it was soon gone. The Bt, however, remained untouched.

The retired farmer got curious. What if the Bt variety was the squirrels' only choice? To find out, he didn't refill the natural maize. At the time, Iowa was plunged into the coldest days of winter. But day after day, the Bt cob remained intact. The squirrels went elsewhere for their food. After about ten days, the squirrels ate about an inch off the tip of an ear, but that's all. The farmer felt sorry for the squirrels and put natural maize back into the feeders, which the squirrels once again consumed.

From *Seeds of Deception: Exposing Corporate and Government Lies about the Safety of Genetically Engineered Food* by Jeffrey M. Smith, Green Books, £9.95

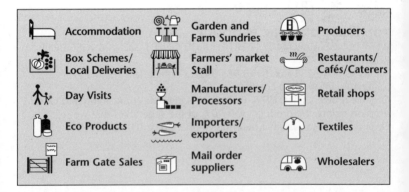

SHROPSHIRE

BEAFRESH LTD
UNIT 2C, ARCHERS WAY, KNIGHTS WAY, BATTLEFIELD ENTERPRISE PARK,
SHREWSBURY SY1 3AB
Tel: 01743 233011 Fax: 01743 233011 Contact: L Beaman
Vegetable processors. Specialists in preparing vegetables for the catering
trade.

BELTON CHEESE CO LTD
BELTON, WHITCHURCH SY13 1JD
Tel: 01948 662125 Fax: 01948 662269 Contact: Brian Gresty
info@beltoncheese.co.uk www.beltoncheese.co.uk
Soil Association registered. Manufacturer of organic cheese, Cheddar and
English Territorials.

BOXFRESH ORGANICS DIRECT
UNIT 5A RODENHURST BUSINESS PARK, RODINGTON,
NR. SHREWSBURY SY4 4QU
Tel: 01952 770006 Contact: Des Walker & Debra Reece
box.fresh@virgin.net
We provide a home delivery service of organic fruit, veg, eggs & apple
juice throughout Shropshire. Also adding meat and diary products in
summer 2004. The accent is on locally grown produce with excellent and
reliable customer service.

BROAD BEAN
60 BROAD STREET, LUDLOW SY8 1NH
Tel: 01584 874239 Contact: Maxwell Miller
Retailers of organic wines, dairy produce, meat, wholefoods and fine foods,
plus essential oils, vitamins, supplements, relaxation tapes, Brita water
filters and cartridges. Collection point for local vegetable box scheme.

THE CHICKEN CAME FIRST

LYNTON MEAD, OUTWOODS, NEWPORT TF10 9EB
Tel: 01952 691418 Contact: Clare Draper
clareword@btconnect.com
Soil Association G7745. Cruelty-free eggs from happy hens. Mixed colours
(chocolate brown, white green and blue shells). One-day workshops on
keeping chickens at home. As seen on Rick Stein's Food Heroes.

CORVEDALE ORGANIC LAMB

CORVE HOUSE, ROWE LANE, STANTON LANE, MUCH WENLOCK SY
Tel: 01746 712539 Fax: 01746 712539 Contact: Paul Mantle
mantlepaul@hotmail.com
Soil Association G4606. Organic lamb direct from farm to customer,
traditional English breeds, traditional taste, no order too small, free delivery
in South Shropshire area.

COW HALL ORGANIC PRODUCE

BETTWS Y CRWYN, CLUN, CRAVEN ARMS SY7 8PG
Tel: 01588 640307 Contact: The Manager
Soil Association producer no. G4116: organic Hereford beef, Clun Forest
and Kerry Hill lamb, and organic seed and eating potatoes. Outlet at
Myriad Organics (see below).

DOGGART, A

THE POPLARS, GWERN-Y-BRENIN, OSWESTRY SY10 8AR
Tel: 01691 652166 Fax: 01691 652166 Contact: A Doggart
Limited box scheme. I supply mainly to local wholefood shop, Honeysuckle
in Church Street, Oswestry, and also other fruit and vegetable outlets in the
area, including Llanfyllin.

EARTHWORM HOUSING CO-OP LTD

WHEATSTONE, LEINTWARDINE SY7 0LH
Tel: 01547 540461 Contact: Hil Mason
Suppliers of willow for basket making, hurdles etc, venue for low cost hire
for camps, courses, meetings. Demonstration wetland system and organ-
ic/veganic gardens. WWOOF host farm.

ELLESMERE ROAD ORGANIC NURSERY

ELLESMERE ROAD ORGANIC NURSERY, COCKSHUTT, ELLESMERE SY12 9AB
Tel: 01939 270270 Contact: RD Anderson
Soil Association G1447. All produce grown on our nursery, vegetables,
salads and fruit fresh picked, also PYO fruit.

FOOD FOR THOUGHT

UNIT 3 HEATH HILL INDUSTRIAL ESTATE, DAWLEY, TELFORD TF4 2RH
Tel: 01952 630145 Fax: 01952 630145 Contact: Alastair Dargue
info@liveorganic.com www.liveorganic.com
Soil Association R2086. Organic food retailers and home delivery service.

GET REAL (ORGANIC FOODS) LTD

SHOTTON FARM, SHOTTON LANE, HARMER HILL, SHREWSBURY SY4 3DN
Tel: 01939 210925 Fax: 01939 210925 Contact: Sue Gwilliam
info@get-real.co.uk www.get-real.co.uk
Soil Association P2616. Britain's leading organic pie makers. Award-winning
frozen pies. Vegetarian specialities: Ambledown, sutaki and masala-raj.
Suppliers to UK's major retailers, independent and health food stores.

GREENVALE AP LTD

WARRANT RD., STOKE HEATH, MARKET DRAYTON TF9 2JJ
Tel: 01630 637444 Fax: 01630 638939 Contact: Craig Sankey
post@greenvale.co.uk www.greenvale.co.uk
Package and trade organic potatoes and make organic dehydrated potato
flake, sell organic potato seed.

GROCONTINENTAL LTD

WHITCHURCH BUSINESS PARK, SHAKESPEAR WAY, WHITCHURCH SY13 1JL
Tel: 01948 666600 Contact: Hugh Jones
hughjones@grocontinental.co.uk www.grocontinental.co.uk
Ingredients and fruit sorting. Multi-temperature storage and distribution
with associated added value services; ingredient sorting; blast freezing and
re-packing.

GUNTON, JOHN & JACKIE
GREEN GORSE WOOD, WHITCHURCH RD, PREES SY13 3JZ
Tel: 01948 841376 Contact: John & Jackie Gunton
We grow organically and by hand, a wide range of vegetables and some
fruit which we pick fresh and sell exclusively at Whitchurch (Shropshire)
traditional Friday Market throughout the year.

HARVEST WHOLEFOODS
LYDHAM, BISHOPS CASTLE SY9 5HB
Tel: 01588 638990 Contact: Susan Jones
Large range of wholefoods, organic and GM-free products, fresh fruit and
vegetables, chilled and frozen foods, herbs, natural remedies, books,
gardening supplies, crystals, special dietary foods. Bulk discounts available.

HONEYSUCKLE WHOLEFOOD CO-OPERATIVE LTD
53 CHURCH ST., OSWESTRY SY11 2SZ
Tel: 01691 653125 Contact: Barbara Farr
hwcl@madasafish.com
Soil Association P5639. Established in 1978, we sell a large range of
organic fresh vegetables and fruit, locally grown when available. Also a
wide selection of organic wholefoods and dairy products, local bread, eggs
and honey.

HOPE ORGANIC PRODUCE
HOPE HOUSE, SANDY LANE, STOKE HEATH, MARKET DRAYTON TF9 2LG
Tel: 01630 638348 Contact: Pete & Sue Bartram
pete@hopeorganicproduce.co.uk www.hopeorganicproduce.co.uk
Soil Association B42M. Herb plants, seasonal vegetables sold in local
shops/garden centres and farmers' markets.

HOPESAY GLEBE FARM

HOPESAY, CRAVEN ARMS SY7 8HD
Tel: 01588 660737 Contact: Nicky & Phil Moore
phil.moore@hopesay.freeserve.co.uk
Soil Association symbol since 1996 and Biodynamic Agricultural Association
Demeter certification (no. 356) since 2001. Organic vegetable production,
organic free range eggs and Shropshire Hills Honey. B&B and self-catering
accommodation.

LONG MOUNTAIN DAIRY

THE HOLE FARM, ASTON PIGOTT, WESTBURY SY5 9HH
Tel: 01743 891231 Contact: Holly Middleton
holly@theholefarm.freeserve.co.uk
Organic dairy producer/processor. Main produce: milk, cheese, yoghurt,
veal, beef, locally available through market stall.

MYRIAD ORGANICS

22 CORVE STREET, LUDLOW SY8 1DA
Tel: 01584 872665 Fax: 01584 879356 Contact: Jane Straker
Soil Association R5414. One-stop organic food shop: all you need for a
family shop plus clothing, seeds, books. Near Ludlow Station, customer
parking. Friendly, well informed staff.

ORGANIC BY ORDER

BENTLEY HOUSE, CLUNGUNFORD, CRAVEN ARMS SY7 0PN
Tel: 01588 660747 Fax: 01588 660126 Contact: G Lambert
enquiries@organicbyorder.co.uk www.organicbyorder.co.uk
Soil Association GCS012, G1915, P1916. Organic vegetables and fruit
delivered throughout Shropshire, north Herefordshire and west
Staffordshire.

THE ORGANIC SMOKEHOUSE

CLUNBURY HALL, CLUNBURY, NR. CRAVEN ARMS SY7 0HG
Tel: 01588 660206 Fax: 01588 660206
Contact: Michael & Deborah Leviseur
info@organicsmokehouse.com www.organicsmokehouse.com
Organic Food Awards Winner 2003/4. Dedicated organic smokehouse
specialising in smoking salmon, various types of cheese, butter and salt.
Smoking is carried out without mechanical intervention using traditional
'draft' method. Soil Association licence no. P8263.

THE SHROPSHIRE ORGANIC WINE COMPANY

GLEBELANDS, 25 KNIGHTON ROAD, CLUN SY7 8JH
Tel: 01588 640442 Fax: 01588 640442 Contact: John Adamson
info@organicwine-online.co.uk www.organicwine-online.co.uk
We import organic wine from personally selected vineyards in Beaujolais,
Burgundy and Cote du Rhone. Nationwide deliveries to individuals and
retail outlets. Emphasis on quality over quantity.

THE SHROPSHIRE SPICE COMPANY

UNIT 10 THE GREEN IND. ESTATE, CLUN, CRAVEN ARMS SY7 8LG
Tel: 01588 640100 Fax: 01588 640900 Contact: The Manager
office@shropshire-spice.co.uk www.shropshire-spice.co.uk
Soil Association P4316. We produce a quality range of four organic stuffing
mixes which we supply to the multiples, wholesalers and retail outlets.

SWIFT, RICHARD C – BAKER & CONFECTIONER

CENTRAL BAKERY, HIGH ST., CLEE HILL, NR. LUDLOW SY8 3LZ
Tel: 01584 890003 Fax: 01584 891317 Contact: Robert Swift
www.bakery.co.uk/swifts
A traditional family craft bakery offering a range of five different organic
breads, including organic white, brown, honey and sunflower, sunflower
and soya and 100% rye. All hand-crafted.

WARD, DE & H

MANOR FARM, CRICKHEATH, OSWESTRY SY10 8BN
Tel: 01691 830262 Contact: David Ward
wardmanorfarm@btinternet.com
Fully organic dairy farm (we grow some organic corn).

WESTHOPE COLLEGE

WESTHOPE COLLEGE, CRAVEN ARMS SY7 9JL
Tel: 01584 861293 Contact: Anne Dyer
www.westhope.org.uk
Soil Association no. G4886. Adult education weekend and weekly courses,
C&G exams. Depth of the country, organic food.

WHEELER, S & SON

BRYNMAWR NEWCASTLE, CRAVEN ARMS SY7 8QU
Tel: 01588 640298 Fax: 01588 640298 Contact: Trev Wheeler
brynmawr@farmersweekly.net www.brynmawrorganics.co.uk
Soil Association G6570. Mixed hill farm with caravan accommodation,
specialising in potatoes, carrots and daffodil bulbs.

Monsanto's outrageous behaviour

*On February 22, 2002, Monsanto was found guilty of negligence, wantonness, suppression of
the truth, nuisance, trespass and outrage. "Under Alabama law," the Washington Post article
explained, "the rare claim of outrage typically requires conduct 'so outrageous in character
and extreme in degree as to go beyond all possible bounds of decency so as to be regarded
as atrocious and utterly intolerable in civilized society.'"
(Published on Saturday, February 23, 2002 in the Washington Post)*

**From *Seeds of Deception: Exposing Corporate and Government Lies about the Safety of
Genetically Engineered Food* by Jeffrey M. Smith, Green Books, £9.95**

ALHAM WOOD CHEESES

HIGHER ALHAM FARM, WEST CRANMORE, SHEPTON MALLET BA4 6DD
Tel: 01749 880221 Fax: 01749 880771 Contact: F Wood
alhamwood@supanet.com www.buffalo-cheese.co.uk
Organic certification with Biodynamic Agriculture Association cert nos. 408
& 408Pr. A variety of soft and hard cheeses from buffalo milk from our own
organic herd, also buffalo meat and buffalo yoghurt (not by mail order).

ALVIS BROS LTD

LYE CROSS FARM, REDHILL, BRISTOL BS40 5RH
Tel: 01934 864600 Fax: 01934 862213 Contact: Mike O'Brien
abl.alvisbros@virgin.net www.lyecrosscheese.co.uk
Soil Association P1542. Organic farmhouse cheesemaker/packer of the
renowned Lye Cross Farm brand. Full range of organic cheddars, UK
territorials and cheese powder. All suitable for vegetarians. Nationwide
distribution and farm shop.

ARCADIA ORGANICS

CLOVER NURSERY, STREAMCROSS, LOWER CLAVERHAM, NR. BRISTOL
BS49 4QA
Tel: 01934 838634 Contact: Rosey Knifton
rosey@arcadiaorganics.com
Soil Association Symbol holder no. G1866. 20-acre organic holding pro-
ducing vegetables for our local box scheme delivering in north Somerset.

AVALON VINEYARD

THE DROVE, EAST PENNARD, SHEPTON MALLET BA4 6UA
Tel: 01749 860393 Contact: Hugh Tripp
pennardorganicwines@mail.com www.pennardorganicwines.co.uk
Soil Association P/T15W. Our organically grown grapes and other fruits we
make into table wine and a range of different fruit wines. We also make
mead from organic honey, traditional Somerset cider, and now produce
bottled apple juice.

BATH ORGANIC COMMUNITY GARDEN

c/o 28 ASHLEY AVENUE, BATH BA1 3DS
Tel: 01225 312116 Contact: TJ Baines
tim@bathorganicgroup.org.uk
Community garden on inner city allotment site providing training, employ-ment and volunteering opportunities for the local community. Courses and workshops. Open days. Plant sales. Open every Saturday 10am to 1pm.

BATH SOFT CHEESE/PARK FARM B&B

PARK FARM, KELSTON, BATH BA1 9AG
Tel: 01225 331601 Fax: 01225 331906 Contact: Graham Padfield
bathsoftcheese@hotmail.com www.bathsoftcheese.co.uk
Soil Association G6169. Handmade soft and blue cheese made from our own milk, also Wife of Bath hard cheese. Mail order available, B&B in charming farmhouse.

BOWERINGS ANIMAL FEEDS LTD

THE DOCKS, BRIDGEWATER TA6 3EX
Tel: 01278 458191 Fax: 01278 445159 Contact: B Bowering
Soil Association P2246. Manufacturers of all types of organic and approved feeds for all systems and all stock.

BRIDIE'S YARD ORGANIC FOOD CO-OP
AND HEALTHY LIVING CENTRE

UNIT 1A, NORTHOVER BUILDINGS, BECKERY OLD RD,
GLASTONBURY BA6 9NU
Tel: 01458 830577 Contact: Simon Ganz
Non-profit-making food co-operative costing one penny to join. Buy and sell organic food for the local community. Home made vegan, raw foods, fresh fruit and vegetables and eco products. Open on Fridays from 11am to 5.30 pm. Mobile no. 07950 664370.

BROWN COW ORGANICS
PERRIDGE FARM, PILTON, SHEPTON MALLET BA4 4EW
Tel: 01749 890298 Contact: Judith Freane
organics@browncoworganics.co.uk
Soil Association G2130, P6108. award-winning beef (Organic Food Awards 2001, 2002, 2003) pork,poultry vegetables, ready prepared meals and dairy products delivered to your door. As featured on Rick Stein's Food Heros and BBC Radio 4's THe Food Programme.

BRYMORE SCHOOL FARM TRUST
BRYMORE SCHOOL, CANNINGTON, BRIDGWATER TA5 2NB
Tel: 01278 652428 Fax: 01278 653244 Contact: A Nurton
We are a secondary school of agriculture, horticulture and engineering with a mixed farm enterprise. We sell beef and table birds through farmers' markets and pork, lamb and free range eggs privately.

BURDGE, JC
FENSWOOD FARM, SAYS LANE, LANGFORD, NR. BRISTOL BS40 5DZ
Tel: 01934 852639 Contact: Jim Burdge
jamesburdge@btopenworld.co.uk
Soil Association G4489. We are producers of organic beef, pork and lamb using traditional breeds, i.e. Devon X Cattle, Hampshire Down sheep, British Saddleback pigs. Organic meat delivered locally at reasonable prices.

CASTLE FARM
MIDFORD, BATH BA2 7BU
Tel: 01225 344420 Fax: 01225 344420 Contact: The Manager
Established organic producer of beef and horticulture.

CERES NATURAL AND ORGANIC FOODS LTD
9–11 PRINCES STREET, YEOVIL BA20 1EN
Tel: 01935 428791 Fax: 01935 426862 Contact: The Manager
info@ceresfoods.com www.ceresfoods.com
Soil Association R1560. Organic and natural foods store. Vegetarian specialists.

COBBS WHOLEFOODS

NO. 7, BRUNEL PRECINCT, SOMERTON TA11 7PY
Tel: 01458 274066 Contact: Jane Close
Cobbs specialise in stocking locally sourced organic produce including fruit, veg and local organic free range eggs; organic specialist breads and gluten-free foods available daily. We also stock all organic wholefoods.

COOMBE FARM

A.H. WARREN TRUST LTD, COOMBE FARM, CREWKERNE TA18 8RR
Tel: 01460 279500 Fax: 01460 77349 Contact: Bob Pearce
info@coombefarm.com www.coombefarm.com
Soil Association P1986. Product category: dairy. Processors and packers of organic milk, mild, medium and mature cheese, cream, milk and butter, fruit recipe products for the ice cream and bakery sectors. Distribution nationally and local deliveries to Devon, Dorset, Somerset, Wilts and Hampshire.

COOMBE FARM FRUITS LTD

COOMBE FARM, CREWKERNE TA18 8RR
Tel: 01460 279500 Fax: 01460 279533 Contact: Tony Moxon
sales@coombefarmfruits.co.uk www.coombefarmfruits.co.uk
Soil Association P1986. Fruit preparations and confectionery sauces for the food industry.

COUNTRY HARVEST

8 ST. JAMES , TAUNTON TA1 1JR
Tel: 01823 252843 Contact: Jill
Wholefoods, organic and gluten-free foods. Supplements, herbal and homoeopathic remedies, pick-up point for box schemes, qualified staff. Local deliveries to post code areas TA1, TA2, TA3, TA4, TA6.

COURT FARM
14 CHAPEL LANE, WINFORD, BRISTOL BS18 8EU
Tel: 01275 472335 Contact: JR Twine
Biodynamic farm for 30 years—products from our own milk production.
Natural and fruit yoghurt, unpasteurised milk, double cream, free range
pork and beef. Local deliveries into Bristol.

CRABTREE & EVELYN
TYLERS END, HIGHBRIDGE TA9 4JS
Tel: 01278 780913 Fax: 01278 795461 Contact: Toni Reed
Manufacturer of high quality organic preserves, marmalades and sauces.
Soil Association reg. no. P4419.

DAISY AND CO
TREE TOPS FARM, NORTH BREWHAM, BRUTON BA10 0JS
Tel: 01749 850254 Fax: 01749 850815 Contact: Richard Harbord
sales@daisyandco.co.uk www.daisyandco.co.uk
Soft cheese made from our own organic Jersey milk. Sold in retail outlets
and on-line by mail order. Other types of cheese available soon.

DEMUTHS RESTAURANT
2 NORTH PARADE PASSAGE, BATH BA1 1NX
Tel: 01225 446059 Contact: Emma Waller
us@demuths.co.uk www.demuths.co.uk
Vegetarian restaurant opened in 1987: vegan, wheat-free, dairy-free,
gluten-free etc.

EDCOMBE FARM
RODNEY STOKE, CHEDDAR BS27 3UP
Tel: 01749 870073 Contact: Robert Mann
Grow a variety of mixed vegetables sold mainly through Bristol Farmers'
Market.

EDWARD, RW & JS

NETHERTON HOUSE, MARSTON MAGNA, YEOVIL BA22 8DR
Tel: 01935 850377 Contact: RW Edward
Soil Association G7206. Cattle breeder: pedigree Simmentals.

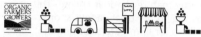

THE ELMS ORGANIC DAIRY

FRIARS OVEN FARM, WEST COMPTON, SHEPTON MALLET BA4 4PD
Tel: 01749 890371 Fax: 01749 890371 Contact: Gillian Stone
elms.organic.dairy@care4free.net
OF&G. Producers of organic sheep and cow dairy products.

FLAXDRAYTON FARM

2 BROOMHILL LANE, LOPEN, SOUTH PETHERTON TA13 5LA
Tel: 01460 241427 Fax: 01460 241427 Contact: Peter Foster
peter@flaxdrayton.fsnet.co.uk www.somersetorganiclink.co.uk
Organic vegetable grower marketing all produce through Somerset
Organic Link, a co-operative formed by organic growers in south Somerset.

GALINGALE

3 VICTORIA GARDENS, HENSTRIDGE BA8 0RE
Tel: 01963 362702 Contact: Susan Place
galingaleorganic@aol.com
Soil Association G4112. Vegetables, fruit, herbs and eggs: 2 acres with
polytunnels, raised beds and small orchard.

GENTLE LENTIL

35 FORE ST., WELLINGTON TA21 8AG
Tel: 01823 400297 Fax: 01823 400297 Contact: Colin Stephenson
A totally organic wholefood shop promoting vegetarianism and vegan
foods. Advice on babies and children is on offer, as well as a huge range of
products.

GODMINSTER VINTAGE

BRUTON BA10 0NE
Tel: 01749 813733 Fax: 01749 812059 Contact: Zara D'Abo
sales@godminster.com www.godminster.com
We are an organic farm selling a creamy mature cheddar cheese. This can be purchased at farmers' markets, by mail order or at various shops throughout the United Kingdom. Visitors for farm gate sales ring in advance.

THE GOOD EARTH

4 PRIORY RD., WELLS BA5 1SY
Tel: 01749 678600 Contact: Andrea Harrington
We have a wholefood shop and restaurant established over 25 years ago. Organic products account for a substantial amount of our business today. We have over 1,000 natural and organic products on sale from a combination of local suppliers and wholesalers.

THE GREEN GROCER

THE OLD DAIRY, POOLBRIDGE ROAD, BLACKFORD, WEDMORE BS28 4PA
Tel: 01934 713453 Contact: Quentin Isaac
greengrocer@madasafish.com
Soil Association G4668. Our own organic fruit and vegetables supplied to local shops and available to order from ourselves for collection.

GREEN, HG CHEESEMAKERS

NEWTON FARM, REDLAKE DAIRY, PAGE LANE, WEST PENNARD,
NR. GLASTONBURY BA6 8NN
Tel: 01458 834414 Fax: 01458 835072 Contact: Lloyd Green
greensofglastonbury@ukonline.co.uk
Soil Association P5176, Organic Farmers & Growers UKF040548. Cheese making.

HARDWICK BROTHERS

COBBS CROSS FARM, GOATHURST, BRIDGWATER TA5 2DN
Tel: 01278 671359 Fax: 01278 671359 Contact: John Hardwick
We produce organic beef, lamb, poultry, potatoes and run a mountain board centre and we run a three-bedroom holiday cottage. Day visits—educational and activity.

HARVEST NATURAL FOODS

37 WALCOT STREET, BATH BA1 5BN
Tel: 01225 465519 Fax: 01225 401143 Contact: Laura Petherbridge
shop@harvest-bath.co.uk
We are a GM-free store selling a wide range of organic produce: wine and champagne, grains and mueslis, veg (all kinds), dried fruits (all kinds), yoghurt, milk, soya milk, tofu, tea, gluten-free, herbs etc. We also have a delicatessen selling fresh vegetarian and vegan produce.

HEART OF DEVON ORGANICS

c/o CROXLEY SUTTON ROAD, SOMERTON, SOMERSET, TA11 6QL
Tel: 01647 24894 Fax: 01647 24894 Contact: Geoff Jones
The largest sole wholesaler of quality organic fresh fruit and vegetables in the south-west. Working closely with local and near continent growers. Deliveries from M4 to Lands End.

HIGH STREET ORGANICS

57A HIGH ST., BRUTON BA10 0AW
Tel: 01749 813191 Fax: 01749 813192 Contact: Lin Scoffin
shop@highstreetorganics.co.uk www.highstreetorganics.co.uk
Soil Association. Small friendly shop offers full range of certified organic foods including fresh fruit and vegetables, frozen, chilled and dry goods, also eco cleaning products and toiletries. Local home delivery service.

HIGHER RISCOMBE FARM

HIGHER RISCOMBE FARM, EXFORD, NR. MINEHEAD TA24 7JY
Tel: 01643 831184 Contact: Rona Amiss
intray@higherriscombefarm.co.uk www.higherriscombefarm.co.uk
Soil Association G4852. Organic farm bed and breakfast in the heart of
Exmoor National Park. Spacious rooms, home cooking, panoramic views.
Specialist producers of organic Christmas geese, ducks and lamb. Mail
order available.

HINDON ORGANIC FARM

HINDON ORGANIC FARM, NR MINEHEAD, EXMOOR TA24 8SH
Tel: 01643 705244 Fax: 01643 705244 Contact: Penny & Roger Webber
info@hindonfarm.co.uk www.hindonfarm.co.uk
Soil Association G2707, P6655. Winners of The Organic Producer of the
Year Award 2003/4. Organic Exmoor hill farm meat produce,
accommodation and farm shop. Only off own farm our quality traditionally
hung Aberdeen Angus beef, hill lamb, Gloucester Old Spot pork, dry cured
bacon, home cured ham and real sausages. B&B: s/c cottage (English
Tourism Council 4 star); luxury organic breakfasts.

HOUSE, DJ, MJ & PW

DYKES FARM, SLOUGH LANE, STOKE ST. GREGORY, TAUNTON TA3 6JH
Tel: 01823 490349 Fax: 01823 491360 Contact: PW House
peterhouse@farming.co.uk
Soil Association G6571. Pedigree Friesian dairy herd. Dairy replacements for
sale, all ages available. Farm gate sales of unpasteurised milk to the public.

HUEGLI INDUSTRIAL FOODS

PRIORYFIELD HOUSE, 20 CANON ST., TAUNTON TA1 1SW
Tel: 01823 350950 Fax: 01823 350953 Contact: Richard Bailey
huegli2@btconnect.com www.huegli.com
Soil Association P6844, OF&G UKP0092. HIF is the European market leader
in the organic bouillon sector. Products include organic bouillons, sauces,
soups, generic seasonings, mustards and desserts.

ILCHESTER CHEESE CO LTD
SOMERTON RD., ILCHESTER BA22 8JL
Tel: 01935 842800 Fax: 01935 842801 Contact: Melvin Glynn
sales@ilchester.co.uk www.ilchester.co.uk
Speciality and traditional cheese manufacturer producing traditional
organic cheeses for the UK and export markets.

IYB PARTNERSHIP
STOWEY ROCKS FARM, OVER STOWEY, BRIDGWATER TA5 1JB
Tel: 01278 733080 Fax: 01278 733080 Contact: Ian & Yta Batchelor
Family partnership farming 82 acres organically. Enterprises include soft
fruit, vegetables, eggs and livestock. Sales via farm gate (PYO) and
wholesale.

JENRO'S
22 WEST STREET, WIVELISCOMBE, TAUNTON TA4 2JP
Tel: 01984 623236 Fax: 01984 629131 Contact: Richard Pakeman
We are a specialist food shop selling a range of organic products including
vegetables, dairy products, beans, pulses, grains, jams, marmalades, pastas,
beverages, pet food etc.

LEIGH COURT FARM
ABBOTS LEIGH, BRISTOL BS8 3RA
Tel: 01275 375756 Fax: 01275 375756 Contact: Chris Loughlin
mail@leighcourtfarm.org.uk www.leighcourtfarm.org.uk
Vegetable box scheme, Bristol Farmers Market (June–December),
volunteers, practical training, working with communities, not for profit,
promoting local food economy, part fully certified remainder due spring
2004, S. A. licence no. G3034. Delivery to Southville, Hotwells, Easton,
Cotham, and offices with more than 20 customers.

LUBBORN CHEESE LTD

MANOR FARM, CRICKET ST. THOMAS, CHARD TA20 4BZ
Tel: 01460 30736 Contact: Christina Baskerville
christina@lubborn.co.uk www.lubborn.co.uk
Sole makers of Somerset Brie, Somerset Camembert and Capricorn goat's
cheese, all traditionally ripened for full flavour and a creamy texture.

LUCAS AND LUCAS ORGANICS

NORWOOD FARM COTTAGE, BATH RD., NORTON ST. PHILIP, BATH BA2 7LP
Tel: 01373 834022 Contact: Dide Lucas
dide@lucasorganics.freeserve.co.uk
Growers of seasonal veg including unusual heritage veg in our show
garden, plants and transplants for sale. Fruit coming soon. Other services
include garden design and planning through to maintenance, advice, tree
planting, hedge laying etc.

LYNG COURT ORGANIC MEAT

LYNG COURT, WEST LYNG, TAUNTON TA3 5AP
Tel: 01823 490510 Contact: R Lloyd Jones
Quality beef and lamb grazed on the Somerset Levels. Farm Gate Sales and
local delivery. Beef in 10kg mixed packs of joints, steaks etc, lamb jointed
and packed to order.

MAGDALEN FARM

MAGDALEN FARM, WINSHAM, CHARD TA20 4PA
Tel: 01460 30144 Fax: 01460 30177 Contact: Peter Foster
Soil Association registered (G932) mixed farm, beef sucklers, pigs, field veg,
polytunnels and cereals, selling vegetables and meat via farmers' markets,
box scheme and farm gate sales.

MARKUS PRODUCTS LTD
MURRAY WAY, WINCANTON BUSINESS PARK, WINCANTON BA9 9RX
Tel: 01963 435270 Fax: 01963 435271 Contact: Simon Clarke
simon@markusproducts.co.uk www.markusproducts.co.uk
Soil Association P4162. Manufacturer of flavoured butters, flavoured soft
cheese portions, crumb coatings, flavoured oils and stuffings in IQF format.

MERRICKS ORGANIC FARM
PARK LANE, LANGPORT TA10 0NF
Tel: 01458 252901 Fax: 01458 252901 Contact: Jane Brooke
simon@merricksorganicfarm.co.uk www.merricksorganicfarm.co.uk
22-acre market garden supplying farm-run box scheme with vegetables and
fruit. Also organic pork, poultry and eggs. Two holiday cottages on farm.

MILES, DJ & CO LTD
PORLOCK HOUSE, STEPHENSON RD., MINEHEAD TA24 5EB
Tel: 01643 703993 Fax: 01643 706303 Contact: John Halls
info@djmiles.co.uk www.djmiles.co.uk
40 Organic Teabags / 80 Organic Teabags. Manufactured in Somerset.

MOLE VALLEY FARMERS LTD
HUNTWORTH MILL, MARSH LANE, BRIDGWATER TA6 6LQ
Tel: 01278 444829 Fax: 01278 446923 Contact: James Trebble
jamestrebble@molevalleyfarmers.com
Soil Association P2332, Organic Farmers & Growers UKP 030463.
Manufacturers of organic feeds for dairy, beef, cattle, sheep, pigs and
poultry, and suppliers of seeds, fertilisers and other inputs for organic
farmers.

NATRACARE – BODYWISE (UK) LTD

UNIT 23, MARSH LANE INDUSTRIAL ESTATE, MARSH LANE, PORTBURY, SOMERSET, BS20 0NH
Tel: 01275 371764 Fax: 01275 371765 Contact: Susie Hewson
info@natracare.com www.natracare.com
Soil Association I303. Feminine hygiene products. Natracare organic cotton tampons and feminine pads made from natural and disposable materials available from health stores and supermarkets nationwide.

NATURAL COLLECTION

GREEN DOT GUIDES, ECO HOUSE, 19A MONMOUTH PLACE, BATH BA1 2DQ
Tel: 01225 404020 Fax: 01225 469673 Contact: Sarah Thorne
sarah@naturalcollection.com www.naturalcollection.com
Green Dot Guides Ltd owns the Natural Collection catalogue and publishes Trees for Life diaries and calendars. The Natural Collection catalogue promotes a huge variety of products that have been manufactured with the environment in mind or traded fairly and which are also desirable both aesthetically and functionally. We are the trading partner for Friends of the Earth and Greenpeace and work with many other worthy organisations.

NEAL'S YARD REMEDIES

7 NORTHUMBERLAND PLACE, BATH BA1 5AR
Tel: 01225 466944 Contact: The Manager
mail@nealsyardremedies.com www.nealsyardremedies.com
Neal's Yard Remedies manufactures and retails natural cosmetics in addition to stocking an extensive range of herbs, essential oils, homoeopathic remedies and reference material.

NORWOOD FARM

BATH ROAD, NORTON ST PHILIP, NR. BATH BA2 7LP
Tel: 01373 834856 Fax: 01373 834765 Contact: Catherine Le Grice-Mack
catemack@norwood.ndo.co.uk www.norwoodfarm.co.uk
Soil Association G814. Organic mixed farm, with rare and native breeds. Open to visitors every day from March 28th–September 19th. Farm shop with organic meat and local produce open all year. Fair trade groceries.

THE ORGANIC HERB TRADING COMPANY
COURT FARM, MILVERTON TA4 1NF
Tel: 01823 401205 Fax: 01823 401001 Contact: Linda Brunsch
info@organicherbtrading.com www.organicherbtrading.com
Soil Association P938. Supplier of certified organic herbs and spices,
essential oils, tinctures and more, for use in the food, beverage, herbal
medicine and cosmetic trades. Quantities from 1kilo/litre to container.

ORGANIC MILK SUPPLIERS CO-OPERATIVE LTD
COURT FARM, LOXTON, NR. AXBRIDGE BS26 2XG
Tel: 01934 750244 Fax: 01934 750080 Contact: Sally Bagenal (C.E.)
enquiries@omsco.co.uk www.omsco.co.uk
UK-wide supplier of organic milk.

ORGANICA
TWEENTOWN CORNER, CHEDDAR BS27 3JF
Tel: 01934 741644 Contact: Sue Gallacher
cheddarorganica@aol.com www.cheddarorganica.com
Organica is a retail outlet for organic wholefoods, fruit and vegetables from
mainly local suppliers. A small range of supplements, boxes and gifts are
also available. Specialist wholefoods available to order.

ORGARDEN PRODUCE
BORDER FARM, CLOSWORTH, YEOVIL BA22 9SZ
Tel: 01935 872483 Fax: 01935 873736 Contact: Jennifer Evans
Soil Association licence no. E07W since 1985. Have eighteen 90-foot
growing houses and specialise in tomatoes, peppers, courgettes,
aubergines, cucumbers and carrots in tunnels.

PITNEY FARM SHOP
GLEBE FARM, PITNEY, LANGPORT TA
Tel: 01458 253002 Fax: 01458 253002 Contact: Rob Walrond
Soil Association G4130. Mixed organic farm producing organic eggs, lamb,
beef, pork, bacon and a range of organic sausages, also interesting seasonal
vegetables. Mostly direct sales through our farm shop or local outlets.

PLOWRIGHT ORGANIC PRODUCE

29 HUNTSTILE, GOATHURST, BRIDGWATER TA5 2DQ
rplowright@tinyonline.co.uk Contact: Richard Plowright
Plowright Organic Produce is a small farm business in Somerset. POP grows
a wide range of vegetables and fruit which it supplies to local homes and
offices through a box scheme.

PROCKTERS FARM SHOP

PROCKTERS FARM, WEST MONKTON, TAUNTON TA2 8QN
Tel: 01823 413427 Contact: M Besley
Farm shop selling a wide range of organic meat and veg. Box scheme
available—collection on Tuesday. Shop situated on mixed organic grass farm
producing organic beef and lamb. B&B accommodation. Wholesale prices
for organic beef and lamb from the farm. Beef and lamb available in packs.

PROVENDER DELICATESSEN

3 MARKET SQUARE, SOUTH PETHERTON TA13 5BT
Tel: 01460 240681 Fax: 08701 694835 Contact: Roger Biddle
www.provender.net
Licensed delicatessen with large organic selection of groceries, cheeses,
dairy and juices. Collection point for Merricks organic farm vegetable box
scheme. Organic frozen vegetables and ice cream.

QUEENSWOOD NATURAL FOODS LTD

2 ROBINS DRIVE, APPLE BUSINESS PARK, BRIDGWATER TA6 4DL
Tel: 01278 423440 Fax: 01278 424084 Contact: Chris Claydon
sales@queenswoodfoods.co.uk www.queenswoodfoods.co.uk
Soil Association P1559. Supplies of bulk and pre-packed organic
commodities, along with a wide range of branded, chilled and frozen
products, with weekly deliveries throughout a large area. Organic
ingredients also available.

RADFORD MILL FARM
TIMSBURY, BATH BA2 0QF
Tel: 01761 479572 Fax: 01761 479572 Contact: Susan Seymour
farm@radfordmill.co.uk www.radfordmill.co.uk
Vegetables, fruit, yoghurt, deli produce, meat and Christmas turkeys.
Award-winning delicatessen foods. All home-produced. Local deliveries,
on-line ordering, farmers' market stalls in Bath (Sat) and Bristol (Wed),
market stall in Glastonbury (Tues).

ROBERT WILSON'S CEYLON TEAS
STONEHAVEN, NUTTREE, NORTH PERROTT, CREWKERNE TA18 7SX
Tel: 01460 77508 Fax: 01460 77508 Contact: Robert Wilson
info@wilstea.com www.wilstea.com
Organic Farmers & Growers UKP 030485. Packers and shippers. Our
business in Sri Lanka works with single estates to have special dry season
manufacture made to our specific requirements. We import for UK
distribution or export internationally from Colombo. Retail shop on the web.

SEASONS WHOLEFOODS
10 GEORGE STREET, BATH BA1 2EH
Tel: 01225 469730 Contact: Peter & Anne Bassil
Take-away salads, savouries, soups etc. A large range of organic products
available in the shop.

SOMERSET ORGANIC LINK
1 BRIDGE FARM COTTAGE, DRAYTON, SOUTH PETHERTON TA13 5LR
Tel: 01460 241427 Fax: 01460 241427 Contact: Peter Foster & Steve Friend
peter@flaxdrayton.fsnet.co.uk www.somersetorganiclink.co.uk
A co-operative of organic farmers in Somerset, SOL supplies fresh organic
produce to outlets in Somerset and beyond. SOL buys produce from
outside the county when necessary to meet demand. Sales and marketing
service for organic vegetable producers in Somerset, forum for crop
planning, opportunities to share labour and equipment.

SOMERSET ORGANICS
GILCOMBE FARM, BRUTON BA10 0QE
Tel: 01749 813710 Fax: 01749 813710 Contact: Andrew Portch
andy@somersetorganics.co.uk www.somersetorganics.co.uk
Organic meat by mail order. Order by internet on-line ordering; we are
the first farmers in Europe to provide a virtual farm tour of the farm.
Nationwide delivery.

SPENCERS GROCERY STORE
4 TUCKER STREET, WELLS BA5 2DZ
Tel: 01749 672357 Contact: J Spencer
shop@spencersofwells.co.uk www.spencersofwells.co.uk
Traditional family grocery store. Free local delivery. Personal counter
service. Locally baked organic bread, cakes. Organic fruit juices, organic
sugar. Local cheeses, cooked hams, honey, pickles. Brand name goods.

SPRING GROVE MARKET GARDEN
SPRING GROVE, MILVERTON TA4 1NW
Tel: 07956 429531
Box scheme for mixed vegetables and eggs.

STILLMANS (SOMERSET) LTD
55 STATION RD., TAUNTON TA1 1NZ
Tel: 01823 272661 Fax: 01823 332270 Contact: C Cook
peter@stillmansbutchers.co.uk www.stillmansbutchers.co.uk
Soil Association P3014. Stillmans is a small welfare-friendly farm abattoir
providing a service to local farmers.

STILLPOINT

OLD OAK FARM, CHAPEL ALLERTON, AXBRIDGE BS26 2PD
Tel: 01934 712726 Contact: Carol Joy
carol@stillpoint.uk.com www.stillpoint.uk.com
Holistic stress management, McTimoney therapy, life coaching, Hawaiian massage. We provide practical on-site stress management and well-being clinics. Chair massage, organic aromatherapy products, nutritious organic snacks and fruit. Clients include OMSCo, Lakewood Conference Centre and local organic farmers. Member of HDRA and Soil Association.

STONEAGE ORGANICS

STONEAGE FARM, COTHELSTONE, TAUNTON TA4 3ED
Tel: 01823 432488 Fax: 01823 432488 Contact: Keith Martin
keith@stoneageorganics.co.uk www.stoneageorganics.co.uk
Soil Association M49W. Organic vegetables, box scheme deliveries from Taunton to Bristol to Shepton Mallet and en route. Organic lamb also available.

SUNSEED

12 SOUTH STREET, WELLINGTON TA21 8NS
Tel: 01823 662313 Contact: Tony Bourne
info@sunseed.co.uk www.sunseed.co.uk
Health and wholefood retailer specialising in all things as natural as possible. Wide variety of usual things and unusual things: organic vegetables, fruit, food, drinks, chilled, frozen etc. Complementary therapies.

SWADDLES ORGANIC

SWADDLES GREEN FARM, HARE LANE, BUCKLAND ST. MARY, CHARD TA20 3JR
Tel: 01460 234387 Fax: 01460 234591 Contact: Sue Alexander
information@swaddles.co.uk www.swaddles.co.uk
Soil Association P1904. Producers of many award-winning meats, pies, bacon, hams, sausages, ready meals. Mail order service of own produce throughout UK, plus full range of organic dairy, grocery, fruit and veg.

THATCHERS CIDER COMPANY LTD
MYRTLE FARM, SANDFORD BS25 5RA
Tel: 01934 822862 Fax: 01934 822313 Contact: Meg Heasman
megh@thatcherscider.co.uk www.thatcherscider.co.uk
Soil Association registered. The Thatcher family has been making cider since 1904, using 100% English apples. Traditional scrumpy, specialist single varieties, and organic ciders, available via the farm shop and website.

TOUCAN WHOLEFOODS
3 THE PARADE, MINEHEAD TA24 5NL
Tel: 01643 706101 Fax: 01643 708624 Contact: Jane Hart
mail@toucan.wholefoods@virgin.net
Independent wholefood shop with a wide range of organic produce, including fresh fruit and veg, specialist breads, dairy and organic wines and beers. Also quality vitamin supplements with free information.

TRUUULY SCRUMPTIOUS ORGANIC BABY FOOD LTD
CHARMBOROUGH FARM, CHARLTON RD., HOLCOMBE, RADSTOCK, BATH BA3 5EX
Tel: 01761 239300 Fax: 01761 239300 Contact: Janice Fisher / Topsy Fogg
sales@bathorganicbabyfood.co.uk www.bathorganicbabyfood.co.uk
Soil Association P8085. A delicious range of freshly prepared, frozen organic meals for babies and toddlers in convenient, tamper-proof containers with ingredients, textures and quantities to suit progress.

TUCKMARSH FARM LTD
MARSTON BIGOT, FROME BA11 5BY
Tel: 01373 836325 Contact: RB Christie
rbonhamchr@aol.com
Soil Association G4078. Suckler herd of Hereford x heifers and stores.

WESTAR & WEEDMACHINE

MANOR FARM, HEWISH, NR. CREWKERNE TA18 8QT
Tel: 07977 206530 Fax: 01460 75317 Contact: George van den Berg
george@weedmachine.co.uk www.weedmachine.co.uk
Soil Association G6756. Producer of organic eggs.

THE WHOLEFOOD STORE

29 HIGH ST., GLASTONBURY BA6 9SX
Tel: 01458 831004 Contact: The Manager
A large wholefood store retailing organic dried, pre-packed foods as well as
fresh fruit and veg, dairy products and drinks. Our aim is to provide the
organic food shopper with everything needed for a weekly shop.

WINCANTON GROUP LTD

CALE HOUSE, STATION RD., WINCANTON BA9 9AD
Tel: 01963 828282 Fax: 01963 31850 Contact: Stuart James
stuart.james@wincanton.co.uk www.wincanton.co.uk
Soil Association P6716. Wincanton Group are specialists in warehousing and
distribution activities including organic milk collected for numerous customers.

THE YEO VALLEY ORGANIC CO LTD

CANNINGTON CREAMERY, CANNINGTON TA5 2ND
Tel: 01761 462798 Fax: 01761 462181 Contact: Mike Pollak
enquiries@yeo-organic.co.uk www.yeo-organic.co.uk
Soil Association P2168. This family-owned independent business won The
Queen's Award for Enterprise for Sustainable Development in 2001. Now
the UK's biggest organic dairy brand, products include yogurts, desserts,
butter and ice cream.

ZUMO ZEST

HAYESWOOD RD., TIMSBURY, BATH BA2 0FQ
Tel: 01761 470523 Fax: 01761 471018 Contact: Mary Young
A family-run business in the heart of the West Country making 'to order'
organic citrus zest and juice, for use as an ingredient to enhance quality of
puddings, cakes etc, by the trade.

STAFFORDSHIRE

ALLIED BAKERIES
LIVERPOOL RD., CROSS HEATH, NEWCASTLE UNDER LYME ST5 9HT
Tel: 01782 717373 Fax: 01782 717392 Contact: Keith Bolton
k_Bolton@alliedbakeries.co.uk www.alliedbakeries.co.uk
We are the UK's largest baking goods manufacturer: customer base
includes all the major UK retailers. Brands include Kingsmill, Allinson, and
organic products are our growth sector.

BELLA HERBS
BROCTON LEYS, BROCTON, STAFFORD ST17 0TX
Tel: 01785 663868 Contact: Beverley Squire
We are a two-acre organic garden licensed by the Soil Association, where
we run leisure courses in organic gardening. We are also producers of
vegetables, fruit and herbs.

BESTFOODS UK LTD – FOOD INGREDIENTS
WELLINGTON ROAD, BURTON-ON-TRENT DE14 2AB
Tel: 01283 511111 Fax: 01283 510194 Contact: Jean Cattanach
jean.cattenach@unilever.com www.unilever.com
Bestfoods Ingredients specialise in the production of stocks and bouillons
for manufacturers of prepared savoury foods. Licensed products include
organic vegetable bouillon and organic light bouillon.

BETTER TASTING SNACK FOODS PLC
UNITS 3–12, BRIDGE STREET IND. ESTATE, TRINITY RD., UTTOXETER ST14 8ST
Tel: 01889 567338 Fax: 01889 562701 Contact: Andy Baldwin
andy@bettertastingsnackfoods.co.uk www.bettertastingsnackfoods.co.uk
Soil Association P2184. Snack manufacturer specialising in batch-fried
potato crisps, vegetable crisps (parsnip, beetroot, carrot and sweet potato),
croutons, crackers and tortillas.

BOOTS HERBAL STORE
5 CASTLE WALK, NEWCASTLE ST5 1AN
Tel: 01782 617463 Fax: 01782 636098 Contact: Keith Woolley
keith.woolley@btinternet.com
Family business, established 1939. Stock organic vegetarian foods wherever possible. Organic herbal tinctures available. Mail order on 01782 617463.

COPE, TH & SON
HUDDLESFORD HOUSE FARM, NR. LICHFIELD WS13 8PY
Tel: 01543 432255 Fax: 01543 433447 Contact: Tom Cope
huddlesford.holsteins@virgin.net
Soil Association G2538. Milking 260 organic cows, processing own milk into organic cheese. Dairy farmer.

HOLGRAN LTD
GRANARY HOUSE, WETMORE ROAD, BURTON-ON-TRENT DE14 1TE
Tel: 01283 511255 Fax: 01283 511220 Contact: Alan Marson
bits4bread@holgran.co.uk www.holgran.co.uk
Industrial bakery ingredients supply: malt, cereal, seed ingredients for the bakery industry. Supplier of ingredients and mixes. Soil Association membership. Delivery to UK, Europe and North America.

THE KERRYGOLD COMPANY LTD
BARNFIELDS IND. ESTATE, SUNNYHILLS RD., LEEK ST13 5SP
Tel: 01538 399111 Fax: 01538 399918 Contact: Chris Proctor
sales@kerrygold.co.uk www.kerrygold.com
Soil Association P5200. Pre-packed natural cheese and grated cheese for retail and industrial applications.

MOORLAND WASTE RECYCLING
CRESFORD FARM, CAVERSWALL LANE, DILHORNE ST10 2PH
Tel: 01782 397907 Fax: 01782 392928 Contact: Anne Wagstaff
anne@moorlands35.freeserve.co.uk
Producers of organic compost, mulches, soil improver, top soil.

PHYTONE LTD

THIRD AVENUE, CENTRUM 100, BURTON ON TRENT DE14 2WD
Tel: 01283 543300 Fax: 01283 543322 Contact: Richard Perry
info@phytone.co.uk
Soil Association P5468. Supplier of a range of organic products including
dried herbs and spices, vegetables and fruit juice concentrates and
powders, caramel syrup and powder, malt extract, molasses and vanilla.

THE REAL FOOD COMPANY

50 SANDBACH ROAD SOUTH, ALSAGER, STOKE-ON-TRENT ST7 2LP
Tel: 01270 873322 Contact: Carol Dines
realfoodco.alsager@virgin.net
Organic wholefoods, vegetables and fruit, including box scheme, frozen
and chilled, herbal, homoeopathic, supplements etc. Large choice to be
found in helpful shop with knowledgeable staff. Local deliveries.

REGENCY MOWBRAY CO LTD

HIXON INDUSTRIAL ESTATE, HIXON ST18 0PY
Tel: 01889 270554 Fax: 01889 270927 Contact: CH Malbon
sales@regencymowbray.co.uk www.regencymowbray.demon.co.uk
Soil Association P4570. Manufacturer of organic food ingredients. Organic
fruit preparations for yoghurt and ice cream. Organic flavourings. Organic
purées and sauces. Natural flavourings for use in organic products. Also
manufacturers of standard flavourings, colours, fruit preparations, chocolate
products, emulsifiers and stabilisers. Visit www.regencymowbray.com.

STAFFORDSHIRE ORGANIC CHEESE

NEW HOUSE FARM, ACTON, NEWCASTLE UNDER LYME ST5 4EE
Tel: 01782 680366 Fax: 01782 680366 Contact: David Deaville
d.deaville@virgin.net
Makers of traditional hand-made, hand-pressed cheeses from organic cow's
milk. Also makers of Whitmore organic sheep's milk cheese.

WOOTTON ORGANIC

RAMSHORN, FARLEY, OAKAMOOR ST10 3BZ
Tel: 01538 703228 Fax: 01583 709900 Contact: Denise Flanaghan
wholesale@woottonorganic.co.uk www.woottonorganic.co.uk
Specialists in the finest organic meats; beef, lamb, venison, pork and
poultry. In our organically certified on-site abattoir our Master Butcher
prepares cuts fresh to order and will happily discuss specific requirements.
Mail order: 0800 652 9469 or email mailorder@woottonorganic.co.uk. See
display ad. See display ad.

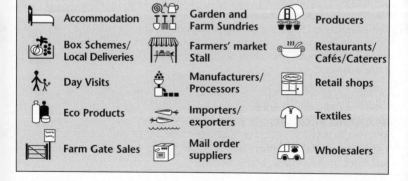

Accommodation	Garden and Farm Sundries	Producers	
Box Schemes/ Local Deliveries	Farmers' market Stall	Restaurants/ Cafés/Caterers	
Day Visits	Manufacturers/ Processors	Retail shops	
Eco Products	Importers/ exporters	Textiles	
Farm Gate Sales	Mail order suppliers	Wholesalers	

SUFFOLK

ASPALL
THE CYDER HOUSE, ASPALL HALL, STOWMARKET IP14 6PD
Tel: 01728 860510 Fax: 01728 861031 Contact: Barry Chevallier Guild
info@aspall.co.uk www.aspall.co.uk
Founder members of the Soil Association and organic producers of apple juice, cyder and cyder vinegar for over 57 years. Our products are widely available through good retail food outlets.

ASTON ORGANIC ORCHARDS
THE ORCHARD, WELHAM LANE, RISBY, BURY ST EDMUNDS IP28 6QS
Tel: 01284 811668 Fax: 01284 700011 Contact: Tony Fuller
tonyfuller@btinternet.com
Soil Association registered organic apple orchard. The following varieties are grown (mainly for the wholesale market). Dessert apples: Spartan & Lord Lambourne. Cooking apples: Bramley & Grenadier.

BARENBRUG UK LTD
33 PERKINS RD., ROUGHAM IND. ESTATE, BURY ST. EDMUNDS IP30 9ND
Tel: 01359 272000 Fax: 01359 272001 Contact: James Ingles
info@baruk.co.uk www.barenbrug.co.uk
Soil Association P6199. Barenbrug are specialist grass and forage seed producers who produce organic grass seed mixtures specifically designed for organic farmers. These include the new white clover Barblanca, which is extremely productive.

BERNARD PAGE WOOD & CO
BY THE CROSSWAYS, KELSALE, SAXMUNDHAM IP17 2PL
Tel: 01728 652000 Contact: The Manager
Soil Association. Organic arable farmers.

BRYDEN ORGANICS

BRYDEN, MINSMERE ROAD, DUNWICH IP17 3DF
Tel: 01728 648960 Contact: Debra Hyatt
debra.hyatt@btinternet.co.uk
Soil Association G9119.Currently in conversion. 10-acre smallholding in
Suffolk Sandlings. We are returning 8 acres to acid grassland in order to
create habitats for woodlark, adder and a range of invertebrates. Our major
enterprise is growing oriental salad leaves. Available from the farm gate.

BUSHY LEY FARM SHOP

ELMSETT, IPSWICH IP7 6PQ
Tel: 01473 658671 Contact: C Thoroughgood
Soil Association T12E. Wide range of vegetables and fruit when in season.
Open July to October, 8am to 8pm seven days a week. All produce sold is
grown on this farm.

CAPEL ORGANIC MUSHROOMS

CAPEL ST. MARY, IPSWICH IP9 2LA
Tel: 01473 310380 Fax: 01473 310380 Contact: Patrick/Damian Hearne
damian@capelmushrooms.co.uk
Growers and packers of organic white cup, button mushrooms. Also
organic Brown Portobello, Portobellini and Brown Cup Mushrooms.
Supermarket approved. Countrywide distribution.

CARLEY AND WEBB

52 THOROUGHFARE, WOODBRIDGE IP12 1AL
Tel: 01394 385650 Fax: 01394 388984 Contact: Mark Balaam
www.carleyandwebb.com
We are a natural food store specialising in organic vegetables, bread and
macrobiotic products. Large delicatessen, fresh fish.

CARLEY AND WEBB
29 MARKET HILL, FRAMLINGHAM IP13 9AN
Tel: 01728 723503 Fax: 01728 724153 Contact: Steve Bax
www.carleyandwebb.com
Specialist delicatessen and natural food store specialising in organic
vegetables, bread and macrobiotic products.

CHURCH (BURES) LTD, WA
HIGH ST., BURES CO8 5JQ
Tel: 01787 227654 Fax: 01787 228325 Contact: Tim Church
organicseed@churchofbures.co.uk www.churchofbures.co.uk
Soil Association P7482. All organic grass mixtures available; vetch, mustard,
red clover, white clover and all organic seed mixtures.

DAGANYA FARM
NUTTERY VALE, HOXNE, EYE IP21 5BB
Tel: 01379 668060 Contact: Michael Knights
Soil Association G2108. Organic fruit and vegetables in season. Founder
member of EOSTRE organics.

DJ PRODUCE LTD
UNIT 1, GRIFFITHS YARD, GAZELEY ROAD, MOULTON, NEWMARKET CB8 8SR
Tel: 01638 552709 Fax: 01638 552709 Contact: Derek Mason
www.djproduce.co.uk
Organic Farmers & Growers 11UKP110089. Fruit and vegetables from
home and abroad, variety of pack sizes available, deliveries to Cambridge
and surrounding area.

ESSENTIAL CARE
SPINNERS, THE STREET, LACKFORD, BURY ST. EDMUNDS IP28 6HW
Tel: 01284 728416 Fax: 01284 728416 Contact: Margaret Weeds
info@essential-care.co.uk http://www.essential-care.co.uk
We create skin & body care with pure, vitamin-rich, biodynamic plant
ingredients. Soil Association certified organic and free from unnecessary
synthetic additives—formulated especially for sensitive skin and eczema.

FOCUS ORGANIC LTD

14 THE THOROUGHFARE, HALESWORTH IP19 8AH
Tel: 01986 872899 Fax: 01986 872995 Contact: Juan Suarez
info@focusorganic.co.uk www.focusorganic.co.uk
Our wholefood shop sells as much organic produce as possible including
cereals, nuts, fruits, flour, seeds, jams, sauces, spreads, juices, pasta and
vegetables. Organic clothes and bed linen, Ecover products, aromatherapy
candles, essential oils, recycled jewellery.

FOCUS ORGANIC LTD

76 HIGH ST, SOUTHWOLD IP18 6DN
Tel: 01502 725299 Contact: Samantha Frost
info@focusorganic.co.uk www.focusorganic.co.uk
Cereals, nuts, fruits, flour, seeds, jams, sauces, spreads, juices, pasta,
essential oils, cosmetics, cleaning materials etc.

GOBBLIN WHOLEFOODS LTD

STATION RD. IND. ESTATE, ELMSWELL IP30 9HR
Tel: 01359 241841 Contact: Peter Dow
Soil Association P5476. Vegetarian sweet and savoury bakery to the retail,
pub and catering trades.

HILLSIDE NURSERIES

HINTLESHAM, IPSWICH IP8 3NJ
Tel: 01473 652682 Fax: 01473 652624 Contact: Roberta Simpson
Soil Association G594. Box scheme (vegetables, fruit, eggs) using local and
own produce wherever possible. Delivery Ipswich, Woodbridge, Felixstowe
and surrounding areas.

HOME FARM NACTON

ORWELL PARK ESTATE OFFICE, NACTON, IPSWICH IP10 0EG
Tel: 01473 659209 Contact: Andrew Williams
Soil Association G4705. Specialising in organic vegetables i.e. broccoli,
cauliflower, carrots, leeks, potatoes and also organic cereals.

HUNGATE HEALTH STORE
4 HUNGATE, BECCLES NR34 9TL
Tel: 01502 715009 Contact: Theresa Hale
Retailers of a wide range of organic foods including fresh bread, biscuits, dried fruit and nuts, beans and lentils, chocolate, drinks. Also essential oils, bath and hair products.

JIM COOPER VEGETABLES
THE CARAVAN, CLARKES LANE, ILKETSHALL ST. ANDREW, BECCLES NR34 8HR
Tel: 07866 960706 Contact: Jim Cooper
Small scale vegetable grower, produce for sale locally as part of forthcoming box scheme. Also grower of 50 mostly old fruit tree varieties under organic conditions.

KOPPERT UK LTD
HOMEFIELD BUSINESS PARK, HOMEFIELD ROAD, HAVERHILL CB9 8QP
Tel: 1440 704488 Fax: 01440 704487 Contact: Matthew Cook
info@koppert.co.uk www.koppert.co.uk
Europe's largest producer of natural enemies. Supplier of organic pesticides such as DIPEL WP for caterpillars and SAVONA, a wide spectrum organic pesticide. Also large range of pest monitoring traps. Delivery to UK & Ireland.

LONGWOOD FARM
TUDDENHAM ST. MARY, BURY ST. EDMUNDS IP28 6TB
Tel: 01638 717120 Fax: 01638 717120 Contact: Matthew Unwin
Soil Association no. G669. Specialist organic meat producers, retailers of fine organic foods—meat, dairy, cheese and provisions. Huge range of over 2,000 items. Delivery nationwide plus local deliveries to postcode areas IP, NR, CB.

MICROCIDE
SHEPHERDS GROVE, STANTON, BURY ST. EDMUNDS IP31 2AR
Tel: 01359 251077 Fax: 01359 251545 Contact: N Balfour
microcide@microcide.co.uk www.microcide.co.uk
Soil Association I1616. Manufacturers of vegetable oil adjuvants which maximise the performance of plant protection products and increase droplet deposition, spread and uptake. Reduces drift and improves rain fastness. They are biodegradable.

NORTON ORGANIC GRAIN LTD
CASTLINGS HEATH COTTAGE, GROTON, SUDBURY CO10 5ES
Tel: 01787 210899 Fax: 01787 211737 Contact: John Norton
john.norton@nortonorganic.co.uk www.nortonorganic.co.uk
Organic grain/pulse supplier, sourcing organic grains and pulses from UK farms and European/third country sourced soya, oilseeds, grains etc. Soil Association licence no. P1674, OFF no. SAL/97. International coverage.

OMEGA INGREDIENTS LIMITED
THE TECHNOLOGY CENTRE, STATION RD., FRAMLINGHAM IP13 9EZ
Tel: 01728 726626 Fax: 01728 726533 Contact: Steve Pearce
sales@omegaingredients.co.uk www.omegaingredients.co.uk
Essential oils, natural extracts, flower and herb waters, fruit juices, flavours and fragrances, ingredients for flavours & fragrances, aloe vera, dried aloe flowers.

OREGANO
169/171 LONDON ROAD NORTH, LOWESTOFT NR32 1HG
Tel: 01502 582907 Contact: Dawn Fellows
Health foods, vitamins, supplements and organic foods are featured in a large section in the store.

QUEEN'S HEAD

THE STREET, BRAMFIELD, HALESWORTH IP19 9HT
Tel: 01986 784214 Fax: 01986 784797 Contact: Mark Corcoran
qhbfield@aol.com www.queensheadbramfield.co.uk
Award-winning dining pub, serving food daily. Many ingredients collected direct from small local organic farms. Close to Southwold and the rest of Suffolk's Heritage Coast.

RED POLL MEATS

CHERRY TREE HOUSE, HACHESTON, WOODBRIDGE IP13 0DR
Tel: 01728 748444 Fax: 07050 600079 Contact: Sebastian Hall
info@redpollmeats.co.uk www.redpollmeats.co.uk
Red Poll Meats supply organic Norfolk Black & Bronze turkeys, organic lamb, organic beef, organic pork, free-range venison and organic fruit & vegetables nationwide. We try where possible to use unusual or rare breeds.

ST. PETER'S BREWERY

ST. PETER'S HALL, ST. PETER SOUTH ELMHAM, BUNGAY NR35 1NQ
Tel: 01986 782322 Fax: 01986 782505 Contact: Colin Cordy
beers@stpetersbrewery.co.uk www.stpetersbrewery.co.uk
Soil Association P5891. Organic brewery. Production of organic beers and ales using organic barley and organic hops, presented in cask or bottle for shipment around the world.

SUFFOLK ORGANIC GARLIC

WHITE HOUSE FARM, UBBESTON, HALESWORTH IP19 0HA
Tel: 01986 798227 Fax: 01986 798179 Contact: Allan Pike
allanpike@farmersweekly.net
Soil Association G6065. Veg production: 2.5 acres of garlic in 2004. Arable: 15 acres of wheat in 2004.

SWALLOW ORGANICS

HIGH MARCH, DARSHAM, SAXMUNDHAM IP17 3RN
Tel: 01728 668201 Contact: Malcolm Pinder
We sell a selection of fruit and vegetables, naturally grown, from our own
market garden. Also pot herbs, fuchsias, pelargoniums etc, organic
fertiliser and compost. Box scheme (not deliveries) for collection only.

WAKELYNS AGROFORESTRY

METFIELD LANE, FRESSINGFIELD IP21 5SD
Contact: The Manager
wolfe@wakelyns.demon.co.uk
Soil Association G2249. Organic arable and agroforestry research undertak-
en largely as part of the Elm Farm Research Centre programme. Vegetables,
potatoes and other produce are sold locally, principally through the Eostre
organic co-operative.

WHITE, JAMES DRINKS LTD

WHITES FRUIT FARM, ASHBOCKING, IPSWICH IP6 9JS
Tel: 01473 890111 Fax: 01473 890001 Contact: James Mwayi
info@jameswhite.co.uk www.jameswhite.co.uk
Soil Association P2648. A producer of premium quality apple juices
including apple and cranberry, apple and crushed ginger and several other
varieties made from freshly pressed fruit.

BIG OZ ORGANIC

126 ACRE ROAD, KINGSTON-UPON-THAMES KT2 6EN
Tel: 020 8541 3636 Fax: 020 8541 5850 Contact: Anne Lotter
bigozorganic@btconnect.com www.bigoz.co.uk
Big Oz puffs organic grains from Australia, for selling wholesale and
packing into display boxes, to make the 'Morning Puffs' range of breakfast
cereals. Wholesome, pure grain cereals with nothing added and nothing
taken away.

BODY AND SOUL ORGANICS

REAR OF 1 PARADE COURT, OCKHAM ROAD SOUTH, EAST HORSLEY KT24
6QR
Tel: 01483 282868 Fax: 01483 282060 Contact: Sarah Webber
bodyandsoul@organic-gmfree.co.uk www.organic-gmfree.co.uk
Collect and delivery service, wide range of fruit and veg, wholefoods, dairy,
wines, beers, meat, poultry etc, gluten-free, dairy-free, special diets, over
2,000 organic lines. Home delivery in Surrey, phone for details.

BROADWAY HEALTH CENTRE

60 THE BROADWAY, CHEAM, SUTTON SM3 8BD
Tel: 020 8643 5132 Contact: R Franeta
Stockists of organic cereals, nuts and dried fruits, drinks, teas, chocolate,
etc. No fresh fruit or vegetables.

CHASE ORGANICS/THE ORGANIC GARDENING CATALOGUE

RIVERDENE BUSINESS PARK, MOLESEY RD., HERSHAM KT12 4RG
Tel: 01932 253666 Fax: 01932 252707 Contact: Mike Hedges
enquiries@chaseorganics.co.uk www.organiccatalogue.co.uk
The Organic Gardening Catalogue contains seeds, composts, pest controls,
sundries and books for organic gardeners. It is the official catalogue of the
HDRA.

CONFOCO (UK) LTD
DUNCAN HOUSE, HIGH STREET, RIPLEY GU23 6AY
Tel: 01483 211288 Fax: 01483 211388 Contact: H Hughes
heidi@confocouk.com www.confocouk.com
Leading supplier of processed fruit and vegetable products for the food
industry, including organic. Soil Association licence no. P2452.

CRANLEIGH ORGANIC FARM SHOP
LOWER BARRIHURST FARM, DUNSFORD ROAD, CRANLEIGH GU6 8LG
Tel: 01483 272896 Fax: 01483 273486 Contact: Ray Parker
organicfarmshop@btopenworld.com
Mixed farm producing vegetables, herbs, meat and poultry. Our farm shop
also sells produce from other local organic farms.

DRYDOWN FARM
HOUND HOUSE RD., SHERE GU5 9JG
Tel: 07941 277545 Fax: 01483 205419 Contact: Jennie Wisher
Established 17 years supplying organic and additive-free meat. Rare breeds
of sheep, pigs and poultry, plus traditional beef suckler herd.

GORDON'S FINE FOODS
GORDON HOUSE, LITTLEMEAD IND. ESTATE, CRANLEIGH GU6 8ND
Tel: 01483 267707 Fax: 01483 267783 Contact: Adam Gordon
info@gordonsfinefoods.com www.gordonsfinefoods.com
Soil Association P2386. Organic mustard, chutney and sauces available
under brand or own label. A private independent family business
producing products to the highest standard.

GROVE FRESH LIMITED
SAXLEY COURT, 121–129 VICTORIA RD, HORLEY RH6 7AS
Tel: 01293 820832 Fax: 01293 822741 Contact: Andrew Shupick
enquires@grovefresh.co.uk www.grovefresh.co.uk
Soil Association P1814. Manufacturer of organic fruit juices.

HEHLIS HOLISTICS

17 LANSDOWNE COURT, BRIGHTON RD., PURLEY CR8 2BD
Tel: 020 8660 7954 Fax: 020 8660 7954
Contact: Andrea Hehlmann & Tim Gunner
info@hehlis-holistics.com
Mail order shop for organic baby sleeping bags, organic teas, organic spices and organic sheepskin yoga mats.

HORTI. HALCYON

HEATH MILL HOUSE, HEATH MILL LANE, FOX CORNER,
WORPLESDON GU3 3PR
Tel: 01483 232095 Fax: 01483 232095 Contact: Halcyon Broadwood
halcyon@heathmillhouse.freeserve.co.uk www.hortihalcyon-organic.co.uk
OF&G 11UKF120202. Over 50 varieties of organic vegetables and herbs are grown by us. Boxes range from £9.50 upwards and contents can be varied to suit customer needs, delivery within 15-mile radius. Farmers' markets in Guildford, Wimbledon and Chiswick. Visitors by appointment.

KALLO FOODS LTD

COOPERS PLACE, WORMLEY GU8 5SZ
Tel: 01428 685100 Fax: 01428 685800 Contact: Charles Eassie
marketing@kallofoods.com www.kallofoods.com
Kallo Foods is the UK's leading supplier of organic breadsticks, organic crackers and biscuits and organic stocks and gravies, as well as organic chocolate and gluten-free products.

LATIN AMERICAN PRODUCE LTD

30 WESTMEADS, ONSLOW VILLAGE, GUILFORD GU2 7ST
Tel: 01483 561719 Fax: 01483 571035 Contact: MSS Namor
lap@mssn.freeserve.co.uk
LAP Ltd is an import house with many contacts in Latin America. We aim to help Latin American producers to sell organic fresh produce (fruit and vegetables) both in UK supermarkets and the European marketplace.

NEAL'S YARD REMEDIES

2 MARKET ST., GUILDFORD GU1 4LB
Tel: 01483 450434 Contact: The Manager
mail@nealsyardremedies.com www.nealsyardremedies.com
Neal's Yard Remedies manufactures and retails natural cosmetics in addition
to stocking an extensive range of herbs, essential oils, homoeopathic
remedies and reference material.

OLIVERS WHOLEFOOD STORE

5 STATION APPROACH, KEW GARDENS, RICHMOND TW9 3QB
Tel: 020 8948 3990 Fax: 020 8948 3991 Contact: Sara Novakovic
sara@oliverswholefoods.co.uk
'This shop is an inspiration. Effortless, curved displays are plumped with
Rococco chocolate, Richmond Park Honey, organic cooking oils and alcohol. The fridges have a wide selection of tofu and tempeh and there's river
trout and organic meat in the freezers. At Christmas organic poultry and
hams, and free game are available. Many things make this store stand out
from the crowd, notably regular bakery deliveries from Cranks and the
Authentic Bakery and the fact that the entire Dr Hauschka range is stocked
including the make-up. Education is the key theme—as well as selling
books galore, Oliver's runs weekly lectures from health experts like John
Briffa.' —Time Out Shopping Guide 2004. Winner of 'Organic Community
Shop of the Year 99' Soil Association Award, 'Health Food Retailer of the
Year—Large Store 99' Natural Products Awards, 'Business of the Year 03'
Richmond Borough Business Awards, 'Retail Shop of the Year 03' Richmond
Borough Business Awards.

ORGANICALLY SPEAKING

33 DENZIL ROAD, GUILDFORD GU2 7NQ
Tel: 01483 531319 Contact: Jessica Hughes
organic-speaking@btclick.com www.organically-speaking.co.uk
A friendly box scheme offering delivery of fruit & vegetables with a
selection of boxes to suit all requirements, wide range of grocery products,
including wheat- & gluten-free varieties, household and skincare products,
meat and ready meals. We offer a personalised service and can deliver
specific fruits and vegetables to suit your needs. We look forward to
hearing from you and are happy to answer any queries.

PIZZA ORGANIC LTD

BARWELL BUSINESS PARK, LEATHERHEAD RD., CHESSINGTON KT9 2NY
Tel: 020 8397 3330 Fax: 020 8974 1298 Contact: Mike Traszko
info@pizzapiazza.co.uk www.pizzapiazza.co.uk
Head office for expanding range of Soil Association accredited restaurants
featuring a menu packed full of organic stonebaked pizza, sautéed pasta,
gourmet burgers, grilled fish and fabulous desserts to die for.

PIZZA ORGANIC LTD

42–46 HIGH ST., KINGSTON KT1 1HN
Tel: 020 8541 5186 Contact: Mike Traszko
info@pizzapiazza.co.uk www.pizzapiazza.co.uk
Expanding range of Soil Association accredited restaurants featuring a
menu packed full of organic stonebaked pizza, sautéed pasta, gourmet
burgers, grilled fish and fabulous desserts to die for.

PIZZA ORGANIC LTD

3 LINKFIELD ST., REDHILL RH1 1HQ
Tel: 01737 766154 Contact: Mike Traszko
info@pizzapiazza.co.uk www.pizzapiazza.co.uk
Expanding range of Soil Association accredited restaurants featuring a
menu packed full of organic stonebaked pizza, sautéed pasta, gourmet
burgers, grilled fish and fabulous desserts to die for.

SUNSHINE ORGANICS

2 KNOWLE LANE GU6 8JL
Tel: 01483 268014 Contact: Amanda Porter
amanda@sunshine-organics.co.uk www.sunshine-organics.co.uk
Specialised home shopping service supporting local organic growers.
Orders taken Mon–Wed for delivery on the following Thursday. Delivery to
some GU & RH postcodes: please check the map on the website.

WHOLE EARTH FOODS LTD

KALLO FOODS, COOPERS PLACE, COMBE LANE, WORMLEY,
GODALMING GU8 5SZ
Tel: 01428 685100 Fax: 01428 685800 Contact: Lisa Lennon
enquiries@wholeearthfoods.co.uk www.wholeearthfoods.co.uk
Since 1976 Whole Earth Foods have led and guided the movement to
organic food. We offer a wide range of organic products: peanut butters,
spreads, breakfast cereals, canned goods, and soft drinks. Available
nationally in major supermarkets and good health food stores.

WILSON & MANSFIELD

HADDON HOUSE, HINDHEAD RD., HASLEMERE GU27 1LH
Tel: 01428 651331 Fax: 01428 641552 Contact: Shirley Humphrey
sales@wmjuice.co.uk www.wmjuice.co.uk
Fruit juices/purées. Wilson & Mansfield are recognised as leaders in the
importation of organic fruit juices and purées. Serving the UK and other
continental European markets.

WINTERBOTHAM DARBY & CO LTD

5–7 NEWMAN RD., PURLEY WAY, CROYDON CR9 3SN
Tel: 020 8664 3000 Fax: 020 8664 3001 Contact: Michelle Watson
www.windar.co.uk
Soil Association P4319. Importing and distributing meat products,
charcuterie, confectionery, snacks and other grocery items to retailers,
wholesalers and food processors.

WINTERSHALL PARTNERSHIP

BRAMLEY, SURREY, GU5 0LR
Tel: 01483 892167 Fax: 01483 898709 Contact: Paul Huntley
susan@huntleygroup.com www.wintershall-estate.com
We are producers of Aberdeen Angus beef and lamb, available retail
through our box scheme delivered to the door. We also sell wholesale and
produce several arable crops.

EAST SUSSEX

AGRIPAL ENTERPRISES 'WICKHAM MANOR FARM'
WICKHAM MANOR FARM, PANNEL LANE, WINCHELSEA TN36 4AG
Tel: 01797 226216 Fax: 01797 226216 Contact: Mason Palmer
mason@wickhammanor.co.uk www.wickhammanor.co.uk
Soil Association G4537. Specialists in quality organic beef, lamb and
mutton. Suckler herd of Simmental x cows producing prime finished cattle
from extensive grazing marshes. Hampshire Down x Lleyn lambs producing
top quality meat with characteristic tender juicy texture and unique flavour.
Breeders of pedigree Lleyn stock. Also growers and retailers of organic
potatoes, cereals, and pulses.

ASHURST ORGANICS
THE ORCHARD, ASHURST FARM, ASHURST LANE, PLUMPTON, LEWES BN7 3AP
Tel: 01273 891219 Fax: 01273 891943 Contact: Peter Haynes
Soil Association G1796. Weekly box scheme for our own and locally grown
seasonal vegetables in Brighton, Lewes, Worthing and surrounding areas.

AVEA ORGANIC
63 BERNARD RD., BRIGHTON BN2 3ER
Tel: 08701993818 Contact: Rick Havemann
rhavemann@avea.co.uk www.avea.co.uk
Avea sells hypoallergenic organic cosmetics and skin care products. We also
sell baby creams and lotions, and cater for men. All ranges and products
are certified organic

BARCOMBE NURSERIES
MILL LANE, BARCOMBE, LEWES BN8 5TH
Tel: 01273 400011 Fax: 01273 400011 Contact: Adrian Halstead
Outdoor and protected growing of vegetables, salads, herbs, well
established box scheme, vegetables, fruit, eggs, with free home delivery
area including Brighton and Hove, Haywards Heath and Lewes.

BATTLE HEALTH STORE

83 HIGH ST., BATTLE TN33 0AQ
Tel: 01424 772435 Contact: N Crawshaw
sussexhealth@hotmail.com
A family-run, local health store selling wholefoods, vegetarian and special diet foods, herbal remedies and supplements. We aim to provide as many organic lines as possible.

BEANS AND THINGS

HARVEST HOME, CHUCK HATCH, HARTFIELD TN7 4EN
Tel: 01273 477774 Fax: 01273 477774 Contact: Dave Flintan
Door to door deliveries of organic fruit, veg, dairy and wholefoods to Brighton, Newhaven, Seaford, Hove etc.

BOATHOUSE ORGANIC FARM SHOP

THE ORCHARD, UCKFIELD RD., RINGMER, LEWES BN8 5RX
Tel: 01273 814188 Contact: Martin Tebbutt
shop@boathouseorganic.fsbusiness.co.uk
www.boathouseorganics.fsbusiness.co.uk
Farm shop. Home-produced beef, mutton, lamb, vegetables, flour and full range of groceries. Quality beef available wholesale and retail. Farm address: Boathouse Organic Farm, Isfield, Uckfield TN22 5TY. Tel: 01825 750641.

CORIANDER RESTAURANT & DELI

5 HOVE MANOR, HOVE STREET, HOVE BN3 2DF
Tel: 01273 730850 Fax: 01273 774555 Contact: Katrin Smale
info@corianderbrighton.com www.corianderbrighton.com
Innovative restaurant serving simple yet exotic food from around the world—absolutely delicious and 90% organic. We promote sustainable living in all aspects of our business. Delicatessen selling prepared foods, cooked meats, dried goods etc.

DAVENPORT VINEYARDS

LIMNEY FARM, CASTLE HILL, ROTHERFIELD, CROWBOROUGH TN6 3RR
Tel: 01892 852380 Fax: 01892 852781 Contact: Will Davenport
info@davenportvineyards.co.uk www.davenportvineyards.co.uk
English wines from Kent and Sussex: dry white 'Horsmonden' wine, quality
sparkling wines sold under the 'Limney Estate' label. Winemaking is done
in-house to completion (organic certified). All wines comply with the UK
wine quality assurance scheme. Suppliers to trade and retail customers (by
mail order).

EMERSON COLLEGE

HARTFIELD ROAD, FOREST ROW RH18 5JX
Tel: 01342 822238 Fax: 01342 826055 Contact: Alysoun Barrett
mail@emerson.org.uk www.emerson.org.uk
Soil Association & Demeter registered. Emerson College runs a three year,
full-time training in Biodynamic Organic Agriculture, as well as short
courses in biodynamics. Students at the college run a commercial
biodynamic market garden through spring and summer.

FRANCHISE MANOR FARM

SPRING LANE, BURWASH
Tel: 01435 883151 Fax: 01435 883151 Contact: Simon Bishop
simon@thenetherfieldcentre.co.uk
Organic mixed farm: arable, beef, sheep, pigs, laying hens. Has on-site
meat chiller store and butchery room with Soil Association licence.

FULL OF BEANS

96 HIGH STREET, LEWES BN7 1XH
Tel: 01273 472627 Fax: 01273 472627 Contact: Sara Gosling
tempeh@globalnet.co.uk
We manufacture organic tofu, tempeh, wholegrain mustard, miso. Shop
has home-made vegetarian/vegan snacks, cakes, pulses, dried fruit, nuts,
herbs, spices and many more delights.

GOSSYPIUM

GOSSYPIUM HOUSE, ABINGER PLACE, LEWES BN7 2QA
Tel: 01273 488221 Fax: 01273 488721 Contact: Thomas Petit
info@gossypium.co.uk www.gossypium.co.uk
Gossypium is about understanding the real value of clothing. All
Gossypium products are made with organic and fairly traded cotton. The
collection includes yogawear, casual wear, nightwear, underwear and
babywear.

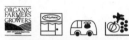

HARVEST SUPPLIES

HARVEST HOME, CHUCK HATCH, HARTFIELD TN7 4EN
Tel: 01342 823392 Fax: 01342 825594 Contact: Dave Flintan
Distribute for local growers. Retail business at home, door to door
deliveries, wholesale deliveries to shops, restaurants etc. Full selection of
veg, fruit, herbs and wholefoods in Sussex and Kent.

HENLEY BRIDGE INGREDIENTS LTD

UNIT 1 FOORDS FARM, FOORDS LANE, VINES CROSS, HEATHFIELD TN21 9EX
Tel: 01435 812808 Fax: 01435 813808 Contact: Tony Mycock
sales@hbingredients.co.uk www.hbingredients.co.uk
Soil Association P4239. Suppliers of organic ingredients to food processors:
sugars, chocolate, cocoa products, cereal syrups, dextrose, starch, dried
fruits, nuts, praline paste, marzipan, fondant, milk powders. Will source
anything on request.

HERONS FOLLY GARDEN

HERONS FOLLY, FLETCHING STREET, MAYFIELD TN20 6TE
Tel: 01435 873608 Contact: Patrick Treherne
Organic vegetables in all seasons. We sell wholesale but have started selling
directly to the public through a box scheme and farm shop.

HIDDEN SPRING VINEYARD & ORGANIC ORCHARDS
VINES CROSS ROAD, HORAM TN21 OHF
Tel: 01435 812640 Fax: 01435 813542 Contact: Sue Mosey
info@hiddenspring.co.uk www.info@
Soil Association G1459. Hidden Spring Vineyard and Organic Orchards set
in gentle Sussex countryside. Visitors can sample the wine and seasonal
fruit: 10 apple varieties and 3 pear varieties. Phone first.

HIGHLANDS ORGANIC FARM
HORAM, HEATHFIELD TN21 0LG
Tel: 01435 812461 Contact: Peter Mason
petermason_uk@yahoo.com
We produce very traditional Sussex beef, Jacob and Texel lamb, really high
quality farmyard organic free range chicken and pond reared ducks. We are
Soil Association registered and we farm in conjunction with conservation
principles. Alternative telephone: 07802 314494.

HODSON, JHW & SE
HIGHAM FARM, BELLS YEW GREEN, TUNBRIDGE WELLS TN3 9AU
Tel: 01892 750363 Fax: 01892 752179 Contact: Sarah Hodson
Soil Association G4555. Organic beef from our own pedigree Sussex herd
and organic lamb from our pedigree Poll Dorset flock. Self-catering granary
accommodation in High Weald area of outstanding natural beauty.

INFINITY FOODS CO-OPERATIVE LTD
25 NORTH RD., BRIGHTON BN1 2AA
Tel: 01273 603563 Fax: 01273 675384 Contact: Grahame Mayo
www.infinityfoods.co.uk
Organic and wholefoods, cruelty-free cosmetics, fresh fruit and vegetables,
organic bread baked on the premises.

INFINITY FOODS COOPERATIVE LTD
FRANKLIN RD, PORTSLADE, BRIGHTON BN41 1AF
Tel: 01273 424060 Fax: 01273 417739 Contact: Charlie Booth
sales@infinityfoods.co.uk www.infinityfoods.co.uk
Leading UK wholesaler of organic foods. Soil Association no. P1465. Over 3,500 organic lines in stock offering the most comprehensive range of organic products available anywhere. Delivery to the trade throughout the UK. See display ad.

IZZARD, MRS MARGARET
GIFFORD FARM COTTAGE, BATTLE RD., DALLINGTON TN21 9LH
Tel: 01424 838210 Fax: 01424 838210 Contact: M Izzard
I have poultry, eggs, single cows and calves, do B&B, plus gardening.

KAI ORGANIC CAFE
52 GARDNER ST., BRIGHTON BN1 1UN
Tel: 01273 684921 Fax: 01273 604021 Contact: Simon & Carol Thompson
kaiorganic@btinternet.com www.kaiorganic.com
Fast moving café using only organic ingredients. Fresh salad bar, sandwiches, including wheat-free selection, seasonal soups and daily specials. Superb cakes including unique wheat- and gluten-free range.

LANSDOWN HEALTH FOODS
44 CLIFFE HIGH ST., LEWES BN7 2AN
Tel: 01273 474681 Contact: Cindy Holmes
Health food and wholefood shop, wide range of organic products, special diets, fruit and vegetables, box scheme, herbal remedies, ordering service, locally produced organic body care range.

MARIPOSA ALTERNATIVE BODYCARE
15A SHELLDALE RD., PORTSLADE BN41 1LE
Tel: 01273 242925 Fax: 08701 300481 Contact: Steve Brown
enquiries@mariposa.co.uk www.mariposa-alternative-bodycare.co.uk
Natural and organic skin care, body care and perfumes. Organic and
demeter essential oils. Animal and earth friendly plus the most divine
fairtrade incense. All of our products are vegetarian. Most are suitable for
vegans. All available to buy here and at our secure on-line shop.

NEAL'S YARD REMEDIES
2A KENSINGTON GARDENS, BRIGHTON BN1 4AL
Tel: 01273 601464 Contact: The Manager
mail@nealsyardremedies.com www.nealsyardremedies.com
Neal's Yard Remedies manufactures and retails natural cosmetics in addition
to stocking an extensive range of herbs, essential oils, homoeopathic
remedies and reference material.

THE NETHERFIELD CENTRE
NETHERFIELD PLACE FARM, NETHERFIELD, NR. BATTLE TN3 9PY
Tel: 01424 775615 Fax: 01424 775616 Contact: Topsy Jewell
simon@thenetherfieldcentre.co.uk
The Netherfield Centre for Sustainable Food and Farming runs education
courses, training and networking for those interested in sustainable
agriculture. The Netherfield Centre is located on an organic farm and
linked to a network of farms sharing a cutting room and marketing meat
locally.

NHR ORGANIC OILS
5 COLLEGE TERRACE, BRIGHTON BN2 0EE
Tel: 0845 310 8066 Fax: 0870 135 2711 Contact: Kolinka Zinovieff
organic@nhr.kz www.nhrorganicoils.com
Organic essential oils, organic aromatherapy oils, trade and direct. The
purest organic aromatherapy oils sold at affordable prices, organic
aromatherapy chocolates, kit boxes, organic shampoo, a huge range. USA
tel: 1866 562 0890. International tel: (+44) 1273 236524.

THE NICE NAPPY COMPANY

61 NEW MOORSITE, WESTFIELD TN35 4QP
Tel: 08453 457193 Fax: 0870 0560165 Contact: Helen Armfield
info@nicenappy.co.uk www.nicenappy.co.uk
WAHM business selling washable nappies and covers, organic and Fairtrade
children's clothes, washable sanitary products, slings and the Bravado! range.
Products in cotton and hemp, organically produced wherever possible.

NOANAHS ORGANICS

NOLANDS FARM, STATION RD., PLUMPTON GREEN BN7 3BT
Tel: 01273 890295 Contact: Noanah Hall
Seasonal mixed organic vegetable grower selling to shops, restaurants and
at farmers' markets.

OAKWOOD FARM

POPPINGHOLE LANE, ROBERTSBRIDGE TN32 5BL
Tel: 01580 830893 Fax: 01580 830201 Contact: Matthew Wilson
Soil Association G2575 & P6079. Top fruit, soft fruit, apple juice, pear juice,
cider and potatoes. Also attend Lewes Farmers' market.

OLIVER, EM & RJH

BLACKLANDS, CROWHURST, BATTLE TN33 9AB
Tel: 01424 830360 Fax: 01424 830360 Contact: Robb & Marianne Oliver
architects@mnroliver.fsbusiness.co.uk
HDRA 55251, Soil Association (personal membership) 8718. An organic
smallholding producing vegetables and goat's milk for family, any surplus
for sale to B&B, campers and holiday guests. Architects (RIBA) to
environment-conscious designs. Camping.

ORCHIDWOOD MUSHROOMS LTD

HOBBS LANE, BECKLEY TN31 6TS
Tel: 01797 260411 Fax: 01797 260603 Contact: Colin F Bell
sales@orchidwood.co.uk
Soil Association P4568. Manufacturer and marketer of processed
mushrooms in frozen, chilled, to the manufacturing trade.

ORGANIC BOTANICS

PO BOX 2140, HOVE BN3 5BX
Tel: 01273 773182 Fax: 01273 773182 Contact: Celsi Richfield
richfield@cwctv.net www.organicbotanics.com
Manufacturer/supplier of organic skin care. Superb organic skin care made
with organic, cold-pressed plant oils and extracts. Organic essential oils,
natural vitamins, natural UV filter. Telephone 01273 773182 for further
information and free sample.

PASKINS HOTEL

18/19 CHARLOTTE ST., BRIGHTON BN2 1AG
Tel: 01273 601203 Fax: 01273 621973 Contact: R Marlowe (Director)
welcome@paskins.co.uk www.paskins.co.uk
Most of our food is organic and we are justly proud of our varied
vegetarian breakfasts. Our tasteful rooms are individually designed and we
have a welcoming bar.

PILE, JOHN S (FARMS) LTD

MIDDLE FARM, WEST FIRLE, LEWES BN8 6LJ
Tel: 01323 811411 Fax: 01323 811622 Contact: Helen Marsh
info@middlefarm.com www.middlefarm.com
Soil Association P6214 (shop), G5831 (beef). Open family farm with own
butchery, bakery, specialist food and cheese sections, restaurant and The
National Collection of Cider and Perry, producing and selling raw milk from
pedigree Jersey herd, and organic beef.

REAL FOOD DIRECT

UNIT 4, LEVEL 3, NEW ENGLAND HOUSE, NEW ENGLAND STREET,
BRIGHTON BN1 4GH
Tel: 01273 621222 Fax: 01273 626226 Contact: Kate Baker
info@realfood-direct.com www.realfood-direct.com
Organic food home delivery for Brighton and Hove: fruit and vegetables,
fresh bread, meat and fish, dairy, wholefoods, baby food, green cleaning
products and lots more.

RYE HEALTH STORE

90 HIGH ST, RYE TN31 7JN
Tel: 01797 223495 Contact: NC Crawshaw
sussexhealth@hotmail.com
A busy local shop selling a full range of wholefoods, special diet foods, supplements and natural remedies. Many organic wines are stocked.

SCHMIDT NATURAL CLOTHING

CORBIERE, NURSERY LANE, NUTLEY TN22 3NS
Tel: 0845 3450498 Fax: 01825 714676 Contact: Glenn Kositzki-Metzner
glenn@naturalclothing.co.uk www.naturalclothing.co.uk
Catalogue of organic clothing, nappies, bedsheets, duvets, toys and toiletries for babies, children and adults by mail order. Eczema, sensitive skin, chemical allergy specialists. Emphasis is placed on hygiene and comfort of products, fair trade practice, and attentive personal service. Products certified by International Natural Textile Association, Biodynamic Agricultural Association (Demeter), Real Nappy Association.

SEASONS FOREST ROW LTD

10–11 HARTFIELD ROAD, FOREST ROW RH18 5DN
Tel: 01342 824673 Fax: 01342 826119 Contact: John Walden
seasonsforestrow@btinternet.com www.seasons-forest-row.co.uk
Two shops. Large range of wholefoods and fresh produce, most organic, many biodynamic. Also natural cosmetics, wooden toys, large range of books on biodynamics and anthroposophy. Separate shop for organic fruit and vegetables. Wholesale to shops, restaurants and institutions in Sussex. Business owned by charitable trust.

SEASONS OF LEWES

199 HIGH STREET, LEWES BN7 2NS
Tel: 01273 473968 Contact: Carol Mercer
Vegetarian/vegan restaurant, 75% ingredients organic. GM-free. Outside catering available. Weddings, buffets etc. Food from the freezer (vegetarian meals, soups, pies). Family business. Open Tues–Sat 10am–5pm.

SEDLESCOMBE VINEYARD
CRIPP'S CORNER, SEDLESCOMBE, NR. ROBERTSBRIDGE TN32 5AS
Tel: 0800 980 2884 Fax: 01580 830122 Contact: Roy Cook
www.englishorganicwine.co.uk
Soil Association PC11S. We produce and sell organic alcoholic and
non-alcoholic drinks, organic wine, cider, juices and liqueur.

SIMPLY WILD FOOD COMPANY
SCRAGOAK FARM SHOP, BRIGHTLING RD., ROBERTSBRIDGE TN32 5EY
Tel: 01424 838454 Fax: 01424 838800 Contact: Howard Lee
enquiries@simplywildorganics.co.uk www.simplywild.biz
Simply Wild at Scragoak Farm is a retail outlet for organic fruit, vegetables,
eggs, home-produced meat and freshly baked bread. A large selection of
other organic products is also available.

ST. MARY'S RETREAT HOUSE
CHURCH STREET, HARTFIELD TN7 4AG
Tel: 01892 770305 Contact: Rose Moore
Restore body, soul and spirit in a peaceful setting near the Ashdown Forest.
Vegetarian home cooking with organic produce. Not a B&B!

WEALDEN WHOLEFOODS
PILGRIMS, HIGH ST., WADHURST TN5 6AA
Tel: 01892 783065 Fax: 01892 783351 Contact: Barbara Godsalve
barbara@wealdenwholefoods.co.uk www.wealdenwholefoods.co.uk
Wholefood shop and café selling mostly organic products. We also stock
fair traded and environmentally friendly products. In the process of
expanding both the shop and café, and the range of goods carried.

WOODEN WONDERS

FARLEY FARM HOUSE, CHIDDINGLY BN8 6HW
Tel: 01825 872856 Fax: 01825 872733 Contact: Kerry Negahban
info@woodenwonders.co.uk www.woodenwonders.co.uk
Wooden Wonders was the first wooden craft gift manufacturer in the UK
with Forest Stewardship Council accreditation making practical and
ornamental gifts—all suitable for customisation with our in-house laser
engravers.

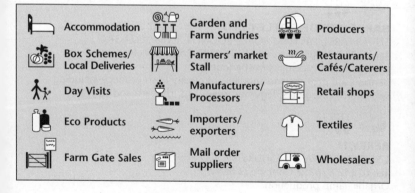

Accommodation	Garden and Farm Sundries	Producers
Box Schemes/ Local Deliveries	Farmers' market Stall	Restaurants/ Cafés/Caterers
Day Visits	Manufacturers/ Processors	Retail shops
Eco Products	Importers/ exporters	Textiles
Farm Gate Sales	Mail order suppliers	Wholesalers

THE ACORN CENTRE

TODHURST SITE, NORTH HEATH, PULBOROUGH RH20 1DL
Tel: 01798 873533 Fax: 01798 873533 Contact: Rachel Smither
michellewykes@aldingbournetrust.co.uk
Training centre for adults with learning disabilities. We grow our own
organic vegetables which are sold through our farm shop. Other organic
produce also available. Coffee shop. Soil Association G2586, P5118.

ALDINGBOURNE COUNTRY CENTRE

BLACKMILL LANE, NORTON, CHICHESTER PO18 0JP
Tel: 01243 542075 Fax: 01243 544807 Contact: Linda Thompson
acc@aldingbournetrust.co.uk www.aldingbournetrust.co.uk
Soil Association G4375. Training centre for adults with learning disabilities.
Retail shop, coffee shop, woodland walk.

BARFOOTS OF BOTLEY LTD

SEFTER FARM, PAGHAM ROAD, BOGNOR REGIS PO21 3PX
Tel: 01243 268811 Fax: 01243 262842 Contact: Peter Gimbel
peterg@barfoots.co.uk www.barfoots.com
Barfoots are growers and suppliers of quality fresh produce including
sweetcorn, courgettes, legumes, pumpkins, rhubarb and squash.

BERRY, N

GREAT WATER FARM, ASHURSTWOOD RH9 3PQ
Tel: 01342 826752 Contact: N Berry
Organic lamb production.

BIOWISE

HOYLE DEPOT, GRAFFHAM, PETWORTH GU28 0LR
Tel: 01798 867574 Fax: 01798 867574 Contact: Sue Cooper
post@biowise-biocontrol.co.uk www.biowise-biocontrol.co.uk
International Biocontrol Manufacturers Association. Biological controls for
growers and gardeners.

CORNERWEIGHS

ELM LODGE, CAUDLE STREET, HENFIELD BN5 9DQ
Tel: 01273 492794 Contact: Susie Marjoribanks
cornerweighs@aol.com
An Aladdin's cave for natural and organic foods specialising in dietetic needs, with a state of the art computer enquiry system for health concerns putting you in control of your purchases.

COTTON BOTTOMS LTD

UNITS 7–9, WATER LANE IND. ESTATE, WATER LANE,
STORRINGTON RH20 3XX
Tel: 08707 778899 Fax: 08707 778700 Contact: Joanne Freer
sales@cottonbottoms.co.uk www.cottonbottoms.co.uk
Exciting and innovative modern cotton nappies and accessories. Leading the way in environmental systems, helping parents care for their baby and its future.

DOWN TO EARTH

GOLDRINGS, WEST STREET, MIDHURST GU29 9NQ
Tel: 01730 815133 Fax: 01730 815133 Contact: Jan Start
Friendly organic shop with range of Sussex sheep and goat cheeses and yoghurts, organic fruit and vegetables, wholefoods, frozen meat, fish, ice cream, eco-friendly washing products, nappies.

FARGRO LTD

TODDINGTON LANE, LITTLEHAMPTON BN17 7PP
Tel: 01903 721591 Fax: 01903 730737 Contact: J McAlpine
promos@fargro.co.uk www.fargro.co.uk
Horticultural wholesaler providing organic fertiliser and a full range of biological and organic pest control products.

G&G FOOD SUPPLIES LTD

VITALITY HOUSE, 2/3 IMBERHORNE WAY, EAST GRINSTEAD RH19 1RL
Tel: 01342 311401 Fax: 01342 301904 Contact: Jeremy Stephens
jstephens@gandgvitamins.com www.gandgvitamins.com
Soil Association approved contract encapsulator of herbal and vitamin
capsules. Own label product ranges created.

GREEN PEOPLE

BRIGHTON ROAD, HANDCROSS RH17 6BZ
Tel: 01444 401444 Fax: 01444 401011 Contact: Sue Losson
organic@greenpeople.co.uk www.greenpeople.co.uk
Manufacturer of handmade organic health and beauty products for all the
family. Sun care, dental care, body care, baby care, skin care, hair care and
home care products. No petrochemicals, sodium lauryl sulphate or
parabens. Approved by the Vegan Society. Call for a free catalogue and trial
sachet.See display ad.

THE GOODWOOD ESTATE CO LTD

HOME FARM, GOODWOOD, CHICHESTER PO18 0QF
Tel: 01243 771615 Fax: 01243 536699 Contact: Karl Barton
www.goodwood.co.uk
Beef, lamb and pork: quarter, half or whole beasts. Native breeds finished
to a high standard. Also quality ice cream. Registered with the Soil
Association.

HIGH WEALD DAIRY

TREMAINS FARM, HORSTED KEYNES, HAYWARDS HEATH RH17 7EA
Tel: 01825 791636 Fax: 01825 791641 Contact: Mark Hardy
info@highwealddairy.co.uk www.highwealddairy.co.uk
Soil Association P1772. High Weald make a wide range of cheeses from
organic sheep milk and organic cow's milk, and supply outlets throughout
the UK. Telephone for your nearest stockist.

KPS COMPOSTING SERVICES LTD

AWBROOK PARK FARM, HAM LANE RH17 7PR
Tel: 01444 831010 Fax: 01444 831340 Contact: Edward Watson
ed@kps.uk.com www.kpscomposting.com
Contract hire of green waste processing machinery. Organic compost also supplied.

LAINES ORGANIC FARM

47 NEWBURY LANE, CUCKFIELD RH17 5AA
Tel: 01444 452480 Fax: 01444 452480 Contact: Toos Jeuken
Soil Association J04S. Producer of organic outdoor traditional and seasonal field vegetables. Family business, self-service farm shop.

LANGMEADS OF FLANSHAM LTD – ROOKERY FARM EGGS

ROOKERY FARM, FLANSHAM, BOGNOR REGIS PO22 8NN
Tel: 01243 583583 Fax: 01243 585354 Contact: Rupert Langmead
Soil Association G7241, OF&G 11UK F02075. Our organic eggs are available wholesale from the farm or via our delivery rounds and retail from the farm or via farmers' markets.

MONTEZUMA'S CHOCOLATES

THE OLD PIGGERY, THE KINGLEY CENTRE, DOWNS ROAD, WEST STOKE PO18 9BQ
Tel: 01243 576 589 Fax: 01243 576 516 Contact: Simon Pattinson
simon.pattinson@montezumas.co.uk www.montezumas.co.uk
Soil Association P6067. Manufacturer and retailer of hand-made organic chocolates.

MYRTLEGROVE LTD
MYRTLEGROVE FARM, PATCHING, NR. WORTHING BN13 3XL
Tel: 01903 871334 Fax: 01903 772747 Contact: Jill Angell
jillmangell@aol.com
Soil Association G7054. Producers of pedigree Sussex cattle from
single suckler herd on downland farm also participating in the South
Downs Environmentally Sensitive Area scheme. Cattle reared on grass and
silage and outwintered. Store cattle and replacement heifers available mid
summer 2004.

NATURAL WAY
33A CARFAX, HORSHAM RH12 1EE
Tel: 01403 262228 Fax: 01403 262228 Contact: Jean Earl
Offer wide range of pre-packed wholefoods and produce sold by well
known names in the wholefood industry. Not vegetables or eggs.

OCEANS OF GOODNESS/SEAGREENS
1 THE WARREN, HANDCROSS RH17 6DX
Tel: 01444 400403 Fax: 01444 400493 Contact: Simon Ranger
post@seagreens.com www.oceansofgoodness.com
Soil Association P2446. Oceans Of Goodness markets Seagreens®
(www.seagreens.com) food products, which are harvested from remote
wild seaweeds and are nutritionally outstanding. Consumer, healthcare,
catering.

PASTA REALE
FLEMING WAY, CRAWLEY RH10 9JW
Tel: 01293 649700 Fax: 01293 649741
Contact: Michelle Jeffrey/ Chris Redman
michelle.jeffrey@pastareale.com www.pastareale.com
Soil Association P5554. Pasta Reale specialise in the manufacture of fresh
pasta and fresh sauce to the retail sector. All products are made using
natural ingredients.

STEEPWOOD FARM
BROADFORD BRIDGE RD., ADVERSANE, BILLINGSHURST RH14 9EG
Tel: 01403 785434 Fax: 01403 784730 Contact: AJ Challis
val@steepwoodfarm.fsnet.co.uk
Soil Association G7049. Producer, wholesaler and retailer of the finest
quality meat and game.

ST. MARTIN'S TEA ROOMS
3 ST. MARTIN'S ST., CHICHESTER PO19 1NP
Tel: 01243 786715 Fax: 01243 786715 Contact: Keith Nelson
info@organictearooms.co.uk www.organictearooms.co.uk
Medieval tea room in centre of Chichester, sensitively restored in 1979
by Keith Nelson (present proprietor). No smoking throughout. No
convenience or tinned foods. Three cosy log fires and walled garden.

WAYSIDE ORGANICS
WAYSIDE, WOODHORN CORNER, OVING, CHICHESTER PO20 2BT
Tel: 01243 779716 Fax: 01243 779716 Contact: Bart Ives
bart.ives@talk21.com
Soil Association G1510; P5555. Local deliveries, farm gate sales, stall at old
Spitalfields market, Sundays. Growers of salads, vegetables, herbs and top
and soft fruits to Soil Association standards.

THE WHOLE FOOD SHOP
12 THE HORNET, CHICHESTER PO19 7JG
Tel: 01243 790901 Contact: Jackie Manners
We sell a wide range of loose and pre-packed organic food including wheat-
free and dairy-free. We are also the collection point for a local box scheme.

WILLOW NURSERY
44 HILL LANE, BARNHAM PO22 0BL
Tel: 01243 552852 Fax: 01243 552852 Contact: David & Michele Wheeler
Soil Association W31S & PW31S. Grow a wide range of vegetables and
salad crops sold through a year round box scheme. Also supply fruit boxes.
Deliveries within West Sussex and East Hampshire.

TYNE AND WEAR

BLENDEX FOOD INGREDIENTS LTD
HETTON LYONS INDUSTRIAL ESTATE, HETTON LE HOLE DH5 0RG
Tel: 0191 517 0944 Fax: 0191 526 9546 Contact: NJ Robinson
blendex@blendex.co.uk www.blendex.co.uk
Blenders of organic herbs and spices for the food industry, specifically
meat, poultry and bakery. Soil Association certified no. P1654.

BRITISHECO.COM
15A GRANVILLE GARDENS, JESMOND, NEWCASTLE UPON TYNE NE2 1HL
Tel: 0191 209 4161 Contact: Nick Pringle
britisheco@hotmail.com www.britisheco.com
On-line shop selling solar powered lights, panels, water features and
rechargers. Wildlife products, organic fertiliser, mulch and lawn feed, wind-
up radios, composters, garden furniture plus loads more.

F.M. (FOODS) LTD (TROPICAL WHOLEFOODS)
50 SOUTHWICK IND. ESTATE, SUNDERLAND SR5 3TX
Tel: 0191 548 0050 Fax: 0191 516 9946 Contact: The Manager
info@fmfoods.co.uk www.fmfoods.co.uk
Soil Association P4707. Importation of Fairtrade and organic dried fruit and
vegetables. Packing of imported products into retail display packs.
Processing of imported products into snack bars, for own and private label.

NEAL'S YARD REMEDIES
19 CENTRAL ARCADE, NEWCASTLE UPON TYNE NE1 5BQ
Tel: 0191 232 2525 Contact: Lynda Airey
mail@nealsyardremedies.com www.nealsyardremedies.com
Neal's Yard Remedies manufactures and retails natural cosmetics in addition
to stocking an extensive range of herbs, essential oils, homoeopathic
remedies and reference material.

OUT OF THIS WORLD

106 HIGH ST., GOSFORTH, NEWCASTLE UPON TYNE NE3 1HB
Tel: 0191 213 5377 Fax: 0191 213 5378 Contact: Jon Walker
info@ootw.co.uk www.outofthisworld.coop
Head office of small chain of ethical and organic supermarkets in Newcastle
upon Tyne, Nottingham and Leeds. Selling over 5,000 products, most food
products certified organic plus fairly traded crafts, recycled paper and
bodycare products etc. Delivery scheme from Newcastle shop. Consumer
co-op with over 16,500 members.

OUT OF THIS WORLD

GOSFORTH SHOPPING CENTRE, HIGH ST., GOSFORTH, NEWCASTLE
UPON TYNE NE3 1JZ
Tel: 0191 213 0421 Fax: 0191 213 0429 Contact: Simon Critchley
info@ootw.co.uk www.outofthisworld.coop
Small chain of ethical and organic supermarkets in Newcastle upon Tyne,
Leeds and Nottingham. Selling over 5,000 products, mostly certified
organic food plus fairly traded crafts, recycled paper and bodycare
products etc. Consumer co-op with over 16,500 members.

PUMPHREYS COFFEE LTD

BRIDGE ST., BLAYDON NE21 4JH
Tel: 0191 414 4510 Fax: 0191 499 0526 Contact: Archer
www.pumphreys-coffee.co.uk
Soil Association P4547. Roasters and blenders of the finest quality coffees
and teas to the wholesale, retail and catering sectors, established 1750.

RISING SUN FARM

KINGS RD. NORTH, WALLSEND NE28 9JL
Tel: 0191 234 0114 Contact: D Shanks
organics@risingsunfarm.freeserve.co.uk
Soil Association producer no. P1490. Cereals, horticultural, pigs, cattle.
Urban fringe farm providing education, day service for special needs. Open
farm for community. Livery yard for diy liveries.

TRAIDCRAFT PLC
KINGSWAY, GATESHEAD NE11 0NE
Tel: 0191 491 0591 Fax: 0191 482 2690 Contact: Joe Osman
joeo@traidcraft.co.uk www.traidcraft.co.uk
Importer and distributor of organic honey, tea, chocolate. Soil Association
no. P2321.

TWINING, R & CO LTD
EARL GREY WAY, NORTH SHIELDS NE29 6AR
Tel: 0191 296 0000 Contact: Hector Galley
www.twinings.com
Soil Association P4121. 295-year-old tea manufacturer. Offers a wide variety
of organic tea and infusions.

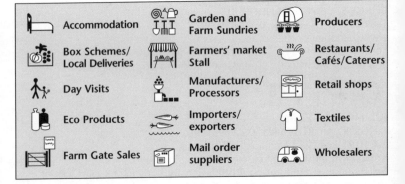

Accommodation	Garden and Farm Sundries	Producers
Box Schemes/ Local Deliveries	Farmers' market Stall	Restaurants/ Cafés/Caterers
Day Visits	Manufacturers/ Processors	Retail shops
Eco Products	Importers/ exporters	Textiles
Farm Gate Sales	Mail order suppliers	Wholesalers

WARWICKSHIRE

BROWNING, GNF & GA

FELDON FOREST FARM, FRANKTON, RUGBY CV23 9PD
Tel: 01926 632246 Contact: George Browning
georgebrowning@farmersweekly.net www.feldon-forest-farm.co.uk
Soil Association G2209. Organic mixed farm with rare breeds. Produce
includes beef, eggs, flour, fruit, herbs, vegetables, lamb, wheat, wool,
sheepskins and wood. Local delivery possible. We only sell our own produce.

CHARLECOTE MILL

HAMPTON LUCY, WARWICK CV35 8BB
Tel: 01789 842072 Contact: John Bedlington
john@charlecotemill.co.uk www.charlecotemill.co.uk
Soil Association P1555. Watermill producing wholemeal flour, including
organic.

CITADEL PRODUCTS

32 ST. ANDREWS CRESCENT, STRATFORD-UPON-AVON CV37 9QL
Tel: 01789 297456 Fax: 01789 297456 Contact: K Heming
info@citadelpolytunnels.com www.citadelpolytunnels.com
Manufacturers of polytunnel greenhouses for over 30 years. Suitable for
horticulture, livestock housing, storage etc.

ELMHURST ORGANIC FARM

BOW LANE, WITHYBROOK, COVENTRY CV7 9LQ
Tel: 01788 832233 Fax: 01788 832690 Contact: Ann Pattison
Soil Association G761. Organic meat producer and retailer. Beef, sheep,
pigs and poultry and eggs. Shop retails only own produce, open Monday,
Tuesday, Friday and Saturday, 9am–4pm.

GAIA

7 REGENT PLACE, LEAMINGTON SPA CV31 1EH
Tel: 01926 338805 Contact: Joanna
shop@gaia.coop www.gaia.coop
Soil Association P5739. Vegetarian workers co-op selling organic vegetables
and wholefoods, locally produced where possible, Fair Trade foods (mainly
organic) and eco-friendly household products. Box scheme three days a
week delivered by bicycle.

HDRA, HENRY DOUBLEDAY RESEARCH ASSOCIATION, RYTON ORGANIC GARDENS

RYTON-ON-DUNSMORE, COVENTRY CV8 3LG
Tel: 024 7630 3517 Fax: 024 7663 9229 Contact: Susan Kay-Williams
enquiry@hdra.org.uk www.hdra.org.uk
Soil Association G1092. Standards for organic products for amenity
horticulture. HDRA is Europe's largest organic gardening organisation. It is
dedicated to researching and promoting organic gardening, farming and
food. Ryton Organic Gardens, ten acres displaying all aspects of organic
horticulture for gardens, plus The Vegetable Kingdom, an interactive
exhibition for all ages on the history and role of vegetables.

IMPLEMENTATIONS

PO BOX 2568, NUNEATON CV10 9YR
Tel: 0845 330 3148 Contact: Jane Cobbald
sales@implementations.co.uk www.implementations.co.uk
Beautiful hand-crafted copper garden tools. Hard-wearing, kind to the soil,
hand-made in Austria by craftsmen coppersmiths, with shafts of European
hardwoods and bronze blades, hand-beaten for added durability.
Alternative telephone: 024 7639 2497.

KITCHEN GARDEN

DAIRY HOUSE, STONELEIGH ABBEY, KENILWORTH TQ5 9AR
Tel: 01926 851415 Fax: 01926 851997 Contact: Mike Jack
michael.jack@fourseasonsfoods.fsnet.co.uk www.kitchen-garden.co.uk
OF&G registered. Range of organic condiments, herbs, spices, nut butters,
herbal teas, essential oils. Established 10 years.

MYTHE FARM ORGANIC PRODUCE

MYTHE FARM, PINWALL LANE, SHEEPY MAGNA, ATHERSTONE CV9 3PF
Tel: 01827 712367 Fax: 01827 715738 Contact: Joe & David Garland
garland_joseph@hotmail.com
Premium organic beef and lamb for sale. Organic feed barley, feed wheat,
malting barley produced. Organic wheat and barley straw available.
Organic ware/baking potatoes delivered to wholesalers. B&B, organic
produce used occasionally.

PIZZA ORGANIC LTD

33 JURY ST., WARWICK CV34 4EH
Tel: 01926 491641 Contact: Mike Traszko
info@pizzapiazza.co.uk www.pizzapiazza.co.uk
Expanding range of Soil Association accredited restaurants featuring a
menu packed full of organic stonebaked pizza, sautéed pasta, gourmet
burgers, grilled fish and fabulous desserts to die for.

REALITY BITES ORGANIC MARKET GARDENS

4 RAILWAY COTTAGES, SOUTHAM RD., LONG ITCHINGTON CV47 9RA
Tel: 07780 688271 Contact: Tristan Coverdale
tristan@tesco.net
We grow a wide range of vegetables including up to 10 varieties of
tomatoes. Not open to the public.

REVITAL HEALTHFOOD
UNIT 1, GREENHILL ST, STRATFORD UPON AVON CV37 6LF
Tel: 01789 292353 Contact: The Manager
www.revital.com
Health shop.

SHAKESPEARE BIRTHPLACE TRUST
MARY ARDEN'S HOUSE & THE SHAKESPEAR COUNTRYSIDE MUSEUM,
STRATFORD UPON AVON CV37 9XL
Tel: 01289 293455 Fax: 01789 415404 Contact: Joe Moore
joemoore@farmersweekly.net www.shakespeare.org
Soil Association registered. We are an organic farm surrounding the
childhood home of William Shakespeare's mother, displaying rare breeds
and open throughout the year to visitors.

WARWICK HEALTH FOODS
40A BROOK ST, WARWICK CV34 4BL
Tel: 01926 494311 Contact: PR Gooding
Family-run business, 25 years, stockists of all kinds of organic foods, fresh
fruit and vegetables always in stock, yeast-free bread and other speciality
organic breads available.

WELLESBOURNE WATERMILL
KINETON ROAD, WELLESBOURNE CV35 9HG
Tel: 01789 470237 Contact: Andrew Hamilton
hamilton.a@btconnect.com
Traditional water-powered mill that produces organic and non-organic
wholemeal stoneground flour, and organic and non-organic plain white
flour, semolina and bran.

THE WHOLEFOOD SHOP

c/o ST ANDREWS CHURCH HOUSE, CHURCH STREET, RUGBY CV21 3PT
Tel: 01788 567757 Contact: Dave Kerruish
d.kerruish@ntlworld.co.uk
Retailing organic wholefoods, veg, fruit, bread, cakes, savouries—all
organic; also eco products, box scheme, local deliveries. Focal point for
environmental groups. Open Thursday and Friday.

WILD & FREE

2 CENTRAL BUILDINGS, RAILWAY TERRACE, RUGBY CV21 3EL
Tel: 01788 570400 Fax: 01788 570400 Contact: Steve Prime
info@wildandfree.net www.wildandfree.net
Retail shop offering a full range of organic vegetables, sourced wherever
possible from the UK, together with organic fruit, locally reared organic
meats, wide range of organic groceries. Delivery service available to local
area.

WEST MIDLANDS

BIRMINGHAM FARMERS' MARKET
NEW STREET, NEAR VICTORIA SQUARE, BIRMINGHAM B1
Tel: 0121 303 3004 Contact: Sam Ghera
citycentre@birmingham.gov.uk www.birmingham.gov.uk/farmers
1st and 3rd Wednesday of the month, 10am to 4pm.

DOWN TO EARTH
96A EARLSDON STREET, EARLSDON, COVENTRY CV5 6EJ
Tel: 024 7667 7500 Contact: Suzanne Bristow
downtoearthorganic@compuserve.com www.downtoearthorganic.co.uk
Soil Association GCS079, P6189. Small, friendly retail shop selling
organic, local (wherever possible) fruit and veg, dairy, eggs, bread, meat
and fish, nuts, seeds, rice and pulses, groceries, eco household products.
Home delivery and organic box scheme.

DROP IN THE OCEAN
17 CITY ARCADE, COVENTRY CV1 3HX
Tel: 024 7622 5273 Fax: 024 7622 5273 Contact: Paula Harris
We specialise in wholefoods, herbal remedies, vitamins and vegetarian
foods. We stock a large range of organic produce including nuts, fruit,
cereals, and grains.

EVANS ORGANICS, RYAN
Tel: 01902 762785 Contact: Ryan Evans
Can supply organic meat and fish. Very competitive prices.

FINN BUTCHERS, M
19 STANTON ROAD, GREAT BARR, BIRMINGHAM B43 5QT
Tel: 0121 357 5780 Contact: Vaughan Meers
Organic, chemical and hormone-free meat and poultry specialists. Maynards
dry cure bacon and ham. Mail order available: phone for price list.

GROUNDWORK BLACK COUNTRY

WOLVERHAMPTON ENVIRONMENT CENTRE, WEST ACRE CRESCENT,
FINCHFIELD, WOLVERHAMPTON
Tel: 01902 766199 Fax: 01902 574600 Contact: Terry Bird
terry_bird@groundwork.org.uk www.groundwork-bc.org.uk
Soil Association G5900. Enterprises in organic food production including
protected salads, environment-considered decorative/native horticultural
products, recycled timber/green wood products, training, education and
community links, open days.

HEALTH FOOD CENTRE

146–148 HIGH ST., SOLIHULL B91 3SX
Tel: 0121 705 0134 Fax: 0121 705 0134 Contact: H Hards
barbara@healthfoodcentre.com www.healthfoodcentre.com
Dairy, meat, poultry, vegetables, bread, cakes, eggs, chocolates, dried fruit.
Retail organic vegetables, pulses, etc; also bread and supplements.

HOPWOOD ORGANIC FARM

BICKENHILL LANE, CATHERINE-DE-BARNES, SOLIHULL B92 0DE
Tel: 0121 711 7787 Fax: 0121 704 4033 Contact: John Cattell
sales@hopwoodorganic.co.uk www.hopwoodorganic.co.uk
Soil Association P5539 & G5540. Farm shop and home delivery of our own
produce plus meat, poultry, cheeses, wholefoods, juices, jam and cereals.

MOODY, JACK

HOLLY BUSH FARM, WARSTONE RD., SHARESHILL,
WOLVERHAMPTON WV10 7LX
Tel: 01922 417648 Fax: 01922 413420 Contact: Robert Moody
sales@jackmoodylimited.co.uk
Soil Association I4369. Producer of soil conditioners/compost. Centralised
composting of green materials for the production of compost, soil
conditioners and top dressings supplied locally around the West Midlands,
Staffordshire and Shropshire.

MOSELEY FARMERS' MARKET

VILLAGE GREEN, JUNCTION AT ALCESTER RD. TRAFFIC LIGHTS, MOSELEY,
BIRMINGHAM B13
Tel: 0121 449 3156 Contact: David Isgrove
david@isgrove.co.uk
4th Saturday of the month except December, when it's the Saturday before
Christmas. Organic produce includes, meat, ice cream, cheese, butter,
yoghurt, salmon, fruit, vegetables and soft fruit in season.

ONE EARTH SHOP

54 ALLISON STREET, DIGBETH, BIRMINGHAM B5 5TH
Tel: 0121 632 6909 Contact: Tina Rickards & John Beddowes
Vegan shop with large range of organic products; wholefoods, chilled,
confectionery etc.

ORGANIC ROOTS

CRABTREE FARM, DARK LANE, KINGS NORTON, BIRMINGHAM B38 0BS
Tel: 01564 822294 Fax: 01564 829212 Contact: Bill Dinenage
info@organicroots.co.uk www.organicroots.co.uk
Soil Association G1880. Organic Roots is the only organic shop in the West
Midlands wholly dedicated to supplying organic food of all types. Home
delivery service based on our 500 lines of organic produce.

A.R. PARKIN LTD

UNIT 8, CLETON STREET BUSINESS PARK, CLETON STREET, TIPTON DY4 7TR
Tel: 0121 557 1150 Fax: 0121 522 4086 Contact: Peter Gregory
enquiries@arparkin.co.uk www.arparkin.co.uk
Soil Association licence number P2508. Manufacturer and supplier of
organic seasoning blends, ingredients, herbs, spices, peppers and crumbs.

ROSEMARY'S HEALTH FOODS

2/3 MANDER SQUARE, MANDER CENTRE, WOLVERHAMPTON WV1 3NN
Tel: 01902 427520 Fax: 01902 426147 Contact: Duncan Gillan
enquiries@rosemaryshealthfoods.co.uk www.rosemaryshealthfoods.co.uk
We sell an extensive range of organic healthy, dried, fresh, chilled, frozen
foods and herbal remedies.

ROSSITER, S & A – TRADITIONAL FAMILY BUTCHERS

247 MARYVALE ROAD, BOURNVILLE, BIRMINGHAM B30 1PN
Tel: 0121 458 1598 Fax: 0121 458 1598 Contact: Stephen Rossiter
sjv.rossiter@tinyonline.co.uk
Soil Association R2037, NFMT. Meat and poultry, bread, cheeses, eggs,
cooked meats, pickles, preserves, trout and salmon. Small friendly family-
run business with emphasis on customer satisfaction and confidence.

SAGE WHOLEFOODS

148 ALCESTER RD., MOSELEY, BIRMINGHAM B13 8HS
Tel: 0121 449 6909 Fax: 0121 449 6909 Contact: George Howell
sagewholefoods@talk21.com www.sagewholefoods.com
A not-for-profit workers co-operative retailing a wide range of organic
foods including fruit and vegetables, fair trade goods, specialist dietary
food, supplements and remedies. Mon–Sat 9.30am–6.30pm.

AGRALAN GARDEN PRODUCTS

THE OLD BRICKYARD, ASHTON KEYNES, SWINDON SN6 6QR
Tel: 01285 860015 Fax: 01285 860056 Contact: Alan Frost
sales@agralan.co.uk www.agralan.co.uk
Agralan offer a range of non-poisonous and effective treatments for many
pest problems: vegetables can be grown without pesticides. New products
allow control of slugs, ants and flies.

BARKER, DI & AM

PURTON HOUSE, PURTON, SWINDON SN5 4EB
Tel: 01793 770219 Fax: 01793 772750 Contact: DI & AM Barker
rowie@purton-house.co.uk www.purton-house.co.uk
Beef, eggs, vegetables and fruit box scheme.

BERKELEY FARM DAIRY

BERKELEY FARM, SWINDON RD., WROUGHTON, SWINDON SN4 9AQ
Tel: 01793 812228 Fax: 01793 845949 Contact: N Gosling
Soil Association G4670, P4891. Using organic Guernsey milk from our own
organic herd, we make organic butter (salted & unsalted), organic cream
and organic milk.

CLOTHWORKS

PO BOX 3233 BA15 2WB
Tel: 01225 309 218 Contact: Linda Row
clothworks.info@virgin.net www.clothworks.co.uk
Clothworks' aim is to produce clothes ethically from eco textiles, obtaining
colour from natural sources and eco dyes (containing no heavy metals).
The Mail Order catalogue includes 'organic essentials', clothing for women
and a small range of clothing and bedding for 1–3 year olds. Clothworks
'Unique' designer range for women is made from silk, hemp and organic
cotton.

COLESHILL ORGANICS

59 COLESHILL, SWINDON SN6 7PT
Tel: 01793 861070 Fax: 01793 861070 Contact: Sonia Oliver
coleshillorganics@msn.com www.coleshillorganics.co.uk
Home-grown organic vegetables, fruit and eggs: boxes of seasonal produce
delivered weekly within radius of 25 miles. Also farm shop within the
walled garden. Shop closed Sun, Mon, Tues and Wed am.

DIBBLE, G & E

EASTROP FARM, HIGHWORTH SN6 7PP
Tel: 01793 762196 Contact: Guy Dibble
guy@dibble18.freeserve.co.uk
Organic beef sold direct, freezer ready, vacuum packed, handy box sizes
£100 & £200 per box. School visits by arrangements.

EASTBROOK FARMS ORGANIC MEAT

EASTBROOK FARM, THE CALF HOUSE, CUES LANE, BISHOPSTONE,
SWINDON SN6 8PL
Tel: 01793 790460 Fax: 01793 791239 Contact: Barbara Rayner
orders@helenbrowningorganics.co.uk www.helenbrowningorganics.co.uk
Soil Association PH53S. Nationwide home delivery service of organic meat.
Supplier to the major supermarkets. The Helen Browning's Totally Organic
range of cured organic pork products is sold through Sainsbury's.

FURZE COTTAGE

TEFFONT MAGNA, NR. SALISBURY SP3 5QU
Tel: 01722 716285 Fax: Contact: Carol Jacobs
Soil Association approved organic fruit, vegetables and herbs,
mid June–March. Please telephone first.

GREEN CUISINE

PILLAR HOUSE, THE STREET, CHARLTON SN16 9DL
Tel: 01666 824584 Contact: Anna Ross
anna@greencuisine.org.uk
Delivery service. Local fresh organic veg delivered weekly to your door.

THE GREEN HOUSE
120 FISHERTON ST., SALISBURY SP2 7QT
Tel: 01722 325515 Contact: Sana Stephens
sanastephens@yahoo.co.uk www.loveorganic.com
Organic clothing from well established organic companies such as People Tree, Bishopston Trading and many more. All the companies we use have their own certified cotton. We also sell Green Baby clothing and other organic products such as bedding.

HAMBLEDEN HERBS
PO BOX 2711, MARLBOROUGH SN8 4ZR
Tel: 01672 811145 Fax: 01672 811863 Contact: Lyn Seymour
lyn@organicmanufacture.com www.hambledenherbs.co.uk
The Hambleden Herbs range of over 135 organic herbal products includes teas, culinary herbs and spices, infusions, tinctures and Christmas products. The range has won over 30 trade and consumer awards in the last nine years. High quality, unadulterated herbal products ethically produced and traded, using only essential processing and minimal recycled packaging. Hambleden Herbs are produced on a working organic farm in Somerset and can be purchased from health food stores, organic farm shops and delicatessens.

HARVEY, M & A
GOULTERS MILL, NETTLETON, NR. CHIPPENHAM SN14 7LL
Tel: 01249 782555 Fax: 01249 782555 Contact: A Harvey
We produce Lleyn sheep for breeding and for meat. Eggs for sale from the farm gate. Light Sussex chicks also available from farm gate. We also have paying guests to stay. Soil Association no. G2641. Deliveries made all over UK.

HAZELBURY PARTNERS
HAZELBURY MANOR, BOX, CORSHAM SN13 8HX
Tel: 01225 812088 Fax: 01225 810875 Contact: The Manager
Soil Association G1825. Delicious organic lamb, pork, and beef, hens and duck eggs, produced on family-run farm using rare breed lambs and pigs.

THE HERBARY

THE HERBARY, 161 CHAPEL STREET, HORNINGSHAM, WARMINSTER BA12 7LU
Tel: 01985 844442 Contact: Pippa Rosen
info@beansandherbs.co.uk www.beansandherbs.co.uk
Organic seed, specialising in herbs and vegetables. Very large number of
unusual varieties of french bean seed, climbing and dwarf. Suitable for the
home grower or allotment holder. Mail order all year. Visit our website, or
send A4 first class SAE for catalogue.

HIGGINS, R & S

CHURCH FARM, MAIDEN BRADLEY, WARMINSTER BA12 7HN
Tel: 01985 844221 Fax: 01985 844221 Contact: Sally Higgins
Milk for OMSCo and a local dairy, farm gate sales of lamb to order.

KENSONS FARM

SUTTON MANDEVILLE, SALISBURY SP3 5NG
Tel: 01722 714815 Fax: 01722 714815 Contact: Hugh Collins & Liz Barrah
Soil Association G5971. Intensive and field scale organic vegetables,
including asparagus.

KIT FARM

SOUTHVIEW, LITTLE CHEVERELL, DEVIZES SN10 4JJ
Tel: 01380 818591 Fax: 01380 818591
Contact: Lynn Rooke & Peter Edwards
lynnrooke6@aol.com
We produce top quality beef animals. They are sired by Sussex bulls, single
suckled and finished on grass. They yield tender, succulent, marbled meat.
Soil Association symbol no. G1941.

LAKESIDE EGGS

LAKESIDE STABLES, STEEPLE LANGFORD, SALISBURY SP3 4NH
Tel: 01722 790786 Contact: John Delaney
Soil Association G2215. We have free ranging laying hens.

LANGLEY CHASE ORGANIC FARM
KINGTON LANGLEY, CHIPPENHAM SN15 5PW
Tel: 01249 750095 Fax: 01249 750095 Contact: Jane Kallaway
post@langleychase.co.uk www.langleychase.co.uk
Pedigree flock of rare breed Manx Loghtan sheep carefully reared to produce
organic whole, half lambs or joints. Nationwide delivery. Organic Food
Awards winner 2001, 2002, Winner of Best Lamb Organic Food Awards
2003. Farm visits welcome.

LOTMEAD FARM
WANBOROUGH, NR. SWINDON SN4 0SN
Tel: 01793 790260 Contact: Norman Parry
200-acre organic dairy farm specialising in milk from grass. Pick your own
fruit and vegetables. Business village on farm.

MANOR FARM PARTNERSHIP
MANOR FARM, EAST GRAFTON, MARLBOROUGH SN8 3DB
Tel: 01672 810735 Fax: 01672 810749 Contact: Pip Browning
pip.james@btopenworld.com
Organic beef and cereals.

NEAL'S YARD REMEDIES
27 MARKET PLACE, SALISBURY SP1 1TL
Tel: 01722 340736 Contact: The Manager
mail@nealsyardremedies.com www.nealsyardremedies.com
Neal's Yard Remedies manufactures and retails natural cosmetics
in addition to stocking an extensive range of herbs, essential oils,
homoeopathic remedies and reference material.

THE ORGANIC EXPERIENCE
7 THE BRIDGE, CHIPPENHAM SN15 1HA
Tel: 01249 720274 Contact: Steve Cronin
We sell an extensive range of food, drink, ecological cleaning and body
care products including our own and others fresh fruit and vegetables,
fresh meat, dairy, frozen, ice cream, and a full range of groceries including
cereals, pulses etc. Home delivery available.

PERTWOOD ORGANIC CEREAL CO LTD

LOWER PERTWOOD FARM, NR. HINDON, SALISBURY SP3 6TA
Tel: 01747 820720 Fax: 01747 820499 Contact: Mark Houghton Brown
www.pertwood.co.uk
Range of organic breakfast cereals processed from own produce: oat-based,
wheat-free, GMO-free muesli with delicious fruits, porage oats, crunchy
with raisins and almonds, crunchy with mixed nuts. UK coverage. Large
quantities available.

PERTWOOD ORGANICS LTD

THE OLD BARN AT LORDS HILL, LOWER PERTWOOD FARM, LONGBRIDGE
DEVERILL, WARMINSTER BA12 7DY
Tel: 01985 840646 Fax: 01985 840649 Contact: Chloe Fox Lambert
mail@pertwood-organics.co.uk www.pertwood-organics.co.uk
Soil Association certified farm-based box scheme, wholesale, market stalls
and special diets catered for. Price list on application. Internet shopping
service via website. Full range of local organic food.

PURE ORGANICS LTD

STOCKPORT FARM, STOCKPORT RD., AMESBURY SP4 7LN
Tel: 01980 626263 Fax: 01980 626264 Contact: Pauline Stiles
pauline@pureorganics.co.uk www.pureorganics.co.uk
Soil Association P2269. We specialise in the production of organic,
additive-free foods for children, with minimal processing, using the very
best ingredients, including chicken nuggets, burgers, sausages and
vegetarian products. We specialise in addressing dietary intolerances, and
recently have started to produce food for school meal services.

PURELY ORGANIC

DEVERILL TROUT FARM, LONGBRIDGE DEVERILL, WARMINSTER BA12 7DZ
Tel: 01985 841093 Fax: 01985 841268 Contact: Tony Free
trout@purelyorganic.fsnet.co.uk www.purelyorganic.co.uk
Trout farm and shop selling a full range or organic produce, smoked trout,
paté, watercress, etc.

RUSHALL FARM

DEVIZES RD., RUSHALL, PEWSEY SN9 6ET
Tel: 01980 630361 Fax: 01980 630095 Contact: Lesley Walford
info@rushallorganics.co.uk www.rushallorganics.co.uk
Grain and organic pigs. Soil Association no. W09S.

STONEGATE LTD

CORSHAM RD., LACOCK SN15 2LZ
Tel: 01249 730700 Fax: 01249 732200 Contact: John Sayer
enquiries@stonegate.co.uk www.stonegate.co.uk
Soil Association P6229, Organic Farmers & Growers 12UKCP030028.
Stonegate Ltd currently produce, pack and deliver organic eggs to the UK.
We supply all large retailers and specialise in special breed organic eggs
such as Columbian Blacktail and Speckledy.

SUMMERLEAZE GALLERY

EAST KNOYLE, SALISBURY SP3 6BY
Tel: 01747 830790 Fax: 01747 830790 Contact: Trish Scott Bolton
trish@summerleazegallery.co.uk
Soil Association G4877. Art gallery holding three exhibitions a year,
four-day painting courses and lectures in converted farm buildings on
organic farm. Dinner, bed and breakfast in nearby farmhouse.

SWINDON PULSE WHOLEFOODS

27 CURTIS ST., SWINDON SN1 5JU
Tel: 01793 692016 Contact: Cath Dolling
www.swindonpulse.co.uk
Fresh, local, organic vegetables. Herbal remedies/loose herbs. We are a
friendly specialist wholefood shop, near the town centre, stocking local
organic vegetables, a wide range of organic produce, herbal remedies and
environmentally friendly cleaning products and toiletries. Organic bread
delivered weekly.

TALLYWACKER FARM
50 THE RIDINGS, KINGTON ST. MICHAEL, CHIPPENHAM SN14 6JG
Tel: 01249 750035 Contact: Steve O'Connor
sales@tallywackerfarm.co.uk www.tallywackerfarm.co.uk
Soil Association registered producer/processor. Producers of organic fruit and veg. Home delivery box scheme to Corsham, Chippenham, Devizes, Malmesbury, Tetbury, Wootton Bassett, west Swindon, Calne, Melksham, Neston, Somerfords, surrounding villages and all areas in between.

THOMAS FAMILY BUTCHERS, MICHAEL
51 THE TRIANGLE, MALMESBURY SN16 0AH
Tel: 01666 823981 Fax: 01666 823981 Contact: Steve Cox
www.michaelthomasbutchers.co.uk
Fruit/veg, organic nuts, pulses, dried fruit, dairy products, whole foods, eco cleaning products, vitamins, minerals.

THROOPE MANOR FARM
BISHOPSTONE, SALISBURY SP5 4BA
Tel: 01722 718318 Fax: 01722 718544 Contact: Head
vishead@aol.com
Soil Association G5089. Flock of 500 Mule ewes producing organic texel x fat lambs on ESA chalk downland, lambing out of doors in May. Also from 2005, 60 hectares of spring sown cereals/pulses.

THE TRACKLEMENT COMPANY LTD
THE DAIRY FARM, PINKNEY PARK, SHERSTON SN16 0NX
Tel: 01666 840851 Fax: 01666 840022 Contact: Guy Tullberg
info@tracklements.co.uk www.tracklements.co.uk
Soil Association P4261. Manufacturers of high quality chutneys, sauces, jellies, mustards and dressings (accompaniments to meat, fish and cheese).

UPPER BURYTOWN FARM PARTNERS
UPPER BURYTOWN FARM, BLUNSDON, SWINDON SN26 7DQ
Tel: 01793 700595 Contact: Arend Von Freeden
Soil Association G7025. Beef, cereal, sheep, small amount of direct sale meat.

VITACRESS SALADS LTD
MULLENS FARM, MANNINGFORD, BOHUNE COMMON, NR. PEWSEY SN9 6LY
Tel: 01672 851711 Fax: 01672 851774 Contact: Rob Corlett
rob.corlett@vitacress.co.uk www.vitacress.com
Soil Association G7887. We are producers of baby leaf salads with land in
conversion at present.

WARMINSTER MALTINGS LTD
39 POUND ST., WARMINSTER BA12 8NN
Tel: 01985 212014 Fax: 01985 212015 Contact: Chris Garratt
info@warminster-malt.co.uk www.warminster-malt.co.uk
Soil Association P5961. Manufacture of malt from cereal (barley/wheat)
using traditional floor malting process. For use in brewing and food.

WESTWOOD FARM
RODE HILL, COLERNE, NR. CHIPPENHAM SN14 8AR
Tel: 01225 742854 Contact: J Trotman
Organic farm growing delicious seasonal vegetables, fruit and herbs. The fruit
is used for hand-crafted jams, jellies, marmalades and chutneys. Hand-made
Dundee and rich celebration cakes available by order and direct sales.

WILTSHIRE ORGANIC MILK
HOUSECROFT FARM, EDINGTON, NR. WESTBURY BA13 4NN
Tel: 01380 870985 Fax: 01380 870985 Contact: Julie Osborne
pf.josborne@tinyworld.co.uk
Produce and sell wholesale pasteurised organic milk, whole and
semi-skimmed, also organic cream; ideally to shops, boxes, milkmen,
restaurants, cafés, hotels etc in Wiltshire.

YATESBURY ORGANICS
GR GANTLETT & SON, YATESBURY HOUSE FARM, YATESBURY,
CALNE SN11 8YF
Tel: 01672 539191 Fax: 01672 539039 Contact: Richard Gantlett
yatesbury@farming.co.uk www.easisite.co.uk/yatesburyorganicfarm
Soil Association G2931. Vegetables, pedigree Aberdeen Angus beef, lamb.
All home-grown. Box deliveries. Please come and see us.

WORCESTERSHIRE

BEEWELL
4 ROYAL ARCADE, PERSHORE WR10 1AG
Tel: 01386 556577 Contact: Jen Creese
beewellhealth@hotmail.com
Health food shop, established 1986, specialising in organic wholefoods, fresh organic vegetables and fruit, organic meats and poultry. Small café/coffee shop.

CAVES FOLLY NURSERIES
EVENDINE LANE, COLWALL, MALVERN WR13 6DU
Tel: 01684 540631 Fax: 08700 632805 Contact: Bridget Evans
info@cavesfolly.com www.cavesfolly.com
Specialist growers of perennials, grasses and herbs in peat-free compost. Garden design and advisory service specialising in organics and using environmentally sound products and reclaimed building materials.

THE COTTAGE HERBERY
MILL HOUSE, BORASTON, NR. TENBURY WELLS WR15 8LZ
Tel: 01584 781575 Fax: 01584 781483 Contact: Kim Hurst
www.thecottageherbary.co.uk
Organically and peat-free grown pot herbs and hardy herbaceous—send 4 first class stamps for catalogue and information. Flower shows and food festivals.

CRIDLAN & WALKER
23 ABBEY ROAD, MALVERN WR14 3ES
Tel: 01684 573008 Fax: 01684 566017 Contact: The Manager
Organic Farmers & Growers no. UKP100013. Organic meat, vegetables, milk, cheese and groceries.

DINGLEY, WL & CO

BUCKLE ST., HONEYBOURNE, EVESHAM WR11 7QE
Tel: 01386 830242 Fax: 01386 833541 Contact: Alan Bown
dingley1921@hotmail.com www.wldingley.com
Soil Association 1656. Manufacturer of organic fertilisers to the Soil
Association certification scheme.

ELYSIA NATURAL SKIN CARE

27 STOCKWOOD BUSINESS PARK, STOCKWOOD, NR. REDDITCH B96 6SX
Tel: 01386 792622 Fax: 01386 792623 Contact: Claire Thompson
enquiries@drhauschka.co.uk www.drhauschka.co.uk
Elysia distributes the Dr Hauschka skin care range, holistic products using
organically grown herbs and plants from certified biodynamic farms. The
products and ingredients are not tested on animals.

FERTILE FIBRE

TENBURY WELLS WR15 8LT
Tel: 01584 781575 Fax: 01584 781483 Contact: Rob Hurst
sales@fertilefibre.fsnet.co.uk www.fertilefibre.com
Soil Association 11408. Organic Coir compost. We supply seed,
multi-purpose and potting composts, plus Coir blocks, and fertilisers. Trade
and mail order services available.

GREENLINK ORGANIC FOODS

11 GRAHAM ROAD, GREAT MALVERN WR14 2HR
Tel: 01684 576266 Contact: Mike Gatiss
One-stop organic shop and snack bar with delivery service.

KINGSTON, MAGGIE

THE RETREAT, STOKE BLISS, TENBURY WELLS WR15 8RY
Tel: 01885 410431 Contact: Maggie Kingston
maggie@retreatstokebliss.freeserve.co.uk
Space to be! Hereford/Worcestershire borders. Buzzards, butterflies and
badgers. Holiday cottage 2 + 2. Self-contained to fully supported respite
holiday.

OAKFIELD FARM PRODUCTS LIMITED
NEWTOWN, OFFENHAM, EVESHAM WR11 8RZ
Tel: 01386 425222 Fax: 01386 49835 Contact: Hugh Owens
oakfieldoffice@aol.com
Soil Association Member P2526, P2110, P2253 (UK5) Mushroom grower—
all organic grades of chestnut mushrooms and various exotic varieties of
mushrooms, also organic. Delivery nationwide.

OXTON ORGANICS
BROADWAY LANE, FLADBURY, PERSHORE WR10 2QF
Tel: 01386 860477 Fax: 01386 860477 Contact: Jayne Arnold
boxes@oxtonorganics.co.uk www.oxtonorganics.co.uk
Soil Association E17M. Fruit, vegetables and eggs delivered locally via our
box scheme. Also on-line ordering via our website.

PHOENIX ORGANICS LTD
PULLEN'S FARM, BROMYARD RD., CRADLEY, NR. MALVERN WR13 5JN
Tel: 01886 880713 Fax: 01886 880743 Contact: Geoff Mutton
phoenixorganics@btconnect.com www.phoenixorganics.ltd.uk
We are wholesalers of organic fruits and vegetables, specialising in sales to
box schemes, independent retail outlets, farm shops, caterers, processors
and other non-supermarket outlets. See display ad.

PRICHARD, STEPHEN
WOODCOTE FARM, DODFORD, BROMSGROVE B61 9EA
Tel: 01562 777795 Fax: 01562 777024 Contact: SJ Prichard
woodcotefarm@btinternet.com www.woodcotefarm.com
Soil Association G4109. Woodcote Farm produces organic fat lamb
and Aberdeen Angus beef. We also provide bed and breakfast and
self-contained apartments for holidays or long lets.

PRIMAFRUIT LTD

ENTERPRISE WAY, VALE BUSINESS PARK, EVESHAM WR11 1TG
Tel: 01386 425000 Fax: 01386 425001 Contact: The Manager
www.primafruit.co.uk
Importer of fresh organic fruit including grapes, stone fruit, berries, top
fruit and citrus supplies to the industry. Committed to the organic
market, growers, customers and consumers.

ROSEMARY'S HEALTH FOODS

10 THE SHAMBLES, WORCESTER WR1 2RF
Tel: 01905 612190 Fax: 01905 612190 Contact: Marie Cockill (Manageress)
enquiries@rosemaryshealthfoods.co.uk www.rosemaryshealthfoods.co.uk
We sell an extensive range of organic healthy, dried, fresh, chilled, frozen
foods and herbal remedies.

SONG OF THE EARTH

2 CONISTON CLOSE, POOLBROOK, MALVERN WR14 3SN
Tel: 01684 892533 Fax: 01684 892533 Contact: Fiona Hopes
fiona@song-of-the-earth.com www.song-of-the-earth.com
Garden designer. Individual and special gardens created by a qualified and
experienced designer, working with the subtle energies of the land to
create sustainable landscapes that are ecologically sound, practical,
productive and beautiful. Co-principal of The Earth School.

STEELE, WO & SONS

CHAPEL FARM, NETHERTON, NR. PERSHORE WR10 3JG
Tel: 01386 710379 Fax: 01386 710379 Contact: Adrian Steele
adrian@wosteele.fsnet.co.uk
Soil Association S37M; Organic Arable Marketing Group; Organic Seed
Producers Ltd, Graig Farm. Mixed lowland organic farm specialising in
wheat, oats, beans, potatoes, beef and lamb since 1986. Farm gate sales
and sales to mills, butchers and box schemes. Please phone first.

WALCOT ORGANIC NURSERY

LOWER WALCOT FARM, WALCOT LANE, DRAKES BROUGHTON,
PERSHORE WR10 2AL
Tel: 01386 553697 Fax: 01905 841587 Contact: Kevin O'Neill
enquiries@walcotnursery.co.uk
Soil Association G5594. Producers of organically grown fruit trees. Available
bare-root November to March, and in containers. Mail order anywhere in
mainland UK. Visitors welcome by appointment. Catalogue available.

Accommodation	Garden and Farm Sundries	Producers
Box Schemes/ Local Deliveries	Farmers' market Stall	Restaurants/ Cafés/Caterers
Day Visits	Manufacturers/ Processors	Retail shops
Eco Products	Importers/ exporters	Textiles
Farm Gate Sales	Mail order suppliers	Wholesalers

AARHUS UNITED UK LIMITED
KING GEORGE DOCK, HULL HU9 5PX
Tel: 01482 701271 Fax: 01482 709447 Contact: Steve Tate
steve.tate@aarhusunited.com
Importing, processing and packaging organic extra virgin olive, safflower, sesame and sunflower oils, palm oil (and fractions) certified by the Soil Association, licence no. P966.

ARTHUR STREET TRADING CO LTD
UNIT 2, 23 ARTHUR ST., HULL HU3 6BH
Tel: 01482 576374 Fax: 0870 132 3035 Contact: Graham Brooks
arthursorganics@hotmail.com www.arthursorganics.com
Soil Association P6548. A workers co-operative that makes home deliveries in a solar powered veg-float, supplying a comprehensive range of organic fruit and vegetables, eco-cleaning products, wholefoods, beers, wines and own brand hummus.

BARMSTON ORGANICS
ALLISON LANE END FARM, LISSETT, DRIFFIELD YO25 8PS
Tel: 01262 468128 Fax: 01262 468128 Contact: Tony & Colleen Hunt
barmstontone@aol.com
Soil Association P5571 & G1855. 273-acre mixed farm selling vegetables, flour from our own wheat and lamb & beef. Box scheme and local farmers' markets.

COLEMAN, WG & PARTNERS
WESTFIELD FARM, BURTON FLEMING, DRIFFIELD YO25 3PZ
Tel: 01262 470850 Contact: Jim Coleman
We produce Saddleback/Duroc cross organic pigs reared entirely outdoors. Also wheat.

CRANSWICK COUNTRY FOODS

INGLEMIRE LANE, COTTINGHAM, HULL HU16 4PJ
Tel: 01482 848180 Fax: 01482 876146 Contact: J Brisby
jim.brisby@cranswick.co. uk
Producers of fresh pork, sausage, cooked meats.

FOSTON NURSERIES

FOSTON ON THE WOLDS, DRIFFIELD YO25 8BJ
Tel: 01262 488382 Contact: Jenny Webb
Soil Association W28N. Organic seasonal produce grown under glass.

GREEN GROWERS

1 STATION COTTAGES, WANSFORD RD., NAFFERTON, DRIFFIELD YO25 8NJ
Tel: 01377 255362 Contact: GM Egginton
mail@greengrowers.fsnet.co.uk
Soil Association G2175. Green Growers is an organic nursery, retailing a
wide variety of organic vegetables, fruit and wholefoods, specialising in
fresh salads and herbs, and herb plants.

HNP DIRECT.COM

EVERTHORPE GRANGE, COMMON LANE, NORTH CAVE HU15 2PE
Tel: 01430 425531 Fax: 01430 423196 Contact: Tony Roach
info@hnpdirect.com www.hnpdirect.com
Internet company supplying Coia coir composts, fertilisers, magna therapy.

HUMBER VHB

COMMON LANE, WELTON, BROUGH HU15 1UT
Tel: 01482 661600 Fax: 01482 665095 Contact: Ian Ball
sales@humbervhb.com www.humbervhb.com
Humber VHB are growers and packers of glasshouse grown tomatoes
(including speciality), cucumbers, peppers and herbs for the retail market
and local box schemes.

HUMDINGER LTD
GOTHANBURG WAY, SUTTON FIELDS INDUSTRIAL ESTATE, HULL HU7 0YG
Tel: 01482 625790 Fax: 01482 625791 Contact: Paul Sangwin
paul.sangwin@humdinger_foods.co.uk
Packaging company packing for major brands within the wholefoods
industry.

HURRELL AND McLEAN (HURRELL'S)
BEVERLEY ROAD, CRANSWICK, DRIFFIELD YO25 9PF
Tel: 01377 271400 Fax: 01377 271500 Contact: Nick Gladstone
nick@hurrells.fsbusiness.co.uk www.hmseeds.co.uk
Specialise in supply of organic farm seeds, forage/grass and combinable
crops.

MOTHERHEMP LTD
SPRINGDALE FARM, RUDSTON, DRIFFIELD YO25 4DJ
Tel: 01262 421100 Fax: 421101 Contact: Ria Spencer
info@motherhemp.com www.motherhemp.com
MotherHemp produces a quality range of organic hemp food products.
Hemp's claim as a superfood lies in its balance of essential fatty acids and
high quality protein. The range includes hemp pasta and pesto, Hemp
Ice—a dairy-free ice cream, hemp oil and seeds. MotherHemp products will
be of interest to anyone on a lactose-free, dairy-free, vegan, low sugar and
low gluten diet.

SLATER ORGANICS
16 CROSS ST., ALDBROUGH, HULL HU11 4RW
Tel: 01964 527519 Contact: Bob Slater
slaterorganics@yahoo.co.uk
Soil Association G1917. Family business growing wide range of organic
vegetables in walled garden at Rise Village. Working with other local
growers, we supply box schemes in Hull, Beverley and local villages.

SPRINGDALE CROP SYNERGIES LTD

SPRINGDALE FARM, RUDSTON, DRIFFIELD YO25 4DJ
Tel: 01262 421100 Fax: 01262 521101 Contact: Simon Meakin
info@springdale-group.com www.springdale-group.com
Soil Association P7844. Seed merchant/advisor. Agronomy-based crop
development business offering buy-back contracts and advice on organic
crops. Supplier and trader of organic seeds and the only UK registered
specialist organic oilseed supplier.

Eating Out

*In Europe, restaurants are supposed to list foods which contain GM ingredients,
or have the information available upon request. One eating establishment,
for example, offered the following policy statement in 1999:*

*"In response to concern raised by our customers . . . we have decided to remove, as far as
possible, genetically modified soy and maize (corn) from all food products served in our
restaurant. We will continue to work with our suppliers to replace GM soy and maize with
non-GM ingredients. . . . We have taken the above steps to ensure that you, the customer,
can feel confident in the food we serve."*

The statement was in reference to the cafeteria of Monsanto's UK headquarters in High Wycombe.

From *Seeds of Deception: Exposing Corporate and Government Lies about the Safety of
Genetically Engineered Food* by Jeffrey M. Smith, Green Books, £9.95

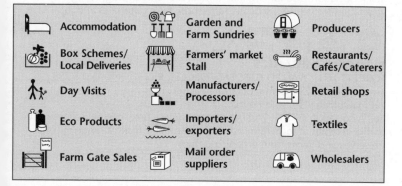

NORTH YORKSHIRE

AGGLOMERATION TECHNOLOGY LTD
UNIT 7, MONKSWELL PARK, MANSE LANE, KNARESBOROUGH HG5 8NQ
Tel: 01423 868411 Fax: 01423 868410 Contact: Enid Rispin
enid.rispin@aggtech.co.uk
Agglomeration (granulation) of sweet and savoury powdered ingredients
and products (soups, gravy, chocolate drinks etc) and spray crystallization
of real chocolate.

ALLIGATOR
104 FISHERGATE, YORK YO10 4BB
Tel: 01904 654525 Contact: Steve Heyman
Tel & Fax: 01904 654525 Contact:
Independent vegetarian & wholefood grocers and greengrocers offering a
wide range of organic fruit, veg and groceries. Speciality diets catered for.
Home delivery service within the York area.

ASPIN ORGANICS
LOW ST., SPROXTON, HELMSLEY, YORK YO
Tel: 01439 771848 Contact: JD Farrar
Soil Association G6005. Organic horticultural enterprise growing organic
vegetables for veg box scheme, farm shop, farm gate sales and local sales.

BLUEBELL ORGANICS
FORCETT HALL WALLED GARDEN, FORCETT, RICHMOND DL11 7SB
Tel: 07759 832234 Contact: Katrina Palmer
katrina@bluebell30.fsbusiness.co.uk
Soil Association G7101. Bluebell Organics run a box scheme, sell fresh fruit
and vegetables at local farmers' markets and also make a range of soups,
preserves and juices from organic produce.

BRUNSWICK ORGANIC NURSERY & CRAFT WORKSHOP

APPLETON RD., BISHOPTHORPE, YORK YO23 2RF
Tel: 01904 701869 Fax: 01904 701869 Contact: Adam Myers
admin@brunswickyork.org.uk
Soil Association G1903, HDRA member. Charity working with adults who
have learning difficulties. Produce includes bedding plants, cottage garden
plants, perennials, herbs, organic fruit and vegetables. All to Soil
Association standards. Also craft workshop.

CAMPHILL VILLAGE TRUST – BOTTON VILLAGE

BOTTON VILLAGE, DANBY, WHITBY YO21 2NJ
Tel: 01287 660871 Fax: 01287 660888 Contact: E Wennekes
botton@camphill.org.uk www.camphill.org.uk
Botton Village is a Camphill Village Trust community for adults with special
needs. It has five mixed farms which are run on biodynamic principles,
several craft and food processing workshops. Day visits are possible, and
there is coffee bar on site.

CAMPHILL VILLAGE TRUST – LARCHFIELD COMMUNITY

STOKESLEY RD., HEMLINGTON, MIDDLESBROUGH TS8 9DY
Tel: 01642 593688 Fax: 01642 595778
Contact: Pink, Smith, Fish, Hodkinson
Producers of real organic meat, vegetables, seasonal fruit, bread, etc. Also
hand crafts: weaving and wooden toys.

CASTLE HOWARD ESTATE LTD

THE ESTATE OFFICE, CASTLE HOWARD, YORK YO60 7DA
Tel: 01653 648444 Contact: Helen Orchison
horchison@castlehoward.co.uk www.castlehoward.co.uk
Soil Association registered organic farmers. Producers of organic meats and
arable crops. Day visits by appointment only.

CORNMILL LODGE VEGETARIAN GUEST HOUSE

120 HAXBY ROAD, YORK YO31 8JP
Tel: 01904 620566 Fax: 01904 620566 Contact: Jen Williams
cornmillyork@aol.com www.cornmillyork.co.uk
Vegetarian/vegan smoke-free B&B, approximately 15 minutes walk from
York Minster. En suite rooms. Off-street car park. Delicious organic
breakfasts using Fairtrade products when possible. Special diets catered for.
Children welcome.

COUNTRY PRODUCTS LIMITED

UNIT 11A & B CENTRE PARK, MARSTON BUSINESS PARK, TOCKWITH,
YORK YO26 7QF
Tel: 01423 358858 Fax: 01423 359858 Contact: Liz Blacker
mail@countryproducts.co.uk www.countryproducts.co.uk
Soil Association P1987. Contract packer. Wholesales and contract packet of
high quality food products, especially wholefoods and organic products.

DEMETER SEEDS STORMY HALL

STORMY HALL FARM, BOTTON VILLAGE, DANBY, WHITBY YO21 2NJ
Tel: 01287 661368 Fax: 01287 661369 Contact: Hans Steenbergen
stormy.hall.botton@camphill.org.uk
Producer, processor, and retailer of biodynamic and organic, vegetable,
herb and flower seeds.

EL PIANO

15–17 GRAPE LANE, YORK YO1 7HU
Tel: 01904 610676 Fax: 01904 643049 Contact: Maggie or Sally
info@elpiano.co.uk www.elpiano.co.uk
Open 10am–midnight Mon–Sat, Sundays midday–5pm. Licensed, hispanic,
informal, vegetarian restaurant. Function rooms, event-catering inside or
out. Children welcome all hours. Organic staples used in restaurant,
Spanish foods. Wheat-free, gluten-free, vegan catered for. 'Hand to Mouth
no ordinary cookbook' published.

FARM-A-ROUND

45 RACECOURSE RD, RICHMOND DL10 4TG
Tel: 020 7627 8066 Fax: 01748 822007 Contact: Isobel Davies
info @farmaround.co.uk www.farmaround.co.uk
Organic Farmers and Growers UKP08009. From their base in Richmond,
Farm-A-Round delivers organic fruit and vegetables boxes to North
Yorkshire and Tyne & Wear. Also a fully organic vegetarian grocery range.
Wholesale enquiries welcome.

FARNDALE FREE RANGE LTD

HILL HOUSES, FARNDALE, KIRKBYMOORSIDE YO62 7LH
Tel: 01751 430323 Fax: 01751 430323 Contact: Barry Sunley
barry@farndale.com www.farndale.com
We produce SA organic eggs to the highest standard, which we deliver to
discerning local shops in North Yorkshire, Cleveland and Teeside. We also
design websites and provide computer services.

FIFE, A M

BRAMPER FARM, THRINTOFT, NORTHALLERTON DL7 0PS
Tel: 01609 770151 Fax: 01609 777436 Contact: Andy Fife
andy@bramper.demon.co.uk
Soil Association G6867. Producer of organic cereals, vegetables and meat.

FIRST SEASON

1 ST. ANN'S LANE, WHITBY YO21 3PF
Tel: 01947 601608 Contact: Keith Mollison
Stock a wide range of organic foods including dairy, eggs, bread, honey,
cereals and convenience food. Our organic vegetable boxes are collected
from the shop. Also organic supplements and cosmetics.

GIBSON, JR & E

PRIEST GARTH FARM, GILLAMOOR, YORK YO62 7HX
Tel: 01751 431872 Fax: 01751 431872 Contact: John & Eileen Gibson
gillamoorganics@yahoo.co.uk
Soil Association G3083. Fully organic mixed farm with Ayrshire dairy herd.
Potatoes and field vegetables for sale, all home-grown.

GOOSEMOORGANICS

WARFIELD LANE, COWTHORPE, NR. WETHERBY LS22 5EU
Tel: 01423 358887 Fax: 01423 358887 Contact: Alex Marsh
vegebox@goosemoor.info www.goosemoor.info
Soil Association G802, P802. Goosemoor grows and distributes organic
fruit, vegetables and vegetarian groceries to shops and restaurants
throughout the north of England, as well as home deliveries via our
veg box scheme.

THE GREEN HOUSE

5 STATION PARADE, HARROGATE HG1 1UF
Tel: 01423 502580 Fax: 01423 505439 Contact: Bob Fisher
Shop selling arguably the best organic food and drink selection in North
Yorkshire. Also vegetarian and special diet foods. Delivery within 5 miles of
shop.

GREENVALE FARMS LTD

LEEMING, NORTHALLERRTON DL7 9LY
Tel: 01677 422953 Fax: 01677 425358 Contact: David Stonebank
Marketing@rooster.uk.com
Soil Association I809. Organic fertilisers. Greenvale produce organic pellets
and fertilisers for garden centres, horticulture and agriculture.

GROWING WITH GRACE

CLAPHAM NURSERIES, CLAPHAM, NR. LANCASTER LA2 8ER
Tel: 01524 251723 Fax: 01524 251548 Contact: N Marshall
info@growingwithgrace.co.uk www.growingwithgrace.co.uk
Soil Association G4295, P5562. We are a Quaker co-operative seeking to provide local people with home/locally produced vegetables and fair trade dried goods, through our bag scheme and farm shop. We cover north and east Lancashire, south-east Cumbria and the southern Yorkshire dales.

HAZELBROW VISITOR CENTRE

LOW ROW, RICHMOND DL11 6NE
Tel: 01748 886224 Contact: Catherine Calvert
hazelbrowfarm@aol.com www.hazelbrow.co.uk
Organic working farm in Yorkshire Dales National Park producing lamb and milk, with visitor centre, shop and café open 11am to 5pm five days a week, March to September (closed Mondays & Fridays).

HOLLINGWORTH, DJ

ADAMSON HILL, CHOP GATE, MIDDLESBROUGH, NORTH YORKS TS9 7HY
Tel: 01642 778284 Fax: 01642 778366 Contact: David Hollingworth
djholl@hotmail.com
Soil Association G5624. Pedigree beef Shorthorn cattle, pedigree North Country Cheviot sheep, and eggs. Farm gate sales for eggs only.

HOOK HOUSE FARM

HOOK HOUSE FARM, PLANE TREE LANE, KIRKBY FLEETHAM,
NORTHALLERTON DL7 0SS
Tel: 01609 748977 Fax: 01609 748686 Contact: Steven Peirson
hookhousefarm@lineone.net
Soil Association G5726. A small, mixed organic farm in the Vale of York, producing Christmas turkeys, lamb, beef and honey.

HUNTERS OF HELMSLEY

13 MARKET PLACE, HELMSLEY YO62 5BL
Tel: 01439 771307 Fax: 01439 771307 Contact: Tony Cowley
info@huntersofhelmsley.com www.huntersofhelmsley.com
High class food specialist stocking cooked meats, bacon, port and game
pies, fish, cheeses, many varieties of jams, chutneys, teas, coffees, Belgian
chocolates. We also offer mail order and specialist hampers.

THE KERFOOT GROUP LTD

MAWSON HOUSE, THE BRIDGE, ASKEW, BEDALE DL8 1AW
Tel: 01677 424881 Fax: 01677 422560 Contact: Robin Frost
packed@kerfootgroup.co.uk www.kerfootgroup.co.uk
Soil Association P5494. Blending, packaging and distribution of vegetable
oils to the food, pharmaceutical, technical and pet food industries.

KIRK, GA & SON

THE ABATTOIR, NUNNINGTON, YORK YO62 5UU
Tel: 01439 748242 Fax: 01439 788546 Contact: Richard Kirk (Director)
ashberrygrangefarm@hotmail.com
We are a small country abattoir able to slaughter any animals, and will
deliver (if a volume) by arrangement.

LARBERRY FARM SHOP

LARBERRY PASTURES, LONGNEWTON, STOCKTON ON TEES TS21 1BN
Tel: 01642 583823 Fax: 01642 582249 Contact: Eileen & Merilyn Wade
larberry@farmersweekly.net
Farm shop selling our own home-reared beef, lamb and organic free range
eggs. Pork from Houghall Agricultural College, fruit and veg, groceries
including flour, dairy, spreads, jams, herbs, spices—you name it, we do it.
Also cater for special diets, gluten-free, dairy-free, wheat-free and diabetic
products.

LAZY DOG TOOL COMPANY LTD

HILL TOP FARM, SPAUNTON, KIRKBYMOORSIDE YO62 6TR
Tel: 01751 417351 Fax: 01751 417351 Contact: Philip Trevelyan
philip@lazydogtoolco.co.uk www.lazydogtoolco.co.uk
Specialist hand tools for removing individual plants (weeds).

THE LITTLE DELICATESSEN

3 HIGH STREET, TADCASTER LS24 9AP
Tel: 01937 833244 Contact: Wendy Preston
High class delicatessen with a wide range of wholefood, organic beer and
organic lager.

LOW GILL BECK FARM

LOW GILL BECK FARM, GLAISDALE YO21 2QA
Tel: 01947 897363 Contact: R&P Drew
Home grown parsnips, carrots, turnips, brassicas, runner beans, dwarf
beans, peas, potatoes. Strawberries & raspberries in conversion.

LOW LEASES ORGANIC FARM

LOW ST., NR. LEEMING BAR, NORTHALLERTON DL7 9LU
Tel: 01609 748177 Fax: 01609 748177 Contact: Elaine McGregor
rjm96@tutor.open.ac.uk www.lowleasesorganicfarm.co.uk
Soil Association G4475. A local family business committed to delivering
quality produce. Our own and partners fresh local veg, fruit, eggs, rare
breed meat, groceries to your door in North Yorkshire, Darlington, Durham
and Teeside. Meat available by mail order.

MERCER, HARVEY

UNIT 15 CLARO COURT BUSINESS CENTRE, CLARO ROAD, HARROGATE
HG1 4BA
Tel: 01423 528822 Fax: 01423 529977 Contact: Paul Mercer
enquiries@harveymercer.com www.harveymercer.com
Soil Association P7691. Producers of Hearty's brand of soy-based foods and
snacks. These are healthy, vegetarian and often organic and gluten-free.

NATURE'S WORLD

LADGATE LANE, ACKLAM, MIDDLESBOROUGH TS5 7YN
Tel: 01642 594895 Fax: 01642 591224 Contact: The Manager
www.naturesworld.org.uk
The north of England's pioneering environmental centre featuring new eco-centre and tropical hydroponicum. Organic demonstration gardens, tearooms and shop. Monthly farmers' market.

NEWFIELDS ORGANIC PRODUCE

THE GREEN, FADMOOR, KIRKBY MOORSIDE YO62 7HY
Tel: 01751 431558 Fax: 01751 432061 Contact: Howard Wass
Farm producing winter vegetables, potatoes, carrots, parsnips, onions, cabbages, swedes, beetroot, parsley, leeks, sprouts, broccoli, cauliflower, celeriac and lettuce.

THE ORGANIC FARM SHOP

STANDFIELD HALL FARM, WESTGATE CARR RD., PICKERING YO18 8LX
Tel: 01751 472249 Fax: 01751 472249 Contact: Mike Sellers
mike@theorganicfarmshop.com
Soil Association PS21N. Specialist retailer or organic goods since 1984.
Home-produced vegetables and beef plus one of the biggest ranges of organic products in Yorkshire. Scarborough/Ryedale free delivery.

THE ORGANIC PANTRY

(NATURAL DELIVERY WHOLEFOODS)
ST.HELENS FARM, NEWTON KYME, TADCASTER LS24 9LY
Tel: 01937 531693 Fax: 01937 834062 Contact: Fanny Watson
organic.pantry@virgin.net www.organicpantry.co.uk
Family-run farm. Complete organic shop selling fruit, vegetables, meat, dairy, bread, wholefoods etc. box scheme, farm shop and website.
Individual diets/special requirements and requests welcome. Deliveries throughout Yorkshire and Derbyshire. Farmers' markets.

PADMORE, CF & ET

BANK HOUSE FARM, GLAISDALE, WHITBY YO21 2QA
Tel: 01947 897297 Fax: 01947 897297 Contact: Chris & Emma Padmore
em-chris-padmore@onetel.net
Soil Association G1135. Organic beef and lamb and woodland reared pork.
All meat home-produced, butchered, bagged and labelled. Please phone
regarding availability.

PASTURE COTTAGE ORGANICS

PASTURE COTTAGE, BOG HOUSE FARM, MICKLEBY, WHITBY TS13 5NA
Tel: 01947 840075 Contact: William Summerson
jenny@yorkshireorganics.freeserve.co.uk
Soil Association G5723. On our small family farm we produce a wide
selection of seasonal vegetables and eggs for retail sale at our farm shop,
through our box scheme and at our farm and local shops.

R & R TOFU

5 RYE CLOSE, YORK ROAD IND. PARK, MALTON YO17 6YD
Tel: 01653 690235 Fax: 01653 699091 Contact: Bruce McKenzie Malarkey
Soil Association P1516. Manufacturers of 'Clear Spot' organic tofu and tofu
products.

ROBINSON, DS

FIR TREE FARM, NORTHALLERTON DL6 2RW
Tel: 01609 772032 Contact: DS Robinson
mail@britishbeef.org www.britishbeef.org
Soil Association G4193. We are a specialist producer delivering organic beef
from our pedigree herd of British White Cattle direct to your home. We
also produce organic pork and lamb.

SMITHY FARM SHOP

BALDERSBY, THIRSK YO7 4BN
Tel: 01765 640676 Fax: 01765 640898 Contact: Susan Brown
Meat, poultry, dairy, vegetables, bread and pasta. Large range of pulses, cereals, sauces, wines and beers.

STAMFREY FARM ORGANIC PRODUCE

STAMFREY FARM, WEST ROUNTON, NORTHALLERTON DL6 2LJ
Tel: 01609 882297 Fax: 01609 882297 Contact: Angus & Sue Gaudie
info@clottedcream.org
Producers of traditionally made clotted cream and yoghurt sold via farmers' markets, farm gate, local farm shops and delicatessens.

STOCKBRIDGE TECHNOLOGY CENTRE LTD

CAWOOD, SELBY YO8 3TZ
Tel: 01757 268275 Fax: 01757 268996 Contact: Rob Jacobson
robjacobson@stc-nyorks.co.uk
STC Ltd. provides contract R&D, technology transfer and related services in all aspects of organic field and glasshouse vegetable production: specialisms include variety evaluation, fertility inputs and pest/disease control.

SUNFLOURS

THE HUTTS MILL, GREWELTHORPE, RIPON HG4 3DA
Tel: 01765 658534 Fax: 01765 658903 Contact: Mark Exelby
info@sunflours.com www.sunflours.com
Soil Association P1495,. We are organic and specialist flour producers and retailers. We mill blend and supply many types of flour including a large range of gluten-free flour.

TAYLORS OF HARROGATE

PAGODA HOUSE, PROSPECT RD., HARROGATE HG2 7LD
Tel: 01423 814000 Fax: 01423 814001 Contact: John Thompson
www.bettysandtaylors.co.uk
Tea blenders and coffee roasters.

TREVELYAN, PE

HILL TOP FARM, SPAUNTON, KIRKBYMOORSIDE YO62 6TR
Tel: 01751 417351/417799 Fax: 01751 417351 Contact: Philip Trevelyan
philip@lazydogtoolco.co.uk
Sheep and cereals.

TWEDDLE, BP & M

FAIRHOLME, MORTON ON SWALE, NORTHALLERTON DL7 9RW
Tel: 01609 774539 Fax: 01609 774539 Contact: Barry Tweddle
Produce potatoes, cereals, pulses.

UK JUICERS LTD

UNIT 3 WATERLINE ESTATE, ACASTER MALBIS, YORK YO23 2UY
Tel: 01904 704705 Fax: 01904 704705 Contact: Nick Ledger
enquiries@ukjuicers.com www.ukjuicers.com
We specialise in supplying high quality fruit, vegetable and wheatgrass
juicers, blenders food dehydraters, water purifiers, books and other health
products.

UNITRITION

OLYMPIA MILLS, BARLBY RD, SELBY YO8 5AF
Tel: 01757 244111 Fax: 01757 244088 Contact: AC Dickins
www.unitrition.co.uk
Soil Association registered. Oilseed crusher. Unitrition are specialist oilseed
crushers and raw material upgraders, supplying crude oils and expeller
cakes to food and agricultural industries.

WENSLEYDALE DAIRY PRODUCTS LTD
GAYLE LANE, HAWES DL8 3RN
Tel: 01969 667664 Fax: 01969 667638 Contact: Phil Jones
creamery@wensleydale.co.uk www.wensleydale.co.uk
Producers of Organic Wensleydale Cheese. Originators & producers of
Organic Wensleydale Cheese with Cranberries.

WESTLER FOODS LTD
AMOTHERBY, MALTON YO17 6TQ
Tel: 01653 693971 Fax: 01653 600187 Contact: Trevor Newbert
trevor.newbert@westler.com www.westlerfoods.com
We manufacture the Chesswood range of organic meals in easy open cans:
vegetable curry and vegetable hot pot.

WILD GINGER VEGETARIAN BISTRO
BEHIND THE GREEN HOUSE, 5 STATION PARADE, HARROGATE HG1 1UF
Tel: 01423 566122 Contact: Rachel Melton
www.wild-ginger.co.uk
100% vegetarian foods, freshly prepared and home made. Large choice for
vegans, also gluten/dairy/wheat/sugar-free and other exclusion diets
catered for. Licensed, selling organic wines and beer. Regular gourmet
evenings and special events. Good Food Best Restaurant in
Yorkshire/Humberside 2004 by public vote from *Guardian/Observer*.

YORK BEER & WINE SHOP
28 SANDRINGHAM STREET, FISHERGATE, YORK YO1 4BA
Tel: 01904 647136 Fax: 01904 647136 Contact: Eric Boyd
ybws@york10.freeserve.co.uk www.yorkbeerandwineshop.co.uk
We are a specialist off-licence selling beer, wine, cider and cheese. We sell
organic lines of all our categories.

YORKSHIRE FARMHOUSE EGGS LTD.

VILLAGE FARM, CATTON, THIRSK YO7 4SQ
Tel: 01845 578376 Fax: 01845 578660 Contact: Adrian Potter
enquiries@yorkshirefarmhouse.co.uk www.yorkshirefarmhouse.co.uk
We produce and pack organic eggs to the highest standards, under the Soil
Association and Organic Farmers and Growers accreditation schemes. Eggs
sold in most multiples and local catering and wholesale businesses.

Kettlewell

Kettlewell was a small village, with about 200 people, two shops (one with the post office), three pubs and a bank—the Yorkshire Penny Bank—and the youth hostel. The youth hostel brought a lot of outside people to the village. The Warden was Mr Gummerson. He was a character. He had taught his dog, a black Labrador, to 'talk'—well at least to count. Many hours were passed playing dominoes with it. It used to bark a number of times to tell Mr Gummerson which domino to play. They say he used to beat very good players! We would often find them in the King's Head, the pub run by Mr Robinson. There was always a big fire and a fine atmosphere. Mr Middlemiss used to go there most nights, and after closing he would go to the back room for supper with one or two of the locals.

A strange thing happened there one night. Mr Robinson had just locked the front door and we were going to have supper when there was a loud banging on the door. Standing there was a young man, very dirty and obviously exhausted. He struggled in and sat down by the fire, saying that he had just crawled under Great Whernside! We thought he must be mad. He said that he had gone down Dowker Cave, north-east of Great Whernside, and had come out in the middle of Kettlewell Beck, which is south of the moor. Well really! This was 1946 or maybe 1947, and it seemed impossible. Now I understand it is done all the time by groups of people. At any rate he got a free pint of beer and a whisky out of it!

From *Working with the Curlew: A Farmhand's Life* by Trevor Robinson, Green Books, £7.95

SOUTH YORKSHIRE

5 A DAY
5 LISTERDALE SHOPPING CENTRE, ROTHERHAM S64 3JA
Tel: 01709 532007 Contact: Michael Mavrakis
Fresh fruit & veg, vegetarian salads and meals, freshly juiced organic fruit, olive oils, sauces etc, all organic.

BEANIES
205–207 CROOKES VALLEY ROAD, SHEFFIELD S10 1BA
Tel: 0114 268 1662 Fax: 0114 268 1555 Contact: Y Williams
Soil Association No R1731. Award-winning workers' co-operative. Shop open seven days a week. Box scheme delivery service within Sheffield, also Doncaster, Barnsley, Chesterfield, Rotherham. Organic greengrocery, wholefoods, bread, chilled and frozen produce, vegan and vegetarian produce and speciality foods.

BEANTREE ORGANICS
663A ECCLESHALL RD., SHEFFIELD S11 8PT
Tel: 0114 266 2972 Fax: 0870 706 2811 Contact: Emma Davies
emma@beantreeorganics.com www.beantreeorganics.com
Beantree specialise in organic delicatessen foods, luxury olive oils, fairtrade coffee and chocolate, biscuits, preserves, wholefoods and other non-perishable mail order foods. 99% of our catalogue is organic. On-line ordering facilities.

DOWN TO EARTH
406 SHARROWVALE RD, HUNTERS BAR, SHEFFIELD S11 8ZP
Tel: 0114 268 5220 Contact: John Leeson
dte@blueyonder.co.uk
Wholefood retailer with wide range of organic produce including dairy, spreads, nuts, beans, pulses, rice, grains, cereals, etc. Not fresh fruit and veg.

THE DRAM SHOP
21 COMMONSIDE, SHEFFIELD S10 1GA
Tel: 0114 268 3117 Contact: Linda Taylor
Specialist off licence: wines, beers, ciders and spirits.

HEELEY CITY FARM
RICHARDS ROAD, SHEFFIELD S2 3DT
Tel: 0114 258 0482 Fax: 0114 255 1400 Contact: The Manager
farm@heeleyfarm.org.uk www.heeleyfarm.org.uk
A community environmental and horticultural project based on an inner
city educational farm. Food produced using organic methods, available in
our farm café and from our garden centre during times of surplus. Local
crafts.

POLLYBELL FARMS
HOLMES FARM, WROOT RD., EPWORTH, DONCASTER DN9 1EA
Tel: 01427 872461 Fax: 01427 874427 Contact: The Manager
pollybell@farmline.com
Producer of large range of organic vegetables.

POTTS BAKERS
STANLEY ROAD, STAIRFOOT, BARNSLEY S70 3PG
Tel: 01226 249175 Fax: 01226 249175 Contact: Andrew Potts
potts.bakers@care4free.net www.pottsbakers.co.uk
Soil Association P4477. Bakers of organic bread, cakes and puddings for
independent and multiple retailers.

THE REAL BREAD BAKEHOUSE LTD
REAR OF 36 CAT LANE, SHEFFIELD S11 9SP
Tel: 0114 249 5459 Fax: 0114 281 7965 Contact: John Coatman
jcoatman@blueyonder.co.uk
Soil Association P4265. Wholesale bakery supplying additive-free organic
bread to local shops.

YORKSHIRE ORGANIC EARTH

33 DEVONSHIRE DRIVE, HALLBALK, BARNSLEY S75 1EE
Tel: 07785 901215 Contact: Stuart Allen
stuartallen@yorkshireorganicearth.fsnet.co.uk
Soil Association G2238. Highly Commended 1998 (vegetables), Highly
Commended 1999 (eggs). Summer seasonal vegetables. Some farm gate
sales.

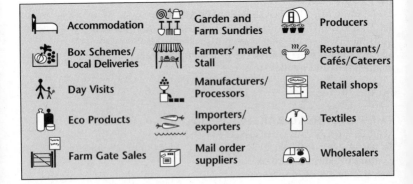

Accommodation	Garden and Farm Sundries	Producers
Box Schemes/ Local Deliveries	Farmers' market Stall	Restaurants/ Cafés/Caterers
Day Visits	Manufacturers/ Processors	Retail shops
Eco Products	Importers/ exporters	Textiles
Farm Gate Sales	Mail order suppliers	Wholesalers

BEANO WHOLEFOODS

36 NEW BRIGGATE, LEEDS LS1 6NU
Tel: 0113 243 5737 Fax: 0113 243 5737 Contact: Carol Tidgewell
info@beanowholefoods.co.uk www.beanowholefoods.co.uk
Soil Association R2282. Vegetarian and vegan wholefood shop, with
specialism in organic products. Organic fruit and vegetables delivered
Monday, Tuesday and Thursday. Fair-traded products stocked. Special diets
catered for.

BEANSTALK ORGANIX

UNIT 9, TOWNHEAD TRADING CENTRE, MAIN STREET,
ADDINGHAM LS29 OPD
Tel: 01943 831103 Fax: 01943 839199 Contact: Helen Roberts
info@beanstalkorganix.co.uk www.beanstalkorganix.co.uk
Soil Association P4995. Yorkshire's leading organic home delivery service
and one-stop organic shop of fresh produce, groceries, meat & poultry,
bread & cakes, eco-baby, personal care & household products. We accept
all major credit and debit cards.

BRADFORD WHOLEFOODS

THE CELLAR PROJECT, THE OLD SCHOOL, FARFIELD RD., SHIPLEY BD18 4QP
Tel: 01422 202648 Contact: Jack First
jackfirstgrove@aol.com
Specialist organic food retailer selling fresh vegetables and fruit, some
locally grown in season, groceries, eco-friendly toiletries and cleaning
products.

BRICKYARD ORGANICS

BRICKYARD ORGANIC FARM, BADSWORTH, PONTEFRACT WF9 1AX
Tel: 01977 617327 Contact: John Brook
Soil Association G598. Organic farm growing cereals, legumes, sheep,
plants, vegetables.

ELYSIUM NATURAL PRODUCTS LTD

UNIT 12, MODERNA BUSINESS PARK, MYTHOLMROYD, HALIFAX HX7 5QQ
Fax: 01422 884629 Contact: G Carroll
elysiumproducts@aol.com
Distribute organic foods: veg in jars, seeds, pulses, cakes, honey, biscuits, tortilla chips, juices, pet food, sweets, chocolate, health bars, gluten-free goods across the whole organic range.

FOOD THERAPY

11 NORTHGATE, HALIFAX HX1 1UR
Tel: 01422 350826 Fax: 01422 362106 Contact: K Benson
www.foodtherapy.freeserve.co.uk
An award-winning store and restaurant with a huge range of organic wholefoods.

FYFFES GROUP LTD

WAKEFIELD 41 IND. PARK, KENMORE RD., WAKEFIELD WF2 0XE
Tel: 01924 826446 Fax: 01924 820109 Contact: Andrew Joyce
dellam@fyffes.com www.fyffes.com
Ripening bananas, preparing and packing bananas. Distributing bananas to wholesalers and retailers.

HALF MOON HEALTHFOODS

6 HALF MOON ST., HUDDERSFIELD HD1 2JJ
Tel: 01484 456392 Fax: 01484 310161 Contact: Judith Beresford & Adrian Midgley
adrian@halfmoonhealthfoods.co.uk www.halfmoonhealthfoods.co.uk
We are a wholefood store specialising in organic lines, vegetables, breads, dairy products, eggs, beers and wines. Our organic box scheme has been established 15 years.

KERSHAW'S GARDEN CENTRE
HALIFAX RD., BRIGHOUSE HD6 2QD
Tel: 01484 713435 Contact: Mark Yates
Garden centre supplying organic composts, seeds, treatments and fertilisers.

LOVE ORGANIC!
4 REGENT ST., CHAPEL ALLERTON, LEEDS LS7 4PE
Tel: 0113 266 3030 Contact: Helen Roberts
A new organic/healthy food shop in the heart of Chapel Allerton. We stock all the organic essentials with a fabulous range of groceries, fresh produce, meat, poultry and fish, baby, personal care and eco-products. We accept all major credit cards.

MEANWOOD VALLEY URBAN FARM
SUGARWELL RD., MEANWOOD, LEEDS LS7 2QG
Tel: 0113 262 9759 Fax: 0113 239 2551 Contact: Susan Reddington
info@mvuf.org.uk www.wwf-leeds.org.uk
Soil Association R27N. Member of the Organic Farm Network. City farm, combining organic market garden, environmental education services to schools. Farm animals, including rare breeds. Purpose-built environment centre, interactive displays. Shop, café and play area. Registered charity, open every day to visitors.

NATURAL CHOICE
72 WESTBOURNE RD., MARSH, HUDDERSFIELD HD1 4LE
Tel: 01484 513162 Fax: 01484 687466 Contact: Graham Rushworth
graham.trudy@rush2001.freeserve.co.uk
Organic fruit and veg and the usual organic products and non-foods. Also class one fruit and veg.

NEAL'S YARD REMEDIES

20 COUNTY ARCADE, VICTORIA QUARTER, LEEDS LS1 6BN
Tel: 0113 243 8924 Contact: The Manager
mail@nealsyardremedies.com www.nealsyardremedies.com
Neal's Yard Remedies manufactures and retails natural cosmetics in addition
to stocking an extensive range of herbs, essential oils, homoeopathic
remedies and reference material.

ORG

79 GREAT GEORGE ST., LEEDS LS1 3BR
Tel: 0113 234 7000 Fax: 0113 242 7201 Contact: Novita Williamson
novita@org-organics.org.uk www.org-organics.org.uk
Soil Association R6296. Treatment centre. Local fruit and vegetables,
deliveries, hot/cold food, eat in/take away, dairy & dairy alternatives, meat
and fish, juice bar, tea, coffees, groceries, cosmetics, frozen foods,
household, alcohol, books, bulk grains, catering.

ORGANIC HOLIDAYS

TRANFIELD HOUSE, 4 TRANFIELD GARDENS, GUISELEY, LEEDS LS20 8PZ
Tel: 01943 870791 Fax: 01943 871468 Contact: Linda Moss
lindamoss@organicholidays.com www.organicholidays.com
Guide to holiday accommodation on organic farms/smallholdings and to
B&Bs, guest houses and small hotels where organic produce is used
according to availability.

ORGANIC HOUSE

2 MARKET ST, HEBDEN BRIDGE HX7 6AA
Tel: 01422 843429 Contact: Ellie
enquiries@organic-house.co.uk www.organic-house.co.uk
Organic retail and refreshment, fresh fruit, veg, bread, dairy, dried goods,
pulses, grains, nuts, cereals, coffees, teas, wines, beers, Fair Trade
products, wide range of vegan, gluten-free and wheat-free produce. Also
bodycare and organic clothing. Vegetarian café with wheat, gluten-free and
vegan options always available.

OUT OF THIS WORLD

20 NEWMARKET ST., LEEDS LS1 6DG
Tel: 0113 244 1881 Fax: 0113 234 1808 Contact: Damian Tapper
info@ootw.co.uk www.outofthisworld.coop
Small chain of ethical and organic supermarkets in Newcastle-upon-Tyne,
Leeds and Nottingham. Selling over 5,000 products, mostly certified
organic food plus fairly traded crafts, recycled paper and bodycare
products etc. Consumer co-op with over 15,000 members.

SALTAIRE WINES & WHOLEFOODS

32 BINGLEY RD, SALTAIRE, SHIPLEY BD 18 4RU
Tel: 01274 583629 Fax: 01274 583629 Contact: Sally Wolfe
len@thewolfes.freeserve.co.uk
Fine foods, luxury chocolates, wines, regional beers, whisky, liqueurs.

SNOWDEN, PA & SJ

HAWTHORNE HOUSE FARM, DUNKESWICK, HAREWOOD, LEEDS LS17 9LP
Tel: 0113 288 6637 Fax: 0113 288 6754 Contact: PA & SJ Snowden
Soil Association G1630. Organic arable farm growing milling wheat, field
beans and fattening lambs. Selling potatoes, carrots, parsnips, leeks and
other vegetables from the farm.

SUMA WHOLEFOODS

LACY WAY, LOWFIELDS BUSINESS PARK, ELLAND HX5 9DB
Tel: 0845 458 2290 Fax: 0845 458 2295 Contact: Chris Sadler
info@suma.co.uk www.suma.co.uk
Soil Association P968. The UK's largest independent wholesaler, of organic,
fair trade & natural foods. We also have extensive ranges of special diet and
environmentally friendly products. Suppliers of RSPB wildlife-friendly foods.
Please contact us for more information & our catalogue.

SWILLINGTON ORGANIC FARM

GARDEN COTTAGE, SWILLINGTON ORGANIC FARM, COACH RD., SWILLINGTON LS26 8QA
Tel: 0113 286 9129 Fax: 0113 286 9129 Contact: Jo Cartwright
jo.cartwright@farming.me.uk www.swillingtonhousefarm.co.uk
Soil Association G5062. Mixed organic farm producing organic eggs, lamb, pork, beef and vegetables from the walled garden. All vegetables freshly harvested to order, to be collected from the farm or can deliver locally. Meat by mail order. Farm shop open Saturdays 10–6 pm phone first at other times. Mob. 07974 826876.

VALLEY GARDEN ORGANICS

31 MARKET ST, HEBDEN BRIDGE HX7 6EU
Tel: 01422 846651 Contact: Mary-Ann Reed
Wide range of fresh organic fruit and veg, priority to local produce, wide range of other organic products including vegan, vegetarian, gluten-free. Organic meat, fair trade products, household and bodycare products.

VINCEREMOS WINES AND SPIRITS LTD

74 KIRKGATE, LEEDS LS2 7DJ
Tel: 0113 244 0002 Fax: 0113 288 4566 Contact: Jem Gardener
info@vinceremos.co.uk www.vinceremos.co.uk
The UK's longest established organic wine specialists. We also supply organic beers, ciders, juices and spirits. Free catalogue, friendly service and nationwide delivery. Trade enquiries welcome. We also run the HDRA Organic Wine Club. See display ad.

WEST RIDING ORGANICS

UNIT 3 NEAR BANK, SHELLEY, HUDDERSFIELD HD8 8LS
Tel: 01484 609171 Fax: 01484 609166 Contact: Julian Chambers
julian@wrorganics.co.uk www.organics.uk.co.uk
Manufacturers of Nature's Own and Bio-Pak organic composts (Soil Association registered). Module, blocking, potting and grow bags all supplied. Volcanic rock dust. Trade enquiries welcome.

WOODVIEW FARM
MANOR RD., FARNLEY TYAS, HUDDERSFIELD HD4 6UL
Tel: 01484 665434 Contact: G Chambers
sales@biogro.co.uk
Soil Association G2468. Aberdeen Angus beef.

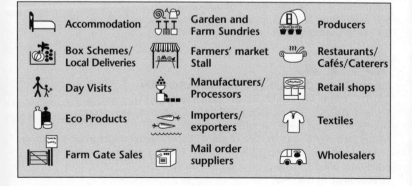

Accommodation	Garden and Farm Sundries	Producers
Box Schemes/ Local Deliveries	Farmers' market Stall	Restaurants/ Cafés/Caterers
Day Visits	Manufacturers/ Processors	Retail shops
Eco Products	Importers/ exporters	Textiles
Farm Gate Sales	Mail order suppliers	Wholesalers

ARKHILL FARM

25 DRUMCROONE ROAD, GARVACH, CO. LONDONDERRY BT51 4EB
Tel: 028 2955 7920 Contact: Paul Craig
arkfarmministry@aol.com
Irish Organic Farmers and Growers licence no. 1003. Organic hen and duck eggs, pork, including bacon, sausages, ham, chops, fillets and roasts, lamb, chickens and turkeys.

BALLYLAGAN ORGANIC FARM

12 BALLYLAGAN RD., STRAID, BALLYCLARE, CO. ANTRIM BT39 9NF
Tel: 028 9332 2867 Fax: 028 9332 2129 Contact: Tom Gilbert
ballylagan@aol.com www.ballylagan.com
Soil Association G1513. Farm shop selling home-produced meat and poultry products, fruit and vegetables, plus full range of organic groceries.
Shop opens: Thursday 2–6.30, Friday 9.30–6.30, Saturday 9.30–5.00.

BULRUSH HORTICULTURE

NEWFERRY RD., BELLAGHY, MAGHERAFELT, CO. LONDONDERRY BT45 8ND
Tel: 028 7938 6555 Fax: 028 7938 6741 Contact: Ann McCann
bulrush@dial.pipex.com www.bulrush.co.uk
Soil Association I2467. Suppliers and manufacturers of organic substrates for use in the horticulture industry.

CAMPHILL COMMUNITY – CLANABOGAN

DRUDGEON ROAD, OMAGH, CO.TYRONE BT78 1TJ
Tel: 028 8225 6111 Fax: 028 8225 6114 Contact: Martin Sturm
sturm@firenet.ws www.camphillclanabogan.com
Mixed Demeter veg farm, sale of some. Experimental underground heating system in polytunnel and 320kw biomass heating systems installed in buildings. Wind turbine producing electricity with solar panels and photovoltaic in planning.

CAMPHILL COMMUNITY – HOLYWOOD

8 SHORE ROAD, HOLYWOOD, CO. DOWN BT18 9HX
Tel: 028 9042 3203 Fax: 028 9039 7818 Contact: Rob van Duin
camphillholywood@btconnect.com
Soil Association certification applied for. Organic café, bakery and vegetable
and dried food, also crafts produced by people with special needs.

GILPINS FARM

72 DRUMILLY RD., LOUGHGALL, CO. ARMAGH BT61 8JJ
Tel: 028 3889 1528 Contact: Drew Gilpin
drewgilpin@hotmail.com
Soil Association G5833. Farmer, fruit grower. Finisher of organic beef cattle
and grower of organic apples, pears, plums.

HELEN'S BAY ORGANIC GARDENS

COASTGUARD AVE, HELEN'S BAY BT18 9DT
Tel: 028 91853122 Fax: 028 90423063 Contact: John McCormick
johneimar.mccormick@btinternet.com www.helensbayorganicgardens.com
Weekly deliveries of fresh organic vegetables from our fields in Helen's Bay.
Our delivery area covers greater Belfast and North Down. We supply large,
medium and small bags to cater for different needs.

LIFE TREE

37 SPENCER ROAD, DERRY, CO. LONDONDERRY BT47 6AA
Tel: 028 7134 2865 Fax: 028 7134 7880 Contact: A Munro
lifetreeshop@hotmail.com
Health food shop run by qualified therapist with medical background,
specialising in foods for special diets. Box scheme weekly with selection of
seasonal fruits and vegetables.

LITTLE EARTHLINGS

RIVERTON HOUSE, 151 DRUMAGARNER RD., KILREA, CO. DERRY BT51 5TW
Tel: 028 2954 1214 Fax: 028 2954 1498 Contact: Shauna Newman
info@littleearthlings.com www.littleearthlings.com
Specialising in the very best quality of organic cotton clothing, nappies and
educational toys for babies up to four. We also have a range of toiletries
especially designed for pregnant mums.

McARDLE ORGANIC MUSHROOMS

KNOCKACONEY, ALLISTRAGH, CO. ARMAGH BT61 8DT
Tel: 028 3889 1506 Fax: 028 3889 1529 Contact: John McArdle
info@mcardle-mushrooms.com www.mcardle-mushrooms.com
We cater for every type of customer of organic mushrooms, from the
individual to multinational multiples.

McGEARY MUSHROOM GROUP

53–58 ARMASH RD., MOY, DUNGANNON, CO. TYRONE BT71 7HR
Tel: 028 3754 8292 Fax: 028 3754 8779 Contact: Thomas & Linda
info@compost-ireland.com www.compost-ireland.com
Soil Association registered. We manufacture organic mushroom compost,
grow organic mushrooms and deliver with a fleet of refrigerated lorries
throughout the UK daily with farms throughout Ireland and Scotland.

MULLEN FARM/PASTURE POULTRY

84 RINGSEND RD., LIMAVADY BT49 0QJ
Tel: 028 7776 4157 Contact: Michael Mullen
jandm@andycameron.com www.pasturepoultry.com
A family business located in Co. Derry, north-west Ireland. Fully organic,
specialising in poultry products, offering free range eggs, bronze turkeys,
geese and chickens. Member of Soil Association and NWO Co-op.

OAKDENE DAIRY/ORGANIC DOORSTEP

125 STRABANE RD., CASTLEDERG, CO. TYRONE BT81 7JD
Tel: 028 8167 1257 Fax: 028 8167 9820 Contact: Glenn Huey
glenn@oakdenedairy.co.uk www.organicdoorstep.co.uk
We specialise in the production, processing, retailing of organic milk from
the farm to the doorstep.

ULSTER WILDLIFE TRUST

JOHN McSPARRAN MEMORIAL HILL FARM, GLENDUN, CUSHENDEN,
CO. ANTRIM BT44 0PZ
Tel: 028 2176 1403 Fax: 028 2176 1403 Contact: Barrie Elkin
ulsterwt@glendunfarm.fsnet.co.uk
Soil Association G6697. Farming together with wildlife in a progressive and
sustainable manner, producing lamb and beef from traditional and native
breeds. Native trees are also produced in our nursery.

ABERDEENSHIRE

BIODYNAMIC SUPPLIES
LORIENEEN, BRIDGE OF MUCHALLS, STONEHAVEN, ABERDEEN AB39 3RU
Tel: 01569 731746 Fax: 01569 731746/739137 Contact: Paul Van Midden
Specialist supplies to biodynamic farmers, gardeners and Demeter symbol holders.

CROFT ORGANICS
SKELLARTS CROFT, DAVIOT, INVERURIE AB51 0JL
Tel: 01467 681717 Contact: Vic Hunter
croftorganics@hotmail.com www.croft-organics.co.uk
Soil Association SP6495, HDRA. Soil Association box scheme; vegetables and soft fruit grown on SA-registered land. Farm shop sales, also organic wines, coffee and tea. Free range eggs.

FRASER, J & M
BURNORRACHIE, BRIDGE OF MUCHALLS, STONEHAVEN AB39 3RU
Tel: 01569 730195 Contact: John Fraser
Biodynamic Agricultural Association (Demeter). Demeter producers: mixed veg, fruit and beef, mainly wholesale. Collection and local delivery service including meat. Farmers' markets in Aberdeen and Forfar.

GOSPEL, TWB
AUCHMACLEDDIE, STRICHEN, FRASERBURGH AB43 6SP
Tel: 01771 637533 Fax: 01771 637533 Contact: Trevor Gospel
Soil Association G1867. North-east Scotland organic farm selling beef, large and small orders.

GRAMPIAN COUNTRY FOOD (BANFF) LTD
TANNERY ST., BANFF AB45 1FR
Tel: 01261 815881 Fax: 01261 818387 Contact: C Barrie
cbarrie@gcfg.com www.gcfg.com
Soil Association P7487, CMI organic standards. Processors of whole chickens.

GREENESS ORGANICS
ROSEBRAE, GREENESS, CUMINESTOWN, TURRIFF AB53 8HY
Tel: 01888 544877 Contact: Victoria Doran
Soil Association G2381. Weekly box delivery of locally grown vegetables and occasionally fruit around Turriff, Banff, Aberchirder and their environs.

HAY, M & M
EDINGLASSIE, HUNTLY AB54 4YD
Tel: 01466 700274 Fax: 01466 700274 Contact: Malcolm Hay
malcolm.hay@btinternet.com
Soil Association SG7519. Quality Angus cross beef store cattle and Shetland Cheviot/Texel cross lambs.

HOWEGARDEN, A DIVISION OF TRUXPLUS LTD
AUCHTURLESS, TURRIFF, ABERDEEN AB53 8EN
Tel: 01888 511808 Fax: 01888 511841 Contact: Adrian Walker
Packing organic produce to major supermarket chains. Specialise in locally grown produce.

LEMBAS
LORIENEEN, BRIDGE OF MUCHALLS, STONEHAVEN, ABERDEEN AB39 3RU
Tel: 01569 731746 Fax: 01569 739137 Contact: Paul Van Midden
Biodynamic Agricultural Association (Demeter) 307; Soil Association P6660. Growers and distributors of organically grown and Demeter food. Wholesale and retail service. Packer.

REID, G & G
CANTERLAND, MARYKIRK AB30 1XJ
Tel: 01674 840316 Fax: 01674 840316 Contact: Gabriela Reid
Organic Aberdeen Angus beef, sold fresh at farmers' market, sold vacuum packed and frozen from farm gate.

SCOTTISH AGRICULTURAL COLLEGE
CRAIBSTONE ESTATE, BUCKSBURN, ABERDEEN AB21 9YA
Tel: 01224 711072 Fax: 01224 711293 Contact: David Younie
d.younie@ab.sac.ac.uk www.sac.ac.uk/organic-farming
Licensed producer of organic crops, beef and sheep. Advice, Research, Education—SAC provides advice on organic farming (including telephone helpline 01224 711072) to Scottish farmers, education and vocational training, and multi-disciplinary research across most aspects of organic farming.

UNITED FISH PRODUCTS
GREENWELL PLACE, ABERDEEN AB12 3AY
Tel: 01224 854444 Fax: 01224 854333 Contact: Alison Chree
chreea@ufp.co.uk
Soil Association P3007. UFP manufactures organic fish meal to Soil Association standards from local fish trimmings. The company is accredited to the Femas standard and can assure safe, pure and traceable fish meal.

WARD, COLIN J
BRIDGEFOOT, NEWMACHER AB21 7PE
Tel: 01651 862041 Contact: Colin Ward
Soil Association no. G1071. A small mixed farm delivering vegetables, fruit and eggs in the Aberdeen area through its prize-winning box scheme.

AIRLIE ORGANICS

AIRLIE ESTATE OFFICE, CORTACHY, KIRRIEMUIR DD8 4LY
Tel: 01575 540294 Fax: 01575 540400 Contact: Susan Dyce
office@airlieestates.com www.airlieestates.com
We are retail and wholesale suppliers of home-produced Aberdeen Angus organic beef.

ANGUS FARMERS' MARKET

WESTBY, 64 WEST HIGH ST., FORFAR DD8 1BJ
Tel: 01307 465454 Contact: Veronica Baillie
jbrewster@ntlworld.com
Angus Farmers' Market held 2nd Saturday March to December. Local farmers interested in selling contact Veronica Baillie, secretary 01307 850207 (tel/fax) or email veronica.baillie@btinternet.com.

ANGUS ORGANICS LTD

AIRLIE ESTATE OFFICE, CORTACHY, KIRRIEMUIR DD8 4LY
Tel: 01575 540294 Fax: 01575 540400 Contact: Susan Dyce
info@angusorganics.com www.angusorganics.com
Scottish organic certified Aberdeen Angus beef and Scottish organic lamb from our own farms. Nationwide deliveries, mail order, retail and wholesale. Traditionally produced, traditionally butchered.

BEE-ORGANIC

THE FENS, DRONLEY RD., BIRKHILL DD2 5QD
Tel: 01382 581186 Contact: Roger Beecroft
roger@bee-organic.co.uk www.bee-organic.co.uk
Locally produced organic veg boxes delivered weekly to the Tayside, Dundee and north Fife areas of Scotland.

SKEA ORGANICS

EAST MAINS OF AUCHTERHOUSE, DUNDEE DD3 0QN
Tel: 01382 320453 Fax: 01382 320454 Contact: Andrew Skea
andrew@skea.sol.co.uk www.skeaorganics.co.uk
Soil Association SP7982. We are specialist growers and wholesalers of
organic seed potatoes. Our range of 25 varieties is especially selected for
taste and suitability for organic and low input farming.

ARGYLL & BUTE

ARGYLL HOTEL

ARGYLL HOTEL, ISLE OF IONA PA76 6SJ
Tel: 01681 700334 Fax: 01681 700510 Contact: Claire Bachellerie
reservations@argyllhoteliona.co.uk www.argyllhoteliona.co.uk
Small friendly hotel on the sea shore of Iona with great views, open fires
and celebrated restaurant serving home-grown organic vegetables and
herbs, local seafood and organic meats.

HODGE, C & C

ACHALIC FARM, LERAGS, BY OBAN PA34 4SE
Tel: 01631 566100 Fax: 01631 571202 Contact: Colin Hodge
achalic@hotmail.com
SOPA Membership no. 430 Certificate no. 1101/02/2101. Approved
producer of organic grass and pure Blackface lambs. Require organic
finisher for lambs Aug/Sept onwards.

KILDALLOIG FARM

KILDALLOIG, CAMPBELLTOWN PA28 6RE
Tel: 01586 553192 Fax: 01586 553192 Contact: Mary Turner
maryturner1@btopenworld.com
Self-catering holiday cottages on organic farm. Organic beef and lamb to
order. Organic breeding stock: Aberdeen Angus heifers, pedigree registered
Blueface Leicester, Blackface and North Ronaldsay rams or ewe lambs.

MILLSTONE WHOLEFOODS

15 HIGH STREET, OBAN PA34 4BG
Tel: 01631 562704 Fax: 01631 562704 Contact: Ray & Linda Grant
Fresh local organic vegetables and bread on Wednesdays to Fridays,
wholefoods, herbal remedies, nutritional supplements, aromatherapy etc.

STONEFIELD FARM – TA GROVES

GLENMASSAN, DUNOON PA23 8RA
Tel: 0136706640 Contact: TA Groves
Soil Association G2325. Organic: Blackface sheep, Highland mules,
Highlander cattle—meat, hay, soft fruit.

VERNON, R & H

RASHFIELD FARM, BY KILMUN PA23 8QT
Tel: 01369 840237 Contact: H Vernon
Soil Association G768. Organically registered since 1985, specialising in the
breeding of the original Black Highland cattle of the Western Highlands,
reared in the traditional manner. Alternative Therapies.

BARWINNOCK HERBS

BARWINNOCK HERBS, BARRHILL KA26 0RB
Tel: 01465 821338 Contact: Dave Holton
herbs@barwinnock.com www.barwinnock.com
Garden and nursery with hardy plants from a cool climate, propagated and grown without any chemical fertilisers or pesticides. Culinary and medicinal herbs available by mail order.

BUTTERWORTHS ORGANIC NURSERY

GARDEN COTTAGE, AUCHINLECK ESTATE, CUMNOCK KA18 2LR
Tel: 01290 551088 or 07732 254300 (mob) Contact: John Butterworth
butties@webage.co.uk www.webage.co.uk/apples
Scottish Organic Producers Association 625G. Organic fruit tree nursery (mainly apples) offering disease-resistant varieties (historic and modern), including many Scottish varieties and those for difficult sites, for garden use. On-line catalogue or 2 x 1st class stamps please.

GLENDRISSAIG HOUSE

GLENDRISSAIG BY GIRVAN KA26 0HJ
Tel: 01465 714631 Fax: 01465 714631 Contact: Kate McIntosh
Modern farmhouse with wonderful views. Peaceful location in Gulf Stream climate. Spacious en suite rooms with one on ground floor. Home cooking with vegetarian option. Organic produce and spring water. Secure parking.

STAIR ORGANIC GROWERS

11 THE YETTS, TARBOLTON KA5 5NT
Tel: 01292 541369 Contact: Steve Hilbourne
sales @organicgrowing.com www.organicgrowing.com
Box scheme and fruit and veg to order. Home delivery service. On-line ordering, no credit cards needed. Locally produced in season.

WILDLY ORGANIC
25 SEAFIELD COURT, ARDROSSAN KA22 8NS
Tel: 01294 472075 Fax: 01294 472075 Contact: Gillian Scott
info@wildlyorganic.co.uk www.wildlyorganic.co.uk
Suppliers of fresh organic fruit, vegetables and groceries. Local box scheme
delivering between Largs and Troon. Mail and internet order of organic
deodorants, natural soaps and personal care goods and organic Active
Manuka honey. Our retail outlet within Stanley plant nurseries at Ardrossan
is open every Friday, Saturday and Sunday.

DUMFRIES & GALLOWAY

BORELAND FARM
DUNSCORE, DUMFRIES DG2 0XA
Tel: 01387 820287 Contact: Simon Barnes
barnes@borelandfarm.co.uk www.borelandfarm.co.uk
Soil Association SG7881. Bed and breakfast accommodation and farm
holidays on an organic sheep farm, set in the rolling hills of Dumfries &
Galloway, south-west Scotland. Pets welcome.

CAMPHILL VILLAGE TRUST – LOCH ARTHUR
LOCH ARTHUR COMMUNITY FARM AND CREAMERY, BEESWING DG2 8JQ
Tel: 01387 760296 Fax: 01387 760296 Contact: Barry Graham
locharthur@supanet.com
Biodynamic Agricultural Association (Demeter). Produce of Demeter
certified cheeses and yoghurt. Organic farm shop selling our own cheeses,
meat, bread and vegetables and much more. Open Monday–Friday. Also
trade enquiries and mail order.

CREAM O'GALLOWAY DAIRY CO LTD

RAINTON, GATEHOUSE OF FLEET, CASTLE DOUGLAS DG7 2DR
Tel: 01557 814040 Fax: 01557 814040 Contact: Wilma Finlay
info@creamogalloway.co.uk www.creamogalloway.co.uk
Soil Association P2928. Farm based manufacturer of organic ice cream and
frozen yoghurt. Open to public with nature trails, tea room and adventure
playground.

FARM FUTURE – JM & PM ANDERSON

NETHERFIELD FARM, BEESWING, DUMFRIES DG2 8JE
Tel: 01387 730217 Fax: 01387 730217 Contact: JM Anderson
www.netherfieldguesthouse.co.uk
BDAA/Demeter certification 325. Small farm guest house in Galloway Hills,
offering own biodynamic and organic vegetarian based catering. Hauschka
massage with rest and care. Self-catering cottages available.

LOW CRAIGLEMINE FARM HOLIDAYS

LOW CRAIGLEMINE, WHITHORN, NEWTON STEWART,
WIGTOWNSHIRE DG8 8NE
Tel: 01988 500730 Fax: 01988 500730 Contact: Kirsty Hurst
cottage@galloway-timber.co.uk www.lowcraiglemine-farm-holidays.co.uk
BDAA Certificate No 354. Self-catering accommodation: organic family
farm, cosy, comfortable cottage and bothy sleeping 6, 3. Warm welcome
and peace await you. Converting to biodynamic, beef available. Bowen
technique available.

THE ROSSAN

THE ROSSAN, AUCHENCAIRN, CASTLE DOUGLAS DG7 1QR
Tel: 01556 640269 Fax: 01556 640278 Contact: Elizabeth Bardsley
bardsley@rossan.freeserve.co.uk www.the-rossan.co.uk
Small guest house in North Solway Shore. Large garden over 20 years
organic. All home cooking, mostly organic. Plus vegetarian, vegan, gluten-
free, med diets. Well behaved dogs welcome free. Stairlift to bedroom floor.
JPC Golden Achievement Award of Excellence for Quality and Service 2004.

SUNRISE WHOLEFOODS
49 KING ST., CASTLE DOUGLAS DG7 1AE
Tel: 01556 504455 Contact: Pauline Tilbury
Wholefood shop, specialising in organic dried and fresh foods; organic
meat, fruit and veg, cheese, wine, bread, books, SOPA symbol holder. Fresh
veg from smallholding in summer.

FIFE

BELLFIELD ORGANIC NURSERY
STRATHMIGO, CUPAR KY14 7RH
Tel: 01337 860764 Fax: 01337 860764 Contact: Irene Alexander
order@bellfield-organics.com www.bellfield-organics.com
Grower of organic vegetables. Home delivery service.

BLINKBONNY ORGANICS
BLINKBONNY COTTAGE, NEWBURGH KY14 6JE
Tel: 01337 840343 Fax: 01337 840343 Contact: Bob McAlpine
shop@blinkbonnyorganics.com www.blinkbonnyorganics.com
Biodynamic Agricultural Association (Demeter) 316.

ORGANIC MEAT & PRODUCTS (SCOTLAND) LTD
JAMESFIELD FARM, ABERNETHY KY14 6EW
Tel: 01738 850498 Fax: 01738 850741 Contact: Alan Dickson
jamesfieldfarm@btconnect.com www.jamesfieldfarm.co.uk
Soil Association. Producers of organic beef, lamb, sausages, pies, ready
made meals, soups, hampers etc. for mail order and farm shop.

PILLARS OF HERCULES FARM

PILLARS OF HERCULES, STRATHMIGLO ROAD, FALKLAND KY15 7AD
Tel: 01337 857749 Contact: Bruce Bennett
bruce@pillars.co.uk www.pillars.co.uk
Soil Association SB26C. Organic farm with on-site shop and café. Selling wide range of fruit, vegetables, salads, herbs, eggs and Christmas turkeys from own farm plus meat, dairy products and wholefoods. Open daily 10am–6pm.

SCOTMED HERBS

113/115 HIGH ST., BURNTISLAND KY3 9AA
Tel: 01592 872689 Contact: Alan Steedman
alan@scotmedherbs.co.uk www.scotmedherbs.co.uk
Grower and retailer of medicinal and culinary herbs (plants and cut herbs), retailer of herbs, spices, organic herbal teas, organic teas and cordials, aromatherapy products, cosmetics, soaps, crystals, CDs, herbal medicines (including Hambledon Herbs Organic Tinctures) and giftware.

SCOTMED HERBS

GARDEN BY THE LOCH, CRAIGENCALT FARM, KINGHORN KY3 3YG
Tel: 01592 872689 Contact: Alan Steedmann
alan@scotmedherbs.co.uk www.scotmedherbs.co.uk
Soil Association G910. Grower and retailer of medicinal and culinary herbs (plants and cut herbs), retailer of herbs, spices and other organic products, aromatherapy products, cosmetics, soaps, crystals, CDs, herbal medicines and giftware.

SPECIALIST POTATOES LTD

GRANARY BUSINESS CENTRE, COAL ROAD, CUPAR KY15 5YQ
Tel: 01334 656360 Fax: 01334 656360 Contact: Alan Romans
Soil Association processor specialising in joint operations with either Soil Association or Scottish Organic Producers Association growers to market best cool stored Scottish organic seed potatoes. Delivery areas covered—mainly UK and Europe.

WONDERMESH LTD.
THE GRANARY, 3RD FLOOR, COAL RD., CUPAR KY15 5YQ
Tel: 01334 657215 Fax: 01334 655290 Contact: Stewart Barnett
sales@wondermesh.co.uk www.wondermesh.co.uk
Wondermesh is the UK's leading supplier of insect crop netting. We offer a
range of mesh sizes for the control of a wide range of insects, birds and
other pests.

HIGHLAND

AQUASCOT GROUP LTD
FYRISH WAY, ALNESS IV17 0PJ
Tel: 01349 880711 Fax: 01349 884162 Contact: Gail Evans
gail.evans@aquascot.com www.aquascot.uk.com
A Highland-based manufacturer of fresh and frozen fish products. Scottish
organic salmon is a key raw material from which the company continues to
base its new product development.

BLACK ISLE BREWERY
BLACK ISLE BREWERY, OLD ALLANGRANGE, MUNLOCHY IV8 8NZ
Tel: 01463 811871 Fax: 01463 811875
Contact: David Gladwin / Jay Jay Gladwin
greatbeers@blackislebrewery.com www.blackislebrewery.com
Soil Association registered. Black Isle Brewery is a small, intensely
independent brewery in the heart of the Scottish Highlands producing a
range of outstanding organic beers.

DANDELION PARTNERSHIP
WALLED GARDEN, BRAHAN, DINGWALL IV7 8EE
Tel: 01349 861982 Contact: J Henderson & S Barclay
Soil Association G5162. Community supported agriculture (no deliveries), growing a complete range of organic vegetables for committed customers and restaurants. Also organic eggs, organic cut flowers. We only sell what we grow ourselves. Experienced teacher/speaker on organic horticulture.

EDINBURGH SMOKED SALMON CO LTD
1 STRATHVIEW, DINGWALL BUSINESS PARK, DINGWALL IV15 9XD
Tel: 01349 860600 Fax: 01389 860606 Contact: J Prentice
essco@btconnect.com
Soil Association P6793. Smoked salmon company specialising in high quality consistent products with a degree of innovation.

THE HEALTH SHOP
20 BARON TAYLOR'S STREET, INVERNESS IV1 1QG
Tel: 01463 233104 Fax: 01463 718144 Contact: Martin Sellar
healthshopinvern@aol.com
We are delighted to offer you a large range of organic products: just get in contact and we'll do the rest! Look forward to hearing from you.

HIDDENGLEN HOLIDAYS
LAIKENBUIE, GRANTOWN ROAD, NAIRN IV12 5QN
Tel: 01667 454630 Contact: Peter & Therese Muskus
muskus@bigfoot.com www.hiddenglen.co.uk
Watch roe deer and woodpeckers from top quality holiday homes with beautiful outlook over loch amid birch woods. Fun for children. Photos on website. Eggs, freezer-ready lamb and weaned calves sold.

MACLEOD ORGANICS

KYLERONA FARM, ARDERSIER, INVERNESS IV2 7QZ
Tel: 01667 462555 Fax: 01667 461138 Contact: Donnie Macleod
macleod.organics@virgin.net macleodorganics.com
Soil Association SP6506, SG8730. Main distributors for organic produce to
and from the Highlands. Organic farm centre including fully certified café,
shop, box scheme and tourist accommodation.

MARCASSIE FARM

MARCASSIE FARM, RAFFORD, FORRES IV36 2RH
Tel: 01309 676865 Fax: 01309 676865 Contact: Betsy van der Lee
marcassie@marcassie.fsnet.co.uk
Soil Association SG7923, Association for Environmentally Conscious
Builders, Association of Scottish Hardwood Sawmillers. Based in Scotland
(near Findhorn), brings together sawmill & woodshop (native timber
building components, bespoke buildings, furniture & street furniture),
organic farm (grains, wheatgrass, eggs, hay), commercial kitchen (being
established), esoteric healing and (at present, occasional) educational
courses.

MILLERS OF SPEYSIDE

STRATHSPEY IND. ESTATE, GRANTOWN ON SPEY PH26 3NB
Tel: 01479 872520 Fax: 01479 872892 Contact: A Milne
info@millersofspeyside.co.uk www.millersofspeyside.co.uk
Millers of Speyside are a small private abattoir situated in the Highlands of
Scotland. Suppliers of quality beef, lamb and pork to the catering and retail
trade.

PHOENIX COMMUNITY STORES LTD

THE PARK, FINDHORN BAY, MORAY IV36 3TZ
Tel: 01309 690110 Contact: David Hoyle
info@phoenixshop.org www.findhorn.org/store/
Full service award-winning food shop plus apothecary, bakery, books, crafts
and music.

POYNTZFIELD HERB NURSERY

BLACK ISLE, BY DINGWALL IV7 8LX
Tel: 01381 610352 Fax: 01381 610352 Contact: Duncan Ross
info@poyntzfieldherbs.co.uk www.poyntzfieldherbs.co.uk
Biodynamic Agricultural Association (Demeter) 326. Over 400 varieties of
rare, unusual and popular herb plants and seeds. Especially medicinal, Scots
natives, Himalayan. Established 1976.

RAASAY WALLED GARDEN

ISLE OF RAASAY, BY KYLE OF LOCHALSH IV40 8PB
Tel: 01378 660345 Contact: Sadie McLeod
raasaywalledgarden@btinternet.com
Soil Association GCS025, G5801; Skye & Lochalsh Horticultural
Development Association, Highlands & Islands Organic Association (HIOA).
An organic garden growing a wide variety of fruits, vegetables, salads,
herbs, cut and dried flowers for sale in season, plus hardy plants, climbers
and shrubs.

RHANICH FARM

RHANICH RD., EDDERTON, TAIN IV19 1LG
Tel: 01862 821265 Contact: Pam Shaw
Fairly isolated hill farm offering camping in summer, farm gate sales (eggs,
fruit, veg) in season. Mail order organic coloured fleece for spinning or
sheepskins.

TIO LTD

CULBLAIR FARM, DALCROSS, INVERNESS IV2 7JJ
Tel: 01667 462189 Fax: 01667 462611 Contact: Kirstine Dinnes
mail@tio.co.uk
Soil Association SP6493. Growers and packers of organic root crops for
supermarket and processors. Specific product range: carrots, bunch carrots,
parsnips, potatoes and broad beans.

LANARKSHIRE

BLACK MOUNT FOODS
8 THE WYND, BIGGAR ML12 6BU
Tel: 01899 221747 Fax: 01899 221518 Contact: John Bryan
orgmeat@aol.com www.scottishorganicmeats.com
Biodynamic Agricultural Association (Demeter) 275. Family-run business
dedicated to the supply of finest Scottish produced organic and
biodynamic beef, lamb, pork and poultry. Sausages and bacon also
available. Wholesale and mail order.

BROUGHTON ALES
BROUGHTON, BIGGAR ML12 6HQ
Tel: 01899 830345 Contact: Alastair Mouat
beer@broughtonales.co.uk www.broughtonales.co.uk
Soil Association P4734. Brewers of Border Gold organic ale, Angel organic
lager, Waitrose Organic Ale and Marks & Spencers Organic Ale and Lager.
All products available in 500ml bottles.

 Accommodation		Garden and Farm Sundries			Producers
Box Schemes/ Local Deliveries		Farmers' market Stall			Restaurants/ Cafés/Caterers
Day Visits		Manufacturers/ Processors			Retail shops
Eco Products		Importers/ exporters			Textiles
Farm Gate Sales		Mail order suppliers			Wholesalers

LOTHIAN

THE CALEDONIAN BREWING CO LTD

42 SLATEFORD ROAD, EDINBURGH EH11 1PH
Tel: 0131 337 1286 Fax: 0131 313 2370 Contact: Robert Burton
info@caledonian-brewery.co.uk www.caledonian-brewery.co.uk
Soil Association P903. Britain's first licensed organic brewer. Caledonian
brews the world renowned Golden Promise organic beer, available in most
UK supermarkets.

CAMPBELL, ALLAN

47 BOSWALD PARKWAY, EDINBURGH EH5 2BR
Tel: 0131 552 3486 Fax: 0131 552 3486 Contact: Dennis Flynn
This is a high street shop selling organic meat and poultry, eggs and
cheeses.

DAMHEAD ORGANIC FOODS

32A DAMHEAD, OLD PENTLAND RD., LOTHIANBURN, EDINBURGH EH10 7EA
Tel: 0131 448 2091 Fax: 0131 448 2504 Contact: Susan Gerard
enquiries@damhead.co.uk www.damhead.co.uk
Biodynamic Agricultural Association (Demeter) 238. Scotland's organic food
specialists: award-winning home delivery service (Soil Association Highly
Commended 2002), farm shop and wholesale division. Vast range of
organic products available to order on-line at www.damhead.co.uk.

DODS OF HADDINGTON

BACKBURN, LETHAM RD., HADDINGTON EH41 4NN
Tel: 01620 823305 Fax: 01620 824406 Contact: G Bonnington
Soil Association P6841. Dods of Haddington Limited established 1782,
suppliers of organic grass seeds, cereal seeds and root seeds for the organic
grower.

EAST COAST ORGANIC BOXES

24 BOGGS HOLDINGS, PENCAITLAND EH34 5BD
Tel: 01875 340227 Fax: 01875 340227 Contact: Mike Callender
ecobox@eastcoastorganics.freeserve.co.uk
Biodynamic Agricultural Association (Demeter) 295. Organic farm box
scheme. Home deliveries to Edinburgh and East Lothian areas. Range of
box sizes to suit every household. Can include fruit, eggs, bread, milk,
meat etc.

THE ENGINE SHED

19 ST. LEONARD'S LANE, EDINBURGH EH8 9SD
Tel: 0131 662 0040 Fax: 0131 667 5319 Contact: M MacDonald
engineshed@aol.com www.engineshed.org.uk
Café, shop, bakers, tofu production unit, outside catering, providing
organic wholefood products. Specialise in production of organic breads
and tofu.

THE ENGINE SHED SHOP

123 BRUNTISFIELD PLACE, EDINBURGH EH10 4EQ
Tel: 0131 229 6494 Contact: Heather Wilson
engineshed@aol.com www.engineshed.org.uk
Small health food shop selling a range of organic dry products, organic
fruit and veg, bread and cakes etc, incorporating a healthy light snacks
take-away service.

GROW WILD

UNIT 10, NEW LAIRDSHIP YARDS, BROOMHOUSE ROAD,
EDINBURGH EH11 3UY
Tel: 0131 443 7661 Fax: 0131 443 7656 Contact: Chris Purser
sales@growwild.co.uk www.growwild.co.uk
Soil Association P2975. Home box/delivery of best of local and imported
fruit and vegetables, throughout central Scotland. Plus quality meats,
bakery, dairy, wines and much more. Wholesale to retailers, box schemes
and caterers. Boxes start from £10.45 or choose your own. Order from our
new website. We like to provide a service as good as we ourselves would
expect.

HELIOS FOUNTAIN
7 GRASSMARKET, EDINBURGH EH1 2HY
Tel: 0131 229 7884 Fax: 0131 622 7173 Contact: Jos Bastiaensen
info@helios-fountain.co.uk www.helios-fountain.co.uk
A shop selling gifts, crafts, toys and beads. Our book selection includes
most works by or about Rudolf Steiner.

HERBARIA PRODUCTS LTD
51BC BRUNSWICK ROAD, EDINBURGH EH7 5PD
Tel: 0131 565 9000 Contact: Monica Wilde
enquiries@herbaria.co.uk www.hedgerowherbals.com
Herbaria makes organic and natural herbal handmade soaps and other
bath & body products. For trade customers we can supply own range or
make to order under your own label. Shoppers can purchase directly from
our website.

MACRAE HOLDINGS
MACRAE EDINBURGH, 50A WEST HARBOUR ROAD, GRANTON,
EDINBURGH EH5 1PP
Tel: 0131 552 5215 Fax: 0131 552 7521 Contact: Katrina Durward
katrina@macrae.co.uk www.macrae.co.uk
A processor of ready to eat seafood products, including organic scottish
smoked salmon, organic salmon paté, organic trout paté, organic hot
smoked trout fillets and organic scottish salmon gravelax. Licence P5868.
Deliveries to UK and EEC.

NATURE'S GATE
83 CLERK STREET, EDINBURGH EH8 9JG
Tel: 0131 668 2067 Contact: Bahram Ajodani
Soil Association R1827. Wholefood shop with large organic range including
bread, cereals, dried fruit, nuts, herbs, spices, coffees, teas, chilled and
frozen, fresh fruit and vegetables, wines, toiletries, vitamin supplements
and herbal remedies.

NEAL'S YARD REMEDIES
102 HANNOVER ST., EDINBURGH EH2 2LE
Tel: 0131 226 3223 Fax: 0131 225 9947 Contact: Gill Hames
mail@nealsyardremedies.com www.nealsyardremedies.com
Retailer of organic essential oils and cosmetics and therapy room offering
herbalist, homoeopath, massage and aromatherapy.

THE NEW LEAF
20 ARGYLE PLACE, MARCHMONT, EDINBURGH EH9 1JJ
Tel: 0131 228 8840 Contact: Linda Goodman
Soil Association R3002. Vegetarian and organic wholefood shop dedicated
to ethical trading. Fine selection of wholefoods including gluten and dairy-
free. Local fresh organic produce; eco-friendly, cruelty-free products and
much more.

SIMMERS OF EDINBURGH LTD
90 PEFFERMILL ROAD, EDINBURGH EH16 5UU
Tel: 0131 620 7000 Fax: 0131 620 7750 Contact: John Holroyd
john@simmersofedinburgh.co.uk www.nairns-oatcakes.com
Producer of organic oat cakes and biscuits.

SIMPLY ORGANIC
19/21 DRYDEN VALE, BILSTON GLEN EH20 9HN
Tel: 0131 448 0440 Fax: 0131 448 0441 Contact: Belinda Mitchell
information@simplyorganic.co.uk www.simplyorganic.co.uk
Simply Organic are an award-winning, all-organic company. We produce
fresh organic convenience products including soups, pasta sauces and
ready meals, all of which are suitable for vegetarians, under the Simply
Organic brand.

ISLE OF MULL

FINDHORN FOUNDATION
ISLE OF ERRAID, FIONNPHORT PA66 6BN
Tel: 01681 700384 Contact: Paul Johnson
paul@erraid.fslife.co.uk www.erraid.com
Spiritual community living lightly on a tiny Hebridean island.

ISLAND BAKERY ORGANICS
TOBERMORY PA65 6PY
Tel: 01688 302223 Fax: 01688 302378 Contact: Joseph Reade
organics@islandbakery.co.uk www.islandbakery.co.uk
Soil Association P6294. Producers of award-winning organic biscuits, first
launched in September 2001. Available in delicatessens, organic stores,
food halls and farm shops across the UK. See our website for more
information.

Wisdom of the Cows

*In 1998, Howard Vlieger harvested both natural maize and a genetically modified Bt variety on his
farm in Maurice, Iowa. Curious about how his cows would react to the pesticide-producing Bt
maize, he filled one side of his sixteen-foot trough with the Bt and dumped natural maize on the
other side. Normally, his cows would eat as much maize as was available, never leaving leftovers.
But when he let twenty-five of them into the pen, they all congregated on the side of the trough
with the natural maize. When it was gone, they nibbled a bit on the Bt, but quickly changed their
minds and walked away.*

*A couple of years later, Vlieger joined a room full of farmers in Ames, Iowa to hear presidential
candidate Al Gore. Troubled by Gore's unquestioning acceptance of GM foods, Vlieger asked Gore to
support a recently introduced bill in congress requiring that GM foods be labelled. Gore replied that
scientists said there is no difference between GM and non-GM foods. Vlieger said he respectfully dis-
agreed and described how his cows refused to eat the GM maize. He added, "My cows are smarter
than those scientists were." The room erupted in applause. Gore asked if any other farmers noticed a
difference in the way their animals responded to GM food. About twelve to fifteen hands went up.*

**From *Seeds of Deception: Exposing Corporate and Government Lies about the Safety of
Genetically Engineered Food* by Jeffrey M. Smith, Green Books, £9.95**

ORKNEY

ORCA HOTEL
76 VICTORIA ST., STROMNESS KW16 3BS
Tel: 01856 850447 Contact: D Fischler
info@orcahotel.com www.orcahotel.com
Two-star guesthouse, six rooms (single, twins, doubles, family), all en suite;
situated in historic harbour village of Stromness, Orkney.

ORKNEY ORGANIC MEAT
NEW HOLLAND FARM, HOLM, ORKNEY KW17 2SA
Tel: 01856 781345 Fax: 01856 781345 Contact: Tony & Elizabeth Bown
info@orkneyorganicmeat.co.uk www.orkneyorganicmeat.co.uk
Organic farm producing Aberdeen Angus beef and lamb with emphasis on
health for both animal and customer. Meat processed here on the farm by
our own butcher. Mail order sales of beef, lamb, speciality sausages and
ready meals, delivered throughout UK. Farm gate sales. Self-catering
holiday cottage.

THE ORKNEY SALMON COMPANY LTD
CROWNESS CRESCENT, HATSTON, KIRKWALL, ORKNEY KW15 1RG
Tel: 01856 876101 Fax: 01856 873846 Contact: The Manager
www.orkneysalmon.co.uk
Soil Association SP2924. The pure waters off the coast of Orkney, where
the North Sea and the Atlantic Ocean collide, are the ideal natural
environment for raising organic salmon. Soil Association approved. See also
www.aquascot.com.

TODS OF ORKNEY
25 NORTH END ROAD, STROMNESS KW16 3AG
Tel: 01856 850873 Fax: 01856 850213 Contact: Eddie Wight
info@stockan-and-gardens.co.uk www.stockan-and-gardens.co.uk
Soil Association P1905. Manufacturer of traditional oatcakes.

THE BEAN SHOP
67 GEORGE ST., PERTH PH1 5LB
Tel: 01738 449955 Fax: 01738 632693 Contact: Lorna Suttie
sales@thebeanshop.com www.thebeanshop.com
The Bean Shop is a coffee roaster and tea specialist shop in Scotland. We offer a range of organic teas, coffees, biscuits and everything to make the perfect cup.

BORLAND FARM
BLACKLUNANS, BLAIRGOWRIE PH10 7LA
Tel: 01932 254855 Fax: 01932 253793 Contact: Keith Howman
100326.641@compuserve.com www.highlandcattleborlandfarm.com
Soil Association G5245. Extensively reared Highland beef cattle and Hebridean sheep including Hebridean woollen products—see www.hebrideanwoolhouse.com.

HIGHLAND HEALTH STORE
7 & 16 ST. JOHN ST., PERTH PH1 5SP
Tel: 01738 628102 Fax: 01738 447541 Contact: John Ritchie
email@highlandhealth.fsnet.co.uk
Vegetarian and health food shop.

HIGHLAND SPRING LTD
STIRLING ST., BLACKFORD PH4 1QA
Tel: 01764 660500 Fax: 01764 682480 Contact: Ruth Nilsson
ruthn@highland-spring.com
Soil Association G5068. Bottled water producer. Highland Spring have gained organic status for 512 hectares, the core of their catchment area in 2001. This accreditation for the land endorses the protection afforded to the Highland Spring source.

HUGH GRIERSON

NEWMILN FARM, TIBBERMORE, PERTH PH1 1QN
Tel: 01738 730201 Fax: 01738 730201 Contact: Sascha Grierson
hgrierson@freeuk.com www.the-organic-farm.co.uk
Finest organic Aberdeen Angus beef (hung for 3 weeks) and organic lamb
from a Perthshire farm. All our beef and lamb is full of the flavour of grass-
fed food. We deliver locally in the evenings or nationwide by courier. You
can order by phone or through our website. Traditional local produce.
Buy local food to safeguard the local economy.

LURGAN FARM SHOP

LURGAN FARM, DRUMDEWAN, BY ABERFELDY PH15 2JQ
Tel: 01887 829303 Fax: 01887 829303 Contact: Sally Murray
sally@lurganfarm.demon.co.uk www.lurganfarmshop.co.uk
Soil Association SP6485. We sell our home-produced organic lamb and
Aberdeen Angus beef. We make ready meals in our shop kitchen with our
meats and bought in organic vegetables. We have a huge range of organic
wholefoods and dairy produce.

ISLE OF SKYE

ACHNACLOICH ORGANIC VEGETABLES

2 & 3 ACHNACLOICH, TARSKAVAIG IV49 8SB
Tel: 01471 855315 Contact: Chris Marsh
chris_marsh@madasafish.com
Soil Association GCS025/G2605. Established 1998, AOV supplies 50
households in South Skye with weekly vegetables (June–October). All
produce grown by us on our 3-acre croft.

GLENDALE SALADS

19 UPPER FASACH, GLENDALE IV55 8WP
Tel: 01470 511349 Fax: 01470 511349 Contact: K&B Hagmann
Salads, herbs, veg and soft fruit to hotels, restaurants and through a
box scheme. Varieties selected for flavour and attractiveness. Delivered
chilled on regular runs several times a week. SA certificate G2263. Mail
order throughout the UK.

RUBHA PHOIL FOREST GARDEN / SKYE PERMACULTURE

RUBHA PHOIL, ARMADALE PIER IV45 8RS
Tel: 01471 844700 Contact: Sandy Masson
sandyrv@tiscali.co.uk www.skye-permaculture.org.uk
Soil Association GCS025/G4609, HDRA, Permaculture Association, Centre
for Alternative Technology Ecosite. Herbs, vegetables, displays and
demonstration of alternative systems, holiday accommodation, woodland
walk, otter/bird hide, solitude in wilderness.

STIRLINGSHIRE

GLENSIDE ORGANICS

2/4 BANDEATH IND. ESTATE, THROSK, STIRLING FK7 7XY
Tel: 01786 816655 Fax: 01786 816100 Contact: Matt Thomson
enquiries@glensideorganics.co.uk www.glensidefarming.co.uk
Glenside's fertility farming system uses the Albrecht soil analysis, natural
soil conditioning fertilisers and seaweed products optimising farm resources
in the profitable production of quality crops and healthy livestock.

STRATHCLYDE

EPO GROWERS
KENNELS COTTAGE, HARDGATE, DUMBARTON G81 5QR
Tel: 01389 875337 Contact: Echo Mackenzie
epo@argonet.uk
We grow and sell organic vegetables, herbs and soft fruit under a
Community Supported Agriculture subscription system. Deliveries to
households in Glasgow and NW area; use compost, manure and rock dust
for fertility.

GRASSROOTS
20–22 WOODLANDS ROAD, CHARING CROSS, GLASGOW G3 6UR
Tel: 0141 353 3278 Fax: 0141 353 3078 Contact: Sarah Duncan
sarah@grassrootsorganic.com www.grassrootsorganic.com
Vegetarian wholefood shop retailing organic produce and groceries. All
your shopping needs, organic where possible, fair trade if we can get it.
Licensed: we stock a range of organic wines and beers.

GRASSROOTS CAFE
97 ST. GEORGES ROAD, CHARING CROSS, GLASGOW G3 6JA
Tel: 0141 333 0534 Fax: 0141 332 9227 Contact: Lesley McNeil
www.grassrootsorganic.com
Grassroots café offers an informal atmosphere in which to enjoy a wide
variety of vegetarian cuisine with plenty of choice for vegans and those
with special dietary requirements.

GREENCITY WHOLEFOODS
23 FLEMING ST., GLASGOW G31 1PQ
Tel: 0141 554 7633 Contact: Lorna Donaldson
sales@greencity.co.uk www.greencity.co.uk
Soil Association P2370. Wholesaler/distributor of wide range of vegetarian
wholefoods, including many organic, Fairtrade and vegan products. Also
stock organic wines and beers and eco-friendly cleaning products.

INGRAM BROTHERS LTD
12 LAWWMOOR PLACE, DIXONS BLAZES IND. ESTATE, GLASGOW G5 0YE
Tel: 0141 429 2224 Fax: 0141 429 2227 Contact: Simon Young
sales.ingrambros@btinternet.com www.ingrambrothers.co.uk
Soil Association P3006. Manufacturers of bakery ingredients including
organic icings, toppings, marzipan and icing sugar. Wholesaler of organic
sugar and cocoa powder.

THE NATURAL FRUIT & BEVERAGE CO LTD
VIEWFIELD PARK, VIEWFIELD RD., COATBRIDGE ML5 5QS
Tel: 01236 429042 Fax: 01236 424234 Contact: Helen Craig
nfbc2000@aol.com
Soil Association P5826. Manufacturer of soft drinks and fruit juices.

NEAL'S YARD REMEDIES
11 ROYAL EXCHANGE SQUARE, GLASGOW G1 3AJ
Tel: 0141 248 4230 Contact: Laurie Heaps
mail@nealsyardremedies.com www.nealsyardremedies.com
Neal's Yard Remedies manufactures and retails natural cosmetics in addition
to stocking an extensive range of herbs, essential oils, homoeopathic
remedies and reference material.

ROOTS & FRUITS, WHOLEFOODS & ORGANICS
455 GREAT WESTERN ROAD, GLASGOW G12 8HH
Tel: 0141 339 3097 Fax: 0141 334 3530 Contact: Wendy Inglis
Stockists of over 1,000 organic products including fruit and vegetables,
fresh meats and breads, dairy and general provisions. A comprehensive
range of baby foods and childcare products. Box scheme and delivery
service throughout the Glasgow area.

TAPA COFFEE AND BAKEHOUSE

21 WHITEHILL ST., DENNISTOUN, GLASGOW G31 2LH
Tel: 0141 554 9981 Contact: Robert Winters
tapa-ltd@tiscali.co.uk
Tapa is a bakery and coffee shop stocking a small but expanding range of organic produce. Bread is baked daily using organic ingredients and includes 2–3 ryes, two sourdoughs and a delicious wholemeal.

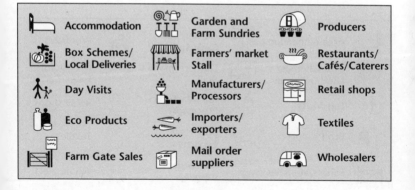

Accommodation	Garden and Farm Sundries	Producers
Box Schemes/ Local Deliveries	Farmers' market Stall	Restaurants/ Cafés/Caterers
Day Visits	Manufacturers/ Processors	Retail shops
Eco Products	Importers/ exporters	Textiles
Farm Gate Sales	Mail order suppliers	Wholesalers

WESTERN ISLES

WEST MINCH SALMON LTD
GRAMSDALE FACTORY, GRAMSDALE, BENBECULA HS7 5LZ
Tel: 01870 602081 Fax: 01870 602083 Contact: Hector Macleod
wmsltd@zetnet.co.uk
Soil Association SG6059 (production), SP5504 (processing). Producers of
organic farmed Atlantic Salmon.

Accommodation	Garden and Farm Sundries	Producers
Box Schemes/ Local Deliveries	Farmers' market Stall	Restaurants/ Cafés/Caterers
Day Visits	Manufacturers/ Processors	Retail shops
Eco Products	Importers/ exporters	Textiles
Farm Gate Sales	Mail order suppliers	Wholesalers

ISLE OF ANGLESEY

ANGLESEY SEA SALT CO
BRYNSIGNCYN, ANGLESEY LL61 6TQ
Tel: 01248 430871 Fax: 01248 430213 Contact: Tanya Geldard
enq@seasalt.co.uk www.seasalt.co.uk
Pure, white, organically certified (by Soil Association) sea salt, produced
from the fresh waters around Anglesey. Also sea salt with organic spices.
Range of eclectic salt bowls. Carriage at cost for small orders, UK-wide.
Free delivery for larger orders.

FOREMAN, HELEN
YSGUBOR BACH, FFORDD CERRIG MAWR, CAERGEILIOG, HOLYHEAD,
ANGLESEY LL65 3LU
Tel: 01407 742293 Contact: Helen Foreman
Soil Association G5882. Fresh organic vegetables, soft fruit and eggs.

GIBBONS, E & M
PEN-YR-ORSEDD, TREFOR, HOLYHEAD, ANGLESEY LL65 3YY
Tel: 01407 720227 Fax: 01407 720227 Contact: E Gibbons
Soil Association G4333. Organic beef producer with pedigree Limousin
herd also offering organic bulls, heifers and cows/calves for breeding
purposes, and store stock for finishing. Unique wooden coffee/occasional
tables.

THE NORTH WALES ORGANIC GROWERS AND PERMACULTURE GROUP
PEN-Y-BRYN, TALWRN, LLANGEFNI, YNYS MON LL77 7SP
Tel: 01248 750029 Contact: Kath Turner
Group of members who put newcomers to the area in touch with existing
organic growers and permaculturists.

PLAS LLANFAIR ORGANICS

PLAS LLANFAIR, TYN-Y-GONGL, YNYS MON LL74 8NU
Tel: 01248 852316 Contact: Mike Parker
mike@plasllanfair.freeserve.co.uk
Anglesey smallholding specialising in soft and top fruit and the processing
thereof, jams, preserves and chutneys. Wide range of vegetable production
on a small scale. Supply direct and local outlets.

ROBERTS, MO & JS

BRON HEULOG FARM, LLANDDEUSANT, HOLYHEAD, ANGLESEA LL65 4AU
Tel: 01407 730292 Contact: Martin Roberts
Soil Association G7296. Producing organic beef calves, Blonde x to sell as
weaned calves and stores, possibility to finish some. Mobile: 07884
213217.

CAERPHILLY

KEDDIE SAUCEMASTERS LTD

PRINCE OF WALES INDUSTRIAL ESTATE, ABERCARN NP11 5AR
Tel: 01495 244721 Fax: 01495 244626 Contact: Lisa Holman
lholman@costa.co.uk www.gcosta.co.uk
Manufacturer of an extensive range of quality sauces for the retail,
industrial and catering sector. We can offer an array of pack formats from
sachets, bottles, jars, catering to bulk formats. We are Soil Association
approved.

CARMARTHENSHIRE

BLACK MOUNTAIN FOODS
CWMCOCHIED, CWMDU, LLANDEILO SA19 7EE
Tel: 01558 685018 Fax: 01558 685185 Contact: Peter Mitchell
mynydddu@aol.com www.blackmountainfoods.co.uk
Soil Association G1802. Specialise in the distribution of organic meat to
retailers in London and South of England. We are now expanding our
operation to include the distribution of organic cheese, vegetables and
other products.

FRANKLANDS FARM FEEDS
UNIT 23 ANTHONY'S WAY, CILLEFWR IND. ESTATE, JOHNSTOWN,
CARMARTHEN SA31 3RB
Tel: 01267 222422 Fax: 01267 237479 Contact: Andrew Morrey
amorrey@countrywidefarmers.co.uk www.countrywidefarmers.co.uk
Manufacturers of blended non-organic approved seed blends for all
ruminants throughout south Wales and the south Midlands.

FRONTLINE ORGANICS
UNIT 4, WHITLAND INDUSTRIAL ESTATE, WHITLAND SA34 0HR
Tel: 01994 241368 Fax: 01994 241063 Contact: Dai Miles
frontline.organics@ukgateway.net www.frontlineorganics.co.uk
Soil Association P16WW. Deliveries direct to individuals, shops, restaurants,
and box schemes of fresh vegetables and fruit, dairy products, bread and
wholefoods, locally produced where possible but we do import to satisfy
year-round demand.

IECHYD DA
11 BROAD ST., LLANDOVERY SA20 0AR
Tel: 01550 720703 Contact: J Nisbett
General health foods etc, organic fresh veg, dried fruit, yoghurts, coffee,
cider vinegar, tofu, bread, tea, soya milk, rice, pasta, flour, oats and bran.

JONES, ORIEL & SON LTD
TEIFY PARK, LLANBYDDER SA40 9QE
Tel: 01570 480284 Fax: 01570 480260 Contact: Meinir Thomas
ojonline@hotmail.co.uk www.oriel-jones.co.uk
Abattoir. Lamb slaughtering and processing. Beef: slaughtering only.

KITE WHOLEFOODS
Y CADW, 38 FFORD ANEURIN, PONTYBEREM SA15 5DF
Tel: 01269 871035 Fax: 01269 871035 Contact: Paul Hartland
sales@kitewholefoods.co.uk www.kitewholefoods.co.uk
Soil Association P5857. Producing award-winning and highly acclaimed
organic mayonnaise in retail and catering packs.

LLANBOIDY CHEESEMAKERS
CILOWEN UCHAF, LOGIN, WHITLAND SA34 0TJ
Tel: 01994 448303 Fax: 01994 448303 Contact: Sue Jones
sue@llanboidycheese.co.uk
Soil Association P7158. Award-winning Cilowen Organic Cheese made by
Llanboidy Cheesemakers on their farm in west Wales using local organic
milk. Milk is pasteurised on farm and cheese hand-made in traditional way,
hard-pressed slowly and matured in their own natural rind to produce a
distinctly different truckle cheese. 'Best New Organic Cheese' & Gold
Medal, British Cheese Awards 2001. 'Best New Cheese Marketed in UK',
World Cheese Awards 2001. Suitable for vegetarians.

MANSE ORGANICS
THE MANSE, CAPEL ISAAC, LLANDEILO SA
Tel: 01558 669043 Contact: Pete & Gary Wignall
info@graftedwalnuts.co.uk www.graftedwalnuts.co.uk
Soil Association G7180. Organic Scheme for Wales member. Specialists in
fruiting and ornamental walnut trees. Native, European and American
(black walnut) varieties and hybrids are grafted on to sturdy walnut
rootstocks selected for UK conditions. Range of sizes available.

PEN PYNFARCH

PEN PYNFARCH, LLANDYSUL SA44 4RU
Tel: 01559 384948 Contact: Eeva-Maria Mutka
enquiries@penpynfarch.co.uk www.penpynfarch.co.uk
Simple, cosy holiday cottage with woodburner, sleeps 4/6. Organic veggie breaks offered. Retreat/course centre with studio, accommodation and catering. Wooded valley with stream and lake, 30 mins to the sea.

PENCAEMAWR TRADITIONAL FARM FOODS

PENCAE MAWR, LLANFYNYDD, CARMARTHEN SA32 7TR
Tel: 01558 668613 Fax: 01558 668613 Contact: John Burgess
pencaemawr@ntlworld.com
As a diversification from our organic farm, we produce certified organic chutneys and preserves using locally produced ingredients wherever possible. Small batches and long cooking times give our chutneys a depth of flavour not possible with mass produced products.

POULSON, JS

BLAENHIRAETH FARM, LLANGENNECH, LLANELLI SA14 8PX
Tel: 01554 773779 Contact: JS Poulson
Organic milk, organic meat and store cattle. Surplus organic livestock usually for sale.

RILEY, JH & TJ

CAEPONTBREN FARM, PONTHENRI, LLANELLI SA15 5PB
Tel: 01269 860930 Contact: John Riley
Soil Association G5983. Produce organic beef, 1 year old, to sell on to finish.

S & J ORGANICS

LLWYNCRYCHYDDOD, LLANPUMSAINT, CARMARTHEN SA33 6JS
Tel: 01267 253570 Fax: 01267 253562 Contact: Juliet Fay
info@sjorganics.co.uk www.sjorganics.co.uk
Soil Association certified poultry specialists. Producers of organic chickens,
Muscovy ducks, Pekin ducks, geese, turkeys & guinea fowl. Whole birds &
portions available. Supplying both retail & trade. Our poultry is processed
through our low throughput on-farm, DEFRA registered, Soil Association
licensed abattoir.

WEALE, MRS S

WAUNGRON, LLANBYDDER SA40 9SB
Tel: 01570 481378 Contact: Sally Weale
Soil Association G6331. A small farm business producing organic beef and
lamb. Organic point of lay completely free range bantam-type hens.

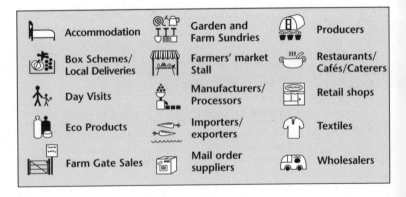

Accommodation	Garden and Farm Sundries	Producers
Box Schemes/ Local Deliveries	Farmers' market Stall	Restaurants/ Cafés/Caterers
Day Visits	Manufacturers/ Processors	Retail shops
Eco Products	Importers/ exporters	Textiles
Farm Gate Sales	Mail order suppliers	Wholesalers

CEREDIGION

CARPENTER, MBP & TWYFORD, CA

TY GWYN, LLWYN RHYDOWEN, RHYDOWEN, LLANDYSUL SA44 4PX
Tel: 01545 590687 Contact: M Carpenter & C Twyford
peasants@care4free.net
Soil Association G4267. Small registered flock Lleyn sheep, meat and
breeding females available. All season mixed vegetables available at home
or group stall at Ceredigion Farmers' markets.

CAWS CENARTH

FFERM GLYNEITHINOG, LANLYCH, BONCATH SA37 0LH
Tel: 01239 710432 Contact: Thelma Adams
thelmaadams@virgin.net www.cawscenarth.co.uk
Soil Association G2093. Hand-made organic farmhouse cheese made on
our Soil Association certified organic farm. Available in many varieties
including Gold Award winners, suitable for vegetarians. Visitors welcome to
watch the cheesemaking.

GARTHENOR ORGANIC PURE WOOL

GARTHENOR, LLANIO ROAD, NR. TREGARON SY25 6UR
Tel: 01570 493347 Fax: 01570 493347 Contact: Chris and Sally King
garthenor@organicpurewool.co.uk www.organicpurewool.co.uk
Soil Association G4388 & X8787. A small mixed farm producing eggs,
lambs and wool from many traditional and rare breeds of sheep from our
own and other certified organic flocks. Fleece: raw; washed; washed &
carded. Beautiful knitting yarns in natural colours—undyed and
unbleached: 4-ply; DK; Aran; Chunky and Super chunky. Others spun to
your specification (for weaving etc.) subject to minimum order. Hand-
knitted garments and babywear. Hand-woven floor rugs, hand-knitted &
hand-woven cushions. Ex-stock or made to order. Commissions welcome.
Visitors by appointment. See display ad.

THE HIVE ON THE QUAY
CADWGAN PLACE, ABERAERON SA46 0BU
Tel: 01545 570445 Contact: Sarah Holgate
hiveon.thequay@btinternet.com www.hiveonthequay.co.uk
Member of the Soil Association. A busy seasonal café/restaurant on the
harbour specialising in regional dishes, local seafood from our own boat
and honey ice creams.

HOLDEN, PH & RM
BWLCHWERNEN FAWR, LLANGYBI, LAMPETER SA48 8PS
Tel: 01570 493244/493427 Contact: Patrick or Becky Holden
pholden@soilassociation.org
Soil Association symbol no. H09WW. Established 1973. Ayrshire dairy herd
of 60, 6 x beef cross Welsh Black, 12 acres of oats, 12 acres of carrots.
Farmed at 720 feet.

INSTITUTE OF RURAL SCIENCES
INSTITUTE OF RURAL SCIENCES, UNIVERSITY OF WALES,
ABERYSTWYTH SY23 3AL
Tel: 01970 624471 Fax: 01970 622238 Contact: Nic Lampkin
organic@aber.ac.uk www.organic.aber.ac.uk
Soil Association certified. Research/demonstration farm. BSc, PgCert and
PgDipl in organic agriculture with student bursary support available,
sponsored by Waitrose and Horizon Organic Dairy. Extensive DEFRA and
EU-funded organic research programme.

JACOBS, CAROLE & ALLEN
BRONIWAN, RHYDLEWIS, LLANDYSUL SA44 5PF
Tel: 01239 851261 Fax: 01239 851261 Contact: Allen Jacobs
broniwan@beeb.net
A 45-acre (19 ha) grassland Aberdeen Angus suckler beef herd with 'tack'
sheep. Small vegetables and soft fruit. A Tir Gofal Conservation Farm.
Developing educational services. Farm guesthouse. Visits by appointment.

THE KNOBBLY CARROT FOOD COMPANY

UNIT 18, LLANBED BUSINESS PARK, TREGARON RD., LAMPETER SA48 8LT
Tel: 01570 422064 Fax: 01570 422064 Contact: Louise Squire
sales@theknobblycarrot.co.uk www.theknobblycarrot.co.uk
The Knobbly Carrot Company supplies a superb range of fresh organic
foods to both retail and catering. Our products include fresh soups, salads
and sandwich fillings. Soil Association certified.

LLUEST GROWERS

LLUEST Y CONSCIENCE, TREFENTER, ABERYSTWYTH SY23 4HE
Tel: 01974 272218 Contact: John Crocker
Soil Association G2225. We produce organic eggs and seasonal organic
vegetables and salads for local customers.

MAETH Y MEYSYDD

16 CHALYBEATE ST., ABERYSTWYTH SY23
Tel: 01970 612946 Contact: DM Parkin
Wholefood shop, organic tea, coffee, milk, dairy products, bread, bakery,
wine, beer, dried fruit, beans and pulses. Friendly Welsh-speaking staff.

MENTRO LLUEST

LLANBADORN FAWR, ABERYSTWYTH SY23 3AU
Tel: 01970 612114 Fax: 01970 612114 Contact: R Allen
mentro.lluest@talk21.com
Soil Association G3081. Mentro Lluest teaches skills to people with special
needs within a framework of organic growing, environmental sustainability
and social cohesion. We specialise in producing salad, seasonal vegetables
and herbs.

MULBERRY BUSH

2 BRIDGE STREET, LAMPETER SA48 7HG
Tel: 01570 423317 Fax: 01570 423317 Contact: Stella Smith
Friendly wholefood vegetarian store, established 1974. Large range of
organic cereals, grains, pulses, fruit, nuts and convenience foods, plus
natural remedies, books and excellent health advice.

NANTCLYD FARM PRODUCE
NANTCLYD, LLANILAR, ABERYSTWYTH SY23 4SL
Tel: 01974 241543 Contact: Liz Findlay
liz.findlay@clara.co.uk
Smallholding producing primarily eggs; also lamb, veg and soft fruit.

ORGANIC FARM FOODS
LLAMBED ENTERPRISE PARK, TREGARON RD., LAMPETER SA48 8LT
Tel: 01570 423099 Fax: 01570 423280 Contact: The Manager
www.organicfarmfoods.co.uk
Widest range of fresh fruit and vegetables available for supermarkets,
wholesalers, retailers and processors.

PENBRYN ORGANIC CHEESE
TY-HEN, SARNAU, LLANDYSUL SA44 6RD
Tel: 01239 810347 Fax: 01239 810347 Contact: A. Degen
penbryn.cheese@talk21.com
Soil Association no. G528, Specialist Cheesemakers Association (SCA).
Family business producing organic cheese since 1989 using unpasteurised
milk from our own Friesian/MRI herd.

RACHEL'S ORGANIC DAIRY
UNIT 63, GLANYRAFON INDUSTRIAL ESTATE, ABERYSTWYTH SY23 2AE
Tel: 01970 625805 Fax: 01970 626591 Contact: Margaret Oakley
enqs@rachelsdairy.co.uk www.rachelsdairy.co.uk
Rachel's Dairy Organic dairy products, made solely from fresh liquid milk,
organic fruit, organic sugar and live cultures. No flavours, colours,
preservatives or stabilisers used. Soil Association member. Nationwide
coverage.

RIVERSIDE HEALTH
ADPAR, NEWCASTLE EMLYN SA38 9EE
Tel: 01239 711440 Contact: Gary & Julie Newman
Wholefood shop, largely organic. Good stock of herbal supplements and
essential oils. Therapy rooms upstairs. Fairtrade products as much as
possible.

STRANG DESIGN & BUILD
CORGAM BWLCHLLAN, LAMPETER SA48 8QR
Tel: 01974 821624 Fax: 01974 821624 Contact: Tim Strang
tstrang@btinternet.com www.strangbuild.co.uk
Soil Association. Mid-Wales based eco-builder, also selling a range of
eco-friendly building materials, including liners/paints.

THE TREEHOUSE
14 BAKER ST., ABERYSTWYTH SY23 2BJ
Tel: 01970 615791 Contact: Jane Burnham
jane@aber-treehouse.com www.aber-treehouse.com
We have a ten-acre market garden growing vegetables and fruit which are
retailed in our organic food shop and made into delicious meals in our
restaurant.

TROPICAL FOREST PRODUCTS LTD
PO BOX 92, ABERYSTWYTH SY23 1AA
Tel & Fax: 01970 832511 Contact: David Wainwright
mail@tropicalforest.com
Importers, packers and sellers of exotic honey. We have a particular interest
in promoting the produce of regional artisans.

COUNTRY KITCHEN
10 SEAVIEW ROAD, COLWYN BAY LL29 8DG
Tel: 01492 533329 Contact: David or Sally Frith
General independent natural food store in business 18 years: vitamin supplements, organic products. Willing to order individual requirements. Free delivery possible within 5-mile radius of shop on orders of £25 minimum.

ELKONLINE.CO.UK
5 OAK DRIVE CLOSE, COLWYN BAY LL29 7YR
Tel: 01492 536396 Contact: Richard Jones
info@elkonline.co.uk www.elkonline.co.uk
Swedish organic jams from the Torfolk Gard company. The jams are made using wild berries with no additives, preservatives or colouring. Blueberry, cloudberry, raspberry and lingonberry jams are available.

DENBIGHSHIRE

BRYN COCYN ORGANIC BEEF & LAMB
BRYN COCYN, LLANNEFYDD, DENBIGH LL16 5DH
Tel: 01745 540207 Contact: Patrick Noble
noblep243@aol.com
Home-produced beef and lamb from our long-established organic upland
farm. Soil Association licence no. G727.

DAVIES, ARWEL REES & LLINOS JONES
BLAENGWNODL UCHAF, CYNWYD, CORWEN LL21 0ET
Tel: 01490 413110 Fax: 01490 413110 Contact: Arwel Rees Davies
davies@peniel.fsnet.co.uk
The production of beef and sheep to organic status.

HAFOD ELWY HALL
BYLCHAU, DENBIGH LL16 5SP
Tel: 01690 770345 Fax: 01690 770180 Contact: Andrea Lee
andrea@hafodelwyhall.co.uk www.hafodelwyhall.co.uk
Soil Association G6524. Peace and tranquillity among lakes and mountains
in former shooting lodge on the edge of Snowdonia. Exclusive 4 Star WTB
accommodation, with breakfast and evening meals using produce from our
organic farm.

HOUSE OF RHUG
RHUG ESTATE OFFICE, CORWEN LL21 0EH
Tel: 01490 413000 Fax: 01490 413300 Contact: Peta Baxter & Philip Hughes
petabaxter@rhugorganicfarm.co.uk or philiphughes@rhugorganicfarm.co.uk
www.rhugorganic.com
The House Of Rhug is an organic café, farm butchery and shop on the A5,
2 miles west of Corwen on Lord Newborough's estate, centred around the
estate's award-winning home-reared meat.

THE ORGANIC STORES
7 MWROG ST., RUTHIN LL15 1LR
Tel: 01244 881209 Fax: 01244 881209 Contact: Allan Hughes
Fruit, veg, meat, fish, poultry and much more. Discount for specialised diets. Ample car parking space and carry out service. Home delivery, not a box scheme. Established in 1996, we only sell organic foods. One stop organic shopping.

FLINTSHIRE

ALEMBIC PRODUCTS LTD
RIVER LANE, SALTNEY, NR. CHESTER CH4 8RQ
Tel: 01244 680147 Fax: 01244 680155 Contact: The Manager
alembic@alembicproducts.co.uk www.alembicproducts.co.uk
Manufacturer of variety of organic mayonnaises and dressings.

ORGANIC STORES
BROOKLYN FARM, SEALAND ROAD, DEESIDE CH5 2LQ
Tel: 01244 881209 Fax: 01244 Contact: The Owners
Retail shop with delivery service selling a range of all organic produce including large variety of fruit and veg, meats, all dried goods, Ecover products, etc.

GLAMORGAN

BEANFREAKS LTD
SWISS HERBAL REMEDY STORE, 18 NOLTON ST., BRIDGEND CF31 1DU
Tel: 01656 661441 Contact: Kevin Bowles
sue@beanfreaks.freeserve.co.uk www.swissherbalremedies.com
Health food stores with organic herbal remedies and friendly service.

BEANFREAKS LTD
3 ST. MARY STREET, CARDIFF CF1 2AT
Tel: 029 2025 1678 Fax: 029 2025 1671 Contact: Kevin Bowles
kevin@feeling-better-already.com www.swissherbalremedies.com
Retail shop with organic dry goods, teas, grains, herbal remedies.

THE CREATIVE COOKING CO LTD
UNIT 4 BRYNMENYN BUSINESS CENTRE, ST. THEODORE'S WAY,
BRYNMENYN INDUSTRIAL ESTATE, BRYNMENYN, BRIDGEND CF32 9TZ
Tel: 01656 722555 Fax: 01656 729977 Contact: Carole Evans
info@creativeorganics.co.uk
Soil Association P7672. Manufacturing a range of organic mustards,
relishes, preserves and dressings combining traditional flavours with
innovative modern twists. All our products are hand-crafted by a
Masterchef of Great Britain: Carole Evans.

GREEN CUISINE
87 WESTVILLE ROAD, PENYLAN, CARDIFF CF23 5DF
Tel: 029 2049 8721 Fax: 029 2049 8721 Contact: A&M Robinson
greencuisine@talk21.com.
A customer choice home delivery service from twelve page price list (meat,
poultry, eggs, dairy, groceries, fruit, veg, baked goods, cleaning products).

JADE GATE ORGANIC PRODUCE
16 HOLTS FIELD, MURTON, SWANSEA SA3 3AQ
Tel: 01792 232643 Contact: Edward Revill
Soil Association G2504 & P4667. Organic vegetable box scheme grown using horses and delivered using a horse and cart in Swansea and Mumbles. Local produce only and reusable packaging. Aiming toward a carbon neutral service.

JUST ORGANIC
CLYNGWYN FARM, YSTRADFELLTE RD, PONTNEATHVAUGHAN, NEATH SA11 5US
Tel: 01639 722930 Fax: 01639 722930 Contact: Alan & Jayne Clements
sales@just-organic.com www.just-organic.com
Organic produce at Clyngwyn Farm, vegetables, fruit, herbs, eggs, farm shop. Bunkhouse accommodation set in glorious scenery in 'waterfall country'; sleeps up to 15. Complementary clinic specialising in osteomyology, acupuncture, meridian therapies, pain control, help with phobias and emotional problems.

MULTIPLE ORGANICS
LAKE FARM BARNS, ST. ATHAN RD, COWBRIDGE CF71 7HY
Tel: 01446 772964 Fax: 01446 772964 Contact: Leighton Maurice
multipleorganics@btinternet.com
Soil Association G6003. Organic herb and wild flower nursery supplying plants, feed, composts; all organically registered. We have a catalogue, weekly 'looking good' list, and are open to the general public.

NEAL'S YARD REMEDIES
23–25 MORGAN ARCADE, CARDIFF CF1 2AF
Tel: 029 2023 5721 Contact: The Manager
mail@nealsyardremedies.com www.nealsyardremedies.com
Neal's Yard Remedies manufactures and retails natural cosmetics in addition to stocking an extensive range of herbs, essential oils, homoeopathic remedies and reference material.

PENRHIW FARM ORGANIC MEATS
PENRHIW FARM, TRELEWIS, TREHARRIS CF46 6TA
Tel: 01443 412949 Contact: John Thomas
penrhiw.farm@virgin.net
Soil Association G4720. Producers of quality Aberdeen Angus beef and
Welsh mountain lamb. Meat is sold at local farmers' markets. A local home
delivery service is operated.

PULSE WHOLEFOODS LTD
171 KINGS ROAD, CANTON, CARDIFF CF1 9DE
Tel: 029 2022 5873 Fax: 029 2023 1694 Contact: Michaela Rosa
pulse@pulsewholefood.co.uk www.pulsewholefood.co.uk
We offer a wide range of organic fruit, vegetables, wines, beers,
wholefoods, and a friendly and helpful service.

THE SOURCE
26, CARDIFF ROAD, CAERPHILLY CF83 1JP
Tel: 029 2088 3236 Fax: 029 2088 3236 Contact: Leigh & Helen Shattock
hebenlee@btopenworld.com www.healthstore24.co.uk
Retail store offering fresh organic fruit and veg box scheme with delivery
service. Health foods, wholefoods, organic ranges, dairy and meat
alternatives. Wheat/gluten-free ranges, organic food supplements.

SPICE OF LIFE
1 INVERNESS PLACE, ROATH, CARDIFF CF2 4RU
Tel: 029 2048 7146 Contact: G Cooksley
www.spiceoflife.co.uk
Wholefood shop running box scheme.

SUNSCOOP PRODUCTS LTD
UNITS K1/K3 COEDCAE LANE IND.ESTATE, PONTYCLUN CF72 9HG
Tel: 01443 229229 Fax: 01443 228883 Contact: John Llewellyn
nuts@sunscoop.co.uk
Manufacturers of natural and processed nut products for retail outlets and
the industrial sector.

UNITED WORLD COLLEGE OF THE ATLANTIC
ST. DONATS CASTLE, LLANTWIT MAJOR, VALE OF GLAMORGAN CF61 1WF
Tel: 01446 799012 Fax: 01446 799013 Contact: AE Davies
estate@uwcac.uwc.org
Soil Association G5656. An international 6th Form College with a
20-hectare farm unit producing organic lamb and beef.

WESTAWAY GALLERY @ JULESGEMS
32 WYNDHAM CRESCENT, CANTON, CARDIFF CF11 9EH
Tel: 029 2040 5050 Contact: Rob Harper
shop@julesgems.com www.julesgems.com
Gallery and bead shop with organic coffee bar. Fair trade coffee freshly
ground, brewed and served in relaxed, inspiring atmosphere.

GWYNEDD

CWM BYCHAN FARM
LLANBEDR, NR. HARLECH LL45 2PH
Tel: 01630 657001 Contact: S Walkden
Soil Association G7384. Sweet mountain lamb and Dexter beef raised
slowly in the Harlech Dome on SSSI land.

DIMENSIONS HEALTH STORE
15 HOLYHEAD RD., BANGOR LL57 2EG
Tel: 01248 351562 Fax: 01248 351562 Contact: Christine Volney
info@dimensionshealthstore.com www.dimensionshealthstore.com
Soil Association no. P1857. Dimensions is an ethical retail store and on-line
business dedicated to providing foods, supplements, remedies and other
goods necessary to create health and well being.

HUGHES, JL & CO
LLWYN, DOLGELLAU LL40 2YF
Tel: 01341 423575 Contact: The Manager
Soil Association G4317. Producing beef and lamb sympathetically with conservation.

LLANGYBI ORGANICS
MUR CRUSTO, LLANGYBI, PWLLHELI LL53 6LX
Tel: 01766 819109 Contact: Val Lynas
info@llangybi-organics.co.uk www.llangybi-organics.co.uk
HDRA, Soil Association G7096. Aims to be a model of sustainable development with vegetables (polytunnel and field) and seasonal fruit. Works in partnership with neighbouring organic farm Ty'n Lon Ychaf. Vegetable box scheme. Educational farm visits by arrangement.

PENTRE BACH HOLIDAY COTTAGES
PENTRE BACH, LLWYNGWRIL, NR. DOLGELLAU LL37 2JU
Tel: 01341 250294 Fax: 01341 250885 Contact: Margaret Smyth
orgd@pentrebach.com www.pentrebach.com
Holiday cottages (two with log fires) in southern Snowdonia. Organic produce, free range eggs. Central heating, scenic Land Rover tours, train station nearby. Secluded, not isolated, between mountains and sea. Magnificent views. Winner, Wales Environment Award for Sustainable Tourism 2003.

RHOSFAWR CARAVAN PARK
RHOSFAWR, PWLLHELI LL53 6YA
Tel: 01766 810545 Contact: Janet Kidd
Small scale home-produced organic produce. Also touring caravan and camping park.

TILL, RICHARD LLOYD
LLWYNGWANADL UCHAF, CLYNNOGFAWR, CAERNARFON LL54 5DF
Tel: 01286 660275 Contact: Richard Till
mefusmelys@hotmail.com
Soil Association G7393. Meat: Cig oen organic Cymreig, wyn stor. Organic Welsh lamb, store lambs and store cattle.

TY'N LON UCHAF
TY'N LON UCHAF, LLANGYBI, PWLLHELI LL53 6TB
Tel: 01766 810915 Contact: Jill Jackson
mike.langley@ntlworld.com
Soil Association G6139. Smallholding producing a wide range of fresh, seasonal, organic vegetables. Together with Mur Crusto, Llangybi we sell through our own box scheme 'Llangybi Organics'—collection from Llangybi only, No delivery. Also produce organic eggs.

WELSH LADY PRESERVES
Y FFOR, PWLLHELI LL53 6RL
Tel: 01766 810496 Fax: 01766 810067 Contact: John Jones
info@welshladypreserves.com www.welshladypreserves.com
Soil Association P5669. A family business producing a premium quality range of organic jams, marmalades and meal accompaniments designed for the grocery, delicatessen and gift markets. We offer bespoke private-label production services.

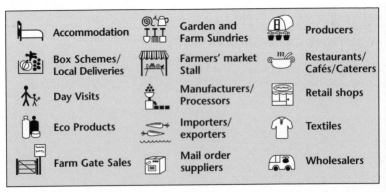

Accommodation	Garden and Farm Sundries	Producers
Box Schemes/ Local Deliveries	Farmers' market Stall	Restaurants/ Cafés/Caterers
Day Visits	Manufacturers/ Processors	Retail shops
Eco Products	Importers/ exporters	Textiles
Farm Gate Sales	Mail order suppliers	Wholesalers

MONMOUTHSHIRE

ABERGAVENNY FINE FOODS
CASTLE MEADOWS PARK, ABERGAVENNY NP7 7RZ
Tel: 01873 850001 Fax: 01873 850002 Contact: BJ Craske
sales@abergavenny.uk.com
Producers and importers of a wide range of organic dairy products
including fresh and aged cheeses in both brand and private label formats.
Supplying wholesale, independent and multiple stores.

BROOKLANDS FARM
CHEPSTOW RD., RAGLAN NP15 2EN
Tel: 01291 690782 Fax: 01291 690782 Contact: Rachel Price
brooklands-farm@raglan.fsbusiness.co.uk
Family-run organic farm 200 metres from Raglan village. Home-cooked
breakfast and evening meal. Children welcome. Pets by appointment.
Spacious garden and ample parking.

CARROB GROWERS
LLANGUNVILLE, LLANROTHAL, MONMOUTH NP25 5QL
Tel: 01600 714529 Contact: Caroline & Robert Boyle
Soil Association G1803. Specialist fruit growers, some vegetables. Produce
picked to order. Local deliveries to Monmouthshire/south Herefordshire.

IRMA FINGAL-ROCK
64 MONNOW ST., MONMOUTH NP25 3EN
Tel: 01600 712372 Fax: 01600 712372 Contact: Tom Innes
tomk@pinotnoir.co.uk www.pinotnoir.co.uk
Shop—wines our speciality. Also olive oil, eggs. Mail order and wholesale
for wines.

HOLT-WILSON, AD & CM

CEFN MAEN FARM, USK RD, RAGLAN NP5 2HR
Tel: 01291 690428 Contact: Holt-Wilson
Soil Association G5270. Producers of bronze turkeys at Christmas. The birds
are slaughtered on-site, dry plucked and hung for ten days as required by
the Traditional Farm Fresh Turkey Association.

JANES, MH & BM

THE WAUN, PENRHOS, RAGLAN, USK NP15 2LE
Tel: 01600 780356 Fax: 01600 780356 Contact: Bronwen Janes
mj@farm80.fsnet.co.uk
Soil Association G6540. Meat producers of beef/lamb, specialising in South
Devon beef.

LITTLE MILL FARM

LLANFAENOR, NEWCASTLE, MONMOUTH NP25 5NF
Tel: 01600 780449 Contact: Ann Eggleton
Soil Association G661. Small ancient organic farm offers friendly comfort in
beautiful Welsh Marches. Chill out in complete peace. B&B £20.26p;
weekend breaks including evening meal £70.82.

UPPER RED HOUSE FARM

LLANVIHANGEL, MONMOUTH NP25 5HL
Tel: 01600 780501 Fax: 01600 780572 Contact: Teona Dorrien-Smith
Soil Association G4969. Tir Gofal. The farm is mainly pasture with some
arable, producing forage and spring cereals with emphasis on conservation
and educational visits to study environment and wildlife. Educational visits,
all ages welcome, but booking essential.

WYEDEAN WHOLEFOODS

113 MONNOW STREET, MONMOUTH NP25 3EG
Tel: 01600 715429 Contact: Barry Cocker
Hundreds of organic lines. Wholefoods, gluten and dairy-free, cruelty-free
cosmetics; SLS-free toiletries. Excellent range of vitamins, minerals and
herbals. Wide range of chilled and frozen products.

NEWPORT

BEANFREAKS LTD
5 CHARTIST TOWERS, UP DOCK ST., NEWPORT NP1
Tel: 01633 666150 Contact: Kevin Bowles
sue@beanfreaks.freeserve.co.uk www.swissherbalremedies.com
Pulses, grains, herbs, teas.

PEMBROKESHIRE

BLACKMOOR FARM
LUDCHURCH, NARBERTH SA67 8JH
Tel: 01834 831242 Fax: 01834 831242 Contact: LT Cornthwaite
ltecornth@aol.com www.infozone.com.hk/blackmoorfarm
Farm-backed tourism, grazing cattle and tack sheep.

BUMPYLANE RARE BREEDS
SHORTLANDS FARM, DRUIDSTON, BROAD HAVEN,
HAVERFORDWEST SA62 3NE
Tel: 01437 781234 Contact: Pam and David Williams
davidandpam@btconnect.com www.bumpylane.co.uk
Soil Association G4793. Recapture the real taste of lamb and beef from the
traditional British breeds born and reared on our organic coastal farm
overlooking St. Bride's Bay, Pembrokeshire.

THE CELTIC HERBAL CO LTD

BALDWINS MOOR, MANORBIER, TENBY SA70 7TY
Tel: 01834 870128 Fax: 01834 870128 Contact: Nicola Dent
info@celticherbs.co.uk www.celticherbs.co.uk
Soil Association G5767/P7499. We grow a wide selection of herbs
organically, and incorporate these in a range of beautiful hand-made
herbal soaps and other bath products.

CLYNFYW COUNTRYSIDE CENTRE

CLYNFYW, ABERCYCH, BONCATH SA37 0HF
Tel: 01239 841236 Fax: 01239 841236 Contact: Jim Bowen
jim.clynfyw@virgin.net www.clynfyw.co.uk
Soil Association G4192. Clynfyw is a residential, all access countryside
activity, education, arts and respite care holiday centre set on a working
organic farm. Animals include Welsh Black cattle and Saddleback pigs. With
excellent Tourist Board approved cottages and a new sculpture trail
through the woods, Clynfyw makes the perfect holiday destination. Walk in
the woods, help make charcoal, explore the decrepit walled garden or
watch the badgers! There are few places more appealing!

DYFFRYN ISAF

DYFFRYN ISAF, LLANDISSILIO SA66 7QD
Tel: 01437 563657 Contact: Bettina Becker & Stephen Jennings
bettina@dyffrynisaf.fsnet.co.uk www.uk.geocities.com/dyffryn2002
Soil Association G7177. Holiday cottage on organic smallholding with
Shetland sheep, goats and chickens. Situated in a quiet valley near Preseli
Mountains and coast with cliffs and beaches. Colourful fleeces for
handspinners.

EGGLETON, SIMON

LEDGERLAND FARM, LLANTEG, NARBERTH SA67 8PX
Tel: 01834 831634 Contact: Simon Eggleton
Organic beef store cattle, Limousin and Hereford available in Spring/early
Summer, dependent on natural weaning.

EVANS, DW & CM

CAERFAI FARM, ST. DAVIDS, HAVERFORDWEST SA62 6QT
Tel: 01437 720548 Fax: 01437 720548 Contact: Wyn Evans
chrismevans69@hotmail.com www.caerfai.co.uk
In the Pembrokeshire coast National Park, 140-acre organic dairy farm
producing unpasteurised milk and home-made cheeses, early potatoes.
Sales from farm shop and box schemes. Camping and self-catering
cottages.

FFYNNON SAMSON

LLANGOLMAN, CLUNDERWEN SA66 7QL
Tel: 01437 532570 Contact: Wendy Lane
Soil Association G7339. Production of organic vegetables, fruit and eggs.
Local box scheme. Please phone for all orders.

FFYNNONSTON ORGANICS

FFYNNONSTON, DWRBACH, FISHGUARD SA65 9QT
Tel: 01348 873004 Contact: Ann Hicks
annhicks@waitrose.com
Soil Association G5836. Small scale organic producers located one mile
from Pembrokeshire coast. Salads, herbs, vegetables and soft fruit. Also
organically grown cut flowers. Self-catering units available.

GROWING HEART WORKERS CO-OPERATIVE LTD

HENPARCAU FARM, BONCATH SA37 0JY
Tel: 01239 841675 Contact: Willow
growingheart2@hotmail.com
Soil Association G6287. We grow fruit and vegetables on 7.5 acres,
wholesaling and retailing locally. We have a fruit tree and bush nursery and
specialise in planting edible forests. Vegetables delivered to cafés, festivals
and events.

HOME FARM BOARDING CENTRE

HOME FARM, EGLWYSWRW, CRYMYCH SA41 3PP
Tel: 01239 891449 Contact: B Rees
Soil Association G5406. Dog and cat boarding centre. Boarding centre
offering best possible care for dogs, cats and other domestic pets. Breeders
of pedigree Aberdeen Angus beef cattle and pure Poll Dorset sheep, stock
sometimes available for sale, also producers of free range organic eggs.

JENKINS, RHGE & TR

MAESYRHEDYDD & PORTIS FARMS, LLANDISSILIO, CLYNDERWEN SA66 7TX
Tel: 01437 563283 Contact: Jenkins
6 month short tenancy lets. Pembs border, main A476 Cardigan to Tenby
road on farm. At Llandissilio, Clynderwen Organic Farm. Dairy farm.

LATTER, TRE & AT

PENRHIW, GOODWICK SA64 0HS
Tel: 01348 873315 Fax: 01348 873315 Contact: Tom Latter
tom.latter@btopenworld.com
Beef, sheep, potatoes, eggs, and cereals. Self-catering visitor accommodation.

THE OLD RECTORY

THE OLD RECTORY, CASTLEMARTIN SA71 5HW
Tel: 01646 661677 Fax: 01646 661677 Contact: Emma Younghusband
www.theoldrectoryweb.com
Comfortable Old Rectory, organic B&B, in wild Pembrokeshire. Sandy
beaches and fabulous walking. Two charming stone cottages available also
for holidays.

PENCRUGIAU ORGANIC FARM SHOP

PENCRUGIAU, FELINDRE FARCHOG, CRYMYCH SA41 3XH
Tel: 01239 881265 Fax: 01239 881265 Contact: Mike Ray
sales@organicfarmshop.com www.organicfarmshop.com
Soil Association R28WW, P5597. Home-grown organic produce of glasshouse, market garden and field crops. Vegetables, salads and herbs. Also
wide range of bought-in organic fruit. Roadside farm shop.

THE RESPONSIVE EARTH TRUST

PLASDWBL BIODYNAMIC FARM, MYNACHLOG DDU,
CLYNDERWEN SA66 7SE
Tel: 01994 419352 Contact: A Kleinjans
Plasdwbl Biodynamic Farm is a charitable trust run for the benefit of
students wishing to gain practical experience in biodynamic farming and
gardening. We have a Welsh Black herd and two Jersey milkers. The farm is
40 ha, and on 4 ha we grow vegetables and forage. We make our own
butter, cheese and bread. Demeter cert. no. 111.

SARRA, MR & T

PEEPOUT FARM, PORTFIELD GATE, HAVERFORDWEST SA62 3LS
Tel: 01437 762323 Fax: 01437 762323 Contact: Romeo Sarra
romeo@fwi.co.uk
150 acres specialising in a wide range of vegetables. Pembrokeshire new
potatoes from May and all year round. Delivered direct to box schemes,
wholesalers. Retail shop, groceries, wines, fruit and veg.

WELLS, WC

PENBACK, LLANDISSILIO SA66 7UP
Tel: 01437 563364 Fax: 01437 563364 Contact: WC Wells
wells.penback@btinternet.com
Soil Association G6198. Pedigree Welsh Black cattle producer, in-calf cows
and heifers available for sale.

WELSH HOOK MEAT CENTRE LTD

WOODFIELD, WITHYBUSH ROAD, HAVERFORDWEST SA62 4BW
Tel: 01437 768876 Fax: 01437 768877 Contact: Emrys Davies
welshhookmeat@talk21.com www.welsh-organic-meat.co.uk
Wholesale and retail butchers specialising in organic pork, beef, lamb, veal,
poultry, bacon and home-made sausages. Deliveries local and M4 corridor
to London. Mail order to anywhere in The UK.

WHOLEFOODS OF NEWPORT

BWYDYDD CYFLAWN, EAST ST., NEWPORT SA42 0SY
Tel: 01239 820773 Fax: 01239 820773 Contact: Lorna & Ian Hipkins
Lively general wholefood grocer, largely organic, healthy snacks, special
diets, dairy-free, gluten-free, wheat-free catered for. Welsh cheeses, cakes,
confectionery, wines, beers, teas, coffees, Pembrokeshire honey, conserves.
Large selection of fresh fruit and vegetables. Complementary remedies.
Bodycare.

POWYS

BACHELDRE WATERMILL
CHURCHSTOKE, MONTGOMERY SY15 6TE
Tel: 01588 620489 Fax: 01588 620105 Contact: Matt & Anne Scott
bacheldre@onetel.net.uk www.bacheldremill.co.uk
17th century watermill, camping site and holiday apartments. Produce award-winning Bacheldre stoneground organic flours.

BHC (HONEY SUPPLIERS) LTD
UNIT 3, FFRWDGRECH INDUSTRIAL ESTATE, BRECON LD3 8LA
Tel: 01874 622335 Fax: 01874 623141 Contact: Anne Preece
bhchoney@aol.com www.bhchoneysuppliers.co.uk
Soil Association P1059. The packing of organic honey into either retail packs or buckets for industrial customers.

BICYCLE BEANO CYCLING HOLIDAYS
ERWOOD, BUILTH WELLS LD2 3PQ
Tel: 01982 560471 Contact: Jane Barnes
mail@bicycle-beano.co.uk www.bicycle-beano.co.uk
Sociable cycling holidays on the idyllic lanes of Wales and the Welsh Borders of England. Delicious vegetarian cuisine, using home-grown organic fruit and vegetables. Relaxed atmosphere. All ages welcome.

BLOOMING THINGS
Y BWTHYN, CYMERAU, GLANDYFI, MACHYNLLETH SY20 8SS
Tel: 01654 781256 Fax: 01654 781256 Contact: Dale & Wyn Garnes
Family-run organic nursery producing herb, vegetable and wild flower plugs and pots for growing on/planting out. Retail through mail order. Wholesale enquiries welcome.

CANNON FARM

LLANERFYL, WELSHPOOL SY21 OJJ
Tel: 01938 820251 Fax: 01938 820136 Contact: Nigel Elgar
nigel@cannonfarm.co.uk www.cannonfarm.co.uk
Soil Association registered. Organic beef and sheep farm in Mid-Wales.
Joint Organic Producer of the Year award winner 2001, Director of Graig
Farm Producers Group Ltd.

CEFN GOLEU ORGANIC TURKEYS

CEFN GOLEU, PONT ROBERT, MEIFOD SY22 6JN
Tel: 01938 500128 Contact: MB Moorhouse
cefngoleuturkeys@btclick.com
Soil Association G2967. Registered packing station, eggs supplied to retail
shops and direct farm gate sales. Oven-ready fresh Christmas turkeys, farm
gate sales. Frozen turkeys, chickens throughout year. Lamb, pork when
available.

CENTRE FOR ALTERNATIVE TECHNOLOGY

MACHYNLLETH SY20 9AZ
Tel: 01654 705950 or 0845 3308355 Fax: 01654 702782 Contact:
Charlotte Cosserat
info@cat.org.uk www.cat.org.uk
Soil Association L09WW. Established in 1974, the Centre for Alternative
Technology is Europe's leading eco-centre, with information on renewable
energy, environmental building, energy efficiency, organic growing and
alternative sewage systems. Services include a visitor centre open 7 days a
week, practical and informative publications, a mail order service of 'green'
books and products, educational services for schools, consultancy for
individuals and businesses, residential courses, membership and a free
information service.

THE CILIAU

THE CILIAU, ERWOOD, BUILTH WELLS LD2 3TZ
Tel: 07887 656887 Contact: Roger Capps
Organic breeding stock, pure breed beef and lamb. Private sales and
deliveries. All feed stuff produced on farm for pedigree North Devons,
Shropshire and Lleyn sheep.

THE CILIAU

LOWER PORTHAMEL, TALGARTH, BRECON LD3 0DL
Tel: 01874 711224 Fax: 01874 711224 Contact: Joel Durrell
joeldurrell@yahoo.com www.smallfarms.co.uk
Two farms combining arable land for own feed, producing pure bred North
Devon & Herefordshire cattle and Lleyn & Shropshire pure bred sheep.
Farm shop and butchery opening October 2004.

CLYRO HILL FARM

CLYRO HILL FARM, CLYRO HR3 6JU
Tel: 01497 820520 Fax: 01497 820520 Contact: Sally Herdman
info@clyrohillfarm.co.uk www.clyrohillfarm.co.uk
Organic Farmers and Growers UKF 001475. Organic poultry, Hereford beef,
Welsh lamb and pork raised on our farm. Free range chickens, turkeys,
goose, duck, guinea fowl, pork, lamb and beef mail order. Eggs and
vegetable boxes delivered locally.

COMPOST TECHNOLOGY LTD

TREWERN, WELSHPOOL SY21 8EA
Tel: 01938 570678 Fax: 01938 570678 Contact: Edwin Kentfield
clucksales@aol.com
Manufacturers of Cluck!, the 100% organic fertiliser. Delivery to UK except
N. Ireland and offshore.

CWM MAWR

HYSSINGTON, MONTGOMERY SY15 6EJ
Tel: 01588 620047 Fax: 01588 620084 Contact: Jon Tanner
jontanner@compuserve.com
Producer of high quality lamb and forage (hay/silage). Cwm Mawr
participates in the Tir Gofal agri-environment scheme.

GEORGE & SONS

DOLL-LLUGAN, BLEDDFA, KNIGHTON LD7 1NY
Tel: 01547 550208 Fax: 01544 230604 Contact: E Gorst
Soil Association G5456. A farm producing quality beef and lamb where extensive farming practices have always been exercised. Root vegetables are also grown.

GOOD FOOD DISTRIBUTORS

35 DDOLE ROAD INDUSTRIAL ESTATE, LLANDRINDOD WELLS LD1 6DF
Tel: 01597 824728 Fax: 01597 824760 Contact: Tracy
gfd.wholesale@btinternet.com www.goodfooddistributors.co.uk
Soil Association P5894. Free delivery service, wholefoods in bulk and pre-packs, free own name labelling service and contract mixing. 100% vegetarian and GMO-free products. Vast range of products listed in our free price list.

GRAIG FARM ORGANICS

DOLAU, LLANDRINDOD WELLS LD1 5TL
Tel: 01597 851655 Fax: 01597 851991 Contact: Bob Kennard
sales@graigfarm.co.uk www.graigfarm.co.uk
Award-winning organic meats, fish and other organic foods available by mail order, internet, retail outlets. Organic Retailer of the Year 2001/2. Livestock supplies through producer group of 200 farmers across Wales and the borders.

GREAT OAK FOODS

12 GREAT OAK ST., LLANIDLOES SY18 6BU
Tel: 01686 413222 Contact: Gareth Davies
gareth@perpetualearth.com
Retail certified organic fruit and veg and non-certified locally grown produce using organic principles. We stock organic cheese, wine and spirits. Local production and low food miles encouraged.

GWALIA FARM

GWALIA CEMMAES, MACHYNLLETH SY20 9PZ
Tel: 01650 511377 Contact: Olivia Chandler
www.gwaliafarm.co.uk
Peaceful, remote smallholding in Welsh hills. Vegetarian/vegan home-cooked wholefood meals using our vegetables, fruit, eggs, milk. Beautiful views, spring water, log fire, therapeutic massage, silence! Lake and conservation area.

MATTHEWS, RG & PARTNERS

ABERHYDDNANT, CRAI, BRECON LD3 8YS
Tel: 01874 636797 Fax: 01874 636797 Contact: Liz Matthews
liz@abercottages.co.uk www.abercottages.com
Two comfortable cottages sleeping 2 to 12 making an ideal location for short breaks and family holidays. Situated on 92-hectare family-run organic beef and sheep farm in Brecon Beacons National Park. Also member of Tir Gofal environmental scheme. Educational farm visits welcome by arrangement. Colour brochure.

NATURAL FOODS LLANIDLOES LTD

17 GREAT OAK ST., LLANIDLOES SY18 6BU
Tel: 01686 412306 Contact: Martine Frost
We are retailers of organic health foods, dietary supplements, herbal remedies and other quality foods including a wide range of chilled and frozen foods. We also do bulk and special orders.

PENPONT

PENPONT ESTATE, BRECON LD3 8EU
Tel: 01874 636202 Contact: Gavin Hogg
penpont@clara.co.uk www.penpont.com
Soil Association G4529. We offer bed and breakfast and self-catering accommodation in a historic listed mansion. We are restoring two Victorian walled gardens where we grow registered organic vegetables. We are now an Organic Demonstration farm, and will host a number of day courses in Horticulture organised jointly by OCW and Farming Connect.

PENTWYN HERBS

c/o 1 CAERLLAN, LLANWRTHWL, LLANDRINDOD WELLS LD1 6NS
Tel: 01597 810113 Contact: Susy Pegrum
susypeg@btopenworld.com
Grow herbs organically as crops (culinary and medicinal) and herbs in pots; herb collection of over 100 different herbs. Herb garden open to the public.

PRESTEIGNE TROUT

THE OLD LEAT, BOULTIBROOKE, PRESTEIGNE LD8 2EU
Tel: 01544 267085 Fax: 01544 267085 Contact: IH Bennett
Soil Association G4310. Producer of organic rainbow trout.

PRESTEIGNE WHOLEFOOD CO-OP

RADNOR BUILDINGS, PRESTEIGNE LD8 2AT
Tel: 01544 267392 Contact: B Reader
A health food shop providing a full range of organic wholefoods, organic bread, organic fruit and veg, delicatessen, natural remedies and suppements.

THE QUARRY SHOP & CAFE

13 & 27 MAENGWYN ST., MACHYNLLETH SY20 8EB
Tel: 01654 702624/702339 Fax: 01654 702624 Contact: Annie Lowmass & Amanda Green
quarry.cafe@cat.org.uk www.cat.org.uk
A vegetarian café and shop including some organic products. We are 25 years old this year and are part of the Centre for Alternative Technology.

RAIKES, D

TREBERFYDD, BWLCH, BRECON LD3 7PX
Tel: 01874 730205 Contact: The Manager
Soil Association G964. Small organic Welsh Black suckler herd.

THOMAS, KP & CS

GYFFOG, LLANFIHANGEL, NANT BRAN, BRECON LD3 9LY
Tel: 01874 638925 Contact: Kate Thomas
Small family farm on the edge of Brecon Beacons. The farm has pedigree
Welsh Black cattle and Beulah Speckleface sheep. Finished store and
breeding stock available.

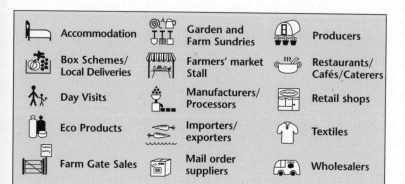

Accommodation	Garden and Farm Sundries	Producers
Box Schemes/ Local Deliveries	Farmers' market Stall	Restaurants/ Cafés/Caterers
Day Visits	Manufacturers/ Processors	Retail shops
Eco Products	Importers/ exporters	Textiles
Farm Gate Sales	Mail order suppliers	Wholesalers

TORFAEN

BEANFREAKS LTD
7 CARADOC RD., CWMBRAN NP44 1PP
Tel: 01633 482507 Contact: Kevin Bowles
Health food stores with organic products and friendly service.

WARMAN, SG & SE
NANT-Y-GOLLEN FARM, FOLLY LANE, TREVITHIN, PONTYPOOL NP4 8TS
Tel: 01495 763780 Contact: S Warman
Soil Association G4651. Aberdeen Angus beef, big bale hay/silage.

WILLIS LTD, JH
GRESFORD BANK, GRESFORD, WREXHAM LL12 8UT
Tel: 01978 852220 Fax: 01978 853737 Contact: RH Willis
j.h.willisltd@roadtransport.net www.j.h.willis.co.uk
Transport. We carry ex-farm organic milk for OMSCO, Calon Wen, South Caernarvon, Dairy Farmers of Britain.

including certification bodies, charities, clubs, local groups, education, research and development

ABERDEEN BIODYNAMIC LAND TRUST
BEANNACHAR, BANCHORY-DEVENICK, ABERDEEN AB12 5YL
Tel: 01224 861200 Contact: Richard Phethean
Community Land Trusts. Purchase of agricultural land to hold in trust for biodynamic or organic food production and support businesses renting that land.

THE ACORN CENTRE
TODHURST SITE, NORTH HEATH, PULBOROUGH, WEST SUSSEX RH20 1DL
Tel: 01798 873533 Fax: 01798 873533 Contact: Rachel Smither
michellewykes@aldingbournetrust.co.uk
Training centre for adults with learning disabilities. We grow our own organic vegetables which are sold through our farm shop. Other organic produce also available. Coffee shop. Soil Association G2586, P5118.

AGROFORESTRY RESEARCH TRUST
46 HUNTERS MOON, DARTINGTON, TOTNES, DEVON TQ9 6JT
Tel: 01803 840776 Contact: M Crawford
mail@agroforestry.co.uk www.agroforestry.co.uk
Research charity producing books and information on fruits, nuts and agroforestry; also plants, seeds and rootrainers.

AINSWORTHS HOMOEOPATHIC PHARMACY
36 NEW CAVENDISH ST., LONDON W1G 8UF
Tel: 020 7935 5330 Fax: 01883 344602 Contact: Tony Pinkus
ainsworth01@btconnect.com www.ainsworths.com
Homoeopathic remedies for prevention and treatment of all your livestock. Books and courses on homoeopathy. All animals can be treated without residues. Help and advice in implementing homoeopathic regimes on the farm. Lectures and seminars by arrangement.

ALDINGBOURNE COUNTRY CENTRE

BLACKMILL LANE, NORTON, CHICHESTER, WEST SUSSEX PO18 0JP
Tel: 01243 542075 Fax: 01243 544807 Contact: Linda Thompson
acc@aldingbournetrust.co.uk www.aldingbournetrust.co.uk
Soil Association G4375. Training centre for adults with learning disabilities.
Retail shop, coffee shop, woodland walk.

APPLIED RURAL ALTERNATIVES

10 HIGHFIELD CLOSE, WOKINGHAM, SURREY RG40 1DG
Tel: 0118 962 7797 Contact: DS Stafford
Education of the general public in organic farming and growing issues by
visits, meetings and publication of papers. Send SAE for details and
programmes.

AVON ORGANIC GROUP

c/o 3 DUBBERS LANE, BRISTOL BS5 7EL
Tel: 0117 935 4261 Contact: Rachel Hudson
aogbristol@yahoo.co.uk www.beehive.thisisbristol.com/avonorganics
Monthly meetings on organic gardening, local food and environmental
themes. Visits to members' allotments. Sale of produce. Run organic
orchard on Horfield Allotment site.

BATH ORGANIC COMMUNITY GARDEN

c/o 28 ASHLEY AVENUE, BATH, SOMERSET BA1 3DS
Tel: 01225 312116 Contact: TJ Baines
tim@bathorganicgroup.org.uk
Community garden on inner city allotment site providing training,
employment and volunteering opportunities for the local community.
Courses and workshops. Open days. Plant sales. Open every Saturday
10am to 1pm.

BIODYNAMIC AGRICULTURAL ASSOCIATION (BDAA)

PAINSWICK INN PROJECT, GLOUCESTER STREET, STROUD,
GLOUCESTERSHIRE GL5 1QG
Tel: 0845 345 8474 Fax: 01453 759501 Contact: Bernard Jarman
office@biodynamic.org.uk www.biodynamic.org.uk
With links across the world, BDAA promotes the unique biodynamic
approach to organic agriculture, operates the Demeter Symbol (UK6),
publishes a journal, sells books and offers training courses and workshops.

BRUNSWICK ORGANIC NURSERY & CRAFT WORKSHOP
APPLETON RD., BISHOPTHORPE, YORK YO23 2RF
Tel: 01904 701869 Fax: 01904 701869 Contact: Adam Myers
admin@brunswickyork.org.uk
Soil Association G1903, HDRA member. Charity working with adults who
have learning difficulties. Produce includes bedding plants, cottage garden
plants, perennials, herbs, organic fruit and vegetables. All to Soil
Association standards. Also craft workshop.

BRYMORE SCHOOL FARM TRUST
BRYMORE SCHOOL, CANNINGTON, BRIDGWATER, SOMERSET TA5 2NB
Tel: 01278 652428 Fax: 01278 653244 Contact: A Nurton
We are a secondary school of agriculture, horticulture and engineering with
a mixed farm enterprise. We sell beef and table birds through farmers'
markets and pork, lamb and free range eggs privately.

CAMPHILL COMMUNITY – HOLYWOOD
8 SHORE ROAD, HOLYWOOD, CO. DOWN, N. IRELAND BT18 9HX
Tel: 028 9042 3203 Fax: 028 9039 7818 Contact: Rob van Duin
camphillholywood@btconnect.com
Soil Association certification applied for. Organic café, bakery and vegetable
and dried food, also crafts produced by people with special needs.

CAMPHILL VILLAGE TRUST – OAKLANDS PARK
OAKLANDS PARK, NEWNHAM ON SEVERN, GLOUCESTERSHIRE GL14 1EF
Tel: 01594 516550 Fax: 01594 516550 Contact: Kai Lange
kaigarden@onetel.com www.oaklandspark.org.uk
Biodynamic Agricultural Association (Demeter) 101, Soil Association V01M.
Working community with people with special needs. Involved with regional
biodynamic land training (2 years), vegetables, herbs and fruit for
wholesaling and box scheme.

CANON FROME COURT
CANON FROME COURT, CANON FROME, LEDBURY,
HEREFORDSHIRE HR8 2TD
Tel: 0870 765 0711 Contact: Membership Secretary
membership@canonfromecourt.org.uk www.canonfromecourt.org.uk
Organic (uncertified) farming community comprising 18 households living
in Georgian house and stable block set in 40 acres of park and farmland.
Cows, goats, sheep, chickens, bees, arable fields, orchard and 2-acre walled
garden. WWOOFers and potential community members welcome.

CENTRE FOR ALTERNATIVE TECHNOLOGY

MACHYNLLETH, POWYS SY20 9AZ
Tel: 01654 705950 or 0845 3308355 Fax: 01654 702782 Contact:
Charlotte Cosserat
info@cat.org.uk www.cat.org.uk
Soil Association L09WW. Established in 1974, the Centre for Alternative
Technology is Europe's leading eco-centre, with information on renewable
energy, environmental building, energy efficiency, organic growing and
alternative sewage systems. Services include a visitor centre open 7 days a
week, practical and informative publications, a mail order service of 'green'
books and products, educational services for schools, consultancy for
individuals and businesses, residential courses, membership and a free
information service.

CLYNFYW COUNTRYSIDE CENTRE

CLYNFYW, ABERCYCH, BONCATH, CEREDIGION SA37 0HF
Tel: 01239 841236 Fax: 01239 841236 Contact: Jim Bowen
jim.clynfyw@virgin.net www.clynfyw.co.uk
Soil Association G4192. Clynfyw is a residential, all access countryside
activity, education, arts and respite care holiday centre set on a working
organic farm. Animals include Welsh Black cattle and Saddleback pigs. With
excellent Tourist Board approved cottages and a new sculpture trail
through the woods, Clynfyw makes the perfect holiday destination. Walk in
the woods, help make charcoal, explore the decrepit walled garden or
watch the badgers! There are few places more appealing!

COMMONWORK

BORE PLACE, CHIDDINGSTONE, KENT TN8 7AR
Tel: 01732 463255 x229 Fax: 01732 740264 Contact: Lyn Kelly
info@commonwork.org www.commonwork.org
Conference and study centre with organic, wildlife and permaculture
gardens on commercial organic farm. Residential accommodation for
groups undertaking their own training and development work.
Environmental education programme and organic farm/food study days
offered by Commonwork. Focus in 2004–05 on hands-on vocational
training in organic farming for people of all abilities. New focus on food
and health (growing, cooking and eating) from 2004 as part of 'The Big
Stir' campaign. Seasonal open days for the public. Development education
centre (global education) in Maidstone.

COMMUNITY COMPOSTING NETWORK
67 ALEXANDRA ROAD, SHEFFIELD S2 3EE
Tel: 0114 258 0483 Fax: 0114 258 0483 Contact: Nick McAlister
ccn@gn.apc.org www.communitycompost.org
We are the national network providing support and representation for
community groups that are in some way involved in the sustainable
management of organic waste resources and community composting.

COMPASSION IN WORLD FARMING
CHARLES HOUSE, 5A CHARLES STREET, PETERSFIELD, HAMPSHIRE GU32 3EH
Tel: 01730 264208 Fax: 01730 260791 Contact: The Secretary
compassion@ciwf.co.uk www.ciwf.co.uk
Pressure group lobbying, campaigning and providing educational materials
with the objective of improving welfare conditions for livestock and poultry.

DARTINGTON TECH – THE REGIONAL CENTRE FOR ORGANIC HORTICULTURE
WESTMINSTER HOUSE, 38/40 PALACE AVENUE, PAIGNTON, DEVON TQ3 3HB
Tel: 01803 867693 Fax: 01803 867693 Contact: Cherry Lyons
clyons@dartingtontech.co.uk www.dartingtontechco.uk
The Regional Centre for Organic Horticulture is an education and resource
centre for the promotion of organic gardening and horticulture. We offer
courses for professionals and amateurs at our Soil Association certified site.

DEMETER COMMITTEE OF THE BDAA
17 INVERLEITH PLACE, EDINBURGH EH3 5QE
Tel: 0131 624 3921 Contact: Fiona Mackie
fionajmackie@hotmail.com www.biodynamic.org.uk
Inspection, certification and information service for biodynamic production.

DEPARTMENT FOR ENVIRONMENT, FOOD AND RURAL AFFAIRS (DEFRA)
NOBEL HOUSE, 17 SMITH SQUARE, LONDON SW1P 3JR
Tel: 020 7238 6000 Fax: 020 7238 6609 Contact: The Help Desk
organic.standards@defra.gsi.gov.uk. www.defra.gov.uk
Defra has taken over responsibility for UK organic standards, previously
monitored by UKROFS.

DERBY COLLEGE
BROOMFIELD HALL, MORLEY, ILKESTON, DERBYSHIRE DE7 6DN
Tel: 01332 836607 Fax: 01332 836601 Contact: Ian Baldwin
eileen.swann@derby-college.ac.uk www.derby-college.ac.uk
Soil Association registered. Full-time and part-time courses in organic
horticulture. Licensed producers of beef, lamb, cereal, and vegetables.
Contact Course Student Services.

DORSET WILDLIFE TRUST

45 HIGH ST., TOLLER PORCORUM, DORCHESTER, DORSET DT2 0DN
Tel: 01300 320573 Contact: Paul Comer
paul@paulcomer.f9.co.uk
Soil Association G898. We run as a farmed nature reserve, producing fat and store lambs and suckled calves/store cattle.

EARTHWORM HOUSING CO-OP LTD

WHEATSTONE, LEINTWARDINE, SHROPSHIRE SY7 0LH
Tel: 01547 540461 Contact: Hil Mason
Suppliers of willow for basket making, hurdles etc, venue for low cost hire for camps, courses, meetings. Demonstration wetland system and organic/veganic gardens. WWOOF host farm.

EAST MALLING RESEARCH

NEW RD, EAST MALLING, KENT ME19 6BJ
Tel: 01732 843833 Fax: 01732 849067 Contact: Jean Fitzgerald
jean.fitzgerald@emr.ac.uk www.eastmallingresearch.com
We carry out research projects on organic apples and strawberries and plan to include more top and soft fruits in our organic demonstration area.

ECLIPSE SCIENTIFIC GROUP LTD

MEDCALFE WAY, BRIDGE STREET, CHATTERIS, CAMBRIDGESHIRE PE16 6QZ
Tel: 01354 695858 Fax: 01354 692215 Contact: S Leavey
sales@esglabs.co.uk www.esglabs.co.uk
Eclipse offers a comprehensive technical support service, providing expert consultancy through to high quality chemical, microbiological and analytical research and testing services.

EMERSON COLLEGE

HARTFIELD ROAD, FOREST ROW, EAST SUSSEX RH18 5JX
Tel: 01342 822238 Fax: 01342 826055 Contact: Alysoun Barrett
mail@emerson.org.uk www.emerson.org.uk
Soil Association & Demeter registered. Emerson College runs a three year, full-time training in Biodynamic Organic Agriculture, as well as short courses in biodynamics. Students at the college run a commercial biodynamic market garden through spring and summer.

FARMS FOR CITY CHILDREN

NETHERCOTT HOUSE, IDDESLEIGH, WINKLEIGH, DEVON EX19 8BG
Tel: 01837 810573 Contact: Jane Feaver
ffcc@nethercott-house.freeserve.co.uk www.farmsforciytchildren.org
Educational Charity. Farms For City Children runs three organic farms where urban children come to stay and help the farmers. They learn to work together for the common good and gain a sense of achievement.

FEDERATION OF CITY FARMS AND COMMUNITY GARDENS
THE GREENHOUSE, HEREFORD STREET, BEDMINSTER, BRISTOL BS3 4NA
Tel: 0117 923 1800 Fax: 0117 923 1900 Contact: Anna Nicholls
admin@farmgarden.org.uk www.farmgarden.org.uk
Charity supporting community farms and gardens. A membership-led organisation working on behalf of community managed farms and gardens. FCFCG works with the Soil Association, NFU and others to promote healthy organic food.

THE FOOD COMMISSION
94 WHITE LION STREET, LONDON N1 9PF
Tel: 020 7837 2250 Fax: 020 7837 1141 Contact: Information Officer
enquiries@foodcomm.org.uk www.foodcomm.org.uk
Public watchdog campaigning for healthier, safer food in the UK. Independent of both government and the food industry. Publishes *The Food Magazine* which includes periodic articles on organic and farming issues. Books, posters and special reports on food issues also available.

FRIENDS OF THE EARTH
26–28 UNDERWOOD STREET, LONDON N1 7JQ
Tel: 020 7490 1555 Fax: 020 7490 0881 Contact: Rita Marcangelo
info@foe.co.uk www.foe.co.uk
Environmental pressure group. Their 'Real Food' campaign asks the government to reform farming and food production to enable farmers to manage the countryside sustainably and provide high quality food for a fair income.

GENEWATCH UK
THE MILLHOUSE, MANCHESTER RD., TIDESWELL, BUXTON SK17 8LN
Tel: 01298 871898 Fax: 01298 872531 Contact: Sue Mayer
mail@genewatch.org www.genewatch.org
Policy research group. Research and analysis on GM crops and foods. Up to date information on latest developments and their implications.

GOULD, JOAN & ALAN
WOODRISING, THORN LANE, GOXHILL, LINCS DN19 7LU
Tel: 01469 530356 Contact: Joan & Alan Gould
alan@agolincs.demon.co.uk
Always willing to help with advice after a lifetime of organic producing.

GREEN CUISINE
PENRHOS COURT, KINGTON, HEREFORDSHIRE HR5 3LH
Tel: 01544 230720 Fax: 01544 230754 Contact: Daphne Lambert
daphne@greencuisine.org www.greencuisine.org
Soil Association E2051. Green Cuisine runs courses on food and health and offers consultations and natural therapies. The company also produce books and educational material. See also Penrhos Ltd and The Penrhos Trust.

GREENACRES ORGANIC PRODUCE
COOMBE BANK, TIPTON ST. JOHN, SIDMOUTH, DEVON EX10 0AX
Tel: 01404 815829 Fax: 01404 815829 Contact: Roger Cozens
roger@greenacres-consultancy.co.uk
Herbs (culinary and medicinal), vegetables, lamb and eggs. Consultancy in arable and horticulture, overseas aid and relief consultancy.

THE GREENHOUSE
42–46 BETHEL ST., NORWICH NR2 1NR
Tel: 01603 631007 Contact: The Members
www.greenhousetrust.co.uk
The Greenhouse is an educational charity providing solutions to environmental problems. The building houses an organic, vegetarian/vegan licensed café and shop plus meeting rooms and herb garden. The shop acts as a contact point for a local veg box scheme and is stockist of a wide range of organic and GMO-free foods. There is a resource centre offering meeting space, offices and other facilities to local and regional voluntary groups.

GREENPEACE UK
CANONBURY VILLAS, LONDON N1 2PN
Tel: 020 7865 8100 Fax: 020 7865 8200 Contact: Charlotte Duggett
info@uk.greenpeace.org www.greenpeace.org.uk
International environmental organisation which fights abuse to the natural world.

GROUNDWORK BLACK COUNTRY
WOLVERHAMPTON ENVIRONMENT CENTRE, WEST ACRE CRESCENT, FINCHFIELD, WOLVERHAMPTON
Tel: 01902 766199 Fax: 01902 574600 Contact: Terry Bird
terry_bird@groundwork.org.uk www.groundwork-bc.org.uk
Soil Association G5900. Enterprises in organic food production including protected salads, environment considered decorative/native horticultural products, recycled timber/green wood products, training, education and community links, open days.

GUILDEN GATE SMALLHOLDING
86 NORTH END, BASSINGBOURN, ROYSTON, CAMBRIDGESHIRE SG8 5PD
Tel: 01763 243960 Contact: Simon Saggers
simon.saggers@home.pipex.com www.guildengate.co.uk
Soil Association G5970. Mixed organic smallholding offering local 'veggie box' scheme and guided tours. Wildflower meadow, veg & herb fields, woodland, pond and orchards. Interesting on-site water and energy resource cycles. A practical design for living and working in a more ecologically sound and sustainable way.

HAZELBROW VISITOR CENTRE
LOW ROW, RICHMOND, NORTH YORKS DL11 6NE
Tel: 01748 886224 Contact: Catherine Calvert
hazelbrowfarm@aol.com www.hazelbrow.co.uk
Organic working farm in Yorkshire Dales National Park producing lamb and milk, with visitor centre, shop and café open 11am to 5pm five days a week, March to September (closed Mondays & Fridays)

HDRA, HENRY DOUBLEDAY RESEARCH ASSOCIATION, RYTON ORGANIC GARDENS
RYTON-ON-DUNSMORE, COVENTRY CV8 3LG
Tel: 024 7630 3517 Fax: 024 7663 9229 Contact: Susan Kay-Williams
enquiry@hdra.org.uk www.hdra.org.uk
Soil Association G1092. Standards for organic products for amenity horticulture. HDRA is Europe's largest organic gardening organisation. It is dedicated to researching and promoting organic gardening, farming and food. Ryton Organic Gardens, ten acres displaying all aspects of organic horticulture for gardens, plus The Vegetable Kingdom, an interactive exhibition for all ages on the history and role of vegetables.

HDRA, HENRY DOUBLEDAY RESEARCH ASSOCIATION, YALDING ORGANIC GARDENS
BENOVER RD., YALDING, NR. MAIDSTONE, KENT ME18 6EX
Tel: 01622 814650 Fax: 01622 814650 Contact: Susan Kay-Williams
chiefexecutive@hdra.org.uk www.hdra.org.uk
Yalding Organic Gardens trace the course of garden history through 16 landscaped displays, illustrating the organic techniques used to maintain them. Shop for browsing and organic café for refreshments.

HEELEY CITY FARM
RICHARDS ROAD, SHEFFIELD S2 3DT
Tel: 0114 258 0482 Fax: 0114 255 1400 Contact: The Manager
farm@heeleyfarm.org.uk www.heeleyfarm.org.uk
A community environmental and horticultural project based on an inner city educational farm. Food produced using organic methods is available in our farm café and from our garden centre during times of surplus. Local crafts.

HOLME LACY COLLEGE
HOLME LACY, HEREFORDSHIRE HR2 6LL
Tel: 01432 870316 Fax: 01432 870566 Contact: Peter Savidge
holmelacy@pershore.ac.uk www.pershore.ac.uk
Holme Lacy College is host to 'Project Carrot', which aims to create a leading European centre for sustainable agriculture and land management on its 600-acre farm and woodland estate.

THE HORTICULTURAL CORRESPONDENCE COLLEGE
LITTLE NOTTON FARMHOUSE, 16 NOTTON, LACOCK,
CHIPPENHAM, WILTSHIRE SN15 2NF
Tel: 01249 730326 Fax: 01249 730326 Contact: Kay Pidgeon
info@hccollege.co.uk www.hccollege.co.uk
Home study courses in garden- and horticulture-related subjects, including
a Soil Association approved organic gardening course. Also organic arable
farming.

INSTITUTE OF RURAL SCIENCES
INSTITUTE OF RURAL SCIENCES, UNIVERSITY OF WALES,
ABERYSTWYTH, CEREDIGION SY23 3AL
Tel: 01970 624471 Fax: 01970 622238 Contact: Nic Lampkin
organic@aber.ac.uk www.organic.aber.ac.uk
Soil Association certified. Research/demonstration farm. BSc, PgCert and
PgDipl in organic agriculture with student bursary support available,
sponsored by Waitrose and Horizon Organic Dairy. Extensive DEFRA and
EU-funded organic research programme.

INTERNATIONAL FEDERATION OF ORGANIC AGRICULTURAL MOVEMENTS (IFOAM)
CHARLES-DE-GAULLE-STR. 5, 53113, BONN, GERMANY
Tel: +49 (0) 228 926 5010 Fax: +49 (0) 228 926 5099
Contact: Bernward Geier
headoffice@ifoam.org www.ifoam.org
IFOAM is the world umbrella organisation of the organic agriculture
movement with 750 members. It offers publications like the directory
'Organic Agriculture Worldwide' and the magazine *Ecology And Farming*,
and organises international conferences and workshops.

INTERNATIONAL SOCIETY FOR ECOLOGY AND CULTURE
FOXHOLE, DARTINGTON, TOTNES, DEVON TQ9 6EB
Tel: 01803 868650 Fax: 01803 868651 Contact: Carole Powell
info@isec.org.uk www.isec.org.uk
ISEC is a non-profit organisation concerned with the protection of both
biological and cultural diversity. Our emphisis is on education for action:
moving beyond single issues to look at the more fundamental influences
that shape our lives.

IPSWICH ORGANIC GARDENERS GROUP

BABOUSHKA, 223 MERSEA ROAD, COLCHESTER, ESSEX CO2 8PN
Tel: 01206 570859 Contact: Jill Carter
tetley@macunlimited.net www.irene.org.uk
Gardening group affiliated to the HDRA, meeting once a month September
to May, speaker each month. Bi-monthly newsletter, discount seeds and
bulk purchasing scheme. Also attend local events to promote organic
gardening.

IRISH ORGANIC FARMERS AND GROWERS ASSOCIATION (IOFGA)

HARBOUR BUILDING, HARBOUR RD., KILBEGGAN, CO. WESTMEATH,
IRELAND
Tel: (+353) 0506 32563 Fax: (+353) 0506 32063 Contact: Angela Clarke
iofga@eircom.net www.irishorganic.ie
IOFGA is a company limited by guarantee, open to farmers, growers,
consumers and others interested in the production of healthy food and the
protection of the environment. IOFGA operates an inspection and
certification scheme, publishes a magazine, *Organic Matters*, and other
practical information for organic farmers and growers. Producers and
processors registered with IOFGA may display the IOFGA symbol on their
products and produce. Details of IOFGA registered producers, processors,
wholesalers and those offering box delivery, market stalls are available
directly from IOFGA.

THE KINDERSLEY CENTRE AT SHEEPDROVE ORGANIC FARM

THE KINDERSLEY CENTRE, SHEEPDROVE ORGANIC FARM, WARREN FARM,
LAMBOURN, BERKSHIRE RG17 7UU
Tel: 01488 674737 Fax: 01488 72285 Contact: Pippa Regan
pippa.regan@thekindersleycentre.com www.thekindersleycentre.com
Sustainable, organic and environmentally sound, the Kindersley Centre
combines exceptional surroundings with the most advanced technology
and attentive service. Set at the heart of award-winning Sheepdrove
Organic Farm, the centre is housed within a beautiful, eco-friendly
building, surrounded by fields and woodlands. A range of meeting places
and adaptable seating for up to 200 people.

THE KINGCOMBE CENTRE

LOWER KINGCOMBE, TOLLER PORCORUM, DORCHESTER, DORSET DT2 0EQ
Tel: 01300 320684 Fax: 01300 321409 Contact: Nigel Spring
nspring@kingcombe-centre.demon.co.uk
www.kingcombe-centre.demon.co.uk
Residential study centre in converted farm buildings beside the river Hooke;
offers courses and holidays in a wide range of subjects for adults and
children, fit and disabled. Day visits for schools and guided walks.
Organically reared pork and lamb.

LACKHAM COLLEGE
LACOCK, CHIPPENHAM, WILTSHIRE SN15 2NY
Tel: 01249 443111 Fax: 01249 444474 Contact: Trevor Arnes
lackham@rmplc.co.uk
A range of qualifications both part time and full time: City & Guilds
Organic Gardening, Certificate in Organic Horticulture, National Certificate
in Organic Horticulture, HND & HNC in organic crop productiion.

LAKEWOOD CONFERENCE CENTRE
RHODYATE, BLAGDON, BRISTOL BS40 7YE
Tel: 01761 463366 Fax: 01761 463377 Contact: Angela Cary-Brown
info@lakewoodcentre.co.uk www.lakewoodcentre.co.uk
A new contemporary conference centre with stunning views over lakes
close to Bristol, Bath, M5. Purpose designed with state of the art audio
visual equipment. Local, fresh and organic food.

LAND HERITAGE
SUMMERHILL FARM, HITTISLEIGH, EXETER, DEVON EX6 6LP
Tel: 01647 24511 Fax: 01647 24588 Contact: Robert Brighton
landheritage@hotmail.com www.landheritage.org
Land-based charitable trust. Seeks to protect and preserve small family
farms creating organic tenancies; promotes community supported
agriculture schemes; supplies educational packs raising awareness of
organic farming; publishes material and provides conversion advice.

LEAFCYCLE
COOMBE FARM, COVE, TIVERTON, DEVON EX16 7RU
Tel: 01398 331808 Fax: 01398 331808 Contact: Michael Cole
www.leafcycle.co.uk
Soil Association C37W. Leafu a highly nutritious vegan organic food
ingredient made from leaves. Leafcycle camps—a green space for green
camps. The Occasional Café, an outdoor organic experience.

LONG CRICHEL ORGANIC WALLED GARDEN
LONG CRICHEL, OPPOSITE LONG CRICHEL ORGANIC BAKERY,
WIMBORNE, DORSET BH21 5JU
Tel: 01258 830295 Contact: Anni Sax
Soil Association G7461. Organic fruit and vegetables growers comprising of
2.5 acres with walled garden using permaculture/forest garden methods,
specialising in oriental salad and herb production. Registered for WOOFERS.

LUPPOLO LTD
42 WESTBOURNE TERRACE, LONDON WC2 6QE
Tel: 020 7262 4562 Fax: 020 7262 9078 Contact: Claudio Bincoletto
ccluppolo@netscapeonline.co.uk
Soil Association P6921. Importing products for the catering industry, day
walks on organic farms, cookery and dietetic courses. Teaching in Tuscany
on local wild herbs, expert on ECC 2092/91.

MARCASSIE FARM
MARCASSIE FARM, RAFFORD, FORRES, HIGHLAND IV36 2RH
Tel: 01309 676865 Fax: 01309 676865 Contact: Betsy van der Lee
marcassie@marcassie.fsnet.co.uk
Soil Association SG7923, Association for Environmentally Conscious
Builders, Association of Scottish Hardwood Sawmillers. Based in Scotland
(near Findhorn), brings together sawmill & woodshop (native timber
building components, bespoke buildings, furniture & street furniture),
organic farm (grains, wheatgrass, eggs, hay), commercial kitchen (being
established), esoteric healing and (at present, occasional) educational
courses.

MEANWOOD VALLEY URBAN FARM
SUGARWELL RD., MEANWOOD, LEEDS LS7 2QG
Tel: 0113 262 9759 Fax: 0113 239 2551 Contact: Susan Reddington
info@mvuf.org.uk www.wwf-leeds.org.uk
Soil Association R27N. Member of the Organic Farm Network. City farm,
combining organic market garden, environmental education services to
schools. Farm animals, including rare breeds. Purpose-built environment
centre, interactive displays. Shop, café and play area. Registered charity,
open every day to visitors.

MENTRO LLUEST
LLANBADORN FAWR, ABERYSTWYTH, CEREDIGION SY23 3AU
Tel: 01970 612114 Fax: 01970 612114 Contact: R Allen
mentro.lluest@talk21.com
Soil Association G3081. Mentro Lluest teaches skills to people with special
needs within a framework of organic growing, environmental sustainability
and social cohesion. We specialise in producing salad, seasonal vegetables
and herbs.

MOLYNEUX ORGANIC MEDICINAL AND AROMATIC PLANT FARM AND RESEARCH CENTRE

MILL HOUSE FARM, EAGER LANE, LYDIATE, MERSEYSIDE L314HS
Tel: 0151 526 0139 Fax: 0151 526 0139 Contact: David Molyneux
sales@phytobotanica.com www.phytobotanica.com
Producers of the first certified organic essential oils in the UK (lavender,
peppermint, roman chamomile, german chamomile) and organic hydrosols.
On-farm commercial hydrodistillation facilities, dispensary and conference
centre for educational days (e.g. aromatherapy and holistic therapies).

NATIONAL FARMERS' RETAIL AND MARKETS ASSOCIATION

PO BOX 575, SOUTHAMPTON SO15 7BZ
Tel: 0845 230 2150 Contact: The Secretary
justask@farma.org.uk www.farmersmarkets.net
A Farmers' Market is one in which farmers, growers or producers from a
defined local area are present in person to sell their own produce direct to
the public. All products sold should have been grown, reared, caught,
pickled, baked, smoked or processed by the stallholder.

THE NATIONAL INSTITUTE OF MEDICAL HERBALISTS

56 LONGBROOK STREET, EXETER, DEVON EX1 6AH
Tel: 01392 426022 Fax: 01392 498963 Contact: The Secretary
nimh@ukexeter.freeserve.co.uk www.nimh.org.uk
Professional body of practising medical herbalists. Offers details/information
on all aspects of western herbal medicine and how to source a qualified
practitioner. Details on education and research available. All members have
undergone a rigorous four-year training.

NATURE'S WORLD

LADGATE LANE, ACKLAM, MIDDLESBOROUGH TS5 7YN
Tel: 01642 594895 Fax: 01642 591224 Contact: The Manager
www.naturesworld.org.uk
The north of England's pioneering environmental centre featuring new
eco-centre and tropical hydroponicum. Organic demonstration gardens,
tearooms and shop. Monthly farmers' market.

THE NETHERFIELD CENTRE

NETHERFIELD PLACE FARM, NETHERFIELD, NR. BATTLE,
EAST SUSSEX TN3 9PY
Tel: 01424 775615 Fax: 01424 775616 Contact: Topsy Jewell
simon@thenetherfieldcentre.co.uk
The Netherfield Centre for Sustainable Food and Farming runs education
courses, training and networking for those interested in sustainable
agriculture. The Netherfield Centre is located on an organic farm and linked
to a network of farms sharing a cutting room and marketing meat locally.

NORFOLK ORGANIC GARDENERS
25 ST. MILDRED'S RD., NORWICH NR5 8RS
Tel: 01603 504468 Contact: Jan Hunt
info@norfolkorganic.org.uk www.norfolkorganic.org.uk
Local group of Soil Association and HDRA. We aim to promote the organic movement in Norfolk by increasing public awareness of organic methods of farming and gardening.

THE NORTH WALES ORGANIC GROWERS AND PERMACULTURE GROUP
PEN-Y-BRYN, TALWRN, LLANGEFNI, YNYS MON,
ISLE OF ANGLESEY LL77 7SP
Tel: 01248 750029 Contact: Kath Turner
Group of members who put newcomers to the area in touch with existing organic growers and permaculturists.

NOTTINGHAM CITY COUNCIL
GREEN'S MILL & SCIENCE CENTRE, WINDMILL LANE, SNEINTON,
NOTTINGHAM NG2 4QB
Tel: 0115 915 6878 Fax: 0115 915 6875 Contact: David Bent
enquiries@greensmill.org.uk www.greensmill.org.uk
Soil Association P4518. Museum: a working tower windmill built in 1807, once operated by the mathematician George Green (1793–1841) Now producing organic stoneground flours, including Organic Foods award-winning wholemeal and white spelt flour.

O&F CONSULTING
THE OLD BAKERY, 8A REPLINGHAM RD. LONDON SW18 5LS
Tel: 020 8870 5383 Fax: 020 8870 8140 Contact: Simon Wright
simon@organicandfair.com www.organicandfair.com
Since 1986 Simon Wright of The Organic Consultancy has worked to develop the organic market in the UK and elsewhere in partnership with ingredient suppliers, manufacturers, supermarkets, independent retailers, certification bodies, government departments and trade bodies. More information from our website.

ORGANIC CENTRE WALES
UNIVERSITY OF WALES, ABERYSTWYTH, CEREDIGION SY23 3AL
Tel: 01970 622248 Fax: 01970 622238 Contact: Neil Pearson
organic@aber.ac.uk www.organic.aber.ac.uk
Operated in partnership with Soil Association, Elm Farm Research Centre, IGER, UWA and ADAS. Advice and demonstration. Dissemination of information on organic farming at all levels from producers, to consumers, through training courses, advice, demonstration farms, discussion groups, publications and website.

THE ORGANIC FARM SHOP
ABBEY HOME FARM, BURFORD ROAD, CIRENCESTER,
GLOUCESTERSHIRE GL7 5HF
Tel: 01285 640441 Fax: 01285 644827 Contact: Hilary Chester-Master
info@theorganicfarmshop.co.uk www.theorganicfarmshop.co.uk
Soil Association G1715, R5253. 100% organic, award-winning farm, shop
and café with garden. Courses, educational visits, trailer rides, woodland
walk. Our own vegetables, meat, eggs and frozen meals, also general
groceries. Greenfield camping.

ORGANIC FARMERS AND GROWERS LTD (OF&G)
ELIM CENTRE, LANCASTER RD., SHREWSBURY SY1 3LE
Tel: 0845 330 5122 Fax: 0845 330 5123 Contact: Christine Rescorla
info@organicfarmers.uk.com www.organicfarmers.uk.com
Certification body. We offer organic inspection and certification services to
farmers and processors.

ORGANIC FOOD FEDERATION (OFF)
31 TURBINE WAY, ECO TECH BUSINESS PARK, SWAFFHAM,
NORFOLK PE37 7XD
Tel: 01760 720444 Fax: 01760 720790 Contact: Julian Wade
info@orgfoodfed.com www.orgfoodfed.com
EC-listed certification body for the organic food industry certifying
producers, processors, caterers and importers. UKAS accredited for
producing and processing. Also able to offer certification against our
private standards for cosmetics and acquaculture. Authorised by DEFRA
under the member state code UK4. Representation and lobbying at
Government, EU and Non-Government level. Personal service offered at all
times with telephones answered between 9.00–5.30 each weekday.

ORGANIC STUDIES CENTRE
DUCHY COLLEGE, ROSEWARNE, CAMBORNE, CORNWALL TR14 0AB
Tel: 01209 722155 Fax: 01209 722156 Contact: Rachel Moss
rachel.moss@cornwall.ac.uk www.organicstudiescentre.co.uk
Soil Association G4694. Organic agricultural research and demonstration
and training. Arable/field vegetables demonstration farm, farm walks, trials
and demos. R&D including farmers' participatory studies in all sectors of
organic agricultural production.

ORGANIC TRUST LTD
VERNON HOUSE, 2 VERNON AVENUE, CLONTEEF, DUBLIN 3
Tel: 00353 1 853 0271 Fax: 00353 1 853 0271 Contact: Helen Scully
organic@iol.ie www.organic-trust.org
Organic inspection and certification service. Publication of quarterly journal,
education and consumer information.

PENPONT

PENPONT ESTATE, BRECON, POWYS LD3 8EU
Tel: 01874 636202 Contact: Gavin Hogg
penpont@clara.co.uk www.penpont.com
Soil Association G4529. We offer bed and breakfast and self-catering
accommodation in a historic listed mansion. We are restoring two Victorian
walled gardens where we grow registered organic vegetables. We are now
an Organic Demonstration farm, and will host a number of day courses in
Horticulture organised jointly by OCW and Farming Connect.

THE PENRHOS TRUST

PENRHOS COURT, KINGTON, HEREFORDSHIRE HR5 3LH
Tel: 01544 230720 Fax: 01544 230754 Contact: Martin Griffiths
martin@penrhos.co.uk www.penrhostrust.org
Charity for the restoration of historic farm buildings regenerated with
organic and ecological small businesses. Education: conservation, food
heritage, organic food production. See also Penrhos Ltd and Green Cuisine
Ltd.

PLANTS FOR A FUTURE

THE FIELD, HIGHER PENPOL, ST. VEEP, LOSTWITHIEL, CORNWALL PL22 0NG
Tel: 01208 873554 Contact: The Manager
www.pfaf.org
Day visits and tours, courses on woodland gardening, permaculture,
nutrition, research, information, demonstration and supply of edible and
otherwise useful plants. Plants for a Future is a registered charity
researching and demonstrating ecologically sustainable vegan organic
horticulture in the form of woodland gardening and other permacultural
practices.

PLOT 21 PERMACULTURE ALLOTMENTS

ALEXANDRA PALACE ALLOTMENTS, OFF ALEXANDRA PALACE WAY N17
Tel: 020 7916 7390 Contact: S Girardi
A loose non-profit-making organisation running courses on permaculture
and producing home-grown crops using permaculture principles.

PROPER JOB

CRANNAFORDS IND PARK, CHAGFORD TQ13 8DJ
Tel: 01647 432985 Fax: 01647 432985 Contact: Jo Hodges
compost@properjob.eclipse.co.uk www.properjob.ik.com
Community business. Holistic co-op. Developing from waste to resource
issues, especially composting, collecting compostables, education/
consciousness raising. Organic veg production and sale in our community
shop/café. Setting up training in related issues. Organic collection round.

PROSPECTS TRUST
SNAKEHILL FARM, REACH, CAMBRIDGE CB5 0HZ
Tel: 01638 741551 Fax: 01638 741873 Contact: Phil Creme
prospect@farming.co.uk www.prospectstrust.org.uk
Soil Association registered. Charitable trust, working together with people
with learning disabilities. Provision of training, work experience and work
opportunities in organic market gardening and horticulture for people with
learning disabilities.

RARE BREEDS SURVIVAL TRUST
NATIONAL AGRICULTURAL CENTRE, STONELEIGH PARK,
KENILWORTH CV8 2LG
Tel: 024 7669 6551 Fax: 024 7669 6706 Contact: Robert Terry
enquiries@rbst.org.uk www.rbst.org.uk
Registered charity for the conservation of rare and endangered livestock
breeds.

REDFIELD COMMUNITY
BUCKINGHAM RD., WINSLOW MK18 3LZ
Tel: 01296 713661 Fax: 01296 714983 Contact: Chrissy Schmidt
info@redfieldcommunity.org.uk www.redfieldcommunity.org.uk
Redfield is an intentional community. We grow and raise our own organic
produce as well as run courses and offer accommodation for groups.

THE RESPONSIVE EARTH TRUST
PLASDWBL BIODYNAMIC FARM, MYNACHLOG DDU,
CLYNDERWEN, PEMBROKESHIRE SA66 7SE
Tel: 01994 419352 Contact: A Kleinjans
Plasdwbl Biodynamic Farm is a charitable trust run for the benefit of
students wishing to gain practical experience in biodynamic farming and
gardening. We have a Welsh Black herd and two Jersey milkers. The farm is
40 ha and on 4 ha we grow vegetables and forage. We make our own
butter, cheese and bread. Demeter cert. no. 111.

RISING SUN FARM
KINGS RD. NORTH, WALLSEND, TYNE & WEAR NE28 9JL
Tel: 0191 234 0114 Contact: D Shanks
organics@risingsunfarm.freeserve.co.uk
Soil Association producer no. P1490. Cereals, horticultural, pigs, cattle.
Urban fringe farm providing education, day service for special needs. Open
farm for community. Livery yard for diy liveries.

ROBERT OWEN COMMUNITIES
LOWER SHARPHAM BARTON FARM, ASHPRINGTON, TOTNES TQ9 7DX
Tel: 01803 732502 Fax: 01803 732502 Contact: B Roodenburg-Vermaat
sharphamfarm@roc-uk.org
Day centre for people with learning disabilities. Dairy, beef, sheep, laying
birds and vegetables. Produce milk, meats, eggs and veg.

RUBHA PHOIL FOREST GARDEN/ SKYE PERMACULTURE
RUBHA PHOIL, ARMADALE PIER, ISLE OF SKYE IV45 8RS
Tel: 01471 844700 Contact: Sandy Masson
sandyrv@tiscali.co.uk www.skye-permaculture.org.uk
Soil Association GCS025/G4609, HDRA, Permaculture Association, Centre
for Alternative Technology Ecosite. Herbs, vegetables, displays and
demonstration of alternative systems, holiday accommodation, woodland
walk, otter/bird hide, solitude in wilderness.

RUSKIN MILL COLLEGE
THE FISHERIES, HORSLEY, GLOUCESTERSHIRE GL6 1PL
Tel: 01453 837500 Fax: 01453 837506 Contact: Julian Pyzer
www.ruskin-mill.org.uk
Biodynamic Agricultural Association 245. Part of special needs further
education college with biodynamic market garden and mixed farm, and
fish farm. Café and shop, crafts, exhibitions, workshops, concerts,
storytelling and talks.

SCOTTISH AGRICULTURAL COLLEGE
CRAIBSTONE ESTATE, BUCKSBURN, ABERDEEN AB21 9YA
Tel: 01224 711072 Fax: 01224 711293 Contact: David Younie
d.younie@ab.sac.ac.uk www.sac.ac.uk/organic-farming
Licensed producer of organic crops, beef and sheep. Advice, Research,
Education—SAC provides advice on organic farming (including telephone
Helpline 01224 711072) to Scottish farmers, education and vocational
training, and multi-disciplinary research across most aspects of organic
farming.

SCOTTISH ORGANIC PRODUCERS ASSOCIATION (SOPA)
SCOTTISH ORGANIC CENTRE, 10TH AVENUE, ROYAL HIGHLAND CENTRE,
INGLISTEN, EDINBURGH EH28 8NF
Tel: 0131 335 6606 Fax: 0131 335 6607 Contact: Christine Robb
sopa@sfqc.co.uk www.sopa.org.uk
SOPA primarily offer an organic certification service to farmer producers.
SOPA is the leading Scottish organic sector body.

SOIL ASSOCIATION
BRISTOL HOUSE, 40–56 VICTORIA STREET, BRISTOL BS1 6BY
Tel: 0117 929 0661 Fax: 0117 925 2504
info@soilassociation.org www.soilassociation.org
The Soil Association is one of the UK's most respected environmental
charities, dedicated to bringing about change by creating a growing body
of public opinion that understands how the health of the soil, plants,
animals, humans and the wider environment link together. Our not-for-
profit subsidiary, Soil Association Certification Limited (see below) certifies
over 70% of the organic food sold in the UK, ensuring food you can trust.
We rely on public support and urge you to make your voice count by
joining or supporting our work. See display ad.

SOIL ASSOCIATION CERTIFICATION LTD (SA CERT)
BRISTOL HOUSE, 40–56 VICTORIA STREET, BRISTOL BS1 6BY
Tel: 0117 914 2405 Fax: 0117 925 2504
info@soilassociation.org www.soilassociation.org
Soil Association Certification Limited is the largest of the UK certification
bodies and currently inspects and certifies over 70% of UK licensed organic
producers and processors. We certify to the Soil Association Standards for
organic food and farming which are well respected worldwide. The well
known Soil Association Organic Symbol, featured in this book and
displayed on much organic food and packaging, is widely recognised and
trusted by consumers.

SOMERSET FOOD LINKS
THE OLD TOWN HALL, BOW ST., LANGPORT, SOMERSET TA10 9PR
Tel: 01458 259485 Fax: 08700 527256 Contact: Vivien Grammer
enquiries@foodlinks.org.uk www.somerset.foodlinks.org.uk
County food links project established in 1999 to encourage thriving local
food economy by supporting Somerset businesses (producers, processors,
retailers, caterers, accommodation providers), schools and community
groups. Advice to local food businesses (including direct marketing, co-
operation, public procurement), advice to community food growing projects,
social enterprise development, advocacy, lobbying and awareness raising.

SOMERSET ORGANIC LINK
1 BRIDGE FARM COTTAGE, DRAYTON, SOUTH PETHERTON TA13 5LR
Tel: 01460 241427 Fax: 01460 241427
Contact: Peter Foster & Steve Friend
peter@flaxdrayton.fsnet.co.uk www.somersetorganiclink.co.uk
A co-operative of organic farmers in Somerset, SOL supplies fresh organic
produce to outlets in Somerset and beyond. SOL buys produce from
outside the county, when necessary to meet demand. Sales and marketing
service for organic vegetable producers in Somerset, forum for crop
planning, opportunities to share labour and equipment.

SOUTH DEVON ORGANIC PRODUCERS LTD
c/o WASH BARN, BUCKFASTLEIGH, DEVON TQ11 0LD
Contact: Ian Noble
Tel: 01803 762100 Fax: 01803 762100
sdop@farmersweekly.net www.sdopltd.co.uk
Co-operative of growers producing organic vegetables.

STOCKBRIDGE TECHNOLOGY CENTRE LTD
CAWOOD, SELBY, NORTH YORKSHIRE YO8 3TZ
Tel: 01757 268275 Fax: 01757 268996 Contact: Rob Jacobson
robjacobson@stc-nyorks.co.uk
STC Ltd provides contract R&D, technology transfer and related services
in all aspects of organic field and glasshouse vegetable production:
specialisms include variety evaluation, fertility inputs and pest/disease
control.

STOCKLEY FARM ORGANICS
SMITHY FARMHOUSE, ARLEY, NORTHWICH, CHESHIRE CW9 6LZ
Tel: 01565 777492 Fax: 01565 777501 Contact: John Walton
organics@stockleyfarm.co.uk www.stockleyfarm.co.uk
Stockley Farm is open to the public and schools from March to October.
Stockley Farm Organics operates a box scheme, hand-delivered throughout
Cheshire and south Manchester.

SUMMERLEAZE GALLERY
EAST KNOYLE, SALISBURY, WILTSHIRE SP3 6BY
Tel: 01747 830790 Fax: 01747 830790 Contact: Trish Scott Bolton
trish@summerleazegallery.co.uk
Soil Association G4877. Art gallery holding three exhibitions a year, four-
day painting courses and lectures in converted farm buildings on organic
farm. Dinner, bed and breakfast in nearby farmhouse.

SUSTAIN
94 WHITE LION ST., LONDON N1 9PF
Tel: 020 7837 1228 Fax: 020 7837 1141 Contact: The Secretary
sustain@sustainweb.org www.sustainweb.org
'Sustain: the alliance for better food and farming' advocates food and
agriculture policies and practices that enhance the health and welfare of
people and animals, improve the working and living environment, promote
equity and enrich society and culture.

THE SUSTAINABLE LIFESTYLES RESEARCH CO-OP LTD
THE OFFICE, POND COTTAGE EAST, CUDDINGTON RD., DINTON,
AYLESBURY, BUCKINGHAMSHIRE HP18 0AD
Tel: 01296 747737 Contact: Mike George
mikegeorge.lara@btinternet.com
Organic Food Federation 0071/01/981. Free range eggs, seasonal
vegetables and fruit, especially Victoria plums. Occasional lamb, mutton
(Jacobs sheep). Selling at Tring Farmers' market and from farm stall. Full
public access to 70 acres. Farm walks through woodland to the riverside.
Run by volunteers.

ULSTER WILDLIFE TRUST
JOHN McSPARRAN MEMORIAL HILL FARM, GLENDUN, CUSHENDEN, CO.
ANTRIM BT44 0PZ
Tel: 028 2176 1403 Fax: 028 2176 1403 Contact: Barrie Elkin
ulsterwt@glendunfarm.fsnet.co.uk
Soil Association G6697. Farming together with wildlife in a progressive and
sustainable manner, producing lamb and beef from traditional and native
breeds. Native trees are also produced in our nursery.

UNITED WORLD COLLEGE OF THE ATLANTIC
ST. DONATS CASTLE, LLANTWIT MAJOR, VALE OF GLAMORGAN CF61 1WF
Tel: 01446 799012 Fax: 01446 799013 Contact: AE Davies
estate@uwcac.uwc.org
Soil Association G5656. An international 6th Form College with a 20
hectare farm unit producing organic lamb and beef.

UPPER RED HOUSE FARM
LLANVIHANGEL, MONMOUTH NP25 5HL
Tel: 01600 780501 Fax: 01600 780572 Contact: Teona Dorrien-Smith
Soil Association G4969. Tir Gofal. The farm is mainly pasture with some
arable, producing forage and spring cereals with emphasis on conservation
and educational visits to study environment and wildlife. Educational visits,
all ages welcome, but booking essential.

THE VILLAGE BAKERY
MELMERBY, PENRITH, CUMBRIA CA10 1HE
Tel: 01768 881811 Fax: 01768 881848 Contact: Chris Curry
info@village-bakery.com www.village-bakery.com
Organic speciality breads, cakes, savoury biscuits, flapjacks, slices, Christmas
goods. Special diet products. Mail order. Nationwide stockists. Baking
courses.

WAKELYNS AGROFORESTRY
METFIELD LANE, FRESSINGFIELD, SUFFOLK IP21 5SD
Contact: The Manager
wolfe@wakelyns.demon.co.uk
Soil Association G2249. Organic arable and agroforestry research undertaken largely as part of the Elm Farm Research Centre programme. Vegetables, potatoes and other produce are sold locally, principally through the Eostre organic co-operative.

THE WATERMILL
LITTLE SALKELD, PENRITH, CUMBRIA CA10 1NN
Tel: 01768 881523 Fax: 01768 881047 Contact: Ana Jones
organicflour@aol.com www.organicmill.co.uk
Soil Association (P632) and Biodynamic Agriculture Association registered. Specialist organic flours, milled by water power in our 18th century watermill to SA and BDAA standards. Mill shop, tea room, mill tours and baking courses.

THE WESSEX ORGANIC MOVEMENT (WORM)
LINDEN COTTAGE, DUCK STREET, HILTON, BLANDFORD,
DORSET DT11 0DQ
Tel: 0845 330 3953 Fax: 0845 330 3953 Contact: Philip Clive
sec@wessexorganic.org.uk www.wessexorganic.org.uk
Soil Association, HDRA, BTCV. We hold a series of talks and visits to promote and educate farmers, producers or consumers about organic methods and to network information, set up projects to meet their needs.

WESTHOPE COLLEGE
WESTHOPE COLLEGE, CRAVEN ARMS, SHROPSHIRE SY7 9JL
Tel: 01584 861293 Contact: Anne Dyer
www.westhope.org.uk
Soil Association no. G4886. Adult education weekend and weekly courses, C&G exams. Depth of the country, organic food.

WILTSHIRE COLLEGE – LACKHAM
LACKHAM PARK, LACOCK, CHIPPENHAM, WILTSHIRE SN15 2NY
Tel: 01249 466800 Fax: 01249 444474 Contact: Trevor Armes
wiltscoll@ac.uk www.wiltscoll.ac.uk
We offer a range of FE & HE courses in organic horticulture at National Certificate/Diploma and National Award in Organic Horticulture. For further details visit the website or telephone 01249 466873.

WOMENS ENVIRONMENTAL NETWORK
PO BOX 30626, LONDON E1 1TZ
Tel: 020 7481 9004 Fax: 020 7481 9144 Contact: Caroline Fernandez
info@wen.org.uk www.wen.org.uk
Educational environmental charity. Educating women and men who care
about the environment from a women's perspective. Projects include local
food, women's food growing groups, health, real nappies and waste
prevention.

THE WORLD LAND TRUST
BLYTH HOUSE, BRIDGE ST., HALESWORTH, SUFFOLK IP19 8AB
Tel: 01986 874422 Fax: 01986 874425 Contact: Vivien Burton
info@worldlandtrust.org www.worldlandtrust.org
The World Land Trust is a UK-based, international conservation organisation
(charity reg. no. 1001291) working to preserve the world's most biologically
important and threatened lands. The Trust has helped purchase and protect
more than 300,000 acres of habitats rich in wildlife, in Belize, Costa Rica,
the Philippines, South America and the UK. For a unique, eco-friendly gift,
save an acre of rainforest for £25. Donations can be made on our website or
by calling the office.

WWF (WORLDWIDE FUND FOR NATURE)
PANDA HOUSE, WEYSIDE PARK, GODALMING, SURREY GU7 1XR
Tel: 01483 426444 Fax: 01483 426409
The WWF works on both global and local environmental issues. Much of
our work is in areas where the most critically endangered wildlife and the
least protected habitats are found. However, the origins of many
environmental problems lie in developed countries, including the UK, and
in our attitudes and behaviour—for example our consumption of natural
resources.

WWOOF (WORLD WIDE OPPORTUNITIES ON ORGANIC FARMS)
PO BOX 2675, LEWES, EAST SUSSEX BN7 1RB
Tel: 01273 476286 Fax: 01273 476286 Contact: Fran Whittle
hello@wwoof.org www.wwoof.org.uk
WWOOF helps volunteers find host farms worldwide to be able to
experience organic growing, meet like-minded people, exchange skills and
get into rural areas. Help in exchange for bed and board.

Many of the organisations in the previous sections also produce their own publications.

COUNTRY SMALLHOLDING
ARCHANT DEVON, FAIR OAK CLOSE, EXETER AIRPORT BUSINESS PARK, CLYST HONITON, EXETER, DEVON EX5 2UL
Tel: 01392 888481 Fax: 01392 888550 Contact: Diane Cowgill
editorial@countrysmallholding.com www.countrysmallholding.com
Smallholding magazine carrying regular articles on organic growing and humane ways of keeping poultry and other animals including broad practical coverage of rural crafts, machinery, weather and environmental issues.

ECO-LOGIC BOOKS
MULBERRY HOUSE, 19 MAPLE GROVE, BATH BA2 3AF
Tel: 01225 484472 Fax: 0117 942 0164 Contact: Peter Andrews
info@eco-logicbooks.com www.eco-logicbooks.com
Publish and sell mail order books that promote practical solutions to environmental problems, organic gardening, permaculture and sustainability.

THE ECOLOGIST
UNIT 18, CHELSEA WHARF, 15 LOTS RD., LONDON SW10 0QJ
Tel: 020 7351 3578 Fax: 020 7351 3617 Contact: The Editor
editorial@theecologist.org www.theecologist.org
The dangers of globalisation, the real reasons behind climate change, the threat of corporate power, the risks of GM food, the truth about global cancer—just some of the issues covered regularly by *The Ecologist*.

FOOD MAGAZINE
THE FOOD COMMISSION, 94 WHITE LION STREET, LONDON N1 9PF
Tel: 020 7837 2250 Fax: 020 7837 1141 Contact: The Editor
enquiries@foodcomm.org.uk www.foodcomm.org.uk
The magazine of The Food Commission reports on genetic engineering, additives, pesticides, food irradiation, food labelling and animal welfare. Sample copies available. For general enquiries, news and submissions to *The Food Magazine* please contact enquiries@foodcomm.org.uk and for press enquiries, including requests to be put on the press release list, please contact press@foodcomm.org.uk.

GREEN BOOKS LTD

FOXHOLE, DARTINGTON, TOTNES, DEVON TQ9 6EB
Tel: 01803 863260 Fax: 01803 863843 Contact: Paul Rossiter
sales@greenbooks.co.uk www.greenbooks.co.uk
Besides publishing *The Organic Directory*, we have a wide range of other
books on organic living, including *The Organic Baby Book, Green Living In
The Urban Jungle* and *Gaia's Kitchen: Vegetarian Recipes For Family And
Community*. Also books on eco-building, organic gardening, green politics
and economics, etc. Mail order and trade catalogues available on request.

GREEN ISP

LEE MILL RD, HEBDEN BRIDGE, WEST YORKSHIRE HX7 8LJ
Tel: 01422 847691 Fax: 01422 847691 Contact: Paul Palmer
info@greenisp.net www.greenisp.net
Green Isp provide environmentally guided internet services, providing
broadband, unmetered dial up, 0845, email and web space, solar-powered
office, advanced solar web hosting. Features and links on green issues.

HDRA, HENRY DOUBLEDAY RESEARCH ASSOCIATION, RYTON ORGANIC GARDENS

RYTON-ON-DUNSMORE, COVENTRY CV8 3LG
Tel: 024 7630 3517 Fax: 024 7663 9229 Contact: Susan Kay-Williams
enquiry@hdra.org.uk www.hdra.org.uk
Soil Association G1092. HDRA is Europe's largest organic gardening
organisation. It is dedicated to researching and promoting organic
gardening, farming and food, and produces many publications.

HEALTH FOOD BUSINESS MAGAZINE

THE OLD DAIRY, HUDSONS FARM, FIELD GATE LANE,
UGLEY GREEN, ESSEX CM22 6HJ
Tel: 01279 816300 Fax: 01279 816496 Contact: Alistair Forrest
info@targetpublishing.com www.targetpublishing.com
Health Food Business trade magazine is sent free of charge to all registered,
named buyers of natural organic foods, drinks, toiletries, herbals and
dietary supplements. Serve UK and Eire.

NATURAL COLLECTION

GREEN DOT GUIDES, ECO HOUSE, 19A MONMOUTH PLACE, BATH BA1 2DQ
Tel: 01225 404020 Fax: 01225 469673 Contact: Sarah Thorne
sarah@naturalcollection.com www.naturalcollection.com
Green Dot Guides Ltd owns the Natural Collection catalogue and publishes
Trees for Life diaries and calendars. The Natural Collection catalogue
promotes a huge variety of products that have been manufactured with the
environment in mind or traded fairly and which are also desirable both
aesthetically and functionally. We are the trading partner for Friends of the
Earth and Greenpeace and work with many other worthy organisations.

ORGANIC & NATURAL BUSINESS MAGAZINE

THE OLD DAIRY, HUDSONS FARM, FIELDGATE LANE,
UGLEY GREEN, ESSEX CM22 6HJ
Tel: 01279 816300 Fax: 01279 816496 Contact: Target Publishing Ltd
Carlota Hudgell
kathryn@targetpublishing.com www.organic-business.com
Organic& Natural Business magazine is the UK's premier platform for
showcasing organic and natural products, reporting authoritatively on
developments within the organic and wider natural food, healthy eating
and fair trade markets. No other magazine is as committed to servicing the
needs of multiple retail buyers, farm shops, convenience and grocery
stores, delis and other food service retailers. To subscribe, email
info@targetpublishing.com.

ORGANIC GARDENING

PO BOX 29, MINEHEAD, SOMERSET TA24 6YY
Tel: 01643 707339 Fax: 01643 707339 Contact: Gaby Bartai Bevan
jeanarmin@orgardening.fsnet.co.uk
The UK's only all organic monthly gardening magazine. Practical hands-on
advice on every aspect of the garden: vegetables, fruit, herbs. Ornamentals,
wildlife. Call for details of our £10 trial subscription offer.

ORGANIC TRADE SERVICES

NORTHORPE HOUSE, NORTHORPE, DONINGTON PE11 4XY
Tel: 07974 103109 Fax: Contact: Neil Butler
info@organicts.com www.organicts.com
The organic industry portal on the internet. Marketplace, news, newsfeeds,
directory, discussion information and more. News and trade offers via
email.

PERMACULTURE MAGAZINE

PERMANENT PUBLICATIONS, THE SUSTAINABILITY CENTRE, EAST MEON,
PETERSFIELD, HAMPSHIRE GU32 1HR
Tel: 01730 823311 Fax: 01730 823322 Contact: Maddy Harland
info@permaculture.co.uk www.permaculture.co.uk
Permaculture Magazine—solutions for sustainable living, published quarterly.
Earth Repair Catalogue of over 500 books, videos, tools and products
available free and on-line at www.permaculture.co.uk.

POSITIVE NEWS

5 BICTON ENTERPRISE CENTRE, CLUN, SHROPSHIRE SY7 8NF
Tel: 01588 640022 Fax: 01588 640033 Contact: Carole Hudson
office@positivenews.org.uk www.positivenews.org.uk
Quarterly newspaper covering organics and organic farming, green energy
and green building, health, peace, recycling, new economics, national and
international news, including book reviews. Magazine, *Living Lightly on the
Earth*, free to subscribers.

RESURGENCE MAGAZINE

FORD HOUSE, HARTLAND, BIDEFORD, DEVON EX39 6EE
Tel: 01237 441293 Fax: 01237 441203 Contact: Angie Burke
ed@resurge.demon.co.uk www.resurgence.org
An international forum for ecological and spiritual thinking, with many
influential contributors. Described by *The Guardian* as 'the spiritual and
artistic flagship of the Green Movement'. Themes include: Organic Living,
Sustainable Development, Deep Ecology, Art and Culture. Read a selection
of articles on-line at www.resurgence.org. Sample copy available on
request. See display ad.

SAWDAY PUBLISHING, ALASTAIR

THE HOME FARM STABLES, BARROW GURNEY, BRISTOL BS48 3RW
Tel: 01275 464891 Fax: 01275 464887 Contact: Paula Brown
paula@sawdays.co.uk www.sawdays.co.uk
Publisher producing and selling guides to Special Places to Stay across
Europe and in India and Morocco. Developing and piloting a Fine Breakfast
Scheme, to celebrate the exceptional quality of breakfasts served in B&Bs
listed in their British B&B guide. Most owners use home-grown, local or
organic produce. Also produces the Fragile Earth Book series, sets of mini-
essays on environmental and social themes.

SEA SPRING PHOTOS

LYME VIEW, WEST BEXINGTON, DORCHESTER, DORSET DT2 9DD
Tel: 01308 897766 Fax: 01308 897735 Contact: Joy Michaud
sales@seaspringphotos.com www.seaspringphotos.com
The slide library contains many images of certified organic products and
scenes on organic agricultural and horticultural holdings.

SMALLHOLDER BOOKSHOP

STOKE FERRY, KING'S LYNN, NORFOLK PE33 9SF
Tel: 01366 500466 Contact: V Charlesworth
bookshop@lodgecottage1.freeserve.co.uk www.smallholder.co.uk
Mail order publisher. Books and videos on smallholding, livestock, poultry,
organics, growing, environment and general rural interests.

SMALLHOLDER MAGAZINE
NEWSQUEST PLC, 3 FALMOUTH BUSINESS PARK, BLICKLAND WATER RD, FALMOUTH, CORNWALL TR11 4SZ
Tel: 01326 213333 Fax: 01326 212108 Contact: Liz Wright / Wendy Symons
liz.smallholder@virgin.net www.smallholder.co.uk
Practical magazine with organic coverage, advice and profiles of producers covering all aspects of livestock and market gardening.

SOIL ASSOCIATION
Produce many publications, reports etc. See above under Associations.

WORLDLY GOODS
10–12 PICTON ST., BRISTOL BS6 5QA
Tel: 0117 942 0165 Fax: 0117 942 0164 Contact: Peter Andrews
wg@eco-logicbooks.com www.eco-logicbooks.com
Specialise in wholesale/trade sales of books that provide practical solutions to environmental problems, permaculture, organic gardening etc. Contact us for free catalogue.

FINANCIAL & COMMERCIAL SERVICES

THE ECOLOGY BUILDING SOCIETY
ECOLOGY BUILDING SOCIETY, REF OD FREEPOST BD714, KEIGHLEY,
WEST YORKSHIRE BD20 0BR
Tel: 0845 674 5566 (local rate) Fax: 01535 636166 Contact: Gillian Ingham
info@ecology.co.uk www.ecology.co.uk
The Ecology Building Society uses the money deposited by savers to
provide green mortgages, such as the purchase of land and construction of
buildings, including homes, that support organic food production.

THE ETHICAL INVESTMENT CO-OPERATIVE LTD
12 ST. NICHOLAS DRIVE, RICHMOND, NORTH YORKS DL10 7DY
Tel: 01748 822402 Fax: 01748 822402
Contact: Ian Harland / Andy Woodmancy
greeninvest@gn.apc.org
Independent financial advisors specialising in ethical/environmental
investments and pensions. Members of Soil Association, Friends Of The
Earth, Sustrans, Amnesty, PETA, CPRE.

O&F CONSULTING
THE OLD BAKERY, 8A REPLINGHAM RD., LONDON SW18 5LS
Tel: 020 8870 5383 Fax: 020 8870 8140 Contact: Simon Wright
simon@organicandfair.com www.organicandfair.com
Since 1986 Simon Wright of The Organic Consultancy has worked to
develop the organic market in the UK and elsewhere in partnership with
ingredient suppliers, manufacturers, supermarkets, independent retailers,
certification bodies, government departments and trade bodies. More
information from www.organicandfair.com.

ORGANIC MONITOR LTD
79 WESTERN RD., LONDON W5 5DT
Tel: 020 8567 0788 Fax: 020 8567 7164 Contact: Tina Gill
postmaster@organicmonitor.com www.organicmonitor.com
Organic Monitor is a leading provider of business intelligence on the
international organic food industry.

THE ORGANIC WORKS
DART'S FARM, CLYST ST. GEORGE, EXETER, DEVON EX3 0QH
Tel: 01392 875678 Fax: 01392 879461 Contact: Fenella Reeves
mail@theorganicworks.co/uk
Organic business management handling everything beyond the farm gate.
Services include: marketing, commercial management, book-keeping,
financial and office administration. Serving producers based in the South-
West. See display ad.

ORGANICA LP
NERINE HOUSE, PO BOX 434, ST. GEORGE'S ESPLANADE, ST. PETER PORT, GUERNSEY GY1 3ZG
Tel: +44 1481 739584 Fax: +44 1481 701619 Contact: Peter R. Geiser
info@organica-guernsey.com www.organica-guernsey.com
Worldwide consultants in marketing of organic farm produce.

SINGLE MARKETING LTD
HIPLEY HOUSE, HIPLEY STREET, WOKING, SURREY GU22 9LQ
Tel: 01483 771152 Fax: 01483 766808 Contact: Jeff Bayley
singlemktg@aol.com
Complete sales and marketing service to regional and national retail chains.

SPRINGDALE CROP SYNERGIES LTD
SPRINGDALE FARM, RUDSTON, DRIFFIELD, EAST YORKSHIRE YO25 4DJ
Tel: 01262 421100 Fax: 01262 521101 Contact: Simon Meakin
info@springdale-group.com www.springdale-group.com
Soil Association P7844. Seed merchant/advisor. Agronomy-based crop development business offering buy-back contracts and advice on organic crops. Supplier and trader of organic seeds and the only UK registered specialist organic oilseed supplier.

TRIODOS BANK
BRUNEL HOUSE, 11 THE PROMENADE, BRISTOL BS8 3NN
Tel: 0800 328 2181 Fax: 0117 973 9303
mail@triodos.co.uk www.triodos.co.uk
Tel: 0800 328 2181 for free information on banking services for organisations. Tel: 0500 008720 for personal savings details. Triodos Bank's unique Organic Saver Account, offered in partnership with the Soil Association, gives you a secure and rewarding way to target your savings to organic enterprises. We provide full banking services for organic food and farming enterprises, including current and investment accounts, overdrafts and loan facilities. As Europe's leading ethical bank we have financed a wide range of organic businesses over many years and understand the needs and dynamics of the sector. Contact us for more details.

Index

Future editions of The Organic Directory

Please contact us if:

- You think your company or organisation should be included in *The Organic Directory*
- You want the details of your entry to be amended
- You know of a company or organisation that you think should be included in *The Organic Directory*
- You have suggestions as to how we can improve *The Organic Directory*

In all cases, please email Clive Litchfield at:

organiceco@aol.com

or write to him c/o Green Books Ltd, Foxhole, Dartington, Totnes, Devon TQ9 6EB.

There is no charge for inclusion in *The Organic Directory*, although we have a section of paid advertising in the printed version.

You can find *The Organic Directory* online at the Soil Association's website:

www.theorganicdirectory.co.uk